E-mail and Ethics

- How is personal identity manifested or conveyed in text?
- Can we know what others are feeling if we utilise computer-mediated communication?
- Can we act on other people when we utilise computer-mediated communication?
- Are computer-mediated friendships and political relations valuable, and what are their limitations?

In *E-mail and Ethics*, Emma Rooksby explores the ways in which interpersonal relations are affected by computer-mediated forms of communication.

For over a decade, computer-mediated communication has been available as an institutional and personal communication technology, and this availability has been increasing ever since its inception. It is often considered an efficient, productive and cost-effective form of communication, and it is claimed to bring many social and personal benefits in fields ranging from political action and formation of friendships, to therapeutic discussion and access to education.

The advent of computer-mediated communication has prompted renewed investigation into the nature and value of forms of human association. Rooksby takes up these issues in her study of the limits and benefits of computer-mediated communication.

With its depth of research and clarity of style, this book will be of great interest to philosophers, scholars of communication, cultural and media studies, and all those interested in the importance and implications of computer-mediated communication.

Emma Rooksby is Research Fellow at the Centre for Applied Philosophy and Public Ethics, Australia. Her research covers computer ethics, including on-line democracy, on-line relationships and the ethics of text-based communication. Her publications include *Habitus: a sense of place* (edited with Jean Hillier, Ashgate, 2001), and 'Empathy in computer-mediated communication' in Mark Wolf (ed.) *Virtual Morality: morals, ethics and new media* (Peter Lang Publishing, forthcoming).

Routledge Studies in Contemporary Philosophy

1 E-mail and Ethics
Style and ethical relations in computer-mediated communication
Emma Rooksby

E-mail and Ethics

Style and ethical relations in
computer-mediated communication

Emma Rooksby

London and New York

177
R77e

First published 2002
by Routledge
11 New Fetter Lane, London EC4P 4EE

Simultaneously published in the USA and Canada
by Routledge
29 West 35th Street, New York, NY 10001

Routledge is an imprint of the Taylor & Francis Group

H   © 2002 Emma Rooksby

Typeset in Baskerville by
HWA Text and Data Management, Tunbridge Wells
Printed and bound in Great Britain by
Biddles Ltd, Guildford and King's Lynn

British Library Cataloguing in Publication Data
A catalogue record for this book is available from the British Library

Library of Congress Cataloging in Publication Data
A catalog record for this book has been requested

ISBN 0-415-28281-0

Contents

Acknowledgements

Many people have contributed to this book. Friends and colleagues have helped me at every stage of research and writing, to think through issues with more depth and clarity, and to tackle some that I might otherwise have left unaddressed.

The book began as part of a doctoral thesis at Murdoch University, Western Australia. I'd like to thank friends and colleagues from that period: Pedro Tabensky, Carolyn Abbs, Antonio Traverso, Peter Kurti, and Bev Murfin, for their thoughtful ideas, advice, and support. Thanks also to the participants at seminars who listened to and commented on earlier versions of Chapters Two, Three and Four. I'd also like to thank Horst Ruthrof for helpful comments and suggestions on Chapter Three, Paula Goulding for constructive discussion of issues raised by Chapter Four, and Niels Nielson and Bruce McClintock for editorial advice and suggestions.

Peta Bowden's careful and critical reading and thoughtful, incisive comments on many earlier drafts of the manuscript helped me immensely in forming the final version, and her support for the project has been invaluable to me. Charles Altieri's and Bob White's comments on the thesis manuscript helped to persuade me that it was worth reworking for publication. The manuscript was rewritten during a research fellowship at the Centre for Applied Philosophy and Public Ethics, and I am grateful to the Centre for giving me the time to complete the task. Thanks also to the editorial team at Routledge.

Particular thanks are due to my family, parents Karen and Dick, and sisters Phillida and Oenone, who were supportive and encouraging at all stages of the writing and editing of the manuscript, and to Keith Horton, who discussed the manuscript with me and provided encouragement and much useful advice during the revision process.

Introduction

This book is an investigation of ethical aspects of computer-mediated communication (or CMC). In it I sort through some important ethical issues that are raised by the prospect of a mediated, textual, social world. I do so by posing and answering a series of questions. How is personal identity manifested (or constructed) in text? Can we know what others are feeling if we communicate with them via CMC? Can we engage in dialogue with others in CMC? Can we act on or with others in CMC? How are computer-mediated (CM) friendships and political relations valuable, and what are their limitations? I explore the ethical possibilities and limitations imposed by the wide geographic reach and textuality of CMC, and consider how the medium sustains or alters social relations, particularly friendships and political relations.

CMC has been available as an institutional and personal communication technology for well over a decade, and has been becoming more widely available ever since its inception. It is particularly popular in the US, where computer networking was pioneered, and is increasingly popular elsewhere. The reasons for its adoption in public, academic and institutional contexts are frequently managerial decisions based on considerations of efficiency, productivity and profit, but the social advantages of CMC are also cited by many people.[1] CMC is claimed to bring many benefits, social and personal, in fields ranging from political action and formation of friendships, to therapeutic discussion and education access.

The value of being able to maintain contact with familiar distant others, and to establish new contact with unknown distant others are two of the major social benefits that people cite for CMC. Further, the organisation of social fora such as mailing lists and discussion groups allows groups of people to keep in touch with each other when they would otherwise be limited from so doing by the time required to engage with participants individually. The comparative novelty of CMC, and the cachet attached to that novelty, no doubt add to the use of CMC, for some people, a particular pleasure not associated with other forms of mediated communication such as telephone conversation.

While social interaction across the panoply of particular personal affiliations, impersonal crowd gatherings, role-based work relations, and political negotiations has been the traditional ground of ethics, the advent of CMC has prompted a renewed investigation into the nature and value of forms of human association. A sense that CMC is radically different from other forms of interaction, and an anticipation of its impact on those other forms, contribute to the belief that our understanding of social interaction needs to be rethought, even as it is being transformed. There are two major reasons for the renewal of interest of social interaction through the lens of CMC. Both relate, I think, more or less directly, to major changes in social interaction already produced by CMC in the countries where it has become prevalent, notably the US, Western Europe and Australia, and increasingly in Asian countries like Singapore and India.

Reach

The first reason is the greatly enlarged geographical area across which social relations, including lengthy, frequent and sustained textual exchanges, can be maintained. CMC permits people to communicate synchronously with anyone else who has access to CMC. Further, it permits large numbers of people to engage socially, in contrast with, say, telephones, which tend to limit the number of participants to two, although more may share a conversation. Regular social textual contact is enabled by CMC over far greater distances than by any other medium except the telephone. The comparatively low cost, by comparison with telephone communication, enhances this possibility for many people. CMC is, for many people, far cheaper than the accessible alternatives. The mechanisms for global interpersonal relations are currently available, to some at least.

Relations may thus be established and maintained across vast distances without requiring any participant to stir out of her or his present location. Like the much more self-evident inter-cultural activity of travelling to other countries, CMC permits meetings of distant minds, and engagement in cross-cultural exploration. CMC may open participants up to what Maria Lugonès calls 'world-travelling', experiencing the lived worlds of others in ways that transform their understanding of their own self and culture (Lugonès 1987).

The maintenance of social relations involves regular contact between people. Ethically valuable social relations, a subset of social relations generally, are relations in which all those involved flourish. There are some important preconditions for ethically valuable social relations.[2] Companionship, that is spending time together, is important for allowing people to establish mutual trust. For intimate relations in particular to flourish, there must be chances for each person to help the other, and for the establishment of mutual understanding. Evidently, there may be some question as to the capacity of textual exchanges to afford mutual trust and understanding. Textuality may conceal much about a writer: she or he may disclose aspects of his or her self, deliberately or unwittingly. But some aspects of the self, such as how someone reacts to social situations that don't occur in CMC, will remain opaque. The question is, then, whether computer-mediated exchanges provide a solid enough foundation for maintaining ethically valuable social relations.

The practical ramifications of the increased capacity for communication with distant others are to be counted as changes in the patterns of human social behaviour. We may maintain intimacy with people whom we rarely if ever see. We may e-mail someone rather than go to visit them. We may e-mail a colleague down the corridor rather than go and talk with them. We may be in touch with many people without ever having to coordinate or disrupt the practical patterns of our lives for each other. The effects on social understandings are less obvious and require far greater caution in interpretation. We may sense that more of those away from us are near us, accessible in a sense that was not previously possible. The possibility of communicating at will with distant others also has discernible effects on our sense of being with those who are near us. We may sense that those near us are distant; that there is no need to talk with them if CMC is more efficient; or that we may not talk with others if CMC allows us to reach them less intrusively.

No discussion of the geographic reach and possibilities of CMC is complete without a consideration of the present limits to CMC, such as equity of access, both in wealthy countries with poor citizens, and in poor countries. The distribution of CMC is irregular across the globe. Access to CMC is limited even in wealthy countries by factors such as institutional wealth, personal wealth, attitudes to technological change and prevailing levels of literacy.[3] In developing countries, distribution is even more patchy, although many international and bilateral aid programmes now fund the provision of Internet services to the poor in developing countries. In both developed and developing countries, only a proportion of the population can take for granted the ongoing possibility of computer-mediated relationships.[4] In addition to access to the technology, CMC use requires access to and familiarity with computers, as well as literacy. The requirement of literacy for using text-based CMC functions both as an excluder of illiterate persons, and as a channel for the sorts of social behaviours that are possible in CMC. Reading and writing practices inherited from other forms of textual interaction are adopted or adapted in textual CMC, adding culture-specific patinas of style to the constraints on using CMC imposed by access restrictions.

A final issue raised by the geographic reach of CMC is the question of the limits of community within which social interaction takes place, and the transformation of communities by the eruption of massive transnational interaction. CMC enables new stable transnational social communities to form, without doing away with former communities, such as those constituted by cities, cultures and nations, and without necessitating a systematic rethinking of the idea of community. Current writing on computer-mediated community can be divided into three broad groups. Members of the first group believe that on-line communities are as legitimate as any other community, and treat on-line communities as associations to which politics is internal, rather than considering the activities of on-line communities as political. Members of the second group see on-line communities as social havens from real political necessities. Members of the third group see on-line communication as part of an emergent diffuse global political community with, as yet, no unified political stance, instead consisting of a multitude of voices on different issues. This third group stresses the current multiculturality of CMC, the ongoing diffusion of CMC into non-English-speaking and developing countries, and the emergence of international political movements and organisations working primarily on-line. I do not address these issues directly in this book, but admit to accepting a version of the third view. Here I do no more than examine the possibilities for sustaining political relations in CMC, without looking at the larger socio-cultural effects of widespread global political communication.

The social and political effects of global use of information transfer and informational capital are readily discernible. CMCs are, for example, forcing changes in national censorship laws, national trade practices, and are affecting leisure practices worldwide. A singular global political community in terms of which individuals and organisations express particular (political) interests has yet to emerge. And yet these interests affect social and political change, through workplace practices, software styles and pervasive ideological influence.[5] The means by which global politics can be conducted via CMC depends in part, as the maintenance of personal relationships does, on the interpretational strengths and weaknesses of the medium.

Textuality

The second reason for the renewed interest in the nature of human relations is the textuality in which almost all computer-mediated relations are conducted. Speech, in full mutual presence, sharing a here and a now, is the mode in which most relationships have traditionally been conducted, and it is a mode to which we appeal as natural or normal despite the prevalence of mediated communications such as letters, telephone, radio, or television. As such, speech has enjoyed normative status as the natural mode for our friendships, political dealings and almost all other social interactions. Despite the increasing domination of media (particularly television) in both our solitary and social leisure activities, as well as in our places of work, this has not been perceived as a variety of 'absence' significantly different in kind from the simpler forms of absence occasioned by travel, or separations between workplaces or homes.

Further, speech has been and is still accepted as primal in human social experience. It is in speech that children are brought up to be individuals within language-using communities. For the overwhelming majority of children, speech comes before writing a language; only when a child is incapable of speech does signed or written language constitute the form in which they learn to know the world, and then it must be specially taught.[6] Despite the prevalence of mediated communication, non-mediated social interaction is still fundamental to human relationships.

Writing and reading are skills that children learn, if at all, only after they have become a member of a speaking community. These skills are often engaged in and furthered in isolation, but learned socially, and brought back to the social world in discussion. A child's reading to her or his self follows being read to aloud by parents, or teachers, and is related back to the world of common, shared experiences in activities of discussion and exploratory questioning. Only slowly do the capacities for silent reflection on text, for appreciation of the structure of texts, for the voice of the author of a text, develop. The history of reading and writing in the West reflects an equally slow social acclimatisation, where reading was at first as often aloud as silent, and as often public as private.[7]

Recent research into the social constraints on language-use also support a strong connection between learning how to use a language and learning how to be a member of a community of people. Learning to use one's first language is necessarily bound up in the process of learning to be a person all together, and the learning of the language consists in large part in understanding in what circumstances, in relation to which social practices, what words are appropriate. Linguistic usage is thus not only a technical achievement, but also a social one, not possible without becoming and having a sense of being a person in a society of persons. Much of what Wittgenstein has to say about learning a language in *Philosophical Investigations* can be read as an illustration of the social, if not ethical, orientation that is acquired in coming to know the linguistic practices of a community.

In light of the primacy of spoken language as the first form of language encountered by children negotiating the world, the textual medium of CMC is aligned with other media as a secondary form of interaction, like other forms of reading, television and telephone. Nevertheless textual CMC is increasingly normalised as a mode of social interaction that is both natural (because socially accepted) and desirable (because efficient, recordable, cheap, productive). It is increasingly employed by public, academic and commercial institutions, as well as being used by many individuals outside institutional frameworks.[8] Its use is increasingly advocated for children, on the grounds that facility with computers will be advantageous for their social and professional later lives. In light of the prevalence of CMC, the connection established between knowing words and knowing the (social) world by reflections such as those of Wittgenstein, suggests that using different interpretational skills, and interacting in differently composed social 'worlds' in CMC may engender quite different social practices and understandings. For example, in so far as language is not a system of communication on its own, but part of a larger semiotic web of intended and unintended signs and phenomena, the sharing of verbal communication alone may curtail or filter the sense we have of others, by altering *what* about people and the way they live is available to us for interpretation.

The emergence of CMC as a medium for social interaction has the potential to reorient the assumed primacy and priority of face-to-face communication. The degree to which CMC can sustain mutually disclosive, supportive and cooperative relations will determine the ethical possibilities and limitations of CMC. The qualities of the medium mean that it is more readily taken up for some forms of social engagement than for others, and that it will encourage some forms of engagement at the cost of others.

Thus the textuality of CMC is of profound importance to how and by whom it is taken up as a mode of communication. I have already mentioned the exclusionary tendencies of text-based communication as something that limits participation in CMC. Users of CMC also have to contend with the ways in which particular textual conventions structure the dynamics of social, and political, interactions. In some fora the pace at which one can type affects the sorts of activities one can engage in, and even the regard in which one is held by other participants.[9] The invisibility of bodily characteristics, by contrast, may figure as either a limitation or as a boon. Many people use their invisibility to other participants for playful purposes, such as impersonation, or establishing quasi-fictive personae. Others find safety in the feeling that they are invisible to those with whom they are in contact, and may gain the courage to speak up where previously they were silent. Thus the textuality of CMC establishes a range of social possibilities and limitations; these in turn intersect with the broadened geographic reach of those using CMC. Together, geographic reach and textuality form the basis of my exploration of ethical issues in CMC.

Two notes about the scope of this book are necessary here. First, the discussion is exclusively of text-based CMC. This is partly because text-based CMC is currently the predominant form of CMC, and is likely to remain so. And it is partly because text-based CMC raises ethical issues to do with the interpretation of others' performances in a particularly sharp and interesting form. Second, my discussion of CMC is limited to English-language exchanges, and largely to exchanges among native speakers of English, in Western cultures. This is partly because of my own status as an English-speaking Westerner, and partly because textual CMC itself remains, at this point, dominated by English-language communication. I hope to address this limitation of scope in future research.

Structure of the book

I begin exploring the ethical possibilities of CMC by developing an account of persons as beings with lifestyles constituted by the gamut of their styled verbal and non-verbal performances, only a small proportion of which is ever witnessed by a single other person. This account is developed in Chapter One. Someone's lifestyle is a performative aspect of their self, and their styled performances display their beliefs and desires to others. The interpretation of others' styled linguistic performances, including textual performances, is thus treated, in my account of persons, as a significant aspect of interpersonal understanding. This account of persons understanding one another through their styled performances encompasses both spoken and written linguistic acts, since both are part of people's lifestyles. Likewise, the interpretation of another's lifestyle is part of the broader social or ethical act of understanding that person, and is engaged in alongside understanding their beliefs and desires.

In Chapter Two I examine the role of empathy in textual relations such as CMC affords. I define empathy as the second-hand experience of the experience of another. Empathy requires an imaginative projection, and an act of attending to the other as a self like oneself. Empathy thus conceived is at once an intuitive orientation towards others, and an ethical stance, deliberately taken, directed towards interpersonal understanding. Empathy has a bodily component (in that persons empathise with the experiences they see expressed in other's physical posture and facial expression) but is facilitated by verbal enunciation (for instance if someone articulates the object of their experience). I then ask how empathy is possible in textual CMC. If, as was argued in the previous chapter, styled textual performances tend to be interpolated as styled texts rather than as expressive of individuals, then persons' intuitively empathic orientation towards others may not be sustained in CMC. Nevertheless, deliberate attending to the experiences of others is possible in CMC, so long as we are aware of the ways in which styled textual performances differ from lifestyle considered more generally.

In Chapter Three I look at the performative possibilities and limitations of CMC. Firstly I take up the question of whether dialogical exchange is possible in CMC. The interpretative requirements for understanding others through their styled textual performances often draw attention to the text itself, and away from the writer. The hermeneutic relation to the text is thus, for both writer and reader, always liable to predominate over the interpersonal relation between reader and writer. Reading geared to hermeneutic interpretation may come to predominate over reading directed to interpersonal understanding. Paul Ricoeur's account of the relation between reader and text can be taken as a study of the degree of distanciation that is possible between reader and writer. I take issue with Ricoeur's account of textual interpretation as non-dialogic and demonstrate that distanciation is a contingent rather than necessary or automatic effect of textuality. Dialogue is constituted in the exchange of texts, rather than through a single text. Within the dialogue established through the exchange of texts, individuals' styled textual performances constitute what I call 'absent presence'.

Having established the conditions for dialogue in CMC, I then use speech act theory to develop an account of text acts (or performative inscriptions) valid for CMC and for other forms of textually-mediated communication. I argue that people can perform text acts in CMC, so long as a shared understanding of 'what is going on' is maintained by those party to the act. The conditions in CMC, however, tend to disrupt the conventions of which locutions (or inscriptions) are but one part. Smooth communication and mutual understanding are both disrupted by what I call modal opacity and the invisibility of bodily movements and social context. In some CMCs, particularly MUDs (Multi-User Dungeons) and MOOs (Multi-User Dungeons, Object Oriented), and anonymous or unmoderated discussion groups or mailing lists, paucity and flexibility of conventions in CMC tend to work against the establishment of conditions of trust in which participants feel confident enough to take each other at their word. Other forms of CMC do not work against the trust necessary for performative utterances: in e-mail exchanged between old friends, for example, trust is already established, as are shared verbal practices. The degree to which text acts are enabled in CMC varies widely with context; exchanges closely allied with workplaces are more likely to allow felicitous acts, aided by familiar conventions, than are exchanges between anonymous strangers in a playful MUD.

In Chapter Four I discuss in greater detail the technical constraints characteristic of all types of CMC. For instance, literacy, computer access, and time are all required for participation in CMC. Further, the communicative good of increased geographic reach comes with the condition of textuality. In order to appreciate the possibilities of CMC fully, it is necessary to consider these constraints, and to give some sense of how participants in CMC have taken up the communicative and social possibilities that they permit. I consider four main constraints: machine-dependency, an unusually flexible temporality of communication, textuality and the proliferation of social 'places'. I address each of these in turn, concluding that the first three tend to elicit stylistic misunderstandings of various sorts, and that the fourth does not so much create misunderstandings in CMC as destabilise the relation between place and physical locations. I conclude that the communicative possibilities of CMC, which include dialogic exchange and text acts, are limited by the structural constraints that currently obtain.[10]

In Chapter Five I move to an application of the theoretical position developed in earlier chapters. I take up the ethical issue of friendship and other intimate relations in CMC. The distance and departicularisation characteristic of the medium conditions the terms on which people meet, so that expectations of friendship may be low, replaced by expectations of other types of relationship, based perhaps on information exchange, academic debate, or discussion of global political issues. Likewise the textuality of CMC prevents friends from sharing a large range of activities in that medium, and from attending to non-textual aspects of others' styles. In CMC we are able to discuss with others as many issues as concern us. But it is with an absence of shared practical and personal experience that we come to know people in CMC.[11] We cannot know much of the practical lives of those we meet there, nor learn of or from their practical comportment as it is outside of the textual computer environment.

If possibilities for establishing and maintaining intimate CMC relations are limited by structural constraints of the medium, there is at least some hope for other, less personal forms of social relations. I take up the question of political relations in CMC in Chapter Six. CMC political relations may not conform to the ideals of political community as a tight-knit group of people making collective decisions face to face. But, then, such political communities (and we know of a few) do not usually resemble the communitarian dream. As Iris Marion Young notes, 'The ideal [of the polity that privileges face to face relations] presumes a myth of unmediated social relations and wrongly identifies mediation as alienation' (Young 1997b: 67). Given the already mediated nature of politics in most countries (through institutions such as voting, proportional representation, advertising and televised parliaments), the addition of CMC to the mix might be seen to be an advantage. Such advantages can perhaps best be thought of in terms of reach, a term which suggests both the global span of CMC networks and the increased speed of interaction that they enable.

Summary

The history of text, the practices of reading and writing, the relation of writing to speaking, and the relation of both to social and political life are currently under critical review. This review, taken up in myriad conversations around the world, is also a textual affair, conducted through CMC discussions and the to-and-fro of academic and journalistic publications and reviews. I hope that the discussion of style and ethical relations in CMC in this book can contribute to that debate in a worthwhile way.

1 Style and ethics

Why, Sir, I think every man whatever has a peculiar style, which may be discovered by nice examination and comparison with others: but a man must write a great deal to make his style obviously discernible. As logicians say, this appropriation of style is infinite *in potestate*, limited *in actu*.

Samuel Johnson (Boswell 1906: 202)

1.1 Introduction

This is a project about interpersonal understanding in the realm of computer-mediated communication (henceforth CMC). The conclusion at which I arrive in this chapter is that the varieties of textual communication, including CMC, transform and in some cases[1] limit people's understandings of one another.

I arrive at this conclusion by an examination of style as a general modifier of all human performances, and its relation to textual style, which can also be considered under the heading of 'artistic style', a self-consciously historical category including artefacts and art objects. Two important findings emerge from the examination of style in general, and two from the comparison of textual style and style in general.

An examination of style in general reveals the significance of style as an aspect of all human activity, expressive of both individual identity and of social belonging. Style is seen as invested in every performance of a person, so that every person could be described as having a 'lifestyle' consisting of the composite of all her or his styled performances. A person's lifestyle, the ways in which they perform social practices, is as significant an aspect of their identity as what they profess to believe, the opinions they hold, or what actions they perform. Its particular significance derives in part from the fact that style is often *less than* chosen, and may express aspects of a person's self that are not deliberately displayed. Knowing another person's style is then argued to be as important for understanding them as is knowledge of their beliefs or their actions. At this point I introduce the ethical importance of attending to style as part of knowing other persons, a theme I take up again at the end of the chapter.

The comparison of textual style with style in general shows that textual style may be seen as one of the subsets of the totality of a person's styled performances, expressing some though not all aspects of a person's lifestyle. But textual style, like the styles of art objects more generally, may also be taken to consist of formal properties attaching to artefacts, without any reference to the performances of those artefacts' creators. Drawing on the claim that textual style is a subset of a person's style in general, I argue that the textual style of a person's communicative inscriptions will often (though by no means always) be less than fully disclosive, even to an intended reader, of a person's interests, attitudes, and intentions, and may lead to misunderstandings. As well as being less than wholly disclosive, textual style has a greatly increased importance as an aspect of a person's self (and self-presentation) in textually mediated social relations such as CMC, in which all a person's performances are textually mediated.

I take these last two claims together to support the conclusion that, while attending to the textual styles of others in CMC is necessary for understanding others as persons, textual style will sometimes be insufficiently disclosive of those others' selves. In other words, the varieties of textual style, by being only a subset of all styled performances, transform the ways we understand others, and may limit that understanding.

The account of style developed in this chapter has ethical implications. Insofar as understanding other people is itself an important and necessary ethical project, part of all cooperative human endeavours, then transformations (particularly limitations) to a project of understanding another person will be of ethical significance. (If understanding a self requires attention to all aspects of a lifestyle, then the limitation of a social relationship to textual exchange may perhaps be problematic for establishing and maintaining understandings that encompass all aspects of persons' selves.) Attention to these transformations may suggest new ways of reading and writing, and ways to avoid the interpretive pitfalls characteristic of textual communication. This chapter, having shown the transformative effects of textual style on textually-mediated social relations, leads on to discussions in subsequent chapters, of how empathy is possible in textually-mediated relationships, and of textually-mediated human agency.

1.2 An expressive theory of style

This chapter begins with a discussion of the nature of style in general. I develop the claim that style is best seen as those qualities of people's performances of social practices that express their attitudes, interests and character, in short their selves, to other people. As human selves grow and develop in social worlds containing both socially normative and idiosyncratic conventions, so individual styles incorporate traits and practices that reflect social norms, and others that reflect individual interests and concerns. Styles are partly but not wholly at the command of individuals, expressive of self as unique and of self in relation to wider social categories. The intersubjectivity of style, like the intersubjectivity of language argued for by Ludwig Wittgenstein, is then a prompt to our attempting to attend to and understand how others perform and express themselves, as 'a specific mode of attending, and caring which makes visible the persons' investments in their expressive activity' (Altieri 1987: 188).

My approach to style could be couched in terms of the common approaches to style. In a book on the evolution of written style in eighteenth-century England, Carey McIntosh describes prevailing approaches to style studies by dividing them into three schools, each treating of one major aspect of style (McIntosh 1998: 225). The groups consist of relations between pairs: between text and writer, between text and reader, between text and world. My focus on style in textual CMC could be classed as the study of style under the aspect of the relation between writer and reader corresponding in text, an approach that necessarily draws on all three relational pairs discussed by McIntosh, and must draw comparisons between textual style and style in social relations more generally.

An expressive sense of style, which takes the social self as the object to which style pertains, is spontaneously expressive to surrounding others of the being, both individual and social, of particular people. This sense of style is not strictly aesthetic but ethical, since both having style and understanding style are activities that occur in the sphere of human relations, and which may lead to either strife or communion. Someone's style, that is, the ways in which they go about their activities in general, is expressive of their particular interests, attitudes, character – it can be seen as individually theirs. Yet their interests, attitudes and character are shared with, and influenced by, many other people; the social practices that they take up are learned from and shared with many other people. Any individual style is neither wholly unique nor wholly independent in its development.

The expressive aspect of style is mirrored in people's everyday grasp of others' styles. We attend to other people's styles as part of understanding them as persons. As all performances are styled, so all attending to other people involves a grasp of their style (or styles) of performance. Further, each individual's style is grasped by others who may have substantially different styles, not to mention different characters, interests, or cultural backgrounds. Differences in style may be productive of new understanding, but may also be significant obstacles to it. This section gives an outline of an expressive theory of style in terms of the expressively styled activities of individuals. The following section outlines the role, and some of the ethical responsibilities, of the interpreter in an expressive theory of style.

The association of style with expressions of self or character has a long history, primarily associated with traditions of rhetoric rather than of writing. Classical discussions of style discuss public oration and focus on excellence of expression and the achievement of desired effects through employment of recognised style, in the form of rhetorical techniques, including manner of delivery.[2] At the same time, style is treated, notoriously by Socrates, as a dangerous tool that can be used as easily for a bad cause as a good. Maud Gleason draws attention to the importance of physiognomic and performance analysis as means of discriminating 'real men' from pretenders in second century BC Greece.[3] A similar attitude can be seen in the 'copious' written Erasmian style of the early Renaissance, in which fullness of expression betokened both erudition and virtue, and afforded the most convivial of literary correspondences.[4] Enlightenment attitudes to style, especially in France and Hanoverian England, associate particular styles of speech and writing with polite society; rigidification of class barriers was accompanied in eighteenth-century Western Europe by prescription in both grammar and style.[5] The same period saw a proliferation of novels in letters, such as Samuel Richardson's *Clarissa* and Choderlos de Laclos' *Les Liaisons Dangereuses*, whose self-conscious stylistic variety allow writers to alternate several authorial voices in single literary productions.[6]

Some more recent approaches to style, such as that of Jacques Derrida, also used by Gregory Ulmer and Tom Conley, and that of writers on rhetoric influenced by Marshall McLuhan, such as David Jay Bolter and Richard Lanham,[7] argue for the ubiquity of style within all (linguistic) discourse without claiming for it the ethical normativity of Classical approaches. Richard Lanham in particular attends to the question of the relation of good literary style[8] and moral goodness, concluding that it is the *purpose* to which style is put, rather than style itself, that is amenable to moral judgement.[9] Berel Lang, who has made particularly detailed explorations of philosophical style, is attentive to the ways in which stylistic genres both enable and channel a writer's intentionality, thus illustrating the historical and cultural embeddedness of many styles of writing.[10] While modern writers are ambivalent about the virtue of any particular style *per se*, there is a general recognition that style, whatever else it is, may be powerfully expressive of character, interests, and intentionality.

Aesthetic expressive theories of style, as in a formulation by Jenefer Robinson in terms of literary works, also treat style as expressive of individual attitudes or feelings. Under Robinson's expressive theory of style, for example, different styles used by the same person are seen as the various attitudes or voices of that person. In 'Style and personality in the literary work', Robinson treats style as 'a way of doing things' in the context of writing a novel, and glosses such things as 'describing character, commenting on the action, and manipulating the plot' (Robinson 1985). Robinson illustrates that we cannot explain why some formal properties count as stylistically important for one literary work, and not for another, unless style refers to something besides formal properties, and then argues that it is the expression of the various attitudes of author (or an authorial voice) that invests formal properties with particular style.

There are some important objections to expressive theories of style, particularly in the expression-of-individual-feeling model. Two important features of style, present both in literary works, and in social comportment generally, that cannot be accounted for by expressive theories, suggest that style is not solely a writer or performer's expression of attitudes and feelings, and that an intersubjective-expressive account of style is necessary. The troubling features are the variety of styles used by individuals, and the relative insignificance, in some social performances, of the author (as opposed to either an authorial voice or the author's subject matter).

On the variety of styles open to any individual, Berel Lang observes that autobiographical narrative, letters, and other textual testimonies have much in common with fiction, in that they may employ a textual style, or a variety of textual styles, that are not recognisably like the social style of their writers.[11] The theatre is the arena *par exemple* of variety of voices, and one in which we can by no means treat all styled performances as expressing the attitudes of a single playwright to her or his creations. Individual performances, in life as well as art, may express attitudes and feelings not those of the performer, or those whose significance is that they are shared by the performer with other people, and so on. This observation renders impracticable the expressivist treatment of all style as expressive of a single unitary self, and suggests a profound modality to individual performances, in the arena of art in particular.[12]

In social life generally, people have a variety of ways of acting available to them, and these may be sufficiently differentiated for any individual to constitute separate roles. We do not usually approach other people as profoundly unique others, but in certain capacities, structured by social rules and possibilities, and as we appear in various capacities, we may have a variety of roles. A person may be said to have a variety of styles of speaking, or of negotiating, or of walking, so that it becomes difficult to treat people as having single, unitary and wholly consistent styles of acting, expressive of singular consistent attitudes.[13] Psychologist Deborah Tannen's observation that impersonation and dramatisation are important and common strategies in ordinary speech and social activity (Tannen 1989; see also Tannen and Lakoff 1994) also makes difficulties for pure expressivist theories of style. Impersonation and dramatisation constitute imitation of others' styles and cannot be said to embody the performer's attitude in any simple way. Certainly their audience may attend to the style of such performances not simply to appreciate the style or character of the performer, but to learn of or laugh at the style of the person imitated.

This last remark is closely related to a second feature of style troublesome to an expressive account. This is that in many cases someone's style in acting or in speaking may be directed toward illuminating some subject matter other than the performing self; as the style of travel writing can sum up the qualities of a place rather than the attitudes of the traveller; as the style of a dramatic performance can capture the character being played rather than the attitude of the actor; that in some cases a performance can express an abstract quality such as lightness or agility rather than an attitude or feeling.[14]

Even the most individual stylistic voice may be so closely attuned, so familiar, with its subject matter that the subject matter becomes more real in the performance than the subject. And then an audience may feel the subject matter come alive for themselves too, as a good mimic can summon her or his subject to an audience. The submergence of subject is particularly evident in some artistic disciplines, such as abstract art, and music, the art at once most abstract and with the greatest corporeal impact. Expressive style in music is only contingently connected with particular emotions, and music itself almost never takes intentional objects (though its lyrics and programmes may do so).

Nelson Goodman's objectivist version of the expressive account of style addresses this limitation, by treating style, as any features of the symbolic functioning of a given performance or object that serve to mark it uniquely.[15] This approach fixes on objective properties of a performance or object as the terms in which its unique style is available to any investigator; it eschews any reference to the emotional or affective qualities of a performance, or to the intentionality of a performer. By not discriminating between expressive voices it avoids the subjectivist troubles of requiring a single expressive authorial voice. However, such an objectivist approach relies on there being a consistent body of features that can be observed in a performance. Yet as Goodman observes, the choice of which objective stylistic features an observer seeks out is coloured by their prior perception of the style of a performance, so that different observers may attribute different styles.[16] Nor can some properties of performances and objects (or indeed of symbols) be satisfactorily explained or accounted for *without* reference to their affective power or emotional import.[17] Goodman emphasises the multiple symbolic functions of performances and objects in an attempt to get away from a theory of style in which style expresses *only* the emotions and attitudes of a single creator.[18] But in making good his escape, he severs symbols from the social world in which they gain and change their significance, which significance cannot be considered merely formal.

The alternative to choosing either subjectivist or objectivist expressivism is to admit that style can incorporate both subjectivist and objectivist traits, just as it encompasses actors and bystanders (or, more properly, groups of people interacting), as well as the objects and texts that often mediate between them. This stance would require relinquishing any pretensions to be able to provide a singular typology of styles (the goal of the objectivist theories), and would cloud the explanatory elegance of singular authorial expression that is the basis of the subjectivist theories. But the expressive aspect of style, and its association with the person who expresses it, rest at the core of style, even if they cannot be given systematic or reductive analysis. The performer may well be, for a viewer or reader, less important than that which is seen through their performance; yet the performer is (or was) that through which the view is instantiated.

This balance between expression and interpretation is the aspect of style that I see as most relevant to social interaction, including the textual social interaction of CMC. It is primarily but not by any means exclusively expressive of, and read as expressive of, individual living selves embedded in social worlds, in relation to which larger canvas both matter and manner ordinarily conceived count as manner. (By comparison, the lack of personal contact and spatio-temporal separation characteristic of works of art may seem to suggest or even to require an objectivist or even formalist approach.[19]) However, any account of style must still take into account the social embeddedness of individuals, and the fact that styled works are not often performed or taken purely as expressions of self, but are created as *about* a separate subject matter, and only obliquely about the performing self. That style is both expressive of individuals, and also read by and important to other individuals is the key to its ethical importance. It suggests an intersubjective expressivist approach.

An intersubjective expressivist approach to style would then comprise a person's expressive acts, and *also* how these acts are understood by other people, by either an intended audience, or by any other audience.[20] That is to say, style covers both the performance and the interpretation of significant objects and actions, and cannot be determined by either producer or a receiver alone. Someone's style, like their attitude, is not determined wholly by either the performer (or 'producer') or his or her audience. Rather, it emerges among interpreters, given its particulars in the performance of the actor, and grasped by other people who bring to it their own conceptions, some of which will be aligned with the speaker's, others of which will not. All, by virtue of being people in contact with one another, are able at least to attempt to understand each other.

Neither speaker nor listener, neither writer nor reader, has absolute control over what is stylistically significant. Style, constituted by individual performances situated within the patterned mass of the social practices of communities, rests on both actors and audience, and its interpretation cannot reliably be arrogated by any one, although some people's interpretations inevitably have more influence than others'. I might try to speak slowly and clearly in order to make myself understood to a large audience, but find afterwards that my style of speech was seen as affected and condescending.

The creation and ascription of style must go on intertwined with, informed and affected by, the other functions of human activity, interaction and communication. Just as language is interpersonal, in that a single person cannot create their first language on their own, or mean whatever they like with a common language, so style is intersubjectively acquired, appropriated and transformed.

1.3 Intersubjectivity of style

This section is about persons as interpreters of others' styled utterances. Starting from the claim that expressivist theories of style consider the interpreter of styled performances to contribute to the judgement of what styles are used, and of what they signify, this section considers how we employ generic stylistic categories as part of coming to understand others' individual styles. It concludes with a discussion of the ethical responsibilities of interpreters towards those they interpret.

Charles Altieri, arguing for a view of style similar to the one I am developing here, draws attention to the importance of audience. Using Wittgenstein's later work, particularly the *Philosophical Investigations*, Altieri argues that someone's style does not simply *display* their self. Their style incorporates both the 'irreducible individuality of the speaking voice while teasing from it insights that make us reconsider familiar subjects'. He argues that this 'irreducible individuality' is neither a self-constructed performative individuality nor a socially constructed artefact, but a mode of seeing the world that is coloured by both individual character and social conditions (Altieri 1987: 186). Style is not the form but the 'life' of the written sentence (Altieri 1987: 184), the artless movement of a body, the concentration embodied in a student's bowed head, of any and every activity of a person. The interpreter then has the work of grasping the relationship between just that performance or sentence, and the person whose expression it is. The interpreter's role involves not just considering the formal stylistic qualities of a performance, but seeing how those qualities are animated by the person who performs them:

> [in his style] the person reveal[s] mental energies as woven into his sense of
> the world as are his physical actions ... Style is a matter of life, not only of art,
> and life is a matter of learning to adapt over time to many things which show
> how crude our frameworks are.
>
> (Altieri 1987: 184)

The idea of interpreters of style attending to the self expressed *through* styled
performances and utterances has important precedents, as Roger Hausheer points
out. The expressivist cultural aesthetics of Johann Gottfried Herder and the
hermeneutics of Friedrich Daniel Ernst Schleiermacher both treat individual
expression as coloured by and expressive of the social world to which that individual
belongs. Both of these writers treat individual performances as expressive of ways
of life at once individual and shared. And both attempt to tackle in some measure
the ethical dilemmas that expressivist theories of style face, the problem of the
hermeneutic circle and the conflict between method (or formal analysis) and
intuition (or empathy) as paths to understanding others.

As Hausheer puts it, Herder's expressivist account of human being and activity
is that 'all men's works and deeds express the social life of their group' (Hausheer
1996). In Herder's work, expressivism is tied to the complementary notion of
Verstehen, humane or empathic understanding, the faculty by which any individual's
expression, through social activity, of his or her group identity and sense of
belonging can be apprehended (Hausheer 1996: 55). For him, the most significant
level at which groups function, and the sense of belonging to a group, was at the
level of the nation, so within his scheme all stylistic qualities of a person's performances express their nationality as well as their individual characteristics.[21]

From Schleiermacher comes an elaboration of hermeneutics as a systematic
discipline of interpretation of individuals that required empathy as well as formal
analysis. Schleiermacher figured individuals as both perfectly unique, and also
capable of empathic understanding (*Verstehen*) of each other through a process of
hermeneutic intuition, enabled by a range of human similarities, and facilitated
by similarity of culture, language or temperament. The task of understanding is
both necessary and infinite, to be taken up again each time we encounter people
who are strange, new, unfamiliar (Schleiermacher 1959: 31; quoted in Hausheer
1996: 59), because in engaging with them we are not attending simply to
grammatical utterances or social performances, but to

> the immediate presence of the speaker, the living expression which conveys
> the immediate participation of his entire mental and spiritual being, the manner
> in which in this situation the thoughts are developed out of the common human
> situation.
>
> (Schleiermacher 1959: 131; quoted in Hausheer 1996: 67)

Schleiermacher starts from the interpretation of the active individual in a social
world, and then extends the hermeneutic process to the interpretation of texts, in
which the absence of a speaker renders it particularly necessary. Texts do not

make themselves out of the body of extant language, but are made by individuals, and count as expressive actions of individuals, each of whom 'makes his own unrepeatable use of the language, for his own specific purpose in his own special circumstances' (Hausheer 1996: 67). While later readers may come to the written text with quite other purposes than to understand its writer, none can ignore that the text itself would not exist but for the person whose expressive action it was. Without some understanding [*Verstehen*] of the person whose expression it is, an interpretation of a performance cannot but be incomplete. So Herder and Schleiermacher both hold versions of stylistic expressivism, and each develops a theory of *Verstehen*, understanding of unique individuals to bridge the gaps between performer and interpreter. Among other things, understanding as *Verstehen* bridges the gap between what we might call generic stylistic categories (such as Georgian, flowery, Baroque, etc) and the unique style of any single person.

The issue of empathy, particularly textually mediated empathy, in understanding others, is a large one, so large that I will take it up in a separate chapter.[22] But I can at this point describe the formalist comparisons that are the second mainstay of Romantic hermeneutics. The method of determining an individual's style by comparing their performances with those of other people requires a distinction between two sorts of style, which I will call generic style and individual style. It is important to draw attention to this distinction because we employ both generic stylistic analysis and the organising concept of individual style in understanding persons through their styled performances. The two play complementary roles, but the former is the more important in social interaction oriented towards understanding of the particular other as a socially situated individual.

Generic styles are abstractions. A generic style consists of a collection of recognised, imitatable stylistic traits, such as pace of speech, type of imagery, choice of subject matter, and so on. As roles are complexes of social practices that occur with sufficient regularity for us to name them or their practitioners (Emmet 1966: 73), so certain ways of performing an activity come to be recognised as generic styles. Richard Wollheim's division of generic styles into universal (such as naturalism), period (such as Social Realism) and school (such as Giotto's style) provides examples of generic styles often employed in aesthetics. We use similar, if less well-known, generic styles to describe people of our acquaintance, and those we know well. Someone might be described as having an 'academic' style of speech, an 'old fogey' style of dress, or as greeting his or her friends in the local style. A generic style is a little like a recipe, in the sense that it is an abstraction that can be employed by anyone to produce performances in the same style.

A style belonging to a single person can be called an individual style.[23] People have styles of dress, speech and address that are quite their own, not conforming to any generic style. Some individual styles are very distinctive, but an individual style may closely resemble a generic style; for example, most people's styles of speech are not remarkable, and even remarkable styles of speech share many features in common with many less remarkable styles. An individual style may also, like a generic style, possess *recognisable* features. However, an individual style is distinct from any generic style, although the features that constitute it may not be sufficiently different from some generic style to warrant its having a separate name. (In some cases an individual style *is* distinctive enough to acquire a separate name, but remains an individual style because it cannot be successfully imitated.)

What is distinctive about individual style for my purposes is that it is instantiated only in the performances of the single person whose style it is, and is *expressive* particularly of the person whose performance it is. Although thousands of singers may have a *bel canto* singing style, each will also have his or her own style of *bel canto* singing; each performance by that person will have some unique constellation of features, and successive performances by that person will have slightly different, unique constellations of features. And although we could formalise the features of the many performances by the person whose style it is, that person's individual style can never successfully be reduced to a set of formal features. This is because the totality of each performance is *more than* the employment of a set of formal features; it is the animation of those formal features in a unique performance, uniquely expressive of the performer.

In coming to understand another person, we have recourse to generalisations of various sorts. As we might use generalisations about a person's class membership, upbringing and so on, generic styles are generalisations that can be used in discerning an individual style. As the primary project of understanding another's style is that of understanding that person (an ethical claim for which I will argue in 1.4.3), generic style analysis is usually subordinate to, performed in aid of, a consideration of someone's individual style. Generic stylistic categories are useful aids as we grope towards familiarity with a person's individual style, and an understanding of that person, though over-generalisation (or stereotyping) is the risk we run in using them.

Performance and interpretation are linked aspects of the social significance of human actions that take place in a social world that cannot properly be said to belong to or be controlled by any single person. This is most clearly seen in cases, such as conversation, in which expression and interpretation are simultaneous activities, part of a social relationship between people. How one person performs some social practice (such as making an apology) depends in large part on how they are seen to perform it by others involved in the performance. So, for example, attending to individuals' particular styles, or inattentively stereotyping people by doing no more than classing their performances as of a generic style, are both varieties of interpretation of style.

Interpreters, as well as performers, have a say in deciding what style performers have; by implication interpreters also have responsibilities that are theirs by virtue of their engaging in social discourse with other people. While these responsibilities are difficult to spell out, a first step would be to specify that interpreters, at least in social exchanges not characterised by physical abuse or gross inequalities of power, already have some sort of social relationship with the person whose styled activities or utterances they are witnessing. As Berel Lang points out in the case of auto-biography, interpreters are at liberty, when reading another's work, to compare the states of affairs described in that work with what they know of states of affairs in the world, and to make judgements about the author's honesty, consistency and self-knowledge on that basis (Lang 1990: 178–84). A corresponding responsibility may be said to obtain, to attend as fully as possible to other persons' style, as these will contain important expressions of those others' selves. Further or different conditions may apply if interpreters are not engaged in social exchanges with a performer, and if a gross inequality of power exists between performer and interpreter. I discuss the first category in section 1.4.4. The second I consider in a discussion of the limitations of speech acts in Chapter Three of this book.

Misunderstandings often occur due to stylistic differences that are difficult to foresee or discount. For example, the style of a person's performance is relative to just what performance other people *think* is being performed. Style is not simply the 'how' of a more substantive 'what'. To begin with, the articulation of social life into distinct social practices is itself always in process and contestable. In other words, whether an action counts as this or that social practice is something that is determined by debate and reflection within the self-adjudicating community that employs that practice,[24] rather than being a priori available to any individual. The 'whats' are themselves less than perfectly stable, in the sense that a single set of physical movements is open to more than one interpretation. One and the same utterance might be considered a greeting, a barrage of insults, or a valiant attempt to master a foreign tongue; on each of these interpretations, the formal features of the action will have different significance to the interpreter.[25] Further, any single action may be considered under different, but not mutually incompatible, aspects. Further, whether something counts as a 'how' or as a 'what' is itself contestable. The topic of conversation on which someone alights may, in some cases but not in others, constitute an aspect of their conversational style. Talking about the weather may, for example, be considered either as a social practice, a 'what' (the practice of talking about the weather) that may be variously styled, or as a style of talking, a 'how' (in this case, perhaps a friendly or phatic style of social discourse).[26] Distinctions into style and content, how and what, or meaning and embellishment, work only for some of the many cases in which we talk about style or employ stylistic categories.[27] Once we put them into place, as when we take someone's conversational contributions as a 'what' and certain formal features of those contributions as 'how', we are in a position to specify and analyse styles fairly clearly. The 'what', whatever counts as the performance, becomes the frame of reference and everything else a 'how', a style of performing, within it.[28]

Differences in the perception of style can result in such confusions as the misperceiving of intent. An example will illustrate how this occurs. Some misunderstandings in CMC occur in relation to the use of block capital letters in exchanges of e-mail, or within discussion groups or chat groups. Some CMC users use block capital letters to suggest emphasis on a particular word, or depth of feeling about a particular topic. Other CMC users do not use block capitals for emphasis, and do not expect to see them used by others in CMC exchanges (or elsewhere). Consequently, some such users find the impression of reading block capital letters akin to being shouted at, and consider their use as a socially inappropriate form of expression. In such cases, which were frequent during the early years of mass CMC, the style of the users of block capital letters, meant to express the emphasis that would appear without effort in the writer's speech patterns, was not recognised as such by many other users of CMC. It often takes time, and considerable care, for an interpreter to come to understand the relation between a performer's styles and the interests, and attitudes that these express.

That we can, by using generic stylistic categories, come to an understanding of an individual's style is not to say that there will not be debate among interpreters about the expressive significance of a person's style of performance. Such debate is common, appearing, for example, in the difference among attributions of style of speech by people with different preconceptions about speech. Familiarity with a subject, experience with Classical or other rhetorical styles, the depth of one's knowledge of someone, one's attitude towards them, and many other factors, inform and distinguish evaluations of style. Some, such as familiarity with a subject, may be of such overriding importance that they quite overshadow others. As Nelson Goodman argues, sometimes the style of a performance or object may be so power-ful that consideration of the intentions or character of the performer or creator is neglected (Goodman 1975: 799–811). The variation in how styled actions and artefacts are read shows that styles are variously constituted by their different receptions.

The variability of attributions of style is described by Hans Robert Jauss as the 'horizonality' of interpretation (Jauss 1982: 200). He writes of the interpretation of literary works and their styles over time, drawing on concepts from sociology to argue that ascriptions of style depend partly on the attitudes and world views of those receiving or understanding a work. In a passage reminiscent of Wollheim's description of the permeable boundary between stylistic and non-stylistic qualities of a work of art, Jauss uses the idea of variable and nested horizons to demonstrate that stylistically important regularities may 'lie dormant' until social conditions render them salient.[29] Appreciation of styles evolves as cultures change and develop.[30] But the variability of interpretations of style is already guaranteed *before* we consider the evolution of interpretation. It is necessitated by the variety of cultures to which people might belong, as well as by what-how permeability, the variety of projects of understanding within which stylistic particulars may be organised.

A fundamental variability pertains to the interpretation of style, since different cultures and contexts of understanding tend to produce different interpretations. Style-words are used to pick out salient aspects of how people act in a particular context of understanding, whereas there are many other aspects that might be stylistically salient, given a different context of understanding. Styles are conven-tionally coalesced descriptions of how people act, set against a background of other regularities. If we accept that the realm of human concern in which we consider style to be significant is broader than any single context of understanding, and we also accept that the salience of particular human behaviours is relative to a particular project of understanding or frame of reference, then we might agree that any attribution of style to a person means picking up on only some aspects of their behaviour (or writing or art), and neglecting others.[31]

There is thus a region of slippage between the existence of conventional semi-regularities which may count as stylistic, and the drawing together of some or all of these regularities under the category of an artistic style, or the style of a person. There is also, necessarily, slippage between one drawing-together and another. Whatever we talk about in terms of style does not constitute the whole realm of style, because the attribution of style occurs within particular projects of under-standing, and so must be relativised within those projects. The recognition of style is crucial to how we treat the behavioural regularities that constitute them. But at the same time style is an organising concept, used for organisation of thought and understanding about other people. And no matter how we approach the issue, we will confront this slippage, between styles conceived within different projects of understanding, and also between recognised styles and unrecognised semi-regularities which might count as styles in some other project of understanding.[32]

In other words, a sophisticated version of stylistic expressivism[33] is rendered most plausible if it also requires of interpreters a careful attention to interpretation or appreciation. (The discussion of empathy as part of that attention must wait until the next chapter of this book.) Indeed, a focus on neither aspect fares well without some attention to the other. In a consideration of the role of style in social relations, neither pole can be neglected, and we must consider style as features of one person's practical and verbal comportment that are, or might be, significant for other people, whether as guides to understanding or obstacles before it. In summary, expressivism is a powerful explanatory account of style, but empathy in interpretation must be brought in to account for how understanding bridges the interpersonal gap presupposed by expressivism's emphasis on the uniqueness of individuals.

1.4 A topography of style

Before considering textual style in CMC in particular I want to provide a topography of style, to illustrate the ethical importance of style for how people understand (and misunderstand) one another. The terrain of style is a complex one, covering not only what is often considered to be the secondary, aesthetic aspect of *how* words are used, but intricately involved in ordinary activities and communications, both signalling normative patterns of expressions, creations and activities, and singling out exceptional or unique expressions, creations and activities. This complexity suggests looking at how we think of style and use style-words as a means of teasing out how the distinctions among their uses may be philosophically important.

This topography serves two purposes. First it allows me to explore further the importance of familiarity with someone's styled performances for knowing their self, styled speech being just one sort of styled performance. Second, through a discussion of style in relation to art objects, it suggests that the artefactuality of people's textual styles affords less of a window for interpersonal understanding than does the broader totality of styled performances. After this analysis we will be in a better position to approach the implications of electronic communications for social interaction.

There are three domains in which style is of especial importance: that of human behaviour generally (lifestyle), that of art (artistic style), and that of language (written, and also spoken). As indicated in the Wittgensteinian approach, this is not to say that style is conceptually triune; the division I have observed indicates less distinct clusters of usage. There are certainly distinctions in how we attend to style in each of these three areas, and the differences are significant. But, as the use of a single word in these three areas indicates, there are also connections among the different uses of style-words as well as distinctions. The relations among the different uses and applications of style words are characteristic of the roughness with which we use this, as any, word. The differences among them are critical to the case that textual style is only one part of lifestyle more generally.

1.4.1 Lifestyle

I have argued that style is expressive of self, and have shown the epistemic value of attending to other people's styles as part of the project of coming to understand them. As I have argued, style may attach not only to writing or artistic performance, but to any of a person's performances, momentous or insignificant, habitual or unique, since all or any of these can be expressive of the person who performs them. I refer to style as attaching to all or any of a person's performances as lifestyle. Familiarity with someone's lifestyle is as important for knowing that person as is familiarity with their claims about their beliefs and desires; its particular significance derives in part from the fact that the styles that a person uses are often *less than* chosen. As noted above, the style of artless movements of the body, or particular postures, can be expressive of aspects of a person's self of which they have less than complete awareness, or about which they do not speak. I argue here that attending to another person's lifestyle is an activity valuable for understanding them.

In the social realm, stylistic categories employed in thinking about others range over the gamut of their performances: we talk of people's styles of relating, their individual styles, work styles and lifestyle. Gesture, rhythm and bodily interactions may figure in our attributions of style to people, almost everything we know about them may figure in what we think of as their style. We could say, then, that the style of any of a person's performances is expressive of their character or something about them, and that familiarity with the styles of many of their performances will therefore permit fuller knowledge of that person.

But there are many styled performances that don't seem to be expressive of a person's character, such as the 'bureaucratese' that someone writes in an official letter, or the impressionist style that I faithfully imitate in my weekend hobby-painting. So some of a person's performances, at least, will not be expressive particularly of them, any more than a cake that they bake following a recipe will be particularly *their* cake. To understand just how and when styled performances are expressive of a particular person, and so can be seen as part of their lifestyle, I need to return to a distinction made above between two types of style.

I distinguished above between individual style and generic style; this distinction can be used to show when and how a performance is expressive of a particular person. A generic style consists of certain recognisable and imitatable formal features. By contrast, an individual style is always more than a collection of recognisable and imitatable features. An individual style is instantiated in an individual's particular performances, the expressive quality of which cannot be captured by any list of formal features.

There are two ways in which an individual's performances will fall outside of some generic style. The first is simply in not conforming completely to any generic style. Thus, while some performances, such as the letter written in 'bureaucratese' mentioned above, will conform closely to a generic style, many others will not, and will be in some individual style. Even in this case, the fact that someone conforms to a generic style *may* be expressive of something about them, although not necessarily something important. Consider the example of clothing fashion. My friend who wears tie-dye tops and kaftans is thereby dressing in a way that falls in line with a fashion (though not a very popular one). That she wears clothes in this fashion may itself have some significance, for example signalling her allegiance to a certain culture or sub-culture; if my friend 'follows the recipe' perfectly, her sartorial style may be expressive of nothing more about her than that she holds allegiance to some sub-culture. Any deviation from the 'recipe', even a slight one, will mark my friend's sartorial style as her own, and allow it to be expressive particularly of herself.

The second way in which an individual's performances fall outside of a generic style is made possible by the introduction of the category of lifestyle, which ranges wider than simply sartorial style, written style or any single other register of style, to encompass the gamut of a person's performances. Once we start looking at a person's lifestyle, rather than at some narrower category of their styled performances, any engagement we have with that person will involve not one but many styled performances, in a range of registers of style, often simultaneous.

Note how very easy it is for a person, even one deliberately employing a generic style of some sort, to perform in an individual style, once we have accepted the claim that style, in the sense of 'lifestyle', attaches to all and any of their performances. Take the example of my friend who wears tie-dye tops and kaftans. Her sartorial style may belong to a pre-existing generic style. But her performances go well beyond that of wearing one fashion or another, and include how she wears the clothes she wears, how she walks, talks, and so on. And I consider *all* these styled performances together, seeing her lifestyle not in any single performance but across the gamut of her performances (or at least those to which I am witness).

Lifestyle is the playing out through a whole life of socially and naturally constrained choices, ways of acting that are expressive of that person. And in its broadest sense, lifestyle is just the accumulated patterns of material and social conditions, deliberate choices, less-than-deliberate choices, and habituated actions involved in becoming and being one sort of person rather than another. Although the broadest category of style within projects of understanding individuals is lifestyle, within this are nested the styles in which someone performs particular practices and activities, which may vary significantly.

On the interpretive side, attributions of lifestyle to somebody are character-istically attempts to sum up something that we think is important about how that person lives, or acts. Because of the significance that many people give to personal deliberation and choice, attributions of lifestyle often refer to significant decisions someone has made about how they will comport themselves, tracing spontaneously styled actions to earlier significant decisions about how they live their lives. But most commonly we take lifestyle to express some amalgam of character, culture and circumstance, not a character chosen in any simple sense.

In interpersonal relations, generic style categories are subordinate to an analysis of another's lifestyle. They are useful approximations, means to the end of grasping that person's style. In understanding another person, we consider any individual styled performance in relation to his or her other styled performances, all within the project of understanding his or her self. Someone's lifestyle can be considered as a composite of all their styled performances; coming to know someone involves having a detailed picture of the relationship between the styles they employ and their interests, attitudes, and character. Familiarity with a person's lifestyle allows us to consider what their style expresses about them, as well as considering the explicit claims that someone makes about themselves (such as claims about their beliefs and desires).

Lifestyle, the broadest form of style, is close to character, in that it reaches most widely across the range of practices of a person, and can incorporate some degree of variety (as I may be voluble in some circumstances and taciturn in others). Style has a significance independent of character, and encompasses the variety of ways that a person's acting may shed light upon that more unitary concept. One person may have different styles in different circumstances and social situations, all of which are consonant with their possessing a single character. The extent to which we come to grasp the relation between people's many styles and their characters is in turn dependent on the attention we give to the people around us, and on the depth of our recognition of the differences and similarities among people.

In attributing a lifestyle to someone, we assume some continuity and regularity in their behaviour. I might talk of the evasive or responsible style with which a friend faces moral choices in her life, but I must observe some consistency in her approach to different particular moral choices to make such an attribution to her. In understanding others' lifestyles we tend to seek continuity and regularity in their practices even if we have no grounds for assuming either. I may observe that someone has a 'green' lifestyle even though I do not know them well, because I *assume* some continuity and consistency in their attitudes and actions in relation to environmental issues. Assumptions of consistency and continuity indicate that there is a temporal dimension to style, and that style, though recognisable in an instant,[34] is more thoroughly grasped over longer periods of time. Appreciation of someone's lifestyle will change, deepen, and become more nuanced as we see that person living and coping in a variety of situations.[35]

Familiarity with someone's lifestyle can thus be identified in large part with knowing that person, although familiarity with that person's claims about her beliefs and desires is also important in knowing her. Coming to know somebody can be achieved in part by finding out what she believes and desires, but examining the style in which these beliefs and desires are expressed also contributes to that process of coming to know somebody. Granted, we may have only a shallow appreciation of someone's lifestyle, as we may know his or her opinions only glancingly. Yet, as by discussion we become familiar with someone by engaging with his or her views, we come to know him or her through seeing him or her engaging in his or her particular way in various social practices.

Further, as I have already argued above, all performances are styled, in the sense that the performance either corresponds to some generic style or is the individual style of the performer. So knowing a person's styles, *how* they act or speak, is as important as knowing their beliefs, although we may learn less if their performance conforms to some generic style than if it is in an individual style. Each of their performances plays out against the background of practical possibilities that we see for them, and its meanings emerge for us against that background. If we mistake their style, then we may mistake their intended meaning and fall as heavily as if we had misheard the words that they uttered. Reasons why beliefs alone do not give whole of character were already given above in the discussion of style as less than fully deliberate expression. Further justification follows in the section below on agency.

1.4.2 Lifestyle and agency

I observed in section 1.2 that a style may be less than deliberately chosen and adopted, and may be expressive of someone's character or attitudes, or social position, quite without their having any intention of displaying either. The observation will be further elaborated in this section. Many human actions are not considered to support a variety of styles at all. Speaking one's mother-tongue is not a style, in an absolute sense; there is simply no way of learning a first language which is not your mother-tongue, and hence there are no different ways of acting in this regard. Some aspects of human nature and behaviour, roughly matching what count as common attributes of humankind, are outside the bounds of attributions of style. So style will inhere in only those aspects of how people act, speak and write, or about what they have created in which we can, and wish to, discriminate different ways of acting. Whether I walk with a stoop or a swagger may be a stylistic matter, expressive of my attitudes, interests, and character, as may be which language a polyglot chooses for thinking.

Style is thus indicative of agency, if not of any particular choice. If we attribute a style to something (an action, an object, a piece of writing) it signals that we perceive the presence of agency in that thing. It is rare to hear someone describe a tree as having a style, or to discuss the style of movement of subatomic particles. Where someone does ascribe style to non-human things or animals (perhaps in poetry, or in some scientific description), it is often a case of deliberate anthropo-morphism on the part of the describer.[36] For example, I may 'wear my hair in a French style', but I cannot 'have a face in a French style' (though I may well have a French cast of features).

The constitution of styles through regularities in the ways people do things means that a person's style is not arrived at by rational decision-making, nor by reflective contemplation. Someone's style consists of spontaneous action following from some mixture of more or less deliberate decisions and more or less unreflective habits. Their style reflects the significance for their life that they act one way or another, but the relation of a particular style to someone's character or identity is more subtle than a reflection of singular deliberate and wholly conscious choices.[37] Indeed in its broadest sense, style is used of a person's life taken *in toto*, so that all styled performances contribute to that person's lifestyle, but no single performance fully expresses it.

The stylistic possibilities open to individuals are neither limitless, nor equally easy to take up. How we go on, linguistically or practically, is not simply *given* by the nature of our situation, and is not determined by individuals entirely in isolation from our relations with others. Hence our responsibility for and to others, our influence upon them, and our vulnerability to them, all help to determine how we comport ourselves. Styles of speaking and acting are not freely choosable by persons who are constituted within webs of relations of power and trust; we are precluded from some, encouraged into others, feel safe with some but not with others, and so on.[38] We acknowledge these pressures when, in attributing a disagreement to a difference of style, we avoid attributing blame or error, but point to differences between people's behaviour without claiming that either is faulty or unacceptable.[39]

The decisions and constraints that produce someone's style may not in themselves be stylistic, or consciously deliberated. Style may thus be regular, but without requiring human behaviour to be regulated by stylistic considerations. Instead, stylistic regularities may be characteristic of someone, in their writing style for instance, without being intentionally styled or contrived. Equally, something deliberately adopted as a stylistic technique, say the use of periodic sentences, may become, with practice, an unprompted activity whose original chosenness may become transparent to both the person concerned and to others around them. For example, in an article on Samuel Johnson's epistolary style, Isobel Grundy observes that, although Johnson spoke in a polished and complex style, what would have appeared mannered or affected in another speaker seemed from him easy and informal (Grundy 1986: 15).

In general, we see the capacity to make significant choices as necessary for, but not, of course, identical with, the capacity to have or act in style. It is not necessary that any debated or abstract choices be made about ways of behaving, living, or making art in order for a life or its products to be styled. We merely need to perceive a degree of latitude, somewhat less strong than any assertion of categorical freedom, but enough to allow that this was not the only way of being or doing things. Style is expressive of a self, but not always in the form of a direct and deliberate statement, or even an indirect intimation. The importance of attending to another's style lies precisely in its expressions of things about a person that they do not show us or say to us explicitly.

1.4.3 Ethical implications of lifestyle as expressive of self

I have argued that style is expressive of self, and shown the epistemic value of attending to other people's styles, as well as their claims about their beliefs and desires, as part of the project of understanding them. With this done, it is now possible to consider the ethical importance of understanding other people's styles.

Attending to and trying to understand what other people do and say is an ethically important activity for many reasons. It helps to avoid misunderstandings, and to avert the conflict that often arises from misunderstandings. Where attending to other people is a reciprocal activity, people may establish understandings with one another that rest upon their mutual knowledge of each other. Understandings established among people, as part of relationships of trust and respect, allow cooperation and independence in working together.

As well as these reasons for knowing other people (advantages for all of coopera-tion) there are also reasons for attending to others that relate directly to the values of respect and consideration for persons *qua* persons. Cultural differences, as I have described, often encourage inattention to other persons, whether this appears as stereotypical or inattentive readings of others' styles, or as inattention to beliefs or actions. Such inattention may count as lack of respect for persons, or as discrimination. It is clear enough that no person could attend to all others with the degree of attentiveness that they reserve for their closest friends and intimates, and that some people are more inclined than others to attend to and try to under-stand the people around them. There are limitations on the number of people anyone might know well, and on the degree to which someone could hope to know the many people they encounter in a lifetime. Such limitations do impose constraints on attention in general, but do not, I think, make the project of attending to and knowing those with whom we live and work any less ethically important. They certainly do not give us a licence to disregard those other people with whom we do not become intimate.

I have argued that understandings between people depend on attention to style, as well as to belief and action. Misunderstandings may likewise arise between people through differences in styles rather than differences of belief, opinion or activity, although these are also important aspects of personal identity. Thus attention to stylistic features, including non-verbal features, of others' words and actions is important in our understanding of others as persons. It is as important as is our understanding of others' beliefs, dispositions, intentions, or actions. If indeed, as I have argued, the project of understanding another person involves attending to their style as well as to their beliefs or actions, then inattention to their style may be as inconsiderate as inattention to what they believe or do.

Attention to style oriented to the project of understanding another as a person is an activity that combines observation of another with openness to their claims, and a careful attempt to discern and overcome stylistic differences that might other-wise lead to misunderstandings. To discern the self expressed by another's styled performances, we need to attend to their performances as *theirs*, within the project of understanding them as persons with whom cooperation is an important, perhaps necessary good. And this attending cannot be a rapid judgement based on a short encounter, or indirect evidence. So, for example, because a style may be expressive of only one mode of a self, attention to the expressive style of another in a single encounter may persuade me that they have a way of life fundamentally at odds with my own. But later, I might see them in other circumstances, and revise my initial opinion. The emphasis here on the ethical aspects of style is an assertion of the value of attending to others' styles of performative and verbal expression as well as to their beliefs, as a way to avoid misunderstandings, and as a way of accounting for disagreements that does not appeal solely to differences in belief.

I shall return to the theme of the ethical importance of attending to other people's styles in relation to textually mediated communication such as CMC after considering artistic style, in which artefacts mediate between performer and interpreter. The project of understanding other people within ordinary social life turns out to be transformed by the artefactuality of textual communication.

1.4.4 The object of genius: artistic style

In this section, I consider style in relation to art objects, where style generally consists of properties of artefacts, and the style of performance of those artefacts' creators secondary, if also necessary, to their creation. I consider ways in which artefactuality may conceal the lifestyle of a performer behind the style of the artefact, and may allow the relationship between interpreter and performer to be overshadowed by that between interpreter and artefact. This overshadowing of the artist's style by that of the artefact has, I argue finally, ethical implications for the kind of understanding of other persons we may have through interpreting their artefactual creations, since those creations are only a small proportion of the totality of their styled performances (or lifestyles).[40]

I defined lifestyle above as those elements of same person's performances that express their interests, attitudes and character, as theirs alone, or theirs by virtue of belonging to some community. Style might also, by metonymy, be considered as the expressive or affective properties of a human-made artefact.[41] Indeed artistic style *is* often considered to be the property of artefacts rather than of people. Many human creations, including printed texts and works of art such as musical compositions, paintings or sculptures, bear little direct trace of the performance, let alone the life, of the person who created them. Nevertheless, they were made by human beings with lives and lifestyles. The relation between a person's lifestyle and the style of an artefact (or collection of artefacts) of theirs remains to be elaborated.[42]

In some respects artistic style is very like the style of persons' performances. We note salient or distinguishing characteristics of a single work or group of works, characteristics that contribute significantly to the affective power of the work. An artistic style is usually taken to consist of representative or characteristic techniques, materials and subjects, one or several of which occur in all works in that style.[43] As I have argued above with reference to what-how permeability, the same stylistic characteristic may indicate different qualities in different works of art, according to the artist and the subject matter.[44]

Style in art, like in life, includes both generic styles, and styles unique to the works of one individual. We can describe works of art as being produced in a socially recognised style, such as 'sonnet' or 'dialogue'. In such cases, we are matching exemplars with already-existing generic styles. These cases are generic, as the styles of fashion are generic, as both these styles are largely delimited by extrapolation from canonical works of major contributors. Since style can refer in this way to abstract and classifiable collections of characteristics it is a powerful and useful way of discriminating and appreciating large numbers of works of art, particularly if their creators are dead or their origins dubious.[45] Alternatively, we can single out an artistic style as characteristic of a single artist, and attempt to specify just what qualities distinguish that style as being uniquely theirs. It is against generic styles that individual styles stand out as irreducibly unique.[46]

An individual's artistic style, like their lifestyle, develops not in a single instance but through iterative practice through which that individual appropriates, or develops, generic styles as her or his own.[47] And since categories of generic style exist as abstractions independent of the works from which their characteristics are drawn,[48] even if I do paint in a symbolist style, I will have developed into this style by practising, and the practice will be my own. Stylistic possibilities (such as the genres with which I am familiar) may form or inform my expression,[49] but my attitudes, interests, and intentions may lead me to employ one genre rather than another. In other words, for artistic style as well as for lifestyle, individual attitudes, interests, character traits, may guide and suggest ways of performing, and may contribute to the particularity that is visible across an individual artist's oeuvre.

But artistic style differs significantly from lifestyle, particularly if we are considering how each may contribute to understanding other persons. The primary object of artistic style, that which appears to express, is the artefact rather than the artist. In social situations, analyses of style tend to be subordinated to the primary project of maintaining interpersonal understandings.[50] In the case of artistic style, the primary project is no longer the understanding of persons, but the understanding of the (aesthetic) meaning or significance of art objects and performances.

Artistic style is not primarily expressive of the life, interests or attitudes of a creator, but to belong to the artefact, to contribute to whatever the purpose of the artefact is (often to move people in a certain way). Formal qualities are characteristically treated as the property of art objects rather than the property of performances of an artist, a condition I call 'artefactuality'. Artefactuality is characterised by three main conditions: the absence of dialogue between artist and audience; the specialised expressive 'languages' of art objects; and the narrow range of the expressive languages of any artistic medium compared with the gamut of styled performances that constitute an individual's lifestyle.

First, the artistic creation is one that can have symbolic significance to an audience in the absence of the artist. To survive as such, works of art must have a significance or resonance that is broader than the understanding between two people, which is meant to appeal to and express the understandings of a community or culture, perhaps to the whole of humankind. The significance of many works of art is theirs because they are addressed to many people, often unknown to the artist, using shapes and forms and subjects that are widely recognisable and evocative. The object stands alone, and is intended to signify alone, not requiring additional intervention or exegesis by the artist (who in many cases is long dead). The performance that constitutes the interpretation of an art object own is in most cases distinct from the performance of its creation: the activity of writing of a book or creating of a sculpture is quite different from the apprehension. Though this is less obviously the case for performance art, or improvisation,[51] it does hold of texts, the artefacts whose status is most important for an understanding of style in CMC.

The separation of artist from audience allows both artistic expression and appreciation freedoms that are not possible in dialogical conversations. Subject matter is often the focus of an attentive, uninterrupted exploration that would not be possible in the cut and thrust of ordinary social life. The artist as subject may, as Goodman argued, disappear from sight as an intentional presence behind a work of art.[52] This may occur for many themes that, like many generic styles, indicate nothing about the person who employs them.[53] The case of music is instructive here, since music's abstract and formal qualities do not convey unambiguously particular emotions, let alone attitudes or character, except insofar as the task of writing music requires a character capable of study and equipped with musical ability. Alternatively, since the work of art allows a creator some liberty from the normative constraints of verisimilitude that govern most of everyday life, a work of art may have the voice of a fictional speaker, or may have rhetorical direction not characteristic of the artist.[54] The artist has considerable leeway to move away from and express attitudes that are not wholly or solely her or his own, although they may be leavened by her or his experience of the world and its inhabitants.

For an audience, too, separation from an artist's life, means that their personal or lifestyle may be secondary to, or eclipsed by, the style of the created object.[55] Having little or nothing to do with the lives of the creators, we may feel ourselves free from any requirement to appreciate the styles of these lives. In many cases these are all but inaccessible through their artistic works.[56] Since single stylistic traits may signify differently to different audiences,[57] the artefact becomes open to many and various interpretations and appropriations.[58] To summarise, we cannot say that an artistic style primarily expresses, or is intended to express, the self of an artist.[59] Yet we can say that (something of) that particular artist's attitudes, interests, and character were necessary and sufficient for making that work, and may be visible in her or his work.

Second, the formal properties and qualities of artistic media may together evolve a range of significations that are quite unlike those that are characteristic of human performative expressions in commonplace situations of social togetherness. For example, the range of musical tonalities employed within a culture constitutes a system of complementary tonalities, complete with conventionally accepted emotional connotations.[60] Classical Greeks categorised the modes known to them, and considered each to excite different emotions, and sometimes actions, in listeners and performers alike. A dominant distinction in European music has been between major and minor tonalities or keys, where major keys are associated broadly with 'happiness' and minor with 'sadness'. Twentieth-century European music includes theories of tonal polarity, in which emotional effects are produced, not by single modes, but by the interplay among modes within a piece of music.[61]

Many other intersecting sets of distinctions also contribute to musical signi-fication: rhythm, pace, pitch (absolute and relative), musical forces used, timbres of voice or instrument, as well as lyrics, which add natural language to musical language.[62] Significatory regularities such as that of tonality, rhythm and pitch (or melody) constitute language-like schemata with which composers can suggest a range of emotive effects to any hearer who is similarly informed or educated.[63] Many of the significatory regularities work by analogy with human bodies – increased tempo, by analogy with the acceleration of heartbeat, signifies and produces excitement. Longer phrases seem calmer by comparison with shorter ones, an analogy with rate of breathing, though very long phrases may no longer brook comparison with breath at all.

So, while the art object is, in effect, an expression of an artist, it is a special sort of performance. It is an artificial expression, in a language or languages that have no clear analogue with natural language, in performances that are ordered and rehearsed. Artistic objects and performances can only rarely be construed as expressive of an artist's interests, attitudes and character. Even when the style of an art object expresses something about the artist, and his or her culture, it is, as Herder specified, only part of the picture.[64]

Third, as the specificity of the expressive languages of artistic media lets us argue, the monologic (or artificially dialogic) world of artistic creation is not an expressive register in which all the life-stylistic particularities of a person could be visible. Artistic expression is at most one of the many strands through which onlookers might discern an artist's character, interests, and person; without knowing the artist as a living being, much of the style of his or her life is invisible. The expressive language of any artistic medium, even writing, rich as it is, is less broad than that of life as a whole, in which linguistic practices are part of social practices more broadly, and in which no piece of talk or writing is the 'last word'. Any life contains a richer range of sets of significant distinctions than those in works of art, no matter how powerfully expressive and universally appealing the latter may be. The scope within which a given artistic performance or object is expressive, while clearly varying from genre to genre, is always narrower than the scope of a life. The significatory schemata of artistic genres are fewer than, as well as different from, the regularities and patterns of performance that constitute a lifestyle.

In the world of art, the lifestyle of an artist has little to do with artistic style, and the attitudes and interests of an artist are often invisible in works of art. The condition of artefactuality encourages focus on objects rather than persons as styled. Artefactuality imposes registers (or media) through which performer (creator) and interpreter may be in touch that are different from those of ordinary social interaction. These registers are also comparatively limited compared with the gamut of registers in which a person's lifestyle may be expressed. Though I have not explored it here, both individuality and deliberate choice have traditionally been privileged in art, and this may also contribute to the separation between artistic style and lifestyle, in which much style is unintended.[65] Art objects, particularly if treated as expressive in their own right, may thus obscure the lifestyle of their creator, and so be a poor guide to understanding the artist as a self.

1.4.5 Linguistic style

Linguistic style crosses into both of the areas already considered. Style is part of our everyday life practices and the tool we use to think reflectively and write about our lives. Further, spoken, written, and recorded language is artistically important, and linguistic expressions may be considered quite separately from the life of the person who performed or created them. Linguistic style may be appreciated either within the frame of the way of life of someone we know, or under the aspect of a literary product, unique, but separate from and independent of the life of the person or people who employed it. In this section I explore how artefactuality, characteristic of some forms of language, may colour our understandings of other people considered purely through their locutions.

First, language figures in artistic style, covering many forms of more or less deliberately styled written and spoken creation, and performance. Works of literature, plays and poetry are typically described as being in particular styles, or conforming to generic styles, or constituting individual styles. The style in which they are written is comparatively worked on or contrived, rather than built up spontaneously in practices of everyday language-use. The language they employ is often, if not always, different from everyday language; even naturalistic styles of expression may be the result of long periods of concentration and effort. Texts that read like dialogues, letters and diaries must be *contrived* to read that way, and often employ a range of para-syntactic markers more varied than the punctuation taken for granted in text. As written creations outlive the time of their origin, their styledness may be thrown into sharper relief, as their use of word or locution ceases to be 'current', striking readers instead as perhaps convoluted, crude or fanciful.

Linguistic art objects, texts, share the objectual or material quality of other art objects, in that they signify in the absence of their author. They can to some extent overcome distance and transcend context, bringing the contexted script of one correspondent into the world of another. They may bear only an oblique relation to their author's attitudes and character, and they may be reinterpreted in a variety of ways, not all in keeping with the author's intentions. Artistic linguistic style is appreciated in relation to the significance of the text or verbal performance, rather than in relation to the author's lifestyle, attitudes and character, which may vanish or be submerged, inaccessible or even irrelevant.

Second, linguistic style has affinity with lifestyle, with the myriad practices associated with significant individual attitudes or interests, and with structuring social preconditions. Language is styled, not only in artistic creations, in which language is worked on and condensed, but also in perfectly ordinary conversations and correspondences, in which it is one aspect of a person's whole life, one part of their lifestyle as understood by those who know them. And here analysing the style of the language used must also include attention to other important aspects of the social situation and its participants. The analysis of linguistic style in a novel or poem can be seen as a freestanding exercise, and can comparatively safely neglect the question of whether any other non-linguistic understandings must be shared by people for one to appreciate the poem of another. But in the case of a conversation, language is not all that passes between people, although it is a very important part of it. People in conversation also share fairly closely overlapping understandings of what is going on between and around them, expressed not only in their words but in every aspect of their comportment in relation to one another.[66]

Linguistic style in social situations is thoroughly intricated with the other aspects of the situation, with what is going on for the people involved, with what is going on between them, and is thus ineluctably part of lifestyle. In this sense then, someone's linguistic style is part of their lifestyle, understood as part of how they express their particular selves.[67] In most situations in which we have linguistic contact with people, and in all of the situations for those people without access to printed books or language-only communication, someone's linguistic style is experienced as part of that person. We pick up and understand people's styles along with their beliefs and opinions, as part of knowing them, and as part of the dance of tolerance that is involved in being members of communities whose composition is heterogeneous, hierarchical and complex.

Conversations are only the most obvious targets for mention of linguistic style. Style-words can be applied to almost any spoken or written material, to public and political speeches, to scientific treatises and even technical manuals (see for instance Koehler, Dupper, Scaff, Reitberger and Paxon 1998). Sociolinguists and psycholinguists have focused on linguistic and performative style in conversations and arguments,[68] and to linguistic style in computer-mediated textual situations, shedding new light on stylistic factors in conversations. Literary theorists have focused on epistolary style, or style in letter-writing, as in the article by Isobel Grundy mentioned above (Grundy 1986). As I suggested above, separation between people does not necessarily result in the absence of dialogue characteristic of the artist–audience relationship, since in many cases separation is merely a temporary gap in an association. Separation may have less drastic impacts on understanding than to orient it away from the expressive subject and towards the expressive object. It may instead suggest techniques of writing designed to produce spontaneity and intimacy such as Grundy discusses: conscious and imaginative shaping of friendship by positive reference to it, or by proffering confidences; representing conversation rather than mimicking it; use of ambivalence to elicit a response from a correspondent (Grundy 1986: 220–1).

Linguistic style stretches across from painstaking textual productions meant for appreciation by a wide and unknown audience, through spontaneous writing, prepared rhetorical speeches, to the spontaneous utterances that are part of ordinary social situations, in which language is just one of the links between people. As the discussion of artistic style above showed, style can be attributed easily to objects independently of their performers, so that there may well be a radical disjunction between the individual style or lifestyle of an artist and what we think of as the style of their creations. To the degree that linguistic performances partake of artefactuality, they are open to interpretations that focus on the artefact rather than the performer. It is here that the ethical importance of attending to the style of another's linguistic performances re-emerges as crucial.

We run the constant risk of overlooking the variety of artless (and sometimes artful) styles of ordinary social practitioners. Sometimes understandings of style are part of mutual understandings between people, serving a primarily social or ethical purpose. At other times, style is part of an analytic or aesthetic understanding that does not necessarily reflect the relation between a styled text or speech and the character and practices of its performer, particularly where the style of the text tends to obscure or overwhelm that of its writer. Texts, whether artful or commonplace, are open to writer-centred or text-centred stylistic readings, as they may share in both the status of art objects as objects, and in the performativity of everyday styled activity. We can analyse style so as to appreciate the character of its author, or to elucidate a text for ourselves. If it is only through text that two people share their lives and come to know one another, as is often the case in CMC, then linguistic style will tend to play a larger role in manifesting character than it would in companionships. I shall now explore textual style in more detail, with specific reference to CMC.

1.5 Textuality and style: CMC

> By the very structural conditions of the letter-writing situation (which involves absence from the addressee and the constitution of a 'present' addressee, removal from events and yet also the constitution of events) epistolary literature intensifies awareness of the gaps and traps that are built into the narrative representation of intersubjective and temporal experience.
>
> (Altman 1982: 212)

In this section I draw together arguments made above, that textual style is one subset of a person's styled performances more generally, and that textual social interactions will be more organised around textual style than other sorts of styled performances. They may also be vulnerable, through their nature as a subset of styled performances, to misinterpretation.

In wholly textual expression, linguistic style takes on an importance that it does not usually have in conversation. A writer uses textual nuances, and techniques of spontaneity in the physically inert textual 'body', to express her or his self. A reader attends to such nuances and techniques, which together go proxy for the work of eye and tone of voice, bodily comportment and relations, in maintaining personal familiarity and the sense of what is at issue, of what is going on in a conversation.[69] As I discussed above in relation to lifestyle, someone's interests, attitude, character, may appear in their prosody, gesture, bodily movement and facial expression, in their performances of any social practices, as well as in their statements of belief or opinion. For example, Iris Young's observation that some people understand others' unreflecting self-confidence as a deliberately intimidatory style (see particularly Young 1990a; 1990b) is a pertinent example of the effects of non-verbal style in social interaction. In the absence of other stylistic registers, textual style can compensate.

But textual style differs from the broader category of lifestyle. Lifestyle, constituted as much in non-verbal (or not wholly) performances as in purely propositional or linguistic assertions, is filtered through a textual medium. Attitudes, interests and character traits that may be bodied forth across a person's styled performances are sometimes inaccessible in printed texts. Such inaccessibility is *not* due to the intrinsic lack of a particular relation between the reader and the writer of texts. This is shown by the existence of all sorts of texts, such as shopping lists, letters and notes, as well as CMCs, that *do* perform particular social functions between people familiar with one another.[70]

The sorts of misunderstandings possible in text result rather from the comparative narrowness of textual style, as well as from differences in style that result, in all media, in misunderstanding or obstruction. This claim hangs on my argument above that there are significant distinctions between performative individual style as part of the social practices of a person and written style, such as that of CMC, as one register in which a person's performances might indicate character. Communication through writing offers occasion for particularly textual forms of misunderstanding, for all that writing allows great precision and clarity of expression. For example, the artefactual nature of textual communications means that the texts, e-mails or letters, function both to bridge the gap of mutual physical absence, and to emphasise the fact of that absence.[71] Styles in textual communication may be directed toward compensating for this absence by employing techniques of intimacy, spontaneity and togetherness that may nevertheless only emphasise the lack of concrete togetherness.

Any attempt to body forth the performative styled self of everyday life pushes the correspondent (of e-mails or of letters) into a more self-consciously performed world than that which they ordinarily inhabit, in which writing does all the work. In textual exchange, self is not bodied forth in a multitude of styled performances, but must be performed in writing, drawing not on all the expressiveness of a self, but only on conscious self-knowledge textually expressed.[72] For example, the styles of greeting and leave-taking available in text are fewer and less varied, and capable of fewer inflections, than those available when people are present to one another. Textual interaction is also a world in which the bounds between creative optimism and self-deception may be perilously blurred;[73] as, for example, people who use MUDs to create fabulous quasi-fictional *alter egos*. I will discuss this blurring in more detail in Chapter Three.

More generally, since writing is the only expressive register available, there is often greater opacity of context (Ruthrof 1992: 15–32) in a written performance than there is in most conversational discourse. Where and when something was written may not appear in the body of a text; why it was written may also not appear, or may appear only as a lacuna, or as a stylistic quality whose significance is ambiguous. While the printing of texts intended for a wide audience encourages conventions such as authorial appeal to a 'generic reader', appeals to objectivity, and the elimination of subjects and expressions considered incapable of transcending context, these methods do not eliminate the contextual nature of writing. Nothing a writer can do will completely or necessarily overcome the gap that exists between the expressive act of their writing and the taking up of that writing by others.

The potential for misunderstanding is partly masked by our more or less spontaneous and unreflective avoidance of some aspects of modal opacity; people tend to avoid or explain easily misinterpretable locutions in writing. For example, we tend to limit the use of indexical expressions such as 'him over there', 'put it underneath', 'I loved the way they did that' and so on. We do not usually *try* to use our bodies as expressive forces in our writing (we do not try to point or smile at our letters); and many CMC users use emoticons, keystrokes conventionally accepted as a 'smile' or a 'wink', to signify how they wish an utterance to be read. But when we comport ourselves socially in text, as is possible in CMC, we who are writing are absent from each other. Many other aspects of people's individual style in conversation are simply absent from textual communication, notably their facial expressions and gestures, the ways in which their physical comportment meshes with verbal expressions, and the prosodic contour of their words. In addition, there is often extra effort[74] required for constructing and interpreting corres-pondence, which may lead either to taciturnity, or to careless writing and reading. They are compensated for by careful written style and by attentive reading; or they find no compensation and lead to misjudgement and misunderstanding.[75]

Since the advent of CMC changes in the communicative possibilities open to us, in the West at least, have affected both how people communicate with each other, and how people envisage communication. There is no longer a single speech-text disjunction to which we can appeal, contrasting orality and literacy as Walter Ong (Ong 1982) has done to great effect. Rather there is a messy complex of oral, textual and electronically-mediated ways of talking to and being with others, taken up and developed by different people in a variety of ways. Widening knowledge of the different roles of text outside dominant Western traditions has necessitated recognition of the multiple ways in which people create, use and understand texts.[76] And the development of CMC, the focus of the current study, has made possible very rapid reciprocal uses of text between people that grant, in some cases at least, a similar degree of spontaneity in textual expression to that which Paul Ricoeur attributes to conversational communication alone. I have argued that, nonetheless, textual styles do not always convey people's interests, attitudes and characters clearly enough for people to avoid misunderstanding each other. Indeed, the types of misunderstandings that occur in CMC (and other textual exchanges) also occur, to a lesser degree, in conversational communication, be it face to face, via a telephone, or via a video link.

I shall now relate the conclusions drawn from this typology of style to the ethical claim I have made, that attending to and understanding other people is an ethically important and valuable part of living in a cooperative society.

1.6 Conclusions: the ethics of understanding

The artefactuality of textual communication has particular implications for how people may know one another in CMC. The textuality of CMC limits its users to textual performances, making invisible or ruling out many non-verbal styled performances or performances with verbal and somatic aspects. Textual communication and physical absence encourage the predominance of textual style, and the eclipse of non-verbal styled performances. That, as I have argued, textual style is a subset of the totality of styled performances, one expressive register of many, with its own characteristic formal properties, limits the sense in which someone's lifestyle can be inferred from his or her textual style. Coming to know people through their textual styles in CMC involves all the risks of inferring from styles of performance to interests, attitudes and character (the problem of empathy to which I have already pointed), and the additional risks of doing so from only one expressive register of the many which we ordinarily employ.

In my approach to style in text, I have drawn on both strands of style already considered (linguistic and artistic style), and considered the case of writing where these areas overlap significantly. The expressive style that is one's own by virtue of being just this self is supplemented by the author's ability, and liberty, to write in many styles, often not characteristically her or his own. Such liberty is available to any writer. And someone's using a range of styles is often taken as just another aspect of their style: we understand as expressive of its author, not the style of the one imitated, but the style of the imitation. Yet, as I have argued, while our imitation and taking up of styles is balanced in ordinary social life by our daily less-than-deliberately expressive styles, the self presented through written style may not be so easily read, as a reader may have little access to a writer's other styled performances.[77] Misunderstanding may occur wherever textual style is taken for someone's whole self: wherever slowness is construed as apathy, stupidity or disrespect; wherever an attempt to be helpful is construed as condescension; wherever attempts at elegance are taken as vulgar or vain.[78]

There are particular difficulties with style in CMC, where conversational pace may be maintained, but without the usual non-verbal aspects of conversation situations. Styles of expression, in any case, may contribute to breakdowns in understanding, as the style of one person, the sense in which they intend their words to be taken may be utterly opaque to another person. Explicit sayings form only a small part of what is going on in most social situations, and in the absence of the myriad other styled performances, may constitute a picture less than fully expressive of a person's self. So, for example, in CMC emphatic block capital letters are sometimes taken as insensitive shouting; a correspondent's silence is taken as offence or as neglect. The leeway of invisibility in CMC, coupled with the potential of textuality for fictional or quasi-fictional performances of various sorts, suggests further that expressions of self may be more self-conscious and yet less than the self that is conveyed in myriad styled performances. If I am less than perfectly aware of what I am like, or of how others see me, or even if I am keen to impress, my descriptions of myself, indeed the self that my styled textual performances imply, may be inaccurate or incomplete, even if I do not mean it to be so. Deliberate attempts to convey the self through text may be partial, through the writer's partial knowledge of his or her self; or too complete, in that they attempt to express verbally what is more usually conveyed without words.

A further stylistic confusion arises from the temporal variability of CMC. This is that CM texts are halfway between being individual performances, contributions to conversations, and being styled textual objects, letters that can be isolated from their original interaction, and used again anew. And, in the past at least, different stylistic conventions have tended to hold for conversation and correspondence. The status of CMC as both conversation and correspondence, as both performance and as object, tends to break down older stylistic categories, at the same time as it makes us highly aware of their artificiality. It allows new styles of textual activity, composites of talk and letter. And it provokes new fears and risks of misinterpretation, as conventions on which people rely for comfort and cooperation cease to hold in their entirety in CMC.

The possibility of misunderstanding through stylistic differences is a layer of possible confusion between people in addition to the possibilities that we more ordinarily recognise, of disagreement on matters of fact or opinion. Misunderstandings may then occur in CMC, not because two people are of different opinions, but often because of stylistic factors that have little to do with what explicitly formulated opinions they hold. An argument designed to persuade, for example, may repel, or not be taken seriously, if its expression is stylistically at odds with the expectations of its reader. People may infer inaccurately from the textual-stylistic qualities of someone's writing to their attitudes, interests, or character, and take what is written more seriously (or less seriously) on that basis. In the wholly textual environment of CMC, the ways in which non-verbal performance allows and constrains the construction and expression of self are limited; hence greater emphasis is thrown on what is actually written.

Lastly, I would like to return to the ethical theme of this project, to draw through the implications of the styled nature of people's performances, textual and otherwise, for CMC. If we accept textuality as a medium through which people come to know one another, then we must also accept that the partiality of such knowledge may have implications for cooperation and social interaction generally.

In CMC we encounter not only a new medium, but also new groupings of people, and new types of interpersonal association. Together, these afford social contacts with a multitude of people previously unknown to us, within the confines of purely textual expression. The qualities of written style noted above give us some idea of how social relations in CMC interaction are structured by textuality, and suggest that attention to written style may go some way towards allowing people to understand each other in writing across social and cultural differences. The structuring power of textuality and the dual conversational/epistolary nature of CMC will suggest ways in which to read the styles of CMC correspondents, so as to avoid misinterpretation and misunderstanding. Indeed, the need to attend with care or empathy to the expressive styles of others emerges as a crucial ethical value in computer-mediated relations generally. It remains to give further details about CMC and its possibilities.

2 Empathy in computer-mediated communication

Now the reason why I do not feel at the present moment so far from you is that I remember your Ways and Manners and actions; I know your manner of thinking, your manner of feeling; I know what shape your joy or your sorrow would take; I know the manner of your walking, standing, sauntering, sitting down, laughing, punning, and every action so truly that you seem near to me.

John Keats (Forman 1935: 246)

2.1 Introduction

The first chapter of this book developed an expressivist theory of style. The ethical importance of stylistic understanding, and some of the unfortunate results of stylistic *misunderstanding*, were shown. While the first chapter concentrated largely on the forms of styled self-expression, including textual and aesthetic expression, this approach left largely unexamined the issue of how we understand others through the gamut of their styled performances. This chapter takes up the issue of understanding of others' lived experiences through their styled performances.[1]

The importance of understanding others through *attending* to their styled performances is an evident corollary to an expressivist theory of style. Because of limitations on our time and our capacities for attending to others, we rest content, for much of our social interaction, and for some ethical deliberation, with generalisations about others' character and personal style that do not require intense and ongoing empathy with others, or attention to their every performance.[2] Synchronic judgements about a person's style are, in effect, always generalisations. And yet we arrive at such generalisations through particular engagements with others; our grasp of these particular engagements (as well as our reflections on them in relation to previous engagements) affects how we understand the persons with whom we engage. There are two prongs to the activity of understanding others' performances in the particular engagements that constitute interpersonal relationships. One, discussed in this chapter, is the value of empathy for understanding people's experiences through their styled performances. The other is the importance of context in determining how we take up the affective aspect of others' performances. This second issue, which involves interpretation as much as the first, is discussed in Chapter Three.

The present chapter's discussion of empathy is directed towards the field of the ethical possibilities of CMC, and particularly with computer-mediated social relationships. At the outset, it is important to specify the scope of discussion. This chapter is concerned primarily with empathy within personal relationships between people, and not with transactions that are designed to be impersonal. Empathy has a significantly smaller role in highly impersonal forms of communication, such as those of information-exchange, that constitute part of interpersonal relations without yet being part of *personal* relationships. This is because it is possible to maintain morally impeccable interpersonal relations with another without having a personal relationship with them.

In preliminary definition, I take empathy to be, most broadly, the experience at second-hand of others' experiences. Empathy has both affective (non-cognitive) and cognitive components. The affective component, sensuous empathy, is associated with observations of another's bodily condition, although does not only occur as an accompaniment to such observations. The cognitive component, reflective awareness of another's experience, can result in and deepen affective empathy, for example by making one's awareness of that experience more vivid. I give a fuller account below.

Empathy is important within all interpersonal relationships that are not entirely impersonal. Empathy facilitates our coming to a more profound understanding of other persons' activities and character as belonging to a self that is like our own, although not our own. Elevated to a consciously practised activity, empathy with the experiences of others can encourage considerate action in relation to others. Reciprocally practised empathy is a part of most intimate relationships, and is valued as such. It can also play an important role in relationships in which barriers to mutual understanding are thrown up by cultural difference, differences in experience, or by novel media of communication such as CMC. Empathy[3] is essential for ethically engaged communication.

In this context, then, the most important questions to ask about empathy are how and in what form empathy is possible in largely or wholly textual relationships. It is to these questions that the current chapter is addressed. I begin by arguing that understandings of and with others, which afford ongoing social relationships and are, in various degrees, essential to their maintenance, are enabled by empathy, that is, by our awareness of the experiences of others. Empathy with particular experiences of others is also necessary to ethically engaged communications within interpersonal relations that are not personal (i.e. not intimate).[4]

Next I give a broadly phenomenological account of empathy as the experience, at second-hand, of the experiences of others. I begin by discussing exemplary experiences of empathy, and the qualities of such experiences. This includes a comparison of empathy with certain broadly similar experiences, memory, anticipation and fantasy. I then show that empathy with the experiences of others is part of, and contributes to, understandings of and with others. Self-understanding and understanding of others develop in tandem, mutually dependent and mutually constitutive, in an intersubjective form.

I add the qualifications that empathy, although essential to interpersonal understandings, is not possible in all circumstances, and its presence is, in any case, not sufficient for ethical comportment. Empathy can occur without producing any practical behaviour in the empathiser. Empathy with the experience of only one person out of many may lead to unjustified partiality, if I do not also take into account the interests of others, and the broader claims of social justice. In other words, empathising with others is only one part of sustaining ethical interpersonal relationships, and of moral behaviour more generally.

The discussion then moves to a consideration of the relationship of language and empathy. I argue that linguistic competence adds significantly to the depth of empathy of which people are capable. Linguistic expression enables deeper empathy by expanding the scope and depth of our appreciation of others' circumstances. Finally, I discuss empathy through text, concluding that empathy with others through text is possible. I conclude that the interpretation of linguistic meanings is an essential and difficult stage in the practice of empathy in textual exchanges such as CMCs. The practical implications of these findings are, first that we should aim to empathise with our interlocutors via CMC, in order to maintain and strengthen personal relationships in that medium. Second, the absence of expressive bodily performances calls for us to develop textual eloquence, in order to flesh out our circumstances and experiences to our interlocutors.

2.2 Attunement and attention

The conclusion I reached in the first chapter was that reading the texts of others within the context of the interpersonal relations of social life involves attending to the person *through* their styled texts, of somehow being aware of another's life and experience through their textual expressions. I focused on style as the gamut of ways in which people perform different sorts of activities, ways that are expressive of their self or character. The textual expressions of one person are grasped in particular ways by other persons; attending to another's style is one of the means by which we grasp their self, a coming to terms that occurs only across a gamut of particular performances.

In the context of social relations conducted via CMC, the question of how we can understand those who are apart from us requires particular examination. I have already remarked the differences between the gamut of styled performances available in shared practical life, and the range of expression and interpretation open to makers and readers of styled textual performances. Yet that earlier conclusion by no means rules out interpersonal understanding via text. And the history of textual relations bears out the possibility of maintaining relationships via text. Older written traditions than CMC have explored ways in which humans may be present to one another across distance, and how we may be aware of the experiences of others despite having no experiential access to these ourselves. Traditions such as those of mediaeval rhetoric, and the humanist world of letters, have accepted and built upon philosophical presuppositions such as that one can produce a true fiction of oneself in writing, and that personal agency may be enacted in letters. More recently, Hannah Arendt drew attention in *The Human*

Condition to the ways in which action and speech intertwine in our practices so that we do not simply perform ourselves as we will, but also disclose ourselves involuntarily as who we are, *as selves* (Arendt 1958: 58–60). Every utterance, every inscription, can be said to disclose at least something of the self who makes it. It is then possible for people to know each other's selves, to be aware of others' experiences, in ways other than through exchanging explicit and deliberately granted self-revelations (verbal or otherwise).

But we need to understand how this happens, how people come to understand how things are going for one another, whether they watch each other's performances or learn about each other's beliefs and desires. The mutual understanding that we have with other people is not some phenomenon that comes 'free' with linguistic or cognitive competence. It is developed and cultivated through connections and relations with particular others, is exemplified and taught to children by their parents. It appears in the kinds and degrees of similarity that allow understanding among people, and recognition of the relations between self and other people, that may exist at different levels and in different intensities. And it appears in our capacity to come to rapid initial understandings with other people.

Understanding of others is, as I argued in the first chapter of this book, ethically important. It provides the grounds for ongoing cooperation, for coordination without disagreement or coercion, for companionable activity, and for shared culture. As Peta Bowden has argued, lived experiences of trusting relationships with dependable other people are essential to a person's capacity to trust others:

> [P]ersonal caring practices provide the experience of continuous relations of being cared for, and of trusting in that care, that is presupposed by such dispositions as being fair to others and fulfilling contractual obligations. Baier points out that willingness to engage in impersonal trust relations, such as those contracted in the public sphere, is encouraged by one's sense of participation in a general climate of trust. Personal experience of the advantages of relations in which one is able to rely on other persons' commitment to care for one's own cares, and awareness of customary relations of trust, are central to the creation of this possibility. Together with more formal conventions and punitive customs, these understandings produce a climate conducive to engaging in long-term exchanges and even choices such as to smile at, speak to, or shake hands with strangers.
>
> (Bowden 1997: 149)

In other words, an individual's capacity to care for other people, and to understand, to know what is going on with them, is a habit (or habits) acquired by attending to the particular conditions, needs and interests of others in many situations over time. The formal rules and agreements on which we rely may contribute much to our awareness of implicit trust, and often enable trust in circumstances where interpersonal connections have little strength. But formal rules would have little power if we did not also already have the capacity to attend to others' conditions, and perceive goodwill in the forms of words used. Mutual understandings between particular people are the base on which more formal and less personal under-standings can also function.[5]

What is the role of empathy in such understandings? As I have said, in coming to understand another person we attend to the gamut of their performances. We listen to their verbal expressions, watch their responses to others, attend to the style of their performances, all in the light of our knowledge of patterns of human character and relations. Social intercourse depends not just on our understanding the words people use, but on our attending to particular people, on seeing how they respond to different situations, and on the understanding and trust that ensue from such histories.[6] In individual performances, we may look at the person performing as if they were another self, and see in their performances the reflection of experiences like our own. This is the experience of empathy. Empathy with the experiences of others is then a key part of the process of grasping the relation between lifestyle and character. This approach then describes empathy as a practice towards others, that is, as a way of attending to others, rather than simply as an experience that may strike us now and then.[7]

Since understandings of others' beliefs and characters requires interpretive effort, it might be asked whether empathy results from engaging in interpretation of others' utterances, or of their actions, rather than contributing to it. This position would make empathy less than fundamental as an object of study in relation to CMC, since it would mean that interpretation was the more fundamental activity in which to engage in interpersonal relations conducted in that medium. Indeed, while empathy between familiars may seem to come spontaneously, even without reflection, in cases of empathy between strangers some interpretation may be necessary to understand clearly the experience of the other. My position is that empathy with others' experiences and interpretation of utterances and actions are intertwined. Empathy with another's experience comes in many cases prior to interpretation, although interpretation is often involved in coming to understand another's experience more fully, and in some cases is essential to our understanding it as an intelligible experience at all.

Empathy is an essential component of a expressivist-interpretive account of human activity, because it allows us second-person knowledge of others' particular experiences, as *theirs*. This knowledge is separate from, and over and above any considerations and principles we might have about the rights and responsibilities of people in the abstract. The mere existence of empathy does not of course guarantee second-person knowledge of others, since we don't know most people well, and may sometimes be mistaken about the experiences that others seem to express in their styled performances. But empathy with the particular experience of others is necessary for understanding their actions as their own responses based on their own experiences, and in turn for guiding one's own comportment in relation to them as other selves. Empathy practised over time in turn contributes to that sort of mutual knowledge of persons that is part of an intimate ethical relationship.

Empathy is essential not only to intimate relations in which empathy helps people to grow closer, but, to some extent to non-intimate relations too. Less intimate relationships still require coordinated action, cooperation, and mutual insight. In less intimate relationships, empathy is directed towards these goals in themselves, rather than the goals of companionship or mutual support. Yet mutual under-standing is of benefit here too, in avoiding conflict, in allowing people to seek and discover non-destructive outlets for tension, and in allowing more harmonious cooperation.[8]

Annette Baier, Cheshire Calhoun and Peta Bowden have all argued that while less personal relations are dependent on a degree of trust produced by more personal relations involving attunement, they are not for all that inadequate (Baier 1994, Calhoun 1988, Bowden 1997). They simply lie in the outer reaches of the circle of caring relationships in which each person lives, with particular caring relationships at its centre, where ethical attention to others is the base on which social relations of trust may be maintained. Attunement also exists among such people, in the sense of their being able to coordinate actions with or not cause offence to others, despite lack of particular mutual attachments. Capacities for trust and attention to others, learned in particular situations, are drawn on in relations with those we do not know well. In the case of CMC where people are only partially 'there' for one another, and where what is going on must be held in the lines of text they share, the particularities of attention to others are somewhat different from those intimate and personal contexts in which ethical attention has typically been described.[9] But that discussion must wait until I have given a general account of empathy.

2.3 A phenomenological account of empathy

2.3.1 Initial definition

Our appreciation of the expressive styles of others is complemented by our capacity to experience in some manner the experiences of others, rather than, say, seeing people, or their writing, as objects, robots or as temporary visual or textual manifest-ations. In people's styled comportment we see something that is partly willed and partly involuntary disclosure of their selves; I have already remarked that we may come to understand other people either through their styled performances or, with more difficulty, through styled objects they have produced. That attributions of style have social and ethical significance stems from their reflecting our awareness of others as other selves. This awareness is more properly known as empathy, since it is not only the appreciation of *how* someone performs, but of the experiences of theirs that lie behind and are expressed in particular performances.

Empathy is the capacity to experience for oneself, in some form or other, the experiences of other people. We may empathise with others' sensations, moods and feelings, although, broadly speaking, it is more correct to say that we empathise with others in their having of these sensations, moods, and feelings, for we experience them as belonging to them, rather than as our own. And it is upon the possibility of interpersonal empathy, on the possibility of perceiving, through the actions and productions of others, their selves, that rest the ethical and social possibilities of mutual understanding, cooperation, and of communication of all sorts. If we did not have the capacity to empathise with the sensations, moods and feelings of others, their styled performances would mean little to us, and would have little ethical significance.

The function and importance ascribed to empathy depend on how it is defined. It is frequently used as a synonym for sympathy. As Daryl Koehn points out, sympathy has connotations of pity that are out of place in the more general experiences possible with empathy (Koehn 1998: 72). Sometimes 'empathy' is used to describe complete agreement or harmony of points of view, or to cover the complete sharing by two or more people of an experience. Max Scheler, for example, described 'complete empathy' in the case of a wife and husband who together mourn at the grave of their child, in which case they share a single experience (Scheler 1971, quoted in Frings 1996: 35). I shall be defining it as experience in which we are re-creatively aware of, or experience at second-hand, the experiences of others. Empathy is not limited to, though it does not preclude, the sense of sharing totally in a single experience with another person. However, it does preclude actually sharing a *single* experience with someone else, since this would require that experience not be constrained by the locus of experience in the singular embodied person.[10]

Of primary importance for the possibility of empathy is the role of the lived, psychically invested body. It is with ourselves, our own psychically invested, reflectively endowed, bodies that we experience and learn about others, as about the non-human world. And it is with the experiencing, feeling, embodied selves of others that we empathise, drawing on our own experiences, and our reflective understandings of these to do so. Even in the matter of interpreting spoken or written words we have recourse to the experiences of our own lived bodies to give practical sense to others' verbal expressions. It is in knowing that other human bodies are psychically-invested, consciously-experiencing bodies like our own that their verbal expressions become intelligible to us. We learn language from the linguistic community to which we are born in conjunction with learning the practical regularities of the world, and our linguistic practices are always very much embedded in our practical relations with the objects, entities and patterns of the social and physical world we inhabit.[11]

The approach to empathy that I am taking here draws from phenomenological work on empathy, but also makes use of other sources, such as recent work by Diana Tietjens Meyers, by Sandra Lee Bartky on Scheler's version of empathy as a political tool (Bartky 1997), and Margaret Walker (Walker 1998). I am relying particularly on Edith Stein's *On the Problem of Empathy* (Stein 1989), which draws on Edmund Husserl's *Ideas on the General Nature of Phenomenology* (Husserl 1931). I diverge, as do many recent theorists employing phenomenological analysis, from both Stein and Husserl on a major point concerning the degree of objectivity obtained in the activity of generalising from single experiences.[12]

Accordingly, I treat the phenomenological method not as transcendental but as experimental, without any final or privileged access to any 'things in themselves', and yet providing insights beyond its methods. I find evidence for the experimental nature of phenomenology inside Stein's own methodology. In particular, the interplay of experiences of self and other, that for Stein constitute the flow of consciousness, is an important indicator of the embeddedness of all individual knowledge and experience in the broader webs of social knowledge and experience. The reasons for my treatment of phenomenology as experimental rather than transcendental, which are based on the claim, held by both Stein and Husserl, that all experience is embodied, will be laid out here.

Edith Stein elucidates the analysis of the act of empathy as arrived at through the phenomenological process of 'bracketing' those parts of the world that are in any way dubitable, leaving only unquestionably 'objective' phenomena of experience. I do not claim to follow her in this process, for example in the general claim that the 'phenomenon forms an exemplary basis for the consideration of essence' (Stein 1989: 6), or in other claims about our having access to the *essence* of objects in reflection; but I do think that her insight into empathy explores important characteristics of empathy.

Instead I intend to take up the intersubjective stream within Stein's thoughts on empathy. Her account of the attainment of subjectivity for any given individual specifies that that path runs through both experiences that are one's own, and experiences recognised as belonging to other people. The weakness of her claim that we can attain complete, objective, context-transcending knowledge of objects, including the phenomena of reflection as employed in phenomenology, is in its conflict with the assumption of a psychophysical person. I shall throughout this chapter treat the site of the experiencing body as being itself situational, so that, while a knowing grasp of phenomena is always possible through experience and reflection, this grasp is always a project in progress.[13]

Taken phenomenologically, empathy is one's own experience of the experiences of others. For example, 'a friend tells me that he has lost his brother and I become aware of his pain' (Stein 1989: 6). I become aware of his pain without myself having outer or bodily awareness of pain. That is, I do not literally experience it myself as a concrete phenomenon; it is not bodily present in me as *my* pain, but available to me *as* the pain of another self. 'I perceive this countenance outwardly and the pain is given "at one" with it' (Stein 1989: 6). The pain is experienced as one with the face, not as an expression of pain, but simply as the pain of that person.[14] In this act of empathy, the inner experience of my friend is somehow also outwardly present to me.

The distinction of self-evident pain on someone's face from gestures and expressions intentionally *indicating* pain, is problematic if it is insisted that there is never any interpretive activity in understanding a face as being in pain, and always interpretive activity in understanding gesture and language. Such a model of affect and its primacy overlooks the possibilities of misinterpretation and deception of faces, although it captures the sense in which our facial expressions are character-istically unforced. The distinction becomes less problematic if we assume that pre-interpretive understanding of someone's face precedes, *as a rule*, the taking of an interpretive stance in relation to them. Since we may also adopt a pre-interpretive stance to bodily gesture and, in some sense, to language-use, the difference is one of degrees of immediacy rather than between a total separation of immediate understanding of facial expression and reflectively mediated interpretation of language and gesture.

It is in this sense that empathy may be a spontaneous (if learned) response to the comportment and expression of others, rather than a response to others that springs from an interpretation of their words or activities. Even spontaneous empathic responses will include some form of interpretation (in that the experience of the other is grasped as being of one sort rather than another); but not all empathic responses involve deliberative interpretation. Interpretation and reflection may deepen an empathic response, or even inspire one in some cases, but empathy is possible without deliberative interpretation.[15] Error, deception and confusion are possible at all levels, but become easier according to the mode of expression. Facial expression, more fully determined by our psychosomatic state, and less conventional than language, is also harder to falsify.[16] Bodily posture and gesture are perhaps somewhere in between language and facial expression in terms of ease of falsification. Questions do arise about the role of language in clarifying the *object* of an affect, but these are related to the issue of language and empathy, and will be dealt with in that context.[17]

There is a similarity between the way in which I am aware of another's pain and how I am aware of objects in the world. I can view an object from many different angles progressively, by moving it, or by moving around it. Different sides of an object can be given to me in turn in my primordial or actually present experience, while I can at the same time co-see or experience in non-primordial absence the sides of things that are not turned to me. For example, I can co-see the parts of a cat or a person that are turned away from me, not in present experience, but imaginatively. In this act '[t]he tactile and visual senses call each other as witnesses, although they do not shift the responsibility on one another' (Stein 1989: 41). Similarly I can consider the expression of my friend's pain from many different angles, and the friend's expressing *face* itself is as immediately present to me as an object. But here the analogy ends. There is no angle from which the friend's pain is given to me as my *own* experience, as it were. Therefore empathic experience of the experience of others does not amount to sharing that experience with them as a single indissoluble whole, but is constituted in some other way, containing both my awareness of my friend as an experiencing self like my self, for whom pain *is* an immediately given experience, and my second-hand co-seeing of their pain.[18]

2.3.2 *Primordial and non-primordial experiences*

Empathic experience of others' experiences is not accessible to us in the same way that our own experiences are accessible to us. Empathic experience can be further explicated with reference to the phenomenological distinction between primordial experiences (experiences of present phenomena) and non-primordial experiences. The major role of non-primordial experiences (that is experience of non-present phenomena) can be used to signal the importance of the imagination in appreciating the experiences of others. Primordial experiences are of three types, the first being that of physically present objects and phenomena. Ideation, or the non-reflective perception of formal or mathematical properties and relations in the matter of the world, is also primordial,[19] as is reflection on past experience. However, Stein herself is quiet on the complexities of reflection.

These different types of primordial experience are wholly one's own and wholly given to the self in the now, though they are not for all that uninfluenced either by each other or by non-primordial types of experience. Nor does primordiality imply that the perception of a phenomenon is categorically free of error; one may perfectly well have a present experience altered or corrected by subsequent experiences. Stein classes perception (say, seeing a friend's face, or hearing their cry) and ideation (appreciating the form of a mathematical proof, or the nature of numbers in general[20]) as primordial because their objects are 'given' to us directly in experience, not because there may not be error in such experience. On a general level, experience as a whole is primordial, ours in immediacy.

However, not all experiences are primordial in their content, since much of what we experience and think about is not actually present before us, available to us, at the time at which we consider it. Experience can also be of things not given and present to me, but remembered, anticipated, fantasised or empathised. Non-primordial experience is of feelings, moods, sensations and beliefs not experienced as bodily present, but given as images or mental representations[21] of those feelings or sensations. While, for example, a remembering has non-primordial content, the experience of remembering is nevertheless as primordial as all other experience. Reliving a favourite time is a primordial *experience*, although the *experiences remembered* are past and no longer primordial themselves. In this sense memory, anticipation and fantasy are, like empathy, two-fold, with both primordial and non-primordial components, the latter available as representation. The non-primordial content of all three is drawn from the past experiences of the individual, although they vary in their particular qualities, since anticipation, fantasy and empathy all involve thinking with the experiences of the past about non-past possibilities. In each variety of experience non-primordiality is the having-present-for-oneself in thought of non-present experiences.

Present and primordial experience, like the non-primordial contents of experience, is understood in an appropriative context consisting of the totality of one's past experiences of all varieties (Stein 1989: 73). These may be actually in one's thoughts, or, more often, exist in a state of non-actuality. (Or, to put it differently, they are present dispositionally rather than occurrently.) Recent accounts of social practice would allow us to supplement Stein's notion of cognitive appropriation with a full account of appropriation of the world through a nexus of social practices (including linguistic practices) within which one's life is intricated. Moreover such an account would allow Stein herself to explain our empathy with others' bodily movements and, importantly, utterances, as well as bodily form.

2.3.3 Empathy as a non-primordial experience

Non-primordial experience, that is the having-present-for-oneself in thought of non-present experiences, can be treated as similar to the commonsense notion of imagination, as enabling us to grasp conceptually things that are not available to be grasped in actuality. Empathy as I have defined it, experience of another's experience, cannot be a form of primordial experience. Rather it is non-primordial, involving, like the other forms of non-primordial experience, the grasping of non-present experiences. I here give a brief account of the non-primordial experiences of memory, anticipation, and fantasy, so as to draw out in the particular way in which non-primordial experience in empathy guides our grasp of others' experiences.

First, it is important to note that non-primordial experience is part of our ordinary experience of the world. Sensuous perceiving, or experiencing the physical qualities of the world, always involves an element of non-primordial as well as of primordial experience. For example, when I see a physical object, most of it is turned away from me, and is out of my sight; many things are out of my hearing, or not within my reach. When I hold part of something I do not touch most of it. Yet I can, because of my accumulated experience of the world, co-experience (not always accurately) those aspects of things that are not directly before me or directly under my hands. This is an example of the functioning of imagination, which is distinct from fantasy in being *guided* by and attempting to be faithful to past experience.

There are parallels between sensuous co-perceiving and empathy as regards the role that is played in each by imaginative co-seeing. One can have sensuous empathy of others in attentively co-experiencing their experiences not as one's own, but representationally as theirs. I may have a feeling of being led, as when, if I see someone's face, I feel or see with them, as it were, although this is not the same as having their experience as primordially my own (Stein 1989: 57). What I *do* have is an imaginative living-after that may be close to, but is never *identical* with, the lived experience with which I empathise, comprehending all the varieties discussed above. Co-perceiving currently absent aspects of the world is essential for the intelligibility of the world and of other people, since it is what allows us to represent things to ourselves, even when they are out of our sight.[22]

To begin with memory:[23] when I recall a past experience, say one of happiness at seeing a friend after an absence, the memory is primordial as an act of representation, summoning to myself that past experience, though the content of the past happiness is not primordial. However, I am guided by that past experience in my representation of it. I may have a sense of being guided, of attending to, or of being faithful to my past self and my past experience. My representation is of a past 'I' whose experience was then primordial, and who is present to me as a subject, but from whom I am nevertheless separated by a gap of time and experience, and which always appears to me differently in the changing light of my historically evolving self. There is continuity between my present self and my past self, but not an identity insofar as I can distinguish my memories from the present self that is doing the remembering.

I can remember, of course, in several ways. I can decide to remember something, or I can have a memory spontaneously appear for me, perhaps evoked by something about which I was thinking. I can remember while being reflectively aware of myself as a remembering subject, 'looking down' as it were, on my remembered self. Or I can become entirely immersed, deliberately or not, in the remembered experience, without having any reflective sense of my present self as doing the remembering. But none of this changes the fact that, while the remembering is primordial, given to me as an experience, the remembered experience is now non-primordial, represented to me in imagination. It may include, for instance, imaginative supplementation (Stein 1989: 11). Or, if I can no longer represent to myself the particular experience I had at some time, I may have to surmise about it, mentally reconstructing rather than re-experiencing it.[24]

Anticipation is similar to memory, but not identical, since the future is not properly part of our experience as the past is, nor is it thought of as part of our past. An experience of anticipation, while involving a second temporally displaced, future 'I', is not one in which my present 'I' can be led or guided by the experience of that other 'I', but one in which possible futures are either summoned deliberately, or evoked unintentionally, either absorbingly experienced, or reflectively considered, by me. My anticipation may be guided, but it will be by surmise about the possibilities held by the future, rather than non-primordial experience of the future. Imagination thus has a larger role to play in anticipation than in memory, as the means by which an anticipated experience is constructed. And I am guided in my anticipation not by any particular experience of the future, but by projection from experience of the past. Anticipated future experiences thus have a wider variety than the pasts that I can recall, since there is no particular experience by which I *must* be guided.[25]

The experience of fantasy is unlike either memory or anticipation, since there is no primordial experience represented at all, but rather a more or less wholly imaginary experience, a non-primordial version of present experience. Most fantasy takes place in an indeterminate time, although one can also fantasise in particular about the past or the future. My representation of the other 'I' is not one guided by a particular past experience, or reliable anticipation of the future, but more loosely by the bounds of my imagination. In this sense, fantasy representation is led neither by the other self's experience, or even by the usual conditions of actuality, such as natural and social laws, and social conventions.[26] In fantasy there is little place for surmise, since I do not have to reconstruct or be guided by any particular experience. While representation involves *my* work in bringing the other 'I' to experience in all three cases, it is only in the case of fantasy that my imaginative representing is not *sensed* as guided by constraints external to it, or as being account-able to external constraints. This analysis suggests in particular that anticipation may shade over easily into fantasy, since imagination plays a strong role in each, and there are no fixed rules as to just what about the future guides my anticipation of it. My anticipated meeting with an e-mail correspondent, for example, might involve a mingling of anticipation and fantasy that would be hard to distinguish, since my understanding of this person as a textually styled self has not had to take stock of her or his non-textual comportment.

Empathy also involves representation, and so is primordial as present experience, but with its non-primordial content taken from the experience of another (perceived first as an object and then empathically as a subject), rather than from other experiences of one's own. Empathy thus has a particular configuration.

> When it arises before me all at once, it faces me as an object (such as the sadness I 'read in another's face'). But when I inquire into its implied tendencies (try to bring another's mood to clear givenness to myself), the content, having pulled me into it, is no longer really an object [just as would be the case if I were pulled into my own past or fantasised present]. I am now no longer turned to the content but to the object of it, am at the subject of the content in the original subject's place. And only after successfully executed clarification, does the content again face me as an object.
>
> (Stein 1989: 10)

In other words, I am guided by what I see of the other to explore their experiences *after them*, as it were, though all the while being other than them.

It is in my turning to and being guided by, not my own experience, but that of another, that constitutes empathy as a unique variety of experience.[27] In empathy as in other representations of experience the emergence of the other's experience for me is followed by my fulfilling explication of it, as I follow through the tendencies and possibilities of the other's experience as I represent it to myself. There may also be what Stein calls a level of comprehensive objectification of the experience through my reflection upon it. This is then a provisional situation of the experience through reflection, rather than an absolute knowledge of it.[28] I draw on my own experiences of fear to understand that of the person with whom I am empathising, as I live their fear after them; the experience of the other is understood in the light of my own experience. My experience serves, in empathy, as material I (re)use in grasping what another person is going through.

But in the case of empathy the second subject that is the object of my representations and towards which I turn, is not my own, and is not joined with me in any continuity of experience, as in my own acts of memory, anticipation or fantasy. Another's fear, as empathised by me, is not mine primordially, nor is it mine in memory or expectation. However, unlike in the experience of fantasy, I am guided by the other's primordial experience, in this case by their fear. The other subject's experience is recognisably primordial, although my experience of it is non-primordial; and it is the other's primordial experience, not given to me as my own, but non-primordially as another's, that guides me.

So empathy, while it requires a non-primordial awareness of the experiences of another, run through the circuit of my own remembered experiences, is nevertheless led by and accountable to, an experience of another that is as particular as one of my own past experiences. Empathising with another's pain does require me to represent intuitively another's experience to myself (an act of imagination), but it does not give me free play in terms of how I do so. This is, in a simple form, what empathy is like as my experience. It is the dual accountability of empathy to my and to the other's selves, that is unique to the imaginative representation involved in empathy. There is in all awareness of the experience of others an element of imaginative intuitive representing to myself of something that is not primordially *there* for me. But this imaginative representation is to be distinguished from the usual sense of 'imagination' as fantasy, because it is a *guided* awareness (however imperfect its realisation in my imagination) of another's experience, rather than being free fantasy curtailed only by one's own wishes. However, it must equally be distinguished from mere repetition or imitation, since my empathic awareness of another's experience has not sufficient grasp on that experience that I might simply copy it.

An important conclusion to be drawn from the non-primordiality of empathised experiences is that empathised experiences are not always *simply* available to us, but often require interpretation and examination, or further discussion with the other person involved. As anticipation and fantasy may be more or less easily come by, according as their themes are familiar or striking to us, so we may need to attend carefully and imaginatively in order to empathise with the experiences of another. The commitment to this sort of attending in being guided by another's experience we might call faithfulness. This unavailability of empathy often requires from us both concerted attending, or faithfulness to the experience of others, and dialogic engagement with them in order to ascertain that our grasp of their experience is adequate. Hence the importance of language for deepening and directing empathy.

2.3.4 Empathy and intersubjectivity

Empathy is intersubjective in that it is essential in persons' self-constitution as subjects, both in the initial phase of maturing as a human being, and later as part of the activity of being a social human being in a community of persons. We come to know ourselves as selves through experience of others' experiences as belonging to other selves, which is learned only through empathy. For developing an understanding of ourselves, we are dependent on being able to recognise other people as selves, and matching this up with our simultaneous lived experience and perceptions of ourselves as living bodies.[29] I experience myself both as a living body (the self or 'I', the reflective experiencer) and as a feeling body (the bearer of experiences). I become intelligible to myself as self, as the world and other people become intelligible to me as other, because I can at once experience something for myself, and 'perceive' myself so experiencing it. I can 'see' (or more properly experience, since this 'seeing' is an awareness composed through several senses) my hand grasping a pen at the same time as I feel the pen in my hand. But I can become for myself a body among bodies, a self among selves, rather than being the experiential centre of the universe, only once I come to see that others who are physically like me also have experiential centres like mine.

In everyday experience, empathy may be very closely interleaved with one's own primordial experiences (as, for example, when I find myself embarrassed and perturbed in the awareness that the person next to me has made a gaffe). The close interleaving of experiences of one's own and of others, enabling under-standing of others' experiences and allowing us to imagine how others might see us, is known as intersubjectivity.[30] Discussion of the particular configuration of interleaved experiences of one's own and others would go beyond the bounds of this chapter; at issue here is the possibility of awareness of others' experiences in text, rather than the problem of the configuration of those experiences.[31] But recognition of the interleaving of any individual's own experiences within the broader expanse of their intersubjective experience is important for understanding the relation of individual experiences of empathy with the broader project of interpersonal understanding with which this book is more directly concerned.

Generally, empathy with a particular experience of another person takes place against the background of the whole of the empathiser's experience, including his or her memories, beliefs and desires. This whole includes the empathiser's prior knowledge, if any, of the other person. In other words, an empathiser brings to the empathic experience a wealth of prior understanding, and in consequence may deepen, either spontaneously, or through reflection or interpretive effort, the empathic experience. For example, my empathy for a friend's sorrow at the death of his brother will probably be more nuanced and more profound than my empathic experience of the sorrow of a stranger who had suffered the loss of a sibling. I might, say, understand the sorrow of my friend as an intermingling of grief and guilt at having failed to make amends for some particular wrong, or as containing an element of relief. Such sensitivity would be unlikely in the case of my empathy with a stranger at the death of a sibling, particularly if I have no knowledge of the circumstances of the death. I shall have more to say about the contribution of dialogue to the deepening of empathy in the section on empathy and language below.

In the light of these observations, empathy is perhaps not well described as an occasional or coincidental experience of the experience of others. It is better considered a frequent, even constant interplay in consciousness between one's own experience and awareness of the experiences of others, without which self-consciousness (that is, consciousness of oneself as a self) would not be possible. So empathy should be seen as a practice rather than simply an (unwilled) experience, and one which individuals subjects might resist if they chose.

Our learning to know other people as selves then takes place within relations with particular other people. If indeed we come to know ourselves as embodied experiencers through our awareness of other people as embodied experiencers, rather than having selfhood available to us a priori, then the particular practices of those other people may be included and predominate in our socially constituted personhood. Such practices include regularities of style, of behaviour, of verbal and emotional self-expression, and regularities in conceptions of personhood. We come, through observation and reflection, to associate people's bodily styles with particular attitudes and emotions, although these associations do not hold universally. Such practices may also include hierarchies of moral worth, and may also limit who is recognised as a person. As Stein notes, we inherit predisposed attitudes that sometimes prevent us from recognising certain people *as* people like us. We may despise and overlook certain minority groups, people with abilities, sexuality, or skin colour different from our own for no other reason than that we grew up surrounded by attitudes of contempt and neglect for such people. We need to encounter people of these groups in meaningful personal circumstances in order to recognise and experience their humanity, which otherwise might not occur to us. These prejudgements, essential to the structure of empathy as context-specific, form part of the limits to empathy as an ethical capacity. These limits are discussed below.

2.4 Limits to empathy

Empathy is, then, a non-primordial experience of the primordial experience of another, relying on imaginative reconstruction. It is also fleshed out by our grasp, often quite independent of the particular occasions on which we empathise with someone, of that person's character, feelings and intentions, and by our grasp of persons generally. Further, empathic experiences are of the experiences of *particular* other people. These considerations suggest together that empathy does not give us universal or unimpeded access to the experiences of others. I will now discuss some limitations to our capacity to empathise with others, as well as limitations of empathy itself as an aspect of our ethical understandings of those with whom we engage. These do not, I conclude, negate the essential importance of empathy as part of ethically engaged communications. They do show, however, why the human capacity for empathy is taxed by textual mediation in communication.

Stein cites the similarity of physical bodies and experiential capacities as enabling empathy. Empathy is possible across difference because my lived body is not sensed as having fixed dimensions or movements, but as being one exemplar of a bodily form that comes in many variants. Once I recognise that I am one person among many, I can see my body, like others' bodies, as being only accidentally in some particular dimensions, and as partaking of a general similitude with the variety of other bodies. Awareness of this variety allows me to appreciate similarity in bodily form and experience across difference (Stein 1989: 59). As the activity of empathic co-experiencing involves a fulfilling explication of the possibilities of the other's experience, as described above, empathy involves at least a spontaneous attending to others' selfhood, and may require increasingly great imaginative effort in investigating others' experiences as those bodies are increasingly different and distant from ours. Attending to the particularity of the sensuous experience of others becomes both more necessary and more difficult as we try to empathise with experiencing bodies increasing unlike our own.

Stein concludes that there are limits on empathy determined by physical similarity, including factors such as similarity of sensory organs. She points to the (at least initial) difficulty, for people who are not blind or deaf, of empathising with the experience of people who *are*, or for those who are blind or deaf, of empathising with people not so incapacitated. Such people are different from one another with regard to their sensory capacities.[32] She also points to situations in which my empathy for a certain class of persons is limited by preconceptions, perhaps about that sort of person, which prevent me from seeing them as relevantly like myself (Stein 1989: 31).

Stein's focus on the necessary embodiment of all human experience, and particularly embodiment as the basis of non-primordial experiences and that to which all knowledge must point, suggests a second axis along which acts of empathy may become increasingly difficult. It is not an axis on which she touches, as she discusses empathy of 'psychic life' as being an objective understanding of the structure of others' souls, without regard for the particularity of psychic experience. The second limitation to empathy results from, and runs along the axis of, culturally habituated differences among experiences and their interpretations in folk psychology and ethics. The importance of such differences in impeding (and so requiring) empathy is implied by Stein's claim that all experience is embodied, together with the claim that all people are born and live out their lives situated in particular cultures.[33] As increasing differences among bodies increasingly tend to impede empathy, requiring greater attention to overcome, so culturally ingrained differences among the psychic aspects of psychophysical persons (such as different expressive or emotional practices, or nexus of beliefs) may tend to impede our capacity to understand the terms in which another's experience is played out for and reflected upon by them.

Recent work on recognition of persons explores this second axis of empathy. Some recent accounts of the recognition of other selves pay particular attention to blindness to the experiences of certain groups or classes of others. If, for example, as Maria Lugonès discusses in her paper 'Playfulness, "world-travelling" and loving perception' (Lugonès 1987), racist and sexist practices inhere in a culture, this may affect the particular sense in which we picture the experiences of others, either imaginatively distorting empathic acts, or preventing them all together. Stereotypes and preconceptions may prevent or distort the experience of another's experience, either limiting the capacity to understand that other person's experience, or limiting the willingness to be guided by the other person. Lugones' account of empathy is, like Stein's, one of maintaining awareness of others' alterity of experience while trying to overcome the interpretive conditioning that allows some sorts of difference to enable moral disregard.

In *Moral Understandings*, Margaret Walker argues, along similar lines, that although 'the human body is the best picture of the human soul',[34] the conditions of the soul we associate with the postures of the body, we are always learning about the relation between bodies and souls. That there are different kinds of persons, in different bodies, means that our readings of some souls may not work for others. We *could* always learn more in our encounters with others, whether by engaging in further dialogue or by attending more closely to how they speak and act. There is never a point at which we have either the epistemic perfection of a total grasp of the states of others' souls nor the moral perfection to judge the state of another's body or soul definitively (Walker 1998: 184–6). I would add to Walker's account the rider that what I have described as cultural and corporeal differences may occasion a stylistic misunderstanding that is not ethically negligent, although ethically engaged communication will involve at least a wholehearted attempt to discern and overcome such stylistic differences.

Certainly, the picture of others' selves (or souls) that we see in their bodies is not always self-evident and it is not always correct. I may puzzle over someone's expression, decide by analogy or induction what they might be feeling. I may make mistakes about how someone is feeling. Or I may not attend particularly to how someone feels in circumstances where it ought to matter to me, for example where I am causing them pain or suffering. We are prone to these errors especially in cases where we do not already care for those whom we encounter, or when I have a negative or dismissive preconception of the sort of person concerned (be that sort the membership of a different race, of a different gender, or the possession of a different pace of speech).

I hold, with Stein, that for the most part we grasp without conscious interpretation what others' facial expressions and gestures say about their emotional states, so that we can be said to understand them rather than to be interpreting them. This is the case particularly for members of the same cultural and social group, and most particularly for those who are familiar with each other's practical lives; but it also extends out significantly from these centres of epistemic privilege. However, I share Lugonès' and Walker's awareness that stereotyping and misrecognition of others are substantial problems, most alive in encounters across social and cultural groupings. There is no guarantee that seeing someone's face guarantees understanding their soul while hearing their words does not. There will be interpretive moments even in seeing faces, and clarity of understanding in hearing another's words. That is all to say that the psychic individual, the soul, is understood through verbal and facial, and bodily phenomena, and that there are risks of error in each, irreducible because of the imaginative and interpretive effort that must accompany our non-primordial experience of the experiences of others.

In terms of emotional and psychical experience generally, my not having experienced the particular events that constitute the situation of another's emotional experience does not rule out empathy, since the empathy is primarily with the intelligible emotional content of experiences, rather than what one goes through to experience them. I may recognise someone's trauma in undergoing a clitoridectomy, or in losing someone else's favourite ring, although I have not undergone just these experiences, if I have *some* experience of trauma myself.[35] I may empathise with experiences that are not, or could never be, my own, through the intelligibility of others' acts to me as meaningful wholes.[36] As I grow older my experience of the qualities of traumas of my own, and of others, allows me to see more fully the tendencies of another's traumatic experience, and to act more appropriately in response to another's trauma. In each case my explication and reflective situating of the empathised experience will take account of my particular history of understanding, and may perhaps be impeded by my ignorance of the particular circumstances of the experience, or by ignorance of the character and the history of the experiencing self.

That empathy is with *experience*, singular, temporally limited and so on, adds a further limitation to the power of empathy as a form of ethical response to others. This is that, even with the contribution of imagination, empathy does not give the empathiser a purchase on the broader historical, and ethical situation of the experience in question. My empathy, for example, with the guilt and shame of my child, caught out in some forbidden act, is unlikely to give me the whole picture of the ethical situation. My response to the child will depend also on my assessment of her character, how often she has done such things in the past, how tractable I have found her in such cases, and so on. And it will also depend on my prior ethical commitments and principles, and the ways in which I live in accordance with these.[37]

A further point arises from these considerations of the limitations of empathy. This is that cooperation and willingness for empathy are required of both persons involved. As I have observed, individuals may fail to empathise with others. That is to say, empathy is not always automatically experienced, and not always intuitively correct. And, from the other direction, even the best-meant attempts to empathise with another may be thwarted by evasion, tergiversation or deception. Acts of empathy depend on the willingness of the other person to share their experience rather than conceal or misdescribe it. In view of these possibilities of failure, it can be said that ethically valuable communication requires, from both participants, a wholehearted attempt to empathise with (to be led by) the experiences of the other, and from both at least an attempt to enable or elicit empathy from the other. Failure by either party in either of these tasks may compromise the ethical value of the relationship between them.

The issues raised by the limitations to empathy highlight the degree to which language, in the forms of reflection and dialogue, is involved in making empathy an ethically valuable sort of experience. My empathy with the experience of another is informed by my awareness of the circumstances of that person, which are often verbally articulated. Furthermore, since empathy with another always takes a path through my own experience, my ethical response to a person with whom I have empathised is also, and should also be, informed by my judgement about what is best for that person. Simply having the other's experience, without reflecting upon it, would not necessarily make for an appropriate response on my part.

To see how it is possible to empathise with moods, emotions and intentions as well as sensations we need to consider sharing of experiences in verbal expression to be, like reflection, essentially a part of human activity. This is particularly important given the major role of language in specifying the *object* of an experience if the object is not immediately discernible, or not present for those empathising. The possibility of empathy includes not only being able to adduce physical causes for other's actions, such as when we see exertion in a blush, but also our awareness of psychic motivation in others, and specifically in terms of their selves. Others' actions and expressions may be intelligible to us as psychically motivated. We may see shame or anger in a blush; we may sense shame in someone's angry public outburst. Additionally, empathy may not only be with others' present experiences but also with others' past or anticipated experiences. I can empathically be aware of a friend's past joys and humiliations, and also of the moods or flavours of larger stretches of their life. As my memories often cover, not particular experiences, but the flavour of a period in my life given in an abridged way,[38] my empathy may be directed towards abridged memories of periods in another's life, when these have been given to me in description.

Linguistic expression thus has a major role in indicating just what aspects of an experience are significant. For Stein the power of language to clarify the object of an experience is only observed in passing:[39] the original example of my friend's sadness at the death of his brother includes his telling me of the death. This speech, showing how language can transform and direct awareness of someone's experience, is not remarked upon in Stein's analysis. Hannah Arendt makes clear that much of what we feel, like much of what we do, needs verbal articulation for it to be distinguishable from movement.[40] Facial expressions without words would often remain ambiguous as indicators of experiences:

> Without the accompaniment of speech, at any rate, action would not only lose its revelatory character, but, and by the same token, it would lose its subject, as it were; not acting men but performing robots would achieve what, humanly speaking, would remain incomprehensible. Speechless action would no longer be action because there would no longer be an actor, and the actor, the doer of deeds, is possible only if he is at the same time the speaker of words.
>
> (Arendt 1958: 160)

Awareness of another's psychic conditions without awareness of the objects of those conditions would give little insight into the state of the other as a person with experiences. In many cases linguistic articulation is essential in order for us to know the objects of another's psychic condition, which often determine my grasp of her or his character and self. And in other cases, although I can determine the object or objects of someone's psychic condition, verbal articulation can deepen my understanding. I understand someone's sadness differently if it is prompted by the unexplained departure of her or his spouse, than if it is prompted by the spouse's departure on discovery of a marital infidelity. Intelligibility of another's state through empathy requires us also to understand more about another than their emotional states, and requires a shared linguistic sense of what is going on for them.

That many experiences of others will be empathically available to me, not in embodied form (the pained face of a friend), but through narrated or typographical (and hence expressive) representational rememberings by other people at or after the event, contributes even more complexity to these acts of empathy. My empathic representation of verbally expressed experiences will depend crucially on how the verbal expressions 'point back' to the experience concerned. With, as in text, the absence of the experiencing body of the other, imaginative representation of the act to which the words point, has a larger and more risky role to play. I have already touched on the temporality of understanding others, which develops through experience of many styled utterances and actions over time. It is now time to consider in more detail the role that linguistic expression plays in empathic awareness of the experience of others.

2.5 Language and empathy

I would like to use some remarks Stein makes in *On the Problem of Empathy* about the relation of language and knowledge to experience, to point her work towards the issue of empathy in textually-mediated communication (including CMC). I start from the position that, broadly, words are expressions and abstractions from (and evolve historically in the context of[41]) human observations about the world, moods, emotions and conditions of utterance/inscription rather than transcendental signs of which we avail ourselves. Stein sees words as expressing (sometimes inaccurately or even deceptively) the moods, experiences and attitudes of word-users. 'One does not arrive at experience by the path leading immediately from verbal expression to meaning' (Stein 1989: 80) but rather by a path of association, where verbal expressions are used in certain more or less conventional ways to evoke in representation certain sorts of experience (Stein 1989: 81).

Firstly a note about Stein's account of language. Her account is brief, and it shares the defects of her account of reflection as enabling transcendental objectivity.[42] She treats words as having ideal meanings beyond the function of their uses, which meanings might be ours to possess if we can divest words of their material forms as utterance or inscription.[43] However, her account of language also emphasises the primacy of primordial experience over conceptual under-standing as the terms in which we make sense of each other's linguistic productions. Stein's ascription of transcendental significance to words does not undermine my claim that bodily experience is primary in linguistic interpretation, since she herself argues that evocation of one's own bodily experience is, in *some form* essential for understanding of the words of others (Stein 1989: 117–18).

Further, in an account of experience as affect such as Stein's, or Scheler's, there is a risk of understating the importance of language in human understanding. Stein's claim that language is empty and points backward to experience suggests a narrow reading in which all we learn is learnt by *living through* sensuously perceived events (that is, through primordial experiences only). It also has a wider, I think more correct reading, in which living through events includes empathised experi-ences, fantasised experiences, and propositional and theoretical understanding, all related, whether by generalisation, analogy or other means, to our own sensuous and ideational experiences.

Natural language has, as I have said above, a particular place in the experience of empathy. Owing to the importance of linguistic communication in human social life, our experience of empathy is bound up with the possibility of our being able to say, and to hear from others 'what the matter is' or 'what has happened' to produce particular experiences. The language that we employ to do this is both our own in that we put it to our own uses, and generic, in that words have generic meaning independently of *individual uses*, if not of usage in general. At the same time, the words available to us to describe our experiences help to construct those experiences for us and others; as Shoshana Felman puts it, we 'do' language, and live through it (Felman 1980: 96).

In linguistic expression our experiences can be given intersubjective formulation, and be related to other events and experiences whose relevance might not be otherwise evident. These experiences themselves are not themselves strictly linguistic, being also sensuous, or involving non-linguistic, sensuous, fantasised representations, but are the linguistically-immersed experiences of embodied psychophysical selves. Language thus has the particular role of making conceptually manifest those aspects of experience that are not apprehended as one with the face, and of allowing us greater insight into the actions and intentions of others, as well as their emotional and affective psychic experiences. Linguistic expressions point back beyond themselves to the world and the experiencing persons in it.

In the verbal expression of particular attitudes and moods, there is twofold distance from the self towards which empathy acts. Words are abstract and conventional symbols, always pointing back to concrete experience, never meaningful in themselves, but only as the markers for that experience, or that sort of experience. They do not *mean*[44] outside of their instantiation in particular circumstances. At the same time ordinary language is comprehensible without the bodily presence of someone using (or who has used) language to express something, and even without reference to the experience of the person who voiced the words. Such pointing, since it is experienced by us primarily as a pointing *to* representations and fantasised variations of our own accumulated remembered experiences, does not need to pass by any empathic awareness of the experiential conditions that prompted a speaker or writer to speak or write as they did. But it does need to point us back to our own experiences (including those we have had empathically) in order for us to see it as intelligible. As Stein puts it:

> Knowledge reaches its object but does not 'have' it. It stands before its object but does not see it. Knowledge is blind, empty and restless, always pointing back to some kind of experienced, seen, act.
>
> (Stein 1989: 19)

She also observes that 'statements can fill the breach and supplement where empathy fails. They may serve as points of departure for further empathy. But in principle they cannot substitute for empathy. Rather their production assumes that of empathy' (Stein 1989: 64). I do not, I cannot speak with others, if I foresee no possibility of mutual understanding. Not even this much holds for some varieties of the practice of reading and writing, since such practices are separate and frequently have no particular person in mind (particularly for the practice of writing). Those occasions of reading and writing, lacking sensuous empathy, must assume the possibility of empathy, or attempt it through textual interpretation of the described or performed experiences of the writer.

The particular characteristic of words is that they can be intelligible in the *absence* of the person who used them on some particular occasion. While they point back to the moods and emotions and dispositions of speakers, words may be understood without access to those particular moods and emotions. Linguistic understanding between people, while it may rely upon empathy, does not always or necessarily take empathy as its goal, or even acknowledge the role empathy plays. Many utterances and inscriptions, while they issue from a particular perspective and context, hold good, and are meant to hold good, for many other perspectives and contexts. The difference of the perspective of a speaker from mine may be irrelevant to our purposes, if we are in agreement about some claim focal to us both. If, for example, someone says to me 'It is raining', it is easy for me to understand this utterance without having to think of their experience of the rain. I can understand it because I am familiar with the practical conventions of English, and its imbrication in the habits of the people who speak it; I can check for rain myself by looking out of the window. I do not need to empathise with the experience of the speaker to understand for myself that it is raining. 'Only if I *want* to have the intuition on which the speaker bases his statement and his full experience of expression, do I need empathy' (Stein 1989: 82).[45]

Thus, though empathy is fundamental in granting each of us access to the intersubjective world, we do not need empathy to understand some types of utterance (such as an easily verifiable factual statement like 'It is raining'). We draw on accumulated understanding of our own and others' experiences and words to make sense of each new utterance, and may do this without necessarily attending in any detail to the particular experience of another that prompted them to use those words *this time*.[46] In many cases of human interaction and communication the attainment of empathy is ignored or treated as negligible, not because it is unimportant or unneeded, but simply because its (as yet unrealised) possibility is presumed.[47] In many cases of empathy, as already described, the second and third stages, in which the other's experience is lived-after them as if one's own, and then situated comprehensively as a certain sort of phenomenon, do not take place; one accepts the experiences of the other as theirs but one does not seek to live them oneself. Likewise, for those cases in which descriptive statements such as 'It is raining' are used, it may be enough for people to presume the possibility of empathy, rather than seeking the experience of the other that gave rise to the utterance.

Linguistic formulations thus give depth and subtlety to empathy, allowing people to specify the objects of their emotional states, and to articulate their experiences precisely. This should not, however, blind us to the continuing importance of the performing body as a site for emotional expression, or of styles that express character, including unvoiced beliefs, desires, and attitudes. Since we 'do' language with our bodies, there may, as Felman points out, be differences, even conflict, between linguistic expressions and overall psychophysical comportment. At times, people may not be up to the task of linguistic articulation at all. As Stein argues, to understand statements, such as 'It is raining', I have *at least* recourse to my own experience, if not that of someone else.

Consequently, we cannot have direct empathic access to the feelings and thoughts of others through language *alone* without some detour through our own personal world of experience, the particularity of which is always with us, even as we presume to commune with others through their words. Imagination thus plays an important role in allowing us empathy with linguistic expression alone. For example, as we comb through the books of those living and dead authors whom we do not meet in person, we cannot but apprehend their verbal expressions through our own understanding of the world (Stein 1989: 117). Without the opportunity to know the writers, we must take up their written expressions in ignorance of their psychic conditions, and supplementing for them those of our own that are evoked as we read. To draw on the argument in the first chapter of this book, without access to the gamut of styled performances of a person, access to their textual performances alone may give us an insufficient or distorted grasp of their life as a whole. Hence it is essential to consider textual empathy, or texts in their role as illuminating the experience of particular persons, rather than in that of expressing general or generic experiences, or exciting such experiences in readers without any empathic circuit past the experiences as those of their writer in particular.

2.6   Empathy and writing

2.6.1   A positive prognosis

As the emphasis on bodily constitution in the discussion above suggests, the physical absence of the other in textual productions is significant for the workings of empathy in textually-mediated communication. Namely, physical absence produces an increase in the importance of imagination, that is of representing for oneself the inner condition of the writer, in textually-mediated empathy. Equally, from the other side, it may require increased care in textual articulation of the self; I shall presently say a little more about the obligations or responsibilities of the reader to enable or elicit empathy. The imagination required for experiencing the other's experience as textually described, alluded to or performed, excludes sensuous empathy, but permits us to surmise about others' experiences from their written expressions.

I have already noted that in the case of text, empathy is presumed in potential, in the separate acts of continuing to write and to read. This is in effect the claim that sensuous empathy is not possible in textually-mediated communication. Each reader/writer assumes that the experiences which are described are accurate reflections of the experiences of the other reader/writer, but is missing any sensuous experience of the other's own particular face and voice. In other words, the work of the imagination in constructing the experience of the other from their styled textual documents is double. It encompasses both the imaginative experiencing for oneself of the other's experience, and the interpretive act of following the pointing of the words back to a textually described, alluded to or performed experience that is not sensuously accessible.

The importance of imagination as a means of co-experiencing and appreciating another's experience, already noted as characteristic of empathy in general, is thus increased in all types of textual interaction. It is further increased, often to an astonishing degree, by temporal separation between CM communicators, who must attend to traces of each other's lives that are long past. Certainly the possibility of discussing an experience as it is present, or of exploring the way, say, a mood unfolds and develops between people, is possible only in completely synchronous CMC, and is impeded by any temporal separation, and especially by uncertainty about the timing of CM contributions.[48]

As I will elaborate further in the following chapter, CMC comes closer to permitting empathy than does the medium of printed texts, because CMC permits textual dialogue, if the exchange of texts is numerous and rapid enough.[49] In this it is unlike the one-way exchange of reading that is our characteristic experience of published books, and it allows people to have ongoing engagements with one another, and to find how the other is faring, to ask and to elaborate on a range of subjects. However, such dialogue is still textual. Textual dialogue, like other texts, describes and points back to people's experiences rather than making them available in sensuous perception. In line with my outline of the generic qualities of language, and its capacity to signify to a reader who does not perform an act of empathy with the writer, textual expressions are sometimes intelligible without the need to consider their experiences at all.

The difficulty can be specified as that of experiencing the specificity of a person's experience in words that are generic, and which *might* equally be interpreted without reference to the particularity of that person's experience. Above I used the statement 'It is raining' as an example of a statement that might be interpreted without detouring through its utterer's (or writer's) experience of the rain; it might as well be interpreted by looking out the window, or by checking the weather forecast for the place and time in question. Stein's elucidation of this example makes clear that the experience of the speaker has no particular importance for someone interpreting the claim, because the statement is not *about* the experience of the speaker.[50] The sentence is not (explicitly at least) making any claims about the speaker, or their experience.[51] So long as the person reading it has some experience of rain of their own, then they can interpret the sentence without attending to the experience of the writer.

Now, something similar *may* happen even in the case of utterances that are about their writer or speaker, and that person's experience. Even passing familiarity with the experience of unhappiness may be enough to grasp the significance of the sentence 'I am in despair'. If I find a piece of paper in the street with that sentence written on it, I have some idea of its significance for its writer, even if I have no idea of who made the inscription. However, significantly, I can find out very little else about the experience of the writer from the piece of paper. Textual expressions, even highly styled or artful expressions, are still generic; if they are printed or typed, they are more generic, and carry fewer features marking them out intrinsically as belonging to, expressive of a particular person.

To return to a theme that I took up in the previous chapter, styled textual performances are simply one aspect of the totality of styled performances of any individual. The role of interpretation of words in conversation is deepened by sensuous empathy with the speaker. In any textually-mediated communication, without this form of empathy, how we are to take someone's text may be in doubt. We are forced to pose ourselves questions that seem impossible to put to the person whose text we cannot interpret, because they fall inside the realm of tacit or non-verbal communication, or because they are issues which in conversation have the normative status of being non-verbal. I might ask: Why are this person's sentences suddenly a lot shorter? How should I understand the phrase 'I've had enough of this', if not as directed towards myself? Is the sentence 'I'm in despair' meant lightly, seriously, or ironically? And how do I find out without further upsetting someone who might already be seriously unhappy? Sensuous empathy, which would have played an important role in understanding the experience of a person speaking such words, is not available to the reader of CMCs.

In other words, people's textually-mediated grasp of what is going on for others, and consequently of their selves, is more approximate and harder to verify in CMC, since the formal properties of words are difficult to particularise if they are not voiced by a particular individual embodied person. This may matter only a little, as when people are not attached to one another; the news that it is raining does not depend on my understanding a great deal about the person who tells me so. But in many cases, it matters a great deal. For example, when two people are attached to each other and care about how the other fares, or when attachment to one another is a possibility not yet developed, a beginning not yet consolidated, or whenever a threat to mutual intimacy and trust is interposed, then the particularity of the person and their experience, of which the text is an expression, is of great significance.

Textual empathy, then, is partial and risky, as it cannot draw on others' embodied styled performances, but only on the textual expressions of those selves. It is partial since we have no possibility of sensuous experience of others in CMC, because we have no experience of the non-verbal comportment or self-disclosure of textually conveyed others, and because the possibilities for expressing a felt empathy are also purely textual. It is difficult, for example, to show willingness to listen in a textual environment, apart from by *putting in writing* phrases such as 'I'm listening' or 'Yes; mmm, hmm'.[52] It is risky because our textual empathy, drawing as it must on our past experiences involving sensuous empathy, requires us to construct, to make real for ourselves, others' comportment through imaginative representations of our own past experiences, but with access only to the textual expression of the experiences and comportment of others. The sheer physical absence of others from their mediated texts effects a transformation in the character of social exchange, by ruling out much of the inarticulate or tacit matter that is part of conversational exchange.[53]

The degree of difficulty to be encountered in textual empathy depends on whether interlocutors have already met. Textual CMC between people who already know one another, while significantly different from conversational contact, will be supplemented for each party by that familiarity they have gleaned, through regular social contact, with the comportment of the other, with 'knowledge of the same routine, people, animals, opinions, anecdotes and jokes' (Grundy 1986: 220). This sort of contact is shared by family, friends and associates, members of groups and affiliations, and by some colleagues and co-workers. Many letter writers observe the particular advantages for correspondents who are already socially familiar with one another.[54] Between those who have not met face to face, exchange will be based around the familiarity gleaned in the solely textual environment, on knowledge of opinions, textual performances and self-descriptions, and shared textual conversations. I shall assume in this section that similar limitations apply, without going once again into the issue of this difference.

In a wholly textual medium, interpreters trying to empathise with writers encounter areas of silence the significance of which is opaque, grounded in but not supplemented by the sensuous empathy so important to our grasp of others' experiences. And the impersonal qualities of language requires them to work harder, not to grasp the generic significance of the words before them (although this might in itself be ambiguous), but to draw from them a faithful understanding of the particular experiences of the person who wrote them.

Equally, the writer of CMCs is at risk of leaving their experiences invisible, and their selves misunderstood if they do not take care to elicit empathy from their readers. If one's experiences are not explained or even referred to, their impact on a writer's style of textual description, self-description and performance may be impenetrable even to a careful reader. For example, it may be impossible to tell if a writer's brusqueness is caused by haste, anger, fear or contempt. Consequently the writer of CMCs (who is in many cases in a relation with another that involves both reading and writing) also has more work to do, in ordering his or her writing in a way that allows or elicits empathy from the reader. If, as I have argued, empathy is an essential part of ethically engaged communication, then there may indeed be some ethical responsibility on writers of CMCs to engage in ways that elicit empathy.[55]

Furthermore, the two axes of difference that I discussed above may both impact on our capacity to empathise with people of different experience from our own. If there is significant difference between people, either in terms of their experiential capacities or their lived histories (and the practices that constitute it), empathy may occur between people in mistaken imaginative terms, so that they end up living-after a largely fictive experience significantly unlike that of the other; my description of an event may evoke quite different emotional responses from others who have different experience from mine, particularly if my language-games are significantly different from theirs. In other words, imaginative co-seeing of another's expressions of their condition may be more likely to be in error when the expressive bodily self is absent from the site at which her or his verbal expression is apprehended and understood.

For example, many encounters across difference occurred in CMC environments in the late 1980s, when discussion groups started that were open to both academics and non-academics. Significantly different conventions of interaction applied to these different groups, and many misunderstandings resulted. In the absence of other terms of reference than that of the discussion groups, it took a long time before participants developed a sense of each other that took into account, rather than running up against, the differences in their experiences, and the textual practices in which they expressed their experiences (Hall 1996: 147–72). Sproull and Kiesler discuss similar encounters in 'Reducing social context cues: electronic mail in organisational communication' (Kiesler and Sproull 1986). Of course, different norms of behaviour hold in different social groups as well; my analysis of style in the first chapter of this book illustrated that such differences in practices often give rise to misinterpretations about others' characters, beliefs and moods. The above account of systematic misunderstandings is an example of confusions about norms of behaviour, transferred to the realm of textual interaction.

2.6.2 *Working towards textual empathy: techniques of spontaneity*

Given that failure of empathy may result from misreadings of textual style in CMC, one possible measure to avoid such failure is for readers to become aware of common interpretive errors and confusions. Codes of conduct for CMC (often known as the rules of 'netiquette') are often designed to make new users aware of some of the traps. Awareness of the temporality of CMC, and of the qualities of purely textual communication may both go some way to assuaging interpretational doubts, and to helping readers avoid errors.[56] The second alternative is for users of CMC to take up their responsibilities as writers in such ways as to elicit or enable empathy, as part of practices of ethically engaged communication. I will explore the second alternative in this section, using historical and contemporary examples, considering how textual media can be used to encourage empathy in a reader.

There are means by which we can maintain ethical responsiveness to absent others, and keep our communications ethically engaged, just as there are also means of coming to know better those with whom we are in textual contact. The lack of sensuous empathy in textuality may be circumvented or played down, particularly for those people who have met in person. There are ways of writing that suggest, to CMC reader, and also to writer, the sense that they are together, may make correspondence more lively and evocative of the experiences of the writer, and may elicit empathic readings of the self whose experiences are described and performed. Empathy, as essential to ethically engaged communications via computers may be promoted by such means, if participants are all willing. While drawing substantially in this section on research into the use of such techniques in earlier exchanges of letters,[57] the pace of exchange possible in CMC, and the use of typed messages certainly differentiate the two media.

Isobel Grundy used the term 'techniques of spontaneity' to describe Samuel Johnson's various means of enlivening his letters for his readers.[58] Interestingly, these occur as much in his intimate letters as in letters in which a polished style was called for. Grundy marks in Johnson's correspondence a gradual increase, especially in personal letters, in informal discussion, such as talk about health, the events of daily life, and other subjects of the moment. As he evolved a style of intimate letter writing distinct from the formal style of his public letters, he drew increasingly on such subjects. At the same time, informality gave opportunities for describing and performing experiences textually, and for mimicking oral linguistic patterns to suggest spontaneous, informal and intimate speech.[59] Such writing also gave the opportunity for Johnson to situate what he wrote, for his reader, in relation to his present mood, and in terms of how things were going for him. Frank and honest situation then set the scene for an empathic grasp of his experiences by his addressees.

Today, using CMC, we may also discuss daily life and subjects of the moment, quite spontaneously, as a way of 'keeping in touch'.[60] The spontaneity of most CMC chat-groups and of many e-mail and discussion group exchanges is Johnsonian, conversational and vivacious, drawing on recent events and described performances as forms of emotional expression and self-presentation, designed to body forth the writing self to the reader. Some of these patterns are used in CMC, sometimes deliberately, often without reflection. The use of colloquialisms, wrong or irregular spelling, hasty construction, and so on, comes quite naturally in informal cultural climates influenced by the colloquial language of film and television. Many e-mail texts draw on conversational patterns of speech rather than the longer, less repetitive and more organised patterns associated with written language, although as I have noted, some e-mail writers follow the comparative formality of published forms of language.[61]

Other ways of evoking the patterns of spoken language are more sophisticated.[62] Evocations of speech in writing, such as the use of ellipsis, suggest the ebb and flow of words, the patterns of breath, the rise and fall of excitement and interest in a subject, the degree of reserve or engagement, the flow of thoughts and ideas of the writer. Unattached exclamations, such as humorous or ironic imperatives, to self or others, and vocative addresses use the short turns and immediacy of conversation. Choices about the use of ellipsis, length and organisation of sentences (number of phrases and clauses, and so on) require effort from a writer, and more labour than the *spontaneous oral expression* that they imitate. They often make textual contributions a pleasure to read, as well as enjoyable, if demanding, to write.[63] And, of course, CMC also gives chances for exchanges within which empathy may become deeper and more nuanced, as interlocutors come to recognise the relation between each other's textual style and how it is going for them at the time of writing. Caroline Bassett gives several interesting examples of imitated orality in CMC: a drawn out 'weell' (Bassett 1997: 545); ellipsis, interrupted sentences and casual pronunciation: 'you aren't a girl ... hate to be the bearer of bad news but hey ... gotta get my kicks somehow' (Bassett 1997: 546).

Indeed, empathy with another's experience, extrapolated indirectly through writing, does not always rely on deliberate or explicit self-performances and positionings, as the relation of intimacy and informality in CMC show. As a general rule, the level of formality of CMC signals its writer's degree of intimacy with its intended reader. For example, a spirit of trust is breathed into letters by the absence of formality (Grundy 1986: 217); correspondingly formality suggests reserve or distrust. Within particular relations the dynamics are similar, with greater formality suggesting greater distance from the interlocutor. Sudden formality after a period of informality may be read as signifying a sudden revelation or brutal betrayal. Since writers writing in a hurry or with some other burden on their mind are prone to being less personable than they would be at other times, this is a juncture at which readers may need to attend with particular care.[64]

CMC has a great advantage over slower epistolary exchanges in that, in *some* of its forms at least, contributors don't need to overcome extended gaps of time between letters, but can write at conversational pace. The mimicry of dialogue, for example, often very effective in letters, is neither necessary nor helpful in a medium that affords conversational-paced dialogue between people, each of whom is both self and other to the other. As Johnson used this sort of feigned dialogue in his daily or twice-daily letters to Hester Thrale as well as in less regular corres-pondence,[65] we might surmise that it will also have a place in e-mail exchanges that run at a slower pace than conversation. As I have noted above, temporal separation and irregularity tend to disrupt empathy in textually-mediated social interactions, since they destroy participants' sense of being together in dialogue, or as going through things together. Feigned dialogue is one way of suggesting togetherness, so as to afford common ground on which further exchanges may rest.

Performances textually described are a mainstay of epistolary exchange. References to the moment of writing occur in Johnson's writing (Grundy 1986: 217), as well as that of contemporary letter writers.[66] They are common in Richardson's epistolary novels as a means of evoking the present at which a letter was written as a present moment.[67] Treating feigned and fancied performances such as are common in Johnson's writing as techniques of spontaneity designed to create the impression of more immediate and intimate social relations could be extended to account for the quasi-fictive performances of MOOs, MUDs and some Internet Relay Chat (IRC) groups.[68] Quasi-fictive performances are often treated as performatively-created 'selves' in wholly detached virtual worlds, that is by deferring the question of how the performances of *personae*, adopted and cast off at will, might affect the enduring selves who adopt and cast. Instead it might be productive to treat these performances as extensions of selves designed to elicit certain types of interaction. The purpose to which performances are put, that is, whether these performances are meant to elicit empathic readings, or entertaining engagements, is not itself determined by the possibility of textual self-performances.

Performance of the self in CMC may extend to imaginary dialogues in which others are depicted, although the configuration of some discussion groups and e-mail programmes tends to discourage both quoting and misquoting.[69] Grundy observes that Johnson 'regularly summons his absent correspondent to take an imaginary place in the letter by supposedly responding to its contents or supplying a contrasting point of view' (Grundy 1986: 220). Such imaginary dialogues are often a gentle form of provocation, designed to elicit an engaged response from a correspondent. The idea of putting words into the mouth of a friend, a reflexive exercise to start with, would tend to produce further reflection by the letter's recipient. E-mail users employ such techniques to spark discussion, either as deliberate antagonism, or in less grave sallies.[70] Caroline Bassett's discussion of interaction in LambdaMOO gives numerous examples of such provocative descriptions and summonses of others, of which 'virtual rape' could be considered a peculiarly manipulative and non-reciprocal variety (Bassett 1997: 542).

As is seen from this catalogue, narratives of all sorts, reminiscence, gossip, fancy, and quasi-fictive descriptions, are important contributors to the flow in CMC, and may allude to or perform the present experiences of the narrating interlocutors. (For example, exhaustion or high spirits may be embodied in sparse or ebullient writing.) Narrative may be vivid and novel, organising the future around plans and propositions, or moving into the realm of fancy.[71] Or it may be of familiar events, invoking writer and reader harmonious as they look backwards together.

Drawing on shared memory is a way of consolidating the present and the future, as it draws reader and writer together in a felt sense of sharing, of being together again in memory. Sharing the memory of particular past conversations and activities can be a great pleasure. A range of memory techniques is used in many letters. Erasmus often recounts shared memories to his correspondents. Jonathan Swift's *Journal to Stella* conjures a range of fancied scenes between Stella and himself, often drawing on shared memories as well as pure imagination. Pietro Aretino describes Venice to a correspondent who has spent time with him there. He mingles descriptions of the events of the day with references to the habits of the city that would be well known to his correspondent, and to the amounts of wine they drank when last together (Aretino 1967: 71–3). Such memories can also be used with the intention to draw separated friends together, as they are used in so much epistolary fiction. In a study of Abigail Adams, Edith Gelles notes that her letters to her husband, often absent, frequently appeal to the memory of their togetherness, perhaps as a means to recreate for herself a sense of his presence, but also in an attempt to persuade him to return to her (Gelles 1992: 32–6).

Perhaps one of the most interesting and subtle means of evoking memories while suggesting their relevance to present circumstances is in the use of evocation. Evocative description may evoke shared memories, for example by allusion rather than reference. Allusion can capture past conversations and shared memories obliquely while also maintaining present conversation. As Grundy observes, Johnson's particular expertise was

> multiple allusiveness to specific, unexplained, shared private memories, to particular writers, to the whole both venerable and mockable literary tradition, the minuter epistolary tradition, and to a broad intellectual background which may also be treated among friends with playful exasperation.
>
> (Grundy 1986: 222)

Even simple repetition of words may evoke memories, particularly if the words have an inherited significance for interlocutors. And the evocation of shared (pleasant) memories is an excellent ground from which people may empathise with the textually-described and -performed current experiences of an interlocutor.

In other words, there are many ways in which the writing of CMCs can be designed to afford and elicit empathy from a reader who is interested in doing so, that is, if participants are equally bent on engaging in ethically engaged communication. To some extent these ways of writing for ethically engaged communication can be described generically. Honesty in writing, situation of the writing self by descriptions of and allusions to how things are going for one, ongoing engagement in dialogue with interlocutors, allusion to shared experiences and interests, and even use of self-performance to suggest the spontaneity of being together, are all useful possibilities for the writer of CMCs. Awareness of such possibilities in turn may make reading for empathy easier, although the translation of the generic techniques into particular strategies leaves room for communications to slip down the axes along which empathy may fail. Participants may have substantially different cultural backgrounds that impede empathy, or substantially different capacities for engaging with the world. Finally, stylistic differences may still get in the way of textual expressions of experiences being legible as such to even the best-meaning interlocutor. That was the original lesson of the first chapter of this book, and, because interpretation is so important for empathising in textually-mediated social interactions, unintelligibility of written meaning may thwart our attempts to empathise through text as much as it does any other interpretive endeavour.

People using CMCs for social interaction are currently situated within and in relation to traditions of letter-writing, social and intellectual traditions, and current US-dominated norms of CMC textual exchange that place particular value on 'freedom of expression'. Our e-mails make references and allusions to the conditions under which we write, by which we are apart from our correspondents. Further, we can ask once again, with the hope of an answer, the question suggested by Keats's letter – if two people can successfully commune spiritually at a distance then is there really anything missing between them? The answer, to judge from this assessment of the role and possibilities of empathy in textual communications, depends in part on the capacity people have for evoking empathy in text; it also depends on their honesty in their self-performances and descriptions. And it depends, to an extent, on the degree to which physical togetherness is important to any individual. To the extent that togetherness is the means by which we may most easily and comprehensively become familiar with someone else's experiences of life, empathy through textual exchange depends, as Keats depicts it, on prior familiarity and intimacy.

2.7 Conclusions

In this chapter I have given a fairly detailed account of empathy, focusing on the relation of individual empathic experiences to the larger panorama of understanding and cooperating with the persons with whom we engage. My purpose in going into such detail was to show how empathy is possible, albeit in partial and risky forms, in CMC. To do this I had to elaborate both the bodily/sensuous component of empathic experience, and the particular contributions and limitations of written language to empathic experience. My initial broad discussion of empathy delimited sensuous empathy, and specified the role of the imagination in bridging the gap between individual embodied experience and the embodied experiences of other individuals. Imagination was shown to be useful for broaching this gap, but not sufficient to guarantee that empathy is always successful or perspicuous. Empathy was shown to have limitations, although these did not make it any the less essential in the project of ethically engaged communication, undertaken so as to develop and maintain interpersonal understandings.

A discussion of language showed that linguistic articulation can deepen empathic experience, allowing us to empathise with others' past experiences, and to determine the object of others' experiences. However, the generic nature of language was, I argued, a barrier to empathising with others through text, particularly through printed text. Interpretation of another's text might be a way to work out the experiences that they describe, allude to or perform textually; but might equally mistake, through well-intentioned ignorance, the particularity of the others' experience as textually expressed. Interpretation itself is not a way out of situations in which empathy is not sufficient; dialogue is perhaps a more ethically acceptable approach. The question, then, to be asked is whether and how dialogue is possible in CMC. This is my task in Chapter Three.

3 Affect and action in CMC

For what subject cannot be committed to a letter? In them we feel joy, pain, hope, and fear. In them we give vent to anger, protest, flatter, complain, quarrel, declare war, are reconciled, console, consult, deter, threaten, provoke, restrain, relate, describe, praise, and blame. In them we feel hatred, love and wonder; we discuss, bargain, revel, quibble, dream, and, in short, what do we not do?

(Erasmus 1985: 71)

3.1 Introduction: style revisited

I have established in previous chapters the importance of appreciating people's style as one aspect of coming to know them, and discussed the structure of empathy in textually-mediated relationships such as CMC. This chapter takes up the issue of the affective and performative possibilities of CMC. Its function is as a twin to the previous chapter, which argued for the possibility of empathetic experience of others in CMC. It aims to establish that textual relations allow people to engage in relationships that allow action and interaction.

The chapter begins with a restatement of the importance of style for understanding persons. I set out some criteria for having a relationship with another person. These are that the relationship be mutually affective, in that each person is able to affect the other in some way or other; that the affect of each be situated within some sort of dialogical exchange; that the terrain of dialogical exchange constitute a field of social action for participants.

The chapter is a discussion of whether and how these three criteria can be satisfied in textually-mediated communication. I consider first whether textuality prevents dialogue, oriented as an address to the Ricoeurian argument that dialogue is not possible at all in text. Ricoeur's position is seen to be powerful but incomplete. I conclude that CMC allows dialogue in the sense of exchange of question and answer, and that it permits affectivity within both impersonal and intimate relations, although not all CMC is either dialogic or affective.

I then analyse the affective capacities of people's uses of text, approaching the subject by way of speech act theory. I argue that the limitation of speech act theory itself to highly conventional types of performance conceals ethical difficulties inherent in the conceptual possibility of speech acts and text acts alike: these problems hinge around the role of the addressee, made more substantial in cases where strong conventions for speech acts are lacking.

People bring to CMC their experiences of physically mediated relationships, to assist them in textually-mediated relationships, and are able to establish and maintain relationships with other people by discussing subjects and projects, as they would in face-to-face relationships. At the same time non-verbal and contextual aspects of social situations such as setting, mood, register, even periods of silence, are transformed or invisible in social relations conducted via CMC. Important aspects of lifestyle, such as people's embodied performances, their voices, the panoply of spontaneous, less-than-fully-intended activities, are accessible in CMC only if they are textually described or enacted. Otherwise they remain inaccessible in textual communication. Accustomed to physically mediated social interaction relying on embodied performances, people participating in CMC are left without significant aspects of others' styles of performance through which their selves are expressed and understood.

At the same time, the increasing popularity of CMC as a social medium attests to its capacity to support some sorts of socially interesting or rewarding interaction. Styles of textual expression develop, spontaneously or through concerted effort, to cope with the absence of shared, ongoing practical activities, and to allow textual activities. People engage together in verbal social activities such as exchange of opinions and understandings, narratives built up in regular discussion, or virtual (simulated) activities.[1] This last category includes the varieties of game-environment (such as MOOs and MUDs), and work-related MUDs that are not dedicated to game playing (such as Media-MOO).

CMC, like other textual media, if it is to allow people to understand one another and to maintain relationships, must be able to support affective interpersonal relations between particular people, and to allow various sorts of social action to occur in a purely verbal context. But how exactly is conversation possible in CMC? And can we do all the things in CMC that we can do in other sorts of conversation, such as make promises, give orders and show willingness?

I address these questions in turn. First I address the question as to the sense in which conversation is possible in CMC. I conclude that dialogue is possible in CMC, in one sense at least. This conclusion sets the stage for me to pose and answer the second question: is social action possible in CMC? This question is also answered with a qualified affirmation, drawing on the account of style in Chapter One to illustrate how limited contextual cues constrain possibilities for textually mediated interaction.

Finally, I look at a specific type of textual performances characteristic of CMC fora such as MOOs and MUDs, cases in which people describe themselves as performing certain physical actions, often in relation to other CMC participants. There are questions as to how to understand these performances, such as a 'bop on the head', a 'promise to be good', or a virtual rape, outside of the fictional game environment. Are such expressions literal, standing for the described real-world action or undertaking? Are they metaphorical, standing for quite *other* actions or undertaking? Or are they to be understood as textual performances with no non-textual analogue at all?

3.2 The hermeneutic gap: does textuality allow dialogue?

In Chapter One I considered the dual nature of style in writing. It appeared from my examination that writing, and language generally, could be considered as part of a writer's comportment in relation to other people, but that there were some significant instances in which this was not the case. In some cases a created artefact was taken not as an object expressive of anything about its creator, but as expressive in its own terms. The exceptions appeared predominantly within the discourse of aesthetics, in which a gap between artist and audience is normalised in the modern West by the mediation of the artefact. Nelson Goodman described cases in which the affective import of a work of art overshadows any appreciation of the work as the expression, let alone the comportment, of a single person. Texts may be, as Jacques Derrida put it, meaningful to readers in the absence of any individual (such as their writer) *willing* them to mean. Enduring communications (such as letters or publications) may no longer function as part of the comportment of their writer, though they once were part of it. Derrida's example of the pernicious use of Nietzsche's writings by National Socialists after his death indicates the importance of the reservation we might have in asserting that whatever follows from someone's writing is somehow *their* activity.[2]

Because written communication is accessible for as long as a text exists, the agency of the author in relation to the effects of 'her' or 'his' text is more nebulous than it would be for an utterance that is grasped on the spot by those to whom it is directed. Once the text becomes a meaningful object separate from its writer, the understandings that it is granted, and the uses to which it is put cannot be straight-forwardly ascribed to the author. Thus the status of the surviving text as part of the comportment of its writer decreases as the ties the text had with its initial context are broken by the passage of time, and traversed by multiple repetitions in subsequent situations.

Paul Ricoeur's post-structuralist account of hermeneutic interpretation is based on a distinction between speech and writing. Ricoeur's account of hermeneutic interpretation treats texts as 'distanciated' from their readers, requiring special interpretive techniques to elevate the text to intelligible discourse. (I will define 'distanciation' presently.) The interpretive act of elevating text to discourse, performed by the reader in relation to the text, is an activity that does not require any attention to the character, attitudes or intentions of the text's writer. Textuality institutes a productive distance between writer and reader.

Ricoeur's position develops from a distinction between conversations and texts in terms of the sorts of understanding available in each. Face-to-face conversation affords the best possibility for mutual understanding between people. Ricoeur describes mutual understanding in face-to-face situations in terms of its immediacy, and its capacity for dialogue, or the exchange of questions and answers. If I don't understand what someone is saying to me, I need only ask, and my interlocutor will give me an explanation that allows me to understand and to go on. The question of alterity or strangeness does not, for Ricoeur, arise in conversation.

Texts on the other hand, by standing in for their writers, rule out the asking-answering relation between writer and reader, and replace it, for the reader, with the prolonged contemplation of the text. The mediation of text between writer and reader is called by Ricoeur 'distanciation'. It comes in four forms: the irrelevance of physical presence for communication; the irrelevance of the writer's intention to the meaning of the text; the irrelevance of the interpretation of any original audience of the text; and the replacement of conversationalists' shared social context by a metaphorical reality contained within the text.

Because of distanciation, the textually mediated relation between writer and reader is thus not a form of dialogue. Conversation and textual expression may both be forms of discourse. However, speech has no privileged status as the primary form of discourse. Just because speech is historically anterior to writing does not mean that each individual piece of writing has, by analogy, its own anterior 'speech' in the thoughts of the writer, or in some imaginary dialogue between writer and another party. Instead, he treats conversation and textual communication as alternative, equally legitimate types of discourse, each with its own distinct qualities, requiring its own form of analysis.

Ricoeur's account of textual interpretation is, broadly, that reading texts is unlike engaging in conversation. Drawing on a metaphorical theory of reference in literary texts, he argues that interpretive practices that are valid for everyday conversations, paradigmatically engaged in conversational dialogue,[3] are not valid for textual analysis. The activity of understanding a text is 'a struggle between the otherness that transforms all spatial and temporal distance into cultural estrangements and the ownness by which all understanding aims at the extension of self-understanding' (Ricoeur 1976: 44). The terms on which we may interpret and understand texts are thus, for Ricoeur, profoundly unlike the dialogicity he attributes to conversation. Understanding of a text is a self-understanding that occurs *across* distanciation, and despite the lack of dialogue.

For writing, the separation of the circumstances of a reader's interpretation from the circumstances of the writer constructs the text as 'independently meaningful' words, that is, words that mean independently of any intention or experience of the writer. Attention to what someone puts in writing can only be given through attention to the resultant text which, though it may be produced by that particular person, holds at the same time the status of independently meaningful linguistic artefact. So, for example, the independently meaningful text may elicit from different readers quite different interpretations. Since the intention and experience of the writer are, for Ricoeur, irrelevant to the validity of the interpretation, there is no single 'correct' interpretation. Interpretations are assessed in terms of productivity or usefulness among self-adjudicating communities of readers.[4]

Ricoeur's work is situated within the discourse of hermeneutics, the primary focus of which has been a particular sort of text – an old, probably fictional or Biblical text difficult to understand, whose principles of organisation and metaphorical language earn it the title of composition. Ricoeur also has a primary target in mind – the Romantic hermeneuticists who aimed to recover the intentions or the genius of a writer through her or his texts, and who conceived of this recovery as a sort of empathic communion or dialogue with the dead writer. This aim of recovery of the genius of an author, which Ricoeur attributes to Schleiermacher, Herder, and Schiller, is one that he describes as naïve.[5] It is against the notion of interpretation as 'a communion of souls' that his non-dialogic account of interpretation is directed.

Unfortunately, Ricoeur's account of hermeneutic interpretation of texts cannot allow that any type of text, including letters, literary exchanges such as articles, and e-mails, permits dialogue. This seems rather a significant obstacle to accepting his theory of textual interpretation as always operating through total distanciation. My conclusion, that dialogue is possible across exchanges of texts, emerges in the light of my larger philosophical project, dealing with interpretation of CMC. There is indubitably exchange of question and answer, often simultaneous or synchronous exchange, between users of CMC. It inheres, not in single texts, but in the exchange of texts between particular people.

But Ricoeur's account of hermeneutic interpretation does shed light on the limitations of textual dialogue. His account of the distanciation of texts from both reader and writer highlights the ways in which texts may be misunderstood, or be considered by reader or writer not to be contributions to dialogue in the first place. Distanciation may, I conclude, occur within dialogue, and is conceptually compatible with the existence of textual dialogue. Ricoeur's account of hermeneutic interpretation describes in detail an extremity of distanciation that is not the characteristic situation of all texts. To establish this, I want to look more closely at the work done by his concept of the fourfold distanciation of texts.

In *Hermeneutics and the Human Sciences*, Ricoeur elaborates the concept of distanciation that he articulated in *Interpretation Theory*. He first notes that there is a gap between someone's saying something and the effects of that saying on other people. He then claims that this gap is instituted in an absolute way in the spatial and temporal separation between the writer and the readers of texts. This distance is so great that the reader of a text simply cannot understand the intentions of the writer.[6] It means that textual interpretation requires special techniques 'in order to raise the chain of written signs to discourse and to discern the message through the superimposed codifications peculiar to the realisation of discourse as a text' (Ricoeur 1981c: 45). These techniques may involve interrogation of a text, but since the (formal) nature of the text is fixed, so these techniques preclude dialogue.

To illuminate the nature of textual hermeneutics, Ricoeur discriminates four types of distanciation that prevent dialogue from occurring between author and reader. I will describe them one by one, before assessing their validity for contemporary and everyday texts such as CMC. The four types, as I have said are: the irrelevance of physical presence for communication; the irrelevance of the writer's intention to the meaning of the text; the irrelevance of the interpretation of any original audience of the text; and the replacement of conversationalists' shared social context by a metaphorical world contained within the text and raised into discourse by the reader.

The first sort of distanciation effected by textuality is the overcoming of the necessity of human presence for an instance of discourse to take place. Unlike meaning in conversation, the meaning of a text endures long after the act of writing. It is not limited as conversation is to the singular situation in which words are uttered. Texts allow what Ricoeur calls the 'intentional exteriorisation' of speech acts by means of technologies of textual expression. A text inscribes, not the event of the writer's speech act, but the 'said' [*énoncé*] of that speech act (Ricoeur, 1976: 27), stripped of its association with an individual's bodily performance of it.[7]

The second sort of distanciation separates the intention of the writing subject from the significance of her or his text. In speech the significance of an utterance is usually closely bound to the significance intended by its utterer, and the speaker has the expectation (or at least the hope) that the listener will grasp that significance. Texts may take on quite different significations in the absence of their authors, to the degree that what the writer meant to say may be deemed irrelevant. Ricoeur puts it this way: 'What the text signifies no longer coincides with what the author meant; henceforth textual meaning and psychological meaning have different destinies' (Ricoeur 1981c: 44). This form of distanciation is a function of the capacity of texts to endure typographically unchanged across changes in social and political conditions subsequent to the time of writing, coupled with the equivocality of written language.[8]

Third, there is distanciation between the original, intended, audience of a text and the interpretive possibilities of the text outside of that audience. Unlike conversations, texts are not constrained to a single spatio-temporal location, and their interpretation may be re-enacted whenever anybody takes up and reads a text. Texts may be multiply reinterpreted. They may be re-read in any number of ways far beyond the interpretations of their first or intended first audience. (Ricoeur uses the example of the letters of St Paul, which he says are addressed to 'us' as much as to the Romans, Galatians, or Corinthians (Ricoeur 1981a: 192).)

Fourth, written discourse liberates texts from the limits of what Ricoeur calls 'ostensive reference' that apply to conversation by virtue of its participants being in the same place (Ricoeur 1977: 3–15). The immediate shared reality or 'social context' of a conversation, which is available to its participants, has no counterpart for a text. Instead textual discourse allows a splayed referentiality that unfolds only through the prolonged hermeneutic interpretation of a text by a reader. The meaning of the text does not depend on its situation in a particular dialogue or conversation but on objective textual properties that afford various interpretive raisings of the text to discourse by different people at different times, or by a single person at different times.[9]

Ricoeur argues that the four forms of distanciation prevent dialogue between writer and reader, because the relation of the reader to the text is 'not a particular case of the speaking-answering relation' (Ricoeur 1981c: 45). If the reader cannot engage with the writer, but only with her or his textual composition, there can be no relation of interlocution, and no dialogue between them.[10] Instead, as Ricoeur sees it, the text discloses an objective *other* world (which is not yet the world of the writer), a world to which the interpreter must open her- or himself. Thus the impossibility of dialogue with a text's author leads to a further normative statement, that we should not seek any such dialogic understanding. In Ricoeur's hermeneutics, the goal is not to understand what the author *means*, because this is faded and gone, but instead, following Heidegger, to open oneself to what the text itself shows, and to learn from that showing. He writes:

> [I]t is necessary to renounce the link between the destiny of hermeneutics and the purely psychological notion of transference into another mental life; the text must be unfolded, no longer towards its author, but toward its immanent sense and towards the world which it opens up and discloses.
>
> (Ricoeur 1981c: 53)

And, following Heidegger, 'The question of the world takes the place of the question of the other' (Ricoeur 1981c: 56). To summarise, the question of what the author meant is replaced by the question of what the text means. Interpreters may inquire into the life of the writer, but all such projects are subordinated to the larger goal of understanding the world that is disclosed by the text.

The four types of distanciation apply well to a variety of reading practices accepted and predominant in the modern academic West. Canonical texts have been the subjects of prolonged and solitary contemplation, and can be indefinitely reproduced in the same (printed) form, without the need for authorial intervention.[11] The authors of most of these texts are dead, their life and times long since vanished. Western copyright laws, which allow authors to cede or sell the ownership of their texts, realise the pattern of distanciation of text from author by permitting the ownership of arrangements of words by those who have not themselves made the arrangement.

3.2.1 Distanciation and the varieties of textual dialogue

But, there are, I think, communicative possibilities to textuality, including CMC, that suggest that Ricoeur's hermeneutic account of textuality as non-dialogic is culturally and historically limited. In particular the neglect of the epistolary genre mars his account. Writing allows textual exchanges to be conducted between particular people, addressed to each, and meant for each, and whose participants often exchange letters over substantial periods of their lives. The expectations of many writers, modern as well as historical, as to how their writing will be read certainly include expectation of responses on particular topics from particular people.[12] Many texts exist as parts of debates expressly directed to asking and answering each other's questions; no single text constitutes a dialogue, but each is a contribution to larger intertextual discussions between specific people.

It is also arguably the case with hypertexts that have no 'final form' but which are continuously re-edited and re-published, in response to textual exchanges that have some of the characteristic of dialogue. Richard Lanham makes this argument, in a defence of the 'orality' of CMC (Lanham 1993: 54–96). Texts contributed by people to initiate or maintain discussions may fail to contribute to or sustain dialogue. Nevertheless dialogue, characterised as the exchange of texts in which people ask and answer to each other as particular persons, is one possibility among the uses of text.

Notably, letters sit on a generic boundary, between 'ordinary' text and 'work of art'. Like diaries, letters may fall into the category of personal documents, or into the category of artistic genre, or into both categories at once. Some of the letters of people such as Samuel Johnson, Mary Wortley Montague, Fanny Burney or Desiderius Erasmus counted as works of art even in their own lifetimes. Ricoeur tries to evade the status of letters as metaphorical texts, and treats them as purely descriptive, writing: 'Letters, travel reports, geographical descriptions, diaries and in general all descriptive accounts of reality ... merely restructure for their readers the conditions of ostensive reference [i.e. as if the reader were there]' (Ricoeur 1981d: 149).

But even by Ricoeur's standards, many letters count as literary works rather than as descriptive accounts of reality. Many letters, and some e-mails, are metaphorical, and worked-upon compositions that embody a strategy for communication using writing – 'a collective multifaceted, polysemic, and highly valorised system of cultural signs' (Valdès 1991: 24). Perhaps the situation of letters at a generic boundary explains why Ricoeur's account of textual interpretation neglects them. But it is precisely the marginality of the letter genre, the existence of letters that are at once part of personal exchanges, and also minor works of art, that requires us to acknowledge the possibility of textual dialogue. The letter genre also alerts us to the existence of degrees of distanciation, even within dialogic exchanges. The enunciating body is absent from a letter, and there is no *physically* shared context in which the exchange is situated and so on.

So Ricoeur's account of distanciation, while representative of hermeneutic understandings of textuality, and indeed of one dominant strand of reading practices in the Western world, overlooks the existence of epistolary exchanges and other forms of textual exchange. Remarking Ricoeur's neglect of certain sorts of texts, notably letters and notes intended for 'immediate consumption', I consider his four types of distanciation to delimit an extreme condition that may befall texts, but which is not intrinsically theirs. The strength of Ricoeur's account of distanciation for understanding CMC is in the clarity with which it articulates the degree of distanciation *possible* for texts.

From the case of epistolary exchange, an interpersonal criterion of dialogicity emerges. Whether a text is or has been dialogic depends not on the *text* itself, but on the relations that obtain between the particular people who send and receive it, and the strategies in which each person engages when writing or reading it. Whether a contribution to dialogue is a text or a speech matters less for the question of its dialogicity than the intentional relation between the speaker-writers who exchange it. Whether a text is or has been dialogic depends rather, in *each particular case*, on the relation between those who read and write, send and receive it. This relation in turn depends on other factors, such as whether the text in question is intended for an audience familiar to the writer, whether its audience sees itself as the intended recipient of the contribution, and whether the audience *is* the intended recipient (however defined) of the contribution.[13] Texts such as letters are thus context-dependent in a way that prevents us from attributing dialogicity (or non-dialogicity) to them *independent of* whether, when and how they are raised into discourse by a reader.

For example, a singular arrangement of words may be at some times part of dialogue and at other times not. A text (a letter, e-mail, or a poem) may start out as part of an epistolary dialogue, be published and read again by others with whom its writer may have *no* dialogue. It may then be quoted in a further dialogic epistolary exchange, in which it takes on the intentional colouring of this new use, but loses that of the original. I might read or quote parts of a poem to someone, to make a point to that person, or to frame a question I have for them. To take a different example, some texts are never dialogic, in the sense that they are not, and not intended as, part of exchanges between two particular people at all. An advertising leaflet is a fairly good example of non-dialogic text.

Whether a text is dialogic also depends on whether it is one of more than one text exchanged between people. Dialogue requires exchange, a series of questions and answers. The position of individual texts as contributions ranged together within an interpersonal relation in which each text is less than every question or every answer, yet all emanating from that constellation of inquiry and certainty which is intrinsic to the human constitution, distinguishes text as part of a dialogue from that same text outside dialogue. (For example, a text may remain a recording or report of a dialogue, or may have been written originally as a fictional dialogue; at the formal level, dialogic and non-dialogic texts cannot be distinguished.) A CMC text may also, incidentally, be part of a 'mixed-media' dialogue, using speech, writing, pictures, or any other media that are available. In a broader sense, it is worth noting that the limits on when a single text is part of a dialogue are rather fluid. A reader of a text must decide, by reference to the interpersonal context in which a contribution is made, whether it is part of a dialogue or not.

In other words, it is the endurance of a text through time, to be read and understood by people distant from the time and context of writing, rather than its being a text *simpliciter*, that increasingly favours its being treated as an artefact, independently meaningful. Certainly, as Ricoeur observes, some texts are not intended as parts of reciprocal exchanges: both text and speech may be non-dialogic in intent, produced for a mass audience with no opportunity to respond, or intended as part of a dialogue but snubbed or overlooked by its recipient. But, as Ricoeur shows, their durability allows texts that were originally dialogic to be read non-dialogically. Such treatment of texts as artefacts, which is merely one of the possibilities for understanding texts, must be qualified to include the possibility of temporally distended epistolary dialogue. This form of dialogue may suffer from some degree of distanciation, but not necessarily its extreme form.

Likewise, although difficulties with ascertaining authorial intention, and interpretations that see texts in quite other terms than those intended by the writer, are common in relations conducted through text, these do not necessitate the substitution of a relation with the text alone for an attempt to understand the text as a 'world' created by its author. Extreme distanciation is possible but contingent. And in many cases, such as in the case of a letter addressed to oneself, to ignore the intention of a writer at the expense of the meaning of the text is possible, but both undesirable and inconsiderate (inconsiderate assuming that the writer has written with the intention that her intention in writing not be ignored).

In textual CMC, for example, a reader seeking to understand a writer's intentions or meaning may ask questions and receive clarificatory answers. He or she understands these answers in the light of what he or she already knows about the writer. If writer and reader do not share the same environment at the time(s) of writing and reading, they may yet live many parts of their lives together, share a common background of beliefs and attitudes, know the same people, be involved in similar webs of practices. Dialogue, exchange of questions and answers between particular persons, is possible between them despite their not being present to each other, in the exchange of a series of texts.

3.2.2 *Contingent textual distanciation*

I now want to draw on my analysis of textual distanciation to develop an account of distanciation as partial and contingent. Ricoeur is right, I think, to argue that there are significant differences between our conversational practices and our practices of textual interpretation, in the academic West at least, and that this difference turns around the decreasing accessibility and importance of the writer's intentions for understanding an enduring text. This is palpably the case with much printed matter intended for mass public consumption. Much literary writing, and much general-interest writing (cookery books, or self-help books) is removed from the everyday context of engagements with particular people. The particularity of the persons who write, and more often, the persons who read such books, is not taken to matter.

Further afield, in the reading practices of cultures that imbue particular texts with ritual importance, a text's significance may rest in continuous reinterpretation through dance and song, rather than inhering in a purely textual 'world'. Here Ricoeur's theory, by focusing on the importance of hermeneutic exegesis simply sidesteps other important and culturally specific functions of texts. There may be no focus on fidelity to the text in exegesis, so that the question of whether the author is important or not remains unasked. Instead, traditions may place emphasis on contemporary performances used to think through current preoccupations and circumstances. This is the case with many Balinese texts, as is described by Clifford Geertz (Geertz 1975). It is also the case with some Tamil texts, considered to be realised only in unique improvised music and dance performances (Kersenboom 1996). Ricoeur's absolute dismissal of the significance of authorial intention for the meaning of a text is meant to counter the claim that text is a form of dialogue; indeed no actual question-and-answer exchange is possible with authors unknown, absent or dead. However, Ricoeur treats distanciation as a quality of all texts necessitating certain reading practices, rather than as just one of many exegetical possibilities.

Even dialogical exchanges between readers and writers, in letters or in CMC, are not in all respects like conversational dialogue, as I will now illustrate. Ricoeur's four types of distanciation can be seen at work in the textual exchanges of CMC, affecting the sorts of relations that people communicating via CMC may share. All four types occur to some extent or at some times, although only the first is essential to textuality in all its forms. I will elaborate on the ways in which they tend to occur.

The first type of distanciation, the overcoming of the necessity of human presence for an instance of discourse to take place, specifies the role of text as mediating artefact, though not necessarily as independently meaningful artefact. Text mediates between reader and writer, playing a greater or lesser role according to whether they communicate *only* in text, and depending on how and how often they use textually-mediated communication.[14] A comparison could be made with telephone communication, which also overcomes the necessity of human presence for discourse to occur; mutual absence, then, does not prevent dialogue in itself. But because written language itself is only one of the many representational systems through which individuals communicate and understand one another, the textual artefact is limited in its expressive capacities.

Two forms of uncertainty in interpretation, common to all epistolary exchanges, can be directly identified with the first form of distanciation. One is the problem of verifiability of authorship: sometimes people cannot identify who, if anyone,[15] is the source of a particular message, because they only have textual clues for validation. So, for example, a message may have several authors, be cobbled together from quotations, or come from an unverifiable address. This difficulty is characteristic of all inscription, particularly typed and printed texts, and disrupts a reader's capacity to come to understand their correspondent by putting into doubt the relation between correspondent and text.[16] A second form of uncertainty is that people cannot always tell who will read a message that they intend to be read only by a particular person or people. This risk pertains to all written communication.[17] It takes a particular form in CMC, because of the ease and breadth of distribution of CMCs, and because of the uncertain moral and legal obligations surrounding them.

The second type of distanciation, that is the separation of the intention of the writing subject from the significance of her or his inscription, is contingent rather than necessary. A reader's engagement with a text is with the intention embodied in the formal properties of the text, not the intention or character of its writer. The particular, temporary intentions of the contributing writer, whatever they may be, recede as their enduring text is taken up at greater and greater remove from its time and place of authorship. And this does seem to occur in CMC. Successive quoted reiterations or re-readings of someone's CMC contribution, by the same or different people count rather, according to Ricoeur's reading, as successive raisings of a text to the level of discourse.

To the extent that his or her contribution is written at a particular time, addressed to particular others, as part of a particular dialogue, someone's intentions may matter for those particular addressed others. But, equally, to that extent will subsequent readings, particularly readings by unintended readers or much later readers, be distanciated. The specificity of epistolary address is noted by Roger Duchêne, who writes: 'The more a letter succeeds as a letter, as a text profoundly adapted to the personality of the writer's complicit addressee, set in a lived context, the more unintelligible it is to anyone else' (Duchêne 1970: 114, my translation).

Even in exchanges between particular people, such as I have described as dialogic CMC, distanciation of the second type may occur. Textual exchanges are not usually as rapid as conversation, and there is sometimes a considerable gap between replies; difference between contexts may discourage harmonisation of intent, make mood and style opaque to a correspondent. As the cases of epistolary relations and academic debate suggest, dialogue through text may not have the degree of immediacy that we associate with *conversational* dialogues. Particular types of misunderstanding may occur through temporal misalignment; for example an e-mail not received (perhaps misaddressed or delayed in transit) may result in a correspondent missing a crucial part of what is going on.[18]

The situation of CMC contributors, who are often writing to each other from quite different physical surroundings and social contexts, may also distort the interpretation of CMC texts of particular persons. It may occur, for instance, if the aspects of the world to which a writer intends a text to point are not clear in contexts other than that in which the text was written. And certainly, in line with Ricoeur, in CMC exchanges the textual fixity of a contribution, even if undermined by semantic indeterminacy, suggests that the textual artefact, rather than its writer, may be the clue to own meaning. If, for example, there is indeterminacy on a sensitive issue (as for example on the degree of affection signalled by a valedictory 'love'), then no question can be asked of the *writer*, and the *text* becomes the only interrogable source on the matter.[19] Re-reading typed words may become for an anxious reader a repetitive reassurance of the hope that they bode well, or may seem like an echo-like answer that is little more than a mirror to any question asked of the text.[20] In such situations dialogue itself seems impossible, and some sort of hermeneutics may take its place.

The third form of distanciation is also associated with the diminishing responsibility of a writer for the interpretations and any practical results they may have. As time passes, the effects of the enduring text become increasingly difficult to ascribe to the writer's responsibility, since the moment in which the writer asserted or performed the text has passed. In another article, 'The model of the text', Ricoeur again contrasts the innate fixity of text with the dialogicity of spoken discourse, by suggesting that text excludes some aspects of verbal communication more completely than others. To do so he refers to Austin's threefold classification of speech acts: locutionary, illocutionary and perlocutionary acts (discussed in more detail below). Ricoeur argues that Austin's locutionary acts are grammatically representable, but that illocutionary acts, comprising 'intonation, delivery, mimicry, gestures', are 'less completely inscribed in grammar'. The perlocutionary act 'is the least inscribable aspect of discourse and by preference ... characterises spoken language'. The perlocutionary act is 'the least discourse in discourse. It is the discourse as stimulus' (Ricoeur 1981b: 200). While there are reasons to reject the 'stimulus' interpretation of perlocutionary acts, these remarks make an apt formulation of the problem of assigning agency or responsibility to a writer for the actions of an audience, intended or unintended, reading what she or he has written.[21] It is difficult to argue for unconditional responsibility for the practical results of readers' textual interpretations if the writer cannot be responsible for its various distributions and appropriations.[22]

However, Ricoeurian attention to text as independently meaningful at the expense of text as intentional expression of a self can be seen, within particular textual exchanges, as unethical reading. Textual mediation allows not only for the malicious but also for the inattentive reader. Ricoeurian hermeneutic interpretation arguably facilitates the easing away of a reader's sense of responsibility to attend to writings as the expressions of other persons. If readers normalise texts as nothing to do with the persons who write them, then they may not see how a text expresses something important about the person who wrote it, or about the intentions. To ignore the meanings or intentions of the writer is one means by which violence may be manifested in writing. Violence in CMC is exemplified in the 'Mr Bungle' case of virtual rape,[23] in which one person treats another's textual expressions as nothing more than textual phenomena with which to play, rather than as expressions of the opinions and attitudes of their writers. This violence, instantiated in neglect of the other person as human participant, must be watched for in particular in a medium in which typographic uniformity and playful anonymity tend to direct attention away from those aspects of persons' selves that are less obvious in textual performance.

The third type of distanciation, between the interpretation of an original audience of a text and the interpretive possibilities of the text outside of that audience, is, like the second, contingent rather than necessary in textual exchanges. It is characteristic of later stages in the life of CMC texts, for example if these are circulated more widely or examined by a third party (such as a sociologist or ethnographer). The original audience of a text is often not the *only* audience for a text. As is the case for canonical writings, and archetypically for the performances that are part of oral traditions, interpretations of texts develop as they are taken up and appropriated by new communities of readers. A text may be the expression of an individual to particular others (an 'audience' in Ricoeur's terms) at some particular time, but also become a publicly accessible document taken up in many ways by many people, some of which ways will be not what that individual had in mind when writing. The original and intended reader of a text may have as little say in the interpretation of that text as the original writer, once a text has been widely distributed.[24] But as the later circulation of texts moves away from the time of the original interpersonal exchange, the third form of distanciation does not have a direct impact on the use of texts in interpersonal exchanges, except by making writers aware that their texts may be quoted and reinscribed.

The fourth type of distanciation, the independence of text from a shared social reality or context, is again only contingent in CMC. There is arguably often some sort of shared social context to CMC discussion, constituted by the presence of two or more people in a single exchange and by the continuity of subjects discussed, if not of physical location, or temporal immediacy. (The temporality of CMC is variable, since participants may be communicating synchronously, as in a chat discussion, or asynchronously, as in e-mail or discussion group communication.) Uses such as 'you', 'we all', 'the one I mentioned before', are straightforward examples of ostensive references used in all these CMC fora, mostly in chat. Personal pronouns and referential definite descriptions (such as 'our friends', or 'that book you told me about'), that would be ambiguous if not part of a dialogue, are common in CMC.

But social context is not wholly or necessarily shared in CMC. CMC participants lack the shared inhabitation of a particular place characteristic of many face-to-face encounters. Dialogues with others via CMC lack some of the characteristics of conversation, such as the experiential quality of what it is like to be with particular other people. Important indicators of personal specificity are missing – typed text does not identify itself, as speech does, as originating with a particular person. Only a return address or name identifies it explicitly. Some affective aspects of speech acts that Ricoeur notes as missing from text are also missing from CMC – gesture, tone of voice, prosody, the authority of the speaking body (Ricoeur 1981d: 148). And, in line with his observations about textuality in general, deictic ostention, uses such as 'that one over there', are not common, because they rely on the coincidence of a naming and monstration, the pointing out of an ostensible (usually visible) object or performance.

Thus the fourth type of distanciation, flagged by Ricoeur's emphasis on conversation as the locus of immediacy, is both partial and contingent. It is produced in part by the temporal separation of writer and reader, and partly by the absence in writing of non-verbal aspects of face-to-face conversations. And, of course, the absence of non-verbal aspects of conversation occurs in synchronous as well as asynchronous forms of CMC.

In synchronous CMC, for example, a person's styled writing is not accompanied by any non-verbal aspects of his or her comportment. A description of my frame of mind, for example, is read by others who cannot see my bodily posture and demeanour. The 'I'm *soooo* tired' or 'I could sleep for a year' that might form part of a conversation, would accompany tired eyes and drooping shoulders. In textual exchange we choose, either to use words bluntly alone, or to elaborate on our feelings so as to summon up to a reader what they might otherwise see in our comportment and demeanour. The latter path could be described as the use of 'techniques of spontaneity', after Isobel Grundy (Grundy 1986). And to perform such 'techniques of spontaneity', we must first judge our bodily condition, and then determine how best, in performing that writerly self-portrayal, to convey that condition. Non-verbal grammatical elements also play parts in the techniques of spontaneity in CMC as in other epistolary exchanges. So, for example, the 'three dots' of ellipsis take on new import, as in the following example:

'Hmmm …

… was only thinking of minidisk. Hence [the reference to] lions etc.

Big comp[uter] – yes you need a giant monster workstation. Cally might say you need an amiga …'

The ellipses represent, in order, a pause for thought, phrasing as the train of thought is taken up again, and a sigh. Ellipsis might also be used to signify (intratextual) absence, pauses for breath, and other sorts of silence and absence. But, as the term suggests, the explicit textual representation of bodily activity requires judgement about what bodily experience or performance to represent, and also requires the writer to use a technique of textual representation. It brings texts such as letters closer to the status of 'composition' that for Ricoeur distinguishes literary texts from literal ones, even as it makes texts *read* more like contributions to conversations.

3.2.3 Conclusions

In conclusion, Ricoeur is correct in claiming that some texts are not dialogic. But non-dialogicity is not due to an absolute or essential distinction between textual and spoken language. Whether a text is dialogic or not is, at least initially, a question of how the textual medium is taken up by its users. That speech and conversation are usually associated with immediacy and communion, while writing is associated with context-independence, artefactuality and indeterminacy, is a distinction sharpened by a circumstantial divergence between the roles of spoken and written language within Western culture. CMC destabilises this divergence. CMC allows exchange, some sense of being with and knowing those with whom one is in textual contact. There is not simply one text and one reader, but the interactions and intersection of understandings of many people. Distanciation functions in various ways in people's interpretations of each other's CMC texts, but does not always prevent dialogue between people who exchange texts.

If we accept that textual dialogue is possible, the remaining fact of partial and contingent textual distanciation leaves us with the necessity of trying to understand, cope and cooperate with others in textual relations as full of political partisanship and the threat of misinterpretation as conversational relations. Within the ethical project of understanding others through their styled text, we understand the texts we encounter as the expressions of particular people at particular times. In line with Ricoeur's argument, seeing texts as expressions of persons becomes with time an increasingly problematic matter. It is, to quote Stanley Cavell, a matter 'of limiting the inevitable extension of the voice, which must always escape me and will ever seek its way back to me' (Cavell 1995: 14). Such problems face users of textual CMC as they do any writer, and any user of language.

I now want to move the discussion of affective relations in CMC a degree closer in, to look at how affective inscriptions *work* in CMC. Working from speech act theory, because it gives a concise formulation of some forms of affect that are significantly, if not wholly, verbal in form, I discuss the workings of verbal affect in CMC. This discussion leads on to a reconsideration of techniques of spontaneity in on-line discussion in Chapter Four.

3.3 Words and actions: text acts with CMCs

3.3.1 Speech act theory

I will explore in this section the questions of whether and how people can use texts analogously to performative utterances, to perform textual acts of various sorts. I answer in the affirmative, and show that people's texts have the capacity for affecting particular readers in particular ways, often if not always broadly in line with the writer's intentions. Given the cooperation that is essential to speech acts, this amounts to saying that some CMC exchanges constitute for their participants a field of social action. I also explore limitations to textual affect.

I shall here follow John Austin's influential formulation of speech act theory. Speech act theory elucidates in particular the idea that with words people can 'do things', as opposed to merely describing states of affairs. The following section illustrates how speech act theory may explicate the practical possibilities of language in CMC.

Speech act theory rests on the presupposition that social conventions may coalesce in which certain forms of words perform symbolic actions. Addressees and utterers of speech acts share, it is assumed, a set of conventions for the performance of speech acts.[25] The verbal conventions that Austin specifies as felicitous speech acts presume a coincidence of intent and understanding between speaker and addressee that, while explanatorily convenient, comes into question in ethically problematic speech situations, involving contestation, coercion or deceptive uses of speech. For some exchanges, including many in CMC, in which a legitimating social context is partly or wholly lacking, we need to go beyond the presumption of shared conventions to explain these exchanges. More generally, people's capacity to affect the social world with their words means that speech, like action, may be put to violent or coercive as well as peaceful or constructive uses.

I conclude that oversights within speech act theory conceal important practical differences between spoken and written performances, which in turn have ethical significance for the use of CMC. My account suggests that some sorts of social stability may permit or preserve unethical and unjust conventions, and that many performative utterances are conventional only in the sense that language itself is conventional. I consider, finally, the notion that some textual performances that describe actions can be treated as functionally equivalent to those actions, as is sometimes argued of CMC texts, concluding that textual performances can be taken only as symbolic of physical performances.

Speech act theory can be summarised in a single claim: we do not use words simply to describe the world, but also to perform actions within it. John Austin, in his formulation of the theory, argues that there are forms of words that do things other than attribute predicates to subjects.[26] These other forms of word use, which Austin called 'performative utterances' may affect the (social) world, by changing what people expect, and how they act (Austin 1962).[27] They are, like non-linguistic actions, subject to ethical appraisal rather than belonging in the realm of 'theory'. Austin's theory of speech acts can be seen as providing an account of cases in which people's use of language constitutes social actions. Austin also suggests that certain uses of language are part of a broad swathe of meaningful social activities, verbal and non-verbal, characterised as ritual (Austin 1962: 18–19).[28]

Austin described speech acts as comprising a hierarchy of locutionary acts, illocutionary acts and perlocutionary acts, resting on linguistic conventions and the acceptance of any other people involved for their felicitous performance. A locutionary act is simply the act of saying any phrase or sentence. The utterance 'I promise to water your garden while you are away', apart from any intention it expresses, is a simple locutionary act. Illocutionary acts are what one intends *in* saying something, but it does not include any reference to the person listening to the speech act.[29] An illocutionary act is something more than locution alone (because some locutions are not performative at all), though still not the whole of doing something with words. A perlocutionary act is one in which the intention of the speaker in performing an illocutionary act is recognised and *taken up*, and acted upon, as such by its addressee. Jonathan Cohen aptly distinguishes illocutionary and perlocutionary acts: 'So, while "She urged him not to shoot" would describe the "force" as Austin called it, of an illocutionary act, "She persuaded him not to shoot" would describe the force of a perlocutionary one, as her speech act has accomplished its intended goal' (Cohen 1975: 22). Simply uttering the words of a promise does not automatically *produce* trust in the person to whom the promise has been given.

That is, the (pragmatic) perlocutionary act of persuasion in the above example is not simply the result of one person's employment of some recognisable social or grammatical convention of persuasion. It is brought about through the successful use of a recognisable speech act of urging, *made successful* by the recognition and taking up in practical terms of that speech act by its addressee. Since a perlocutionary act requires the recognition and acceptance by the addressee of the speaker's intentions in speaking, it is dependent on the amenability of the addressee to the import of the speech act. That is, for example, a person can only make a promise if an addressee accepts it, as an attempted apology is only a successful apology if it is accepted. The 'I do' uttered at a marriage ceremony is the answer to a celebrant's question, and cannot be effective without it.

Attendant on the three-way division of speech acts, which treats illocution and perlocution as functions over and above the literal (or 'ordinary') meaning of the words, is a new sense of the validity of utterances, unlike the true/false dichotomy applicable to descriptive sentences. Prior to Austin's intervention, sentences were usually considered to have two possible values: true and false. Austin added a new pair: the *felicity* and *infelicity* of utterances. Seeing that the efficacy of a speech act depends not only on someone uttering words recognisable as, say, a promise or a threat, but on the circumstances in which they are uttered, Austin specified felicity conditions for certain sorts of speech acts. For Austin, an utterance is felicitous, generally speaking, if no contextual condition, such as the deafness of an addressee, prevents it from being so.

The distinction between felicity and infelicity signals the capacity for speech to *make* something the case rather than merely to observe that something is the case. It also signals the dependence of a speech act's felicity on the context in which it occurs. We cannot achieve anything we wish through our uses of words, but are to some extent constrained by existing conventions for performative utterances, by what we would like to bring about in speaking, and by the states of affairs from which we speak. Uses of words are significant as promises, as christenings or as congratulations in part because of the *conditions* in which they are uttered. Words are the primary focus of Austin's work on speech acts, and he considers cases in which the words to do the *work*,[30] while gestures and conditions enable or impede the words.[31] The significance of a particular speech act is depicted as a function of particular literally meaningful words that, in that context, express (more or less) the intentions of the speaker, which can thus be recognised by the addressee by virtue of the words used, so long as surrounding conditions do not *impede*.[32] The roping off of (linguistic) illocutionary acts from (pragmatic) perlocutionary acts signifies the importance of social context in determining whether a given illocutionary act actually has any social effects.

Felicity and infelicity are not conditions of sentences applicable to different propositions from those to which truth and falsity are applicable, but conditions broader than truth and falsity, applicable to *all* utterances, signifying whether they produce the effects desired by the speaker.[33] Thus felicity conditions apply to all utterances *including* those with truth or falsity conditions, as well as to others not assessed along the axis of truth and falsity, but designed to effect change, to elicit advice or information, to attract attention and so forth. Truth claims, like other speech acts, are made in particular social situations, often with particular intentions, resulting in particular (desired or undesired) effects.[34]

We may conclude that speech act theory can be used to describe some aspects of social interaction in textually mediated exchanges such as CMC. Drawing on my conclusion in section 3.2.2 that dialogicity is possible but not ubiquitous in CMC, we can conclude that in some CMC at least, people may be sufficiently *in relation* to each other to stand in the addresser/addressee relationship required for all social speech acts. That is, in textual dialogues, people may state, ask questions, make apologies and promises to each other. Participants in textual dialogues may accept (or refuse), engage with or ignore these questions, statements, apologies and so on. So it seems reasonable to say that people making such inscriptions are performing 'text acts' (by analogy with speech acts). However, it is not yet clear that text acts will be identical in all particulars with speech acts.

Two general features of speech act theory are relevant to an account of text acts, in CMC and other textual exchanges. I consider these features in turn, seeing how Austin's theory can be modified to take account of them, and so to encompass text acts as well as speech acts. The first feature concerns the conventions employed in performative utterances. Austin's account of speech acts presumes that the grasp by addressees as well as speakers of the convention for performing the type of speech act undertaken by the speaker is enabled by their sharing a single set of conventions for speech acts. He claims that a speech act is infelicitous if the addressee fails to understand the speaker's intention to perform a speech act in uttering certain words. But there are two ways in which an addressee might fail to grasp the speaker's intention. In the trivial case, presumed by Austin, an addressee doesn't recognise the speech act as an instance of that type of speech act, a type that is known to be familiar to all speakers of a language. It can also occur non-trivially when the addressee does not *share* the speaker's convention for performing that type of speech act; cases of this kind are not discussed by Austin. This is the type of case significant for CMC.

The second feature concerns the inherent focus of speech act theory on verbal exchanges. In both verbal and textual communication, the performance of conventional illocutionary acts is intertwined with an array of perlocutionary effects, and non-verbal performances and effects. I give a brief account of the interrelation of verbal and non-verbal performances in interpersonal situations, exploring how the absence of non-verbal performances affects the felicity of the verbal performances.

3.3.2 *Convention, intention and attention*

Within Austin's theory of speech acts, the felicity of a speech act depends partly on the existence of a shared convention for that type of speech act. He holds that the felicity of my speech act depends on whether the person to whom I address it understands my intention in speaking (as well as various other conditions, such as that she accepts that I am sincere, and trusts me to do as I say). Speech acts, Austin holds, are made possible by the fact that certain forms of speech, locutions such as 'I promise' or 'I do', become accepted as 'ritual acts', specific locutions with very specific performative functions.

Austin's specification that speech acts are ritual acts differentiates them from the many non-verbal actions whose functions are not ritual. Verbal conventions, what we say when we perform a speech act, are locutions that are repeatable (Austin 1962: 247). Their function is that of symbolically and publicly extending a person's stance in relation to some matter, for example their responsibility for doing a certain thing, or for behaving in a certain way. Speech acts, such as the 'I do' of a wedding, can do this by virtue of the fact that they are recognisable as such.[35] Each individual verbal performance is recognisable by its similarities to other performances, conforming to one or other ritual.

However, the existence of multiple language-using subcultures in CMC poses a problem that speech act theory needs to account for. A ritual is recognisable only relative to some language-using community or other, in that only members of language-using communities that employ a given ritual will reliably be able to recognise a performance of the ritual as such. Austin's account of speech acts assumes a community that shares the same set of verbal conventions, so that when a speaker uses, say, the verbal convention for promising, she speaks with the reasonable presumption that the addressee is familiar with that convention. But the verbal rituals he discusses are unique to a specific community of speakers, not shared by all speakers. Some locutions, though none of them among the ones discussed by Austin, are not even shared by all English-speakers.

In CMC, as in contemporary society generally, many verbal rituals are by no means universal. For one thing, societies consist of a multiplicity of subcultures, with varying social practices and verbal rituals. Members of any subculture will also be familiar with and capable of using the sorts of performatives discussed by Austin, but may also have their own rituals for performing them. There may thus be confusion across subcultures as to what convention a speaker is invoking in using a particular locution. Additionally, in many cases quite unconventional locutions can be used with performative force, showing that speech acts do not have to be socially recognised ritual locutions. This last point, which I discuss below, suggests that the role of the addressee in recognising a speech act and 'going along' with it is more substantial than Austin's account of speech acts allows.

For the performance of a speech act to count as felicitous, it is necessary that the verbal convention that the speech act employs be recognised and acknowledged as such by the addressee. If we accept that verbal locutions for performatives are not universally shared, then two forms of recognition, rather than Austin's one, are required. The addressee must recognise and accept the verbal convention involved, and must also accept the particular performance of the ritual to which they are party, in the particular circumstances in which it is performed.

In relation to the first form of recognition acceptance, the following should be noted. The existence of a linguistic convention does not guarantee that that convention is an ethically acceptable one, or that it is used in ethically acceptable ways. One may 'felicitously' threaten just as one felicitously promises, if felicity overlooks the attention and intentions of the addressee. The ethical acceptability of many speech acts may also extend beyond particular speech situations, if their effects foreseeably include people not present. My promise that I will deceive or harm a third party is not made acceptable if an accomplice agrees to it. Mere conformity to a verbal convention does not guarantee the moral acceptability of a speech act.

Within whole cultures, conformity to existing conventions, linguistic as otherwise, may be open to criticism. Acceptance of conventions as transparently ethical might on some occasions constitute ethical blindness to their deleterious effects.[36] In a media-saturated cultural environment, where claims and promises are often cynical exaggerations (and accompanied by insinuations of all sorts), it would be foolish to accept Austin's dictum as a general rule. Indeed, the determining by an addressee what performative is being put forward may be a substantial interpretive task. The conventionality of language is sufficient that individual words and word-patterns are often reiterated, while still allowing for substantial variation, even unconventionality in expression.

In relation to the second type of addressee acceptance, discussed by Austin, less needs to be said. Once again, though, the addressee's recognition of the speaker's speech act sometimes (though by no means always) involves the addressee's *acceptance* of the performance, something that Austin does not discuss. In some circumstances, a speaker's locution may not be acknowledged to be an illocutionary act by an addressee. In CMC as elsewhere, an addressee will sometimes not let a performative inscription through, simply by not acknowledging that the writer has written the words associated with a particular performative. An addressee might not acknowledge a speaker's performance of a speech act when, for instance, an addressee feels the act to be a threat. Non-acknowledgement might also occur when the addressee believes that the speaker does not have the necessary status (relative to the addressee) to perform such a speech act; this might happen with insults, or even invitations. The existence of a verbal convention for performing a certain sort of speech act does not guarantee that an addressee will go along with a given performance of a speech act of that sort. Many performatives, particularly those whose significance is or remains unclear to the addressee, remain infelicitous unless or until their significance is clarified to the addressee's satisfaction.

A further point warrants exploration here. Intentions may be less than conventional in their expression by a speaker, which means that an addressee will often be called upon to do interpretive work ascertaining what sort of speech act a speaker is performing. Many performative utterances are less strongly conventional than the ones that Austin describes, in the sense that they are not widely accepted and recognised locutions for effecting certain particular social changes. Explicit performatives are often simply the most obvious aspects of performatives that might also be implied or indicated. I may ask for the salt by saying 'Pass me that thingummy, will you?' Some strongly conventional forms of performatives (such as orders or promises) even tend to be the ones that we use when we believe that less obvious forms will not meet with success.[37] As Annette Baier points out, an explicit promise is often given when unbounded trust is lacking (Baier 1986). People's attitudes and intended undertakings are indicated by the multiple (and sometimes ambiguous) verbal and non-verbal elements of a situation. I may threaten to end a discussion, and in doing so indicate that I wish my addressee to change the topic, or retract something she or he has said. And I may promise with my words while my eyes show (wittingly with a wink or unwittingly with a twitch) my reluctance to do so.

Less strongly conventional uses of language can be recognised as capable, as are gestures (deliberate and spontaneous), facial expressions and prosody, of performative uses. These uses may become strongly conventional, or they may remain marginal; all may be called weakly conventional, in the sense that any natural language is conventional,[38] so long as the addressee has the possibility of grasping what the speaker is getting at. Furthermore, as is shown by the possibility of giving a promise to murder, some 'verbal conventions' are very broad indeed.

The retreat of conventions as guiding the reception of speech acts by addressees reinforces rather than curtails the significance of speech acts. Speech acts do not occur only in highly conventionalised and rule-bound exchanges, but also in discourses that we might classify as informal, or unconventional. And they may still be affective in particular, more or less intended ways. The most particular result of weak conventionality in language-use is that addressees have rather more work to do than Austin suggested. Their role is more thoroughly interpretive than that of simply recognising speech acts. Indications of mood, subtle indirect requests (as in 'Oh, I'm just too tired to cook dinner tonight, darling') and so on, have to be divined by an addressee. Speech acts that are only weakly conventional necessitate particular attention to their speaker and his or her circumstances.

In CMC, the power of linguistic conventions is somewhat constrained in comparison with that of many ordinary social situations. The contexts of performative utterances such as promises, apologies, vows, and christenings often contain many non-verbal means for impressing the importance of the commitment on the person who is making it. What is going on when someone is married is made more obviously important by the solemnity of the vows, the pomp, pace, and presence of many people to whom that person is responsible. Similarly, in situations of moral evaluation or discussion, tone of voice often indicates the seriousness with which people take the issue at hand, and the severity with which they will treat it. Many social conventions are weaker in CMC, as their practical elements (hand shakes, non-verbal signs and so on) are inapplicable; in CMC, not only the nuance of face and voice are missing, but many aspects of the wider social context from which many performances take their sense.

Communicative conventions are developing in many on-line fora. As people continue with the medium, we may expect these to solidify in some areas at least, and to become self-consciously accepted conventions; in other fora they will, no doubt, continue to evolve. On-line fora and e-mail exchanges in CMC develop verbal and communicative regularities that help to establish something of a legitimating context, or at least to establish legitimate paths of verbal action. For example, various tactics, such as flaming (insults) and spamming (junk e-mailing), are broadly considered to be insensitive.[39] In some fora participants recognise certain local conventions, such as not revealing plots to soap opera episodes before other participants have had time to view the episodes.[40]

In CMC, performative utterances may go through without a strongly legitimating social context, whether or not strong conventions do emerge, because, as I have argued above, many performative utterances are not conventional in the sense that a wedding is conventional. In CMC, what is often lacking is any *shared sense* that there is a legitimating context, since none of the usual and familiar signs of context (i.e. physical location, presence of people) are available. Contributors need to establish legitimating contexts for CMC discourse, including the particular attention to other writers that is essential for successful interpretation in weakly conventional communication situations. I discuss these issues in the section on context below.

In this section I have shown that speech act theory as formulated by Austin leaves under-explored the role of the conventions by which speech acts are performed, discussing only 'strong' conventions and ignoring the interpretive difficulties associated with 'weak' conventions when used as performatives. I have also shown that linguistic conventions do not need to be as strong as those highly regulated conventions (of weddings and christenings) employed by Austin; weak conventions require more interpretive effort from addressees, although they too can be felicitous.

I now summarise my account of the role of conventions in enabling felicitous performative inscriptions. First, it will be hard for writers to make felicitous performative inscriptions in the absence of any developed conventions for such inscription. Second, in the absence of developed conventions for performative inscription, addressees may have interpretive difficulties in deciding when an inscription is a text act, and in identifying what text act it is. Some of the limits and oversights within the theory point to a distinction between textual and spoken performances that has implications for the ethics of CMCs. Once again the task of attending to others through their styled textual productions seems both essential and yet insufficient to avoid misunderstanding; the current weakness of many conventions in CMC produces freedom in forms of expression that contribute to interpretive difficulties as often as they resolve them. I now turn to the role of context in the felicity of performatives.

3.3.3 The importance of context

This section highlights some non-verbal aspects of social interaction (such as people's styles of performing non-verbal practices) that differentiate textual performances from performative utterances, and render problematic people's sense of there being a single shared social context into which performative inscriptions are introduced.

Non-verbal performances play an important but unthematised role in speech act theory as felicity conditions. Many of the felicity conditions for Austinian speech acts are non-verbal performances that also contribute to the social situations within which speech acts occur.[41] Austin himself did not thematise non-verbal aspects of communication only because they complicated his book (Austin 1962: 27).[42] Subsequent writers have agreed that non-verbal aspects of communication play significant roles in social interaction, both in signifying intent (signs of impatience might signify intent to change the subject, or to give another participant a turn to contribute), and in contributing to a shared sense of what is going on. Non-verbal aspects of communication are, for example, important in signifying what I have called personal style, and are aspects of how people comport themselves in the world over and above how they use words. They contribute in particular to people's understandings of the uses of words.

Non-verbal aspects of speech situations can be affective. Aspects of social situations that are treated as *felicity conditions* for a performative utterance constitute its affective context.[43] They include the preconditions for successful communication, such as that addressees hear and understand the words of the speaker; non-linguistic aspects of particular communicative situations, such as the presence of a ring or the absence of signs that the speaker is lying, out of their mind, or coerced into speech, or the tacit assent of all those involved.[44] Felicity conditions can be resuscitated as significant performances interdependent with speech acts.

If the speech act is just one aspect of a total speech situation, the performative utterance has (or fails to have) its particular effects only within a particular social context. A sentence, such as 'Watch out!' for example, might seem to contain a purpose in itself. But, as many earlier philosophers simply presumed,[45] the intentionality of the sentence, taken apart from any use of it is secondary to practical human intentionality, and derives from the *uses* to which that sentence is put in particular everyday contexts.[46] What particular sentences can *do* adheres to them through our understanding of the grammar of their *use*, such as the ritual, the conventional, and the possible ways they *might* be used in various situations.

For example, 'Watch out!' can be used for a number of different purposes, some more, some less conventional. Most usually and most obviously, 'Watch out!' is used to warn people to watch out, when the speaker thinks they are endangered by something physical, close-at-hand and avoidable. 'Watch out!' is also used deceptively, to make people believe they are at risk when they are not, and humorously, perhaps to draw attention to the *lack* of danger. In these cases, the purpose with which the phrase is used does not correspond with the purpose usually associated with that phrase in social practices of warning, since nothing about the physical surroundings suggests danger. However, both uses are recognised uses of the phrase. Further, verbal locutions can be abstracted from their usual contexts of employment; 'Watch out!' may be used to describe or exemplify its uses, as I am doing now.[47] It is also used more or less imaginatively as part of historical or fictional narratives in which some character performs one or other of the speech acts described above.

There are other conceivable uses for the phrase, such as for teaching the use of the English imperative; for repeating in order to experience a sense of the meaningless of language; in a game (as in 'Watch out! Coming ready or not!'); as an attempt to persuade someone of one's linguistic competence in English; or for ordering someone to put out (display? remove?) their watch (timepiece? armed guard?). As the uses become less *usual*, my descriptions of them become less straightforward, and more difficult to place in any practical situation. So, overall, the possibilities for using 'Watch out!' are various, encompassing nested intentions, and including deceptive, playful and fictional uses of the phrase, as well as bona fide callings to attention, and relating in various discursively invisible practical relations. The sense in which 'Watch out!' is taken by an addressee depends profoundly on the context in which it is uttered.

Clearly some contextual factors are intertextual, by which I mean that the significance of 'Watch out!' for an addressee depends on other utterances preceding it. But many contextual factors are non-verbal. One speech act theorist, Paul Grice, spells out some of the interrelations of verbal and non-verbal aspects of communication, treating the place of speech acts in *conversation*, a cooperative activity involving two or more people who share some understanding of 'what is going on' (Grice 1975). Grice suggests a 'cooperation principle' that is reflected in (successful) conversations: 'Make your conversational contribution such as is required, at the stage at which it occurs, by the accepted purpose or direction of the talk exchange in which you are engaged' (Grice 1975: 45). This principle states that during conversation we normally adhere to certain conversational maxims (the maxims of quality, quantity, relation, manner) (Grice 1975: 44–5), and that conversation works because all contributors more or less keep to the maxims.[48]

The maxims concern both linguistic and non-linguistic aspects of communication.[49] For example, the maxim of manner is concerned with publicly accessible non-verbal aspects of communication, such as tone of conversation. The efficacy of any speech act is bound, not only into a web of (more or less) conventional uses of language, but into a wide range of social practices, verbal and non-verbal. And people do not always share understandings; Grice's version of speech act theory nests the intention of a speaker inside its interpretation by the addressee as a measure of the dependence of a speaker's intentions on the cooperation and understanding of addressees. Much discussion involves contestation and persuasion, even deception; significant disagreement tends to forestall or destroy conversation all together.

The cooperative principle describes (as it prescribes) weak implicit constraints on the speech of speakers; some intentions, if realised in a particular conversational context, will simply be such as to destroy all conversation.[50] Conversation is constituted precisely in the fact that there is *some* shared understanding of what is going on, even if this shared understanding is limited in many cases, and may not constitute *agreement* about what is going on.[51] At the same time, the shared understanding of 'what is going on' (Grice 1975), that is embedded in particular conversations, prevents too radical a move by anyone who is part of that conversation, for radical moves will tend to disrupt the shared understanding so that further conversation is impossible.[52] It plays, in a more subtle way, the same role played by overtly recognised social conventions in Austin's version of speech act theory, and by the rules of discourse developed by Habermasians such as Robert Alexy (Alexy 1990).

Grice's work is valuable in relating speech act theory to the social situations in which actual speech acts are performed. It makes explicit just how dependent the meanings of words uttered in an ongoing situation are upon particular shared but unspoken understandings and practices of participants in conversation. Understandings can be taken to include shared awareness of 'what is going on', similar maxims of conversation,[53] and a degree of mutual understanding of their own and each other's characters. Understandings are adduced from what is uttered, and also from expressive bodily movement and intonation, and from what I described as style in the first chapter of this book.

The verbal and non-verbal performances that comprise speech situations are not always deliberate, in the sense of being planned or pre-meditated. Nor is their apprehension always a conscious matter, since conscious attention is often directed to one or two aspects of speech situations, rather than concentrating on every nuance. As I have already discussed in relation to styled performance generally, some aspects of people's performances are remarked by other people, others not. And yet unremarked aspects may still be powerful contributors to a speech situation; if I am unaware of a nervous mannerism of mine, it nevertheless informs speech situations in which it manifests. Grice thus incorporates social and non-verbal aspects of meaning and interpersonal understanding into speech act theory. His elaboration shows how firmly embedded speech acts are in contexts or speech situations, in which non-verbal aspects of conversations contribute significantly to participants' knowledge of 'what is going on', and to which simultaneity and mutual presence are both essential contributors.

In the light of the power of non-verbal affective aspects of legitimating social contexts, CMC, which lacks many of these aspects, might seem to be lacking some of the important contributory factors that allow words to mean most fully in ordinary social situations. Indeed, to the extent that CMC lacks singular social contexts, social legitimation tends to be held in abeyance. While Grice's conversational maxims presume an ideal of agreement that is rarely reached in *any* circumstance, the multiplication of contexts in CMC may prevent people from accepting that negotiation, or agreement, is required at all. There are other reasons why social legitimation is a difficult issue in CMC. Prominent is the difficulty of using non-verbal aspects of social situations to signal approval or disapproval, or other moral responses. Verbal signals are often perceived as overly blunt; and this perceived bluntness in turn often leads to heated argument. (See for instance Danielson 1996 or Schuler 1994.)

Likewise, the spatial and temporal splaying of many CMC exchanges limits contributors' capacities to sense what conventions are being used or appealed to. For textual CMC, the absence or invisibility of some non-verbal aspects of social situations, together with the non-simultaneity of some CMC, would seem to be significant. If performative inscriptions function outside of singular shared social contexts, in which their impact can be collectively negotiated in shared time, then they will not be performed and taken up in the same way as performative utterances. Assent or acceptance of an illocutionary text act might have to be given explicitly rather than being granted or denied non-verbally. What is practically at stake in agreeing to a particular verbal performance may be partially or wholly obscure. To the extent that social context, such as the presence of particular important individuals, is required to legitimate some speech acts, the absence of a thick conversational social context in CMC may limit the power of ritual to impress upon people the import of their performative inscription.

So far, we can conclude that, insofar as social relations within CMC avoid distanciation, mutual affectivity is possible through textual exchanges. Contributors to CMC will find themselves together within a field of social action in which each can (at least attempt to) perform text acts, which will be felicitous so long as the relevant conditions are fulfilled. Felicity conditions are more difficult to fulfil in CMC, since due to the existence of multiple subcultures and the predominance of weak conventions for text acts, the addressee's role of recognising the text act will tend to require more interpretation. Within their field of social action, each participant will have a range of performances open to them. However, the range of styled performances available in CMC is narrower than in social performances more generally, since non-verbal performances are invisible to participants.[54] I now move on to the question of how to interpret a particular type of text act: CMC assertions that describe the writer as engaged in physical performance.

3.3.4 *Speech and action*

Here I examine a particular use of performatives common to some CMC social environments. This is the use of assertions in the form of textual *descriptions* of physical performances in CMC, where actual physical performances are invisible. This issue is germane to CMC, because in some CMC environments verbal descriptions of non-verbal acts are taken to have the same significance as the acts would have had if actually performed. I argue that such a view is mistaken, even in cases where the only significance a non-verbal performance has is symbolic.

Several people have argued recently that description of certain actions is, when addressed to a second party, equivalent to performing those actions upon them. Mari Matsuda, Richard Delgado, Charles R. Lawrence III, and Kimberlé Williams Crenchaw have compiled a collection of essays arguing that words may wound through their power to construct or interpellate their addressee. Charles R. Lawrence argues that uses of racist speech are enactments of racial violence, forms of psychological abuse as severe and instantaneous as physical violence. Julian Dibbell has made a similar argument, though with less wholehearted support, in a discussion of 'virtual rape' in a computer-mediated social environment. And Catharine MacKinnon argued that pornography is a representational equivalent to rape.[55] In each case, the argument that the description of certain actions is equivalent to a performance of those actions hangs on the claim that psychological damage is *caused* by verbal abuse, in a manner equivalent to that in which physical violence *causes* physical damage.[56]

This argument can be refuted simply by showing that there are ways in which an individual can turn aside verbal abuse, and thus avoid harmful psychological effects, while there are no such ways of turning aside the harm resulting from physical assault. Judith Butler is one person who has argued for limitations on the identification of speech with action, drawing on Austin's work to do so (Butler 1997). There is, she holds, not such a strong causal link between verbal abuse and psychological damage as there is between physical violence and physical damage. As she points out, people are not compelled to accept the intentions of a person who insults them. Individuals under verbal attack may be in a position to turn the speaker's words back on him- or herself rather than take them as somehow determinative of their being. A fantastical description to someone of their being raped could certainly be both upsetting and demeaning. But Butler's view is that the power relations in a verbal exchange can be more fluid and reversible than those in a physical contest, so that the addressee can resist the offensive intent of the speaker, and speak back in ways that blunt the attack. She claims that representations of demeaning, wounding or murderous acts are best seen as threats or intimations of described acts, and not automatically qualifying as successful abuse.[57]

Butler's position does not require that words have no power; this would be to reject speech act theory all together. Instead she argues that selves are constructed by the various addresses of other people, and also by one's own self-descriptions, performances and takings-up of the addresses of others. She uses Louis Althusser's theory of interpellation to describe how individuals may come to have and act out an identity that is not chosen by them alone but conferred by the address of others. The example that Butler uses from Althusser illustrates the notion of interpellation well. A policeman shouts 'Stop thief!'; all those who turn guiltily are thereby interpellated as thieves (Butler 1997: 25). Butler recognises the power of second parties in delimiting and structuring the performative possibilities for individual selves, both by direct appellation, and indirectly through the broader social web in which certain ways of acting and being are easier and others harder to take up. Sometimes, for example, it may be very difficult to speak back to interpellative abuse; it may be very difficult, for example, for some people not to respond guiltily to a censorious address, or to let the abuse of a racist roll off their back.

Yet Butler argues that the individual also has some say in how his or her self is constructed, and some say in how he or she responds to surrounding social pressures.

It is to this power of self-determination that she appeals in *Excitable Speech* when she argues that speech acts such as descriptions or other representations of rape can be thwarted, and should not be treated as rape proper.[58] It would be inconsistent to say that people can construct others (with interpellative addresses), but are unable to construct themselves, through their own performances, and through their takings-up of, or refusal to take up, the addresses of others. As I might be able to beat off an attacker in the street, I might also be able to turn aside abuse, rather than accepting an insult as a wounding description of myself. Likewise, an addressee will not be as ready to take up negative interpellations as positive ones. An addressee is unlikely to accede to verbal abuse with the readiness with which they would accept a compliment, or accede to suggestions that they imagine being together with absent friends.

To summarise Butler's position, abusive assertoric speech acts can be affective and persuasive, and may persuade their addressees to believe all sorts of things about themselves. But we do not produce an effect similar to performing a given physical action by describing that action, though the description might well function as an intimation, promise, or threat of some future performance of that action. In particular, the causal link between verbal abuse in the form of abusive assertions about an addressee and psychological damage to the addressee is weak, and can be broken by the addressee him- or herself.

Butler's claims about verbal abuse are relevant to CMC exchanges in which verbal self-description (and description of others) is an accepted part of the interaction. Assertions about self take on new significance in CMC, particularly if contributors have not met in person, since people may perform verbally in ways that are not characteristically their own. This may take the form of false or quasi-fictional descriptions of appearance and demeanour. Or it may include quasi-fictional descriptions of actions, such as are characteristic of MUDs, in some chatgroups, and other virtual environments in which social interaction is normalised to include descriptions of actions. CMC spans both comparatively conventional and comparatively self-consciously inventive forms of social interaction. Both involve various sorts of self-construction. But quasi-fictional creative self-descriptions and performances are normalised as such in MUD environments. It is the MUD environment in particular I want to look at, as it is of this sort of environment that claims about the affective (and particularly abusive) power of action descriptions have been taken most seriously.

The first thing to note is that the CMC environments, such as MUDs, in which quasi-fictional self-performance, such as action descriptions, is permitted is simply that, in such environments, participants *recognise* that the self-performances and action descriptions are quasi-fictional. This suggests that the CMC environments in which quasi-fictional descriptions of physical performances are permitted do not enable self-construction in the strong sense theorised by Butler of performance generally. The point can be put this way. The more ambitiously the participants in CMC engagements assume and exuberantly act upon the Butlerian axiom that 'the subject her/himself [is] contingent, formed and reformed in the act of performance', the more the power of each performance to form a subject is compromised by anticipation of other, differing performances, and the less can individual performances be taken as definitive of that subject.[59]

This claim is borne out by studies of CMC environments in which quasi-fictional self-performances and descriptions are normal. For example, in a study of LambdaMOO, an on-line social environment in which participants use quasi-fictional forms of self-expression, Caroline Bassett observes that the existence of a *norm* of quasi-fictional self-expression works against participants' self-descriptions being taken literally by other participants. People's self-described subject-positions are not accepted without question, because common awareness of quasi-fictionality prevents anyone from taking others' descriptions for granted.

> In Lambda, outward 'appearances' are *assumed* to be 'deceptive' – unfaithful iterations of players' Real Life identity, and unstable even in terms of the MUD subculture itself.
>
> (Bassett 1997: 538)

Contests arise, often over the power to define a given self, that prevent individual self-performances from holding; any inconsistencies among on-line self-performances create suspicion or hilarious disbelief; any on-line performance is immediately suspected of differing from the off-line self of the person who performs it. A throwaway line in Caroline Bassett's article suggests the lightness with which 'identities' and 'persons' are read in CMC that takes quasi-fictional self-performances as normal: 'Lambda may be regarded as a low-risk place to play out fantasies with an identity which may be discarded' (Bassett 1997: 547).

In the case of assertoric text acts describing physical performances, the same conditions hold as for quasi-fictional self-descriptions. In any CMC environment in which this sort of performance is accepted, it will be recognised by participants as being accepted, and the claims made in this way automatically treated as quasi-fictional. Hence such claims will be read by participants *as* quasi-fictional, rather than as real, and their interpellative power will be weak.

Of course, it may still be the case that quasi-fictional assertoric text acts describing physical performances have social significance for the participants in CMC environments. For example, one participant might describe an action as undertaken jointly with another participant without asking the other's consent, for example hugging, dancing with or hitting them. Such descriptions, although recognised as literally false or quasi-fictive, may still have some symbolic import to the participants. Quasi-fictive descriptions of physical performances may, for example, be taken to signify the degree of amity or intimacy between participants. So one participant's description of an action jointly performed with another participant might be taken to describe the degree of amity between them, although the second participant has not contributed to the description, and might disagree with it. It should not be held, then, that quasi-fictive assertoric text acts describing physical performances have *no* symbolic significance. However, once again, we can appeal to Butler's argument that verbal interpellation can be turned aside or rejected by a determined addressee; this goes for CMC as for other social exchanges.

In some CMC environments, then, participants are able to perform their selves through a range of self-descriptions and quasi-fictional descriptions of physical performances. However, with the acceptance of quasi-fictional descriptions of physical performances within a CMC environment comes an automatic diminution in the power of such descriptions to affect relations among CMC participants. While such descriptions may retain some symbolic significance, this is far less than that claimed for verbal abuse either on-line or off-line, since addressees are able to resist verbal interpellation in ways not open to them to resist physical assault.

The interpersonal constraints that are significant, if submerged, parts of speech act theory also remain in play in CMC. Cooperation, a shared sense of what is going on, and a background of trust are required for promises and apologies, and self-descriptions, to be taken seriously. People may use the liberty of interpersonal distance, and bodily absence, to perform in new ways, to describe themselves with different characteristics, to play or dissemble. But if deception is common, it is then normalised, and participants may become wary of each other's claims. Participants will trust one another less, or leave a CMC environment all together, rather than be taken in repeatedly.

3.5 Conclusions

We use language in various ways that extend communication beyond immediate social situations, in correspondence, broadcast, textual publication and e-mail. Such uses of language, though they also rely on shared social regularities and trust, do not involve singular social situations, because reader and writer, announcer and listener, are not in the same place, and are often temporally separate as well. The face-to-face spoken communication that figures so highly in speech act theory could be considered to be just one, if primary, way in which words are used, alongside written communication and broadcast media. Text acts may be performed in writing. But granted that, as I have demonstrated above, non-verbal aspects of conversations contribute to the felicity (or infelicity) of performative utterances, and often signify in their own rights, text acts differ from speech acts, both practically and ethically.

Words used via CMCs do not require gesture, simultaneity or physical proximity. Conversations may be stretched out over days or weeks, or may veer between near-simultaneous and separated exchanges. The shared sense of 'what is going on' may be attenuated when participants' takings-up of contributions to an exchange are temporally separated; circumstances may change a great deal between contributions. The bodily absence of participants in textual social situations creates uncertainty as to whether one is 'addressing' a present audience or writing to an absent one, and prevents speaker and writer from sharing a single social context. The relationship between illocution and perlocutionary acts and effects becomes stretched or extended in textual relations, as the spatial and temporal loci of people in communication draw away from one another. Sometimes textual contributions are, by virtue of their artefactuality, entirely extracted from original textual conversations, and read outside of any original intended or hoped-for context;

textual inscriptions may transcend any single context, even if they are directed to and intended for a particular individual.

Such alterations to the locus of communication limit the shared sense of 'what is going on', which in conversation is established cooperatively and simultaneously, by non-verbal and less-than-deliberate means as well as in words. If they limit such a sense of what is going on, and if they preclude important non-verbal (and practical) aspects of being together with others, such alterations will in turn change the scope for ethical attention in CMC. This will be the case particularly for people who have not met and spent time physically together. And insofar as computer-mediation transforms the being together that constitutes social situations, it slows our establishment of understandings with others. That which was taken for granted by Austin, and theorised by Grice and later writers, namely the importance of bodily performance and simultaneous mutual presence for interpersonal understandings, is often invisible to us, simply by virtue of its ordinary obviousness. Its absence in CMC should not be neglected.

In this chapter I have shown that three of Ricoeur's forms of distanciation occur regularly, if not always, in textual exchanges. Despite the separation of correspondents, and in some cases, the lack of any face-to-face mutual familiarity, CMC supports dialogue. I have also argued that this reciprocity and exchange permits 'text acts' that have a greater degree of mutual affect than texts not addressed to particular people, or texts read by a series of differentiated audiences. Reciprocity in textual exchange may be said to open up a field of social action for participants, although it precludes the non-verbal components of social interaction.

In the next chapter of this book, I will discuss some structural constraints particular to CMC. These constraints, such as physical separation and temporal variability, have already been treated briefly in this chapter, in the context of Ricoeur's account of textual distanciation. I want to attend to them more closely, so as to draw out their particular effects in computer-mediated exchanges and social groups, and to look at the ways in which users of CMC cope with them.

4 Technical constraints on CMC

4.1 Introduction

In this chapter I consider some important structural pressures on computer-mediated social interaction, associated with the computerised and textual medium of CMC. I do not argue that any of these pressures precludes friendships or other relationships, nor that they prevent the use of CMC for fostering political activities such as democratic decision-making. However, I argue that they do collectively make the CMC experience significantly different from relationships in which people spend time physically together. CMC social interactions are unique in the degree and type of mediation involved, and in the types of attention required to understand the circumstances of others, so altering the sorts of activities required to build reciprocal relationships. A parallel with relationships in letters would capture many of the social qualities of CMC relationships.

For example, CMC limits the possibilities for many practices that are characteristically associated with friendship. Spending time together, living through situations together, and sharing common projects are all either impossible or substantially limited by CMC. In turn, CMC directs interpersonal interaction towards other types of activity, namely towards discussions abstracted from any physically shared experience and towards action in the forms of discussions, formulation of public statements and sending of petitions. In particular, social interactions via CMC are more oriented around textual activities than in any other relationships save those conducted in letters. What people write to one another constitutes not only their interaction, but also partially constitutes their social environment, in the absence of spatially located places which participants inhabit in common.

It is important to keep in mind throughout this section my earlier argument (in Chapter One) that people's selves are constituted by and through their ongoing activities, rather than being a fixed substrate of activity. Character as style is argued to be (socially situated) activity or practice, condensed for comprehension into simpler categories of personal types. This claim in turn suggests that verbal activities, such as deliberation, correspondence and discussion are best treated as varieties of activity, rather than as non-activity or as reflective stances that are not themselves active. Reciprocally, any person is more than a linguistic subject, and indeed the subject treated as linguistic (or linguistically interpellated) cannot be but an abstractive reduction of the engaged embodied human agent, whose style is sustained in practices never purely linguistic, and never entirely of their own making. Given the primary importance of practical activity as part of people's ethical comportment, the structural pressures of CMC will be significant insofar as they encourage certain social practices and discourage others. For instance, the largely linguistic form of CMC is significant primarily because it signals an increased emphasis on the verbal in computer-mediated social interactions. Likewise it signals a lesser role for the non-verbal aspects of the presentation and appreciation of personal qualities and social practices. The taking-up of the possibilities of CMC constitutes, as in other areas of life an appropriative[1] process that depends on how people approach communicative media, and how their prior practices mesh with the possibilities they see in the new medium.

There are four major structural features of CMC that I shall focus on in this chapter. First, CMC is characterised by machine-dependency. Simply put, nobody can use CMC without a computer and a computer system. CMC requires at least access to a personal computer, and the ability to use it and the associated communication software. Second, CMC is characterised by an unusual temporality of communication. One person's writing a message is temporally separate from another's reading of that message, which has significant implications for interpretation. Third, CMC is characterised predominantly (though not wholly) by textuality. Textuality is characterised by the peripherality of the non-verbal. Fourth, CMC allows the proliferation of inhabited 'places', not all of which are located in physical space. I explain the impact of CMC on place as the diminishing import of place as an element of interpersonal interaction, whether or not this is desired by participants.[2]

These characteristics give CMC interaction its most pervasive qualities. Clearly the characteristics of on-line interactions and relationships depend to a very great degree on the characters and practices of the people involved. For example, the level of trust in an on-line group depends to a great degree on the preparedness of all involved to begin by trusting, and is accordingly great or small. And the purpose for which a group or an interpersonal engagement is initiated has a significant impact on the sorts of relationships that are established through ongoing interaction.[3] Social groups without any single practical goal tend to foster different sorts of relationships from primarily achievement-oriented work-groups (although the distinction is certainly not hard and fast). Groups that allow anonymous posting tend to be different from those on which it is not permitted, in that the former allow people to tie their utterances to a range of personae rather than to themselves as a single person, whereas the latter tie all utterances to a person.[4] Groups in which participants already know each other have different qualities from those in which participants meet on-line.

There has been some debate about whether we can talk at all about structural constraints or conditions in CMC. Some writers, such as Kiesler and Sproull in 'Reducing social context cues', or many of the contributors to *Computerisation and Controversy* (Dunlop and Kling 1996), describe talk of structural constraints broadly as 'technological determinism' and identify it with a naïve naturalism that treats all pre-CMC social interaction as untainted by structural constraints, its participants innocent of any prior technologically-involved practices. Such criticisms are reasonable if levelled at some over-simple utopian or dystopian descriptions of the impact of CMC. They point to the imbrication of CMC, like other techno-logical tools, in the existing social relations, practices and goals of already existing communities, and argue that CMC is appropriated by users already equipped with attitudes and expectations, rather than foisting attitudes, goals and practices upon CMC-users.

These criticisms do not, however, rule out the consideration of structural con-straints all together, since their target is only those accounts of CMC that are truly deterministic. Discussion of structural constraints need not be deterministic, but may leave open the possibility of a range of appropriations.[5] Equally, accounts of CMC that treat its impact as determined largely by how people appropriate the technology still assume that the structural qualities of CMC are significant in determining the range of appropriations possible.[6]

4.2 Machine-dependence

In conceptually straightforward, though practically and politically complex ways, extrinsic factors of computer-use such as cost, free time, and facility with computers, limit access to CMC. CMC requires equipment that many people simply cannot access, and that some people simply cannot use. Although costs for access are low in some countries, such as the US and Australia, they are prohibitively high for most people in many other countries. Many regions, and some countries, lack CMC networks all together. The impact of such differences tends to be on the inequalities of access to timely business information, and so political in a sense only indirectly connected with social interaction. The political significance of a highly commercially-empowering network of CMC that is not available to those who are most in need of material and financial support cannot be included in the present discussion.[7]

Some people are discouraged from being involved with CMC by its machine-dependence.[8] Simply, one cannot share a virtual conversation while engaged in any task that requires movement away from one's computer. CMC does not fit in easily with other non-CMC social relations, but must always take place separately from them: it is difficult to spend time with people via computer at the same time as doing anything else, since the sorts of attention (and the loci of attention) are varied. This exclusivity produces a variety of responses, but it has particular effects on those whose time is not fully their own. Away from the workplace, such people include parents, particularly mothers, of small children, who spend a good deal of time attending to the constant, irregular and practical needs of children. It also includes those whose daily activities demand travel, or whose pastimes do not involve computers. For such people CMC is often difficult and distracting.[9]

In workplaces, where CMC is often freely available, other factors besides the requirements of work structure the use of CMC.[10] Factors such as the possibility of e-mail monitoring mean that co-workers sometimes cannot trust that their e-mail exchanges will remain theirs alone.[11] Administrative and legal ambiguities about the amount of social interaction that is permissible in work hours, and about the use of work equipment for non-work-related purposes make the social component of CMC in the workplace an easy target for criticism. Currently, it is only in exceptional circumstances that personal communications outside workplaces are monitored. As the sorts of abuses to which they are vulnerable are not dissimilar from those familiar from the media of letters and telephone, I shall not discuss them in detail here.[12] It is, however, worth noting that the possibilities for organised surveillance of CMC exceed those of most other forms of communication, because of the comparative ease of gathering, searching and manipulating the digital data of CMC.[13] The impacts of these possibilities are difficult to anticipate, as they hang on the results of current debates about the nature and extent of the workplace, the future of data-encryption, and privacy laws.

A further significant aspect of computer-dependence is to be found in the properties of computers and the communications software they use. It is currently accepted that CMC interaction is influenced by the familiar shape of the personal computer. This consists of screen, mouse, keyboard and network connection: these elements broadly determine the scope of action of someone using CMC. Computer-dependence allows, not only the thinking self, but also eyes, ears, and fingers to be engaged in the activity of communication, but other senses are disengaged from the activity of communication. Tactility is limited to the computer keyboard and the place where one is sitting. It is effectively excluded from the shared context of CMC discussion, and is something marginal to my own experience of the CMC interaction, since it is not an object of common knowledge. Sense and smell are not part of interaction, though they might well engage in the world outside of CMC. (Textuality, treated separately below, is also currently the result of computer-dependence, though this is certain to change.)

Such restrictions are a small price to pay for news from distant friends or strangers, akin to the sort of 'sensory deprivation' suffered in reading a book. They take on more significance in a comparison of on-line interaction with the sorts of interactions we are able to have in actually sharing time with other people, when we can share an environment (often a natural one), walk about, make each other comfortable, look or listen to things together, share food and engage in a whole variety of practical activities that are simply not possible with keyboard and screen. Indeed, the condition of being at a computer is machine-like in itself, because of the fixity and regularity of movement that it requires[14] (although it is not necessarily uncomfortable, given the enormous efforts that have gone into ergonomic seating and PC design). In short, people cannot feel that they live together on-line unless they give little importance to any of those activities that cannot be shared via computers, and unless they accept happily the conditions of computer-use.

Software design also contributes significantly to the experience of using CMC, and indeed to the patterns of textual relationships with others. This is, indeed, an area in which human values are preserved in technical form. The differences among e-mail, discussion groups, chat groups and other formats are produced almost entirely by the design of their programmes. Studies in human–computer interaction support the claim that different software packages encourage significantly different patterns of human interaction. Previously adopted habits of word-processing efficiency, rapid reading, reading for comprehension rather than appreciation, and of treating expressions as manipulable or revisable are, insofar as they become characteristic of computer-users, taken up and appropriated within the context of CMC as part of the apparatus for understanding the situated inscriptions of others. Such habits are usually shed as CMC relationships become established and develop their own pace and focus, but often form the background of such relationships.[15]

Steve Woolgar and Keith Grint argue that economic and technological factors tend to regulate the types of software being used, and also that if we accept that software encourages particular sorts of communicative possibilities, then such regimes may be enduring. They treat technology 'as a cultural artefact or system of artefacts which provides for certain, often new ways of acting and interrelating' (Woolgar and Grint 1996: 90). And they will, the authors claim, endure because of economic and technical considerations, not because they are ideal for those people who are using them:

> Ways of using the software other than those the designers had in mind are possible, but they turn out to be prohibitively costly (since alternative sets of material resources will be needed to counter or offset the effects of the technology) and/or heavily socially sanctioned.
>
> (Woolgar and Grint 1996: 90)

In discussions of on-line anonymity, research by Danielson, Detweiler and Grossman points to ways in which the characteristics of software programmes affect computer-mediated social interaction (Danielson 1996; Detweiler 1999; Grossman 1997). Danielson discusses the effects of allowing anonymity to students contributing to discussion groups. Discussion groups that allow anonymous e-mailing have attracted particular interest, since anonymity[16] in other forms of public communication has allowed some people to speak out in ways that they would not otherwise have dared to do (though with either good or ill intentions).[17] Anonymity allows people comparative impunity to lie or deceive others if they wish to do so; and it allows people to make complaints that might otherwise be withheld through fear of reprisal. Lack of anonymity[18] discourages many forms of on-line dishonesty, since it allows others to see who has said what (though it does not preclude more sophisticated forms of impersonation).

More broadly, whether anonymity is possible on-line affects how we come to know other people we meet there. Anonymity (and, to a lesser degree, varieties of semi-anonymity, such as being able to change at will the name one goes by) affects how we know people, since it limits our ability to associate textual contributions with any single person. If one cannot know which encounters, and sometimes which contributions, belong together as those of a single person, one cannot easily form an understanding of the persons behind all the messages that appear. Thus anonymity tends to interfere with the process of coming to understand the character and style of people in CMC. Without anonymity neither deception nor impersonation is as easy; or rather, neither is so sustainable without anonymity. It is worth noting that anonymity is not always used to deceive, but also supports consistency and honesty, and socially consistent semi-anonymous *personae* (Bacharach and Board 1999: 7–9).

A comparison with unmediated conversation is useful at this point, to highlight some important social qualities of interacting through a computer screen. In conversation, the immediate presence of the other person, particularly the familiar other, allows an empathic understanding of their situation that approaches intuition (though is clearly not identical with it, as discussed in Chapter Two). When I spend time with another person, I live through situations with them, so that our experiences of that situation are bound together as two perspectives on the one happening. Although our perspectives on a situation may not be identical, or even similar, they are recognisably complementary. In conversation I will have an immediate and bodily awareness of another's responses to what I say and do; all my inter-locutor's words are accompanied by and modulated by their bodily performances.[19] That such awareness often only acquires its full import for me in reflective analysis does not detract from its significance as part of the affectivity of conversational relations.

By comparison with spending time in the presence of other people, the computer-dependence of facing a screen cannot but alter the qualities of my social relations with others. The same sort of hermeneutic imagination used in reading a play or a novel is required of me in reading the verbal contributions of others in CMC without the presence of the person before me, in touching distance. There is no person before me, no summons, and often no sense of urgency (or immediacy) conveyed by the words that I see on a screen. The status of textual contributions as social interaction is endangered by their mediated character, by the slackening of the summons of the other. It is up to *me* to contribute, if I will, such a summons in imagination, to read it *into* what appears on my screen. Another person has comparatively little calling power to me via a screen. It is easy for me to ignore a message (something I could not easily do in conversation), to overlook significant aspects of what someone writes to me, or to take lightly their experience as it is expressed to me in their writing.

Philosophers and sociologists have written on the slackening of a sense of other people's existence in CMC relationships (Introna, unpublished). Slackening, or the decreased sense of mutual connection with and obligation to others in on-line relationships is much remarked upon, as having both ethical advantages and disadvantages. I want briefly to consider some claims about the slackening of a sense of other people's humanity on-line, considering it in light of my earlier arguments about empathy and about style. Computer-mediation between people is seen, in the sociological literature, as providing two significant benefits, though by no means in all cases. I shall consider these in turn first.

First, *in absentia*, some physical characteristics often associated with social disadvantage, such as disabilities, disfigurements, or gender, do not appear in an embodied form, and so, the argument goes, do not produce the usual rounds of discrimination. They are invisible to the eye, and so generally imperceptible.[20]

This allows, for example, dialogue among different racial groups who would otherwise revile each other, and permits many handicapped people to have social lives in which their condition is not a major disadvantage. It may stop people from noticing at a first encounter physically or mentally disabled people, people from other racial groups, or people belonging to different generations, and so may prevent some forms of knee-jerk discrimination. But it is problematic to conclude that CMC, despite separating people physically, is a realm comfortably devoid of discrimination, or one in which people are safe from feelings of inferiority or inability. Physical invisibility only affords an advantage insofar as it conceals the *visible* signs of human qualities that provoke negative discrimination.

Physical appearance, while itself sometimes the target of negative discrimination, is often taken as indicative of attributes of persons that are not strictly visual or bodily. Discrimination, or telling apart of all sorts, relies on being able to distinguish whatever attributes are taken to be relevant, by whatever means. In snap judgements dress may be taken as a sign of one's faith, or of one's social status, grey hair as a sign of one's conservatism, a hanging lower lip as a sign of one's stupidity. People often arrive at such judgements by means other than by sight, and just as rapidly. For example, grammatical usage, use of slang or jargons, types of comparison or metaphor used, may all function as indicators of undesirable or discriminable attributes; gender and country of origin are often indicated in people's e-mail addresses. I may be prone to take against strangers who call me 'honey' in e-mails, or who write about 'endeavorily expediting processes' just as I may against people with different coloured skin or a different accent.

The dependence of CMC upon a computer does not provide a permanent screen between the people who use it, unless those people can and are prepared to conceal those things about themselves that are likely to provoke discrimination in the first place. If appearance were all that prompted negative discrimination, then CMC's textuality would indeed be a haven. But since some discriminatory preconceptions about others may come into play when someone finds out about another's characteristics, *regardless of how they are discovered*, invisibility may only defer discrimination to the time when anonymity is shed, or pierced. We can conclude only that existing patterns of discrimination that we associate with bodily appearance may be limited by the invisibility of CMC, and perhaps ameliorated by the establishment of textual relationships before the relevant qualities are discovered.[21] Other forms of discrimination associated, say, with vocabulary, style or speed of writing are not ruled out.[22]

A second benefit claimed for the slackening of the call of the other in CMC is for people who ordinarily have little trust in other people, and who fear the call of others as too demanding or treacherous. Agoraphobic people, or people profoundly wary of others, find that CMC offers social possibilities that they can grasp, where they would otherwise have been too frightened to do so. In such circumstances computer-dependence constitutes not a deprivation of social immediacy, but a relief from the immediate demands of sociality.[23] It may as such afford a means for isolated or fearful people to form relationships less demanding or intimate than ones they might otherwise form, and in turn to develop a capacity for more intimate and trusting relationships. The force of this argument depends on whether CMC is seen as a rehabilitatory measure, or as itself allowing relationships as intimate as any other sort.[24]

The ability of someone's words to appeal to another is significantly dependent on prior knowledge of the person themselves, however this is gleaned. The better I already know a person, the more thoroughly I can envisage their activities, responses, character, in short their personal style, the more intuitive will my reading of their CMC contributions be. When I am familiar with someone through going through life with them, I will already have an understanding of their practices and responses. By comparison, computer-dependent relations give me a weaker grasp of the practices of others, since I am not a party to so much of the activity that constitutes their life. The less well I know a person, the more will I find computer mediation a barrier to my coming to understand their life as a practical whole, or they mine.

4.3 Temporality: synchronous text and asynchronous conversation

A unique aspect of CMC as a medium for social interaction is the possibility of instantaneous text-based communication, something like a textual conversation. Unlike the slower method of mail, or the far slower method of publication, CMC allows texts a hitherto unavailable dynamic quality. Textual communication so nearly approximating conversation has not been possible before. There is some question as to whether CMC allows synchronous communication, because, whether or not people are on-line together, the creation of a message is temporally distinct from its reception. The size of the time gap may be minute, but total immediacy is lacking. However, this distinction hangs not on the asynchronicity of the words in communication, but on the characterisation of CMC as a medium of message transmission. What is missing is not simultaneity as such, but the sense of immediacy or of being *with* someone that is habitually associated with actually being in their presence, and which is precluded by a message-based form of communication. We come to experience telephone calls as having immediacy, since we can sense emotion in others' voices, and we may do so to some extent with written communication such as e-mail and letters. I shall treat CMC as capable, though not wholly comprised, of synchronous textual interaction.[25] The lack of immediacy in CMC is treated below in the section on textuality.

That different rates of communication are possible in CMC is significant for how people understand one another on-line. I want to appeal to the established distinction between conversation and correspondence to illustrate an important technical variability in CMC that translates into a social ambiguity about the sort of interaction that is occurring. Simply put, the rate of exchange of messages determines how we conceive of the sorts of social interaction in which we are engaged. A rapid exchange tends to appear conversational; a slower exchange appears not conversational, but epistolary.

Conversational and epistolary exchanges have different qualities, since we can presume a degree of continuity of subject and mood in conversational exchanges that cannot be presumed in correspondence. These qualities stem from the limits to human memory that prevent people from being able to hold still the references of words, or maintain a particular mood, over the periods of time characteristic of an epistolary exchange. It is difficult, for example, to refer to a particular item with a pronominal or referential definite description if some time has elapsed since the object in question was last mentioned, since the writer cannot presume that the reader will be able to single out the object again after a break. The mood of a conversational exchange will comprise part of the circumstances of the exchange, since participants will be *within* the mood while talking; people in the conversation will be actively engaging with each other in particular moods, and will be thus responsive to, and responsible to, that mood. The mood of an epistolary exchange will tend to be different from that of a conversational exchange, since a correspondence will take place over a longer period of time, so may comprise several moods and changes of mood.

Timing is clearly important in CMC as in conversations (in which waiting for turns, and the development of ideas and positions through ongoing discussion are important elements). But variable and unpredictable timing is characteristic of e-mail and discussion groups. E-mail and discussion groups provide flexibility in terms of when one sends and receives messages. Such flexibility is one of their great communicative advantages, since it obviates the need for several parties to make time in their busy lives to chat with each other; they can chat asynchronously instead. But, by the same token, one can never be certain whether someone will receive one's e-mail straight away or at some later time, whether one is initiating a conversation or not. Unlike the usual hermeneutic presupposition that inscriptions may be read by any person at any time, CMC hermeneutics includes a variant in which the addressee may be fairly clear, but the timing of social interaction with them is unknown.

The unpredictability of the timing of CMC is felt as confusing rather than as constraining. It is frequently brushed over in studies of CMC as being a stage in the formation of on-line friendships.[26] Unpredictability of timing may place significant social stresses on computer-mediated social relations. For one thing, the temporal range of an exchange is never known in advance. There is no guarantee that a conversation will ensue from an e-mail, or whether the e-mail will be received some unknown period later, after the sentiments it expressed have modulated or faded in the life of the writer. If the latter, the communication will have the qualities of a correspondence rather than those of a conversation, as distinguished above.

Textual interaction in CMC, particularly in IRC and MOOs, can provide a sense of being in the presence of other people, largely through the rapidity of response that is possible. That someone is 'there' is indubitable when their response to a message is almost immediate, and particularly when letters appear at the rate at which they are typed. This sense of being together with others is not, however, identical with being with them. The construction of silence in CMC social inter-action is one case in which CMC is significantly different from conversations in mutual presence. On-line, silence appears as nothing more than the passage of time, time without words: much may go on in silence in a face-to-face situation, but silence appears as nothing more than a 'gap' in a textual exchange. In conversations, silence may happen when people are concentrating on an activity together; it may be uncomfortable or comfortable; people may show interest, or lack of interest in their demeanours; people may wait for others to speak, or silently encourage them to do so. Much social interaction is borne in silence, although it is rare for people to communicate solely through a sequence of silent acts unless they are in a situation in which talking is forbidden.

People using CMC have many techniques for representing silence, used to portray discomfort, or hesitancy of speech. For example, pauses are commonly indicated by ellipsis ('…'), by carriage returns, and by transcriptions of non-verbal sounds such as 'oh', 'ah', 'ahem', 'um', or 'unh-hunh'.[27] The mimicking of the pace of thought, or of the passage of concentration, are made possible through the representation of silence, by careful use of punctuation, word order and emphasis. Such representations of silence can only be, by virtue of being the productions of a single person, the representations of their writer's silence. I might use them to portray the gaps in my own train of thought, or to simulate a silence that I conceive as occurring between us. But representations of silence are not identical with actual gaps in conversation, which fall between messages as well as within them, and which are not representational in any sense.[28]

The facial and bodily clues as to what an actual silence, an actual pause on-line might portray, are absolutely absent, just as when a break in correspondence can give no clues as to its cause, being simply an absence.[29] It is thus to be expected that pauses or gaps in the sequence of CMC messages might be a point at which particular discomforts often arise. Silence in discussion groups is often taken as lack of interest;[30] and that if a message does not garner many replies, perhaps simply because it arrives at a forum just as people are engrossed in another message, its sender may think that the message did not interest the group. It is all too easy for the other participant or participants to take the silence as lack of interest, or some sort of deliberate refusal to respond. To summarise: in CMC the sense of togetherness (mutual presence) is maintained in the exchange of e-mails at a pace comfortable for both participants. Each textual contribution is thus read as a sign of the writer's ongoing presence and involvement. It is not surprising that silence in CMC, as in other epistolary exchanges, tends to be taken for a deliberate silence signifying absence.[31]

For example, the conventional bounds of on-line conversations, which, like face-to-face conversations, are often maintained by mutual greetings and leave-takings, may suddenly be suspended by a participant. A person may let conversation drop, unknown to the other (perhaps they have been called from their computer, or are involved in a tricky piece of editing). The other person is left 'lost', expecting a reply, following the conventions of spoken conversation, while the first has turned themselves to another task, out of choice or necessity. For the first, the conversation has become correspondence, a slower exchange. Something that seems simple as moving to answer another e-mail, or to help a co-worker away from one's computer may constitute a breach of expectations or of conventions. In spoken conversation, such breaks tend to be visually self-explanatory, and usually inoffensive. On-line, if their cause is invisible, they count as unexplained disappearances, mysterious and sometimes offensive.

The peculiar transformation of silence in CMC is particularly evident in the CMC version of situations in which speech is either minimal or limited. In times of emotional breakdown or collapse, and particularly for people who are not accustomed to verbal expression of emotions, the textual nature of CMC is particularly inadequate. The requirement for ongoing self-description, or self-performance may form a barrier to togetherness during moments of inarticulacy.[32] Similarly with listening to and being present for a friend in the grip of strong emotions, the absence of a silently expressive face, of a friend who might calm and sooth by his or her steady physical presence, their replacement with a screen, makes comforting difficult to negotiate via CMC. This difficulty with coping with written expression in times of emotional distress has been taken up in terms of CMC by professional counsellors and psychologists,[33] but it has not yet been discussed in terms of ethics and CMC more generally. Here also, representations of silence fail to attain the range of significance and subtlety of facial expressions and of bodily comportment.[34]

The absence of a single e-mail may, for example, throw the sequence of an exchange out of kilter. Its absence might render others unintelligible, or alter their significance to the reader. The more important the missing e-mail, the greater the impact of its absence on a reader's understanding of the e-mail sequence. The disappearance of a reply to a request for a reply, or the disappearance of a promised missive will appear more serious than the absence of an unanticipated contribution. Disappearance of e-mail may impair a relationship conducted entirely in text, if the unreliability of the medium of communication is instead attributed to neglect by the writer. Either may be taken, by a fearful, suspicious or attentive correspondent, as a breach of a tacit commitment to reply, even if the silence is quite unintended.

My claim, in Chapter Three, that distanciation may affect CMCs that endure over time, could also be used to show that variability of timing, particularly in the case of messages lacking time or date indications, problematises the intentional form of particular inscriptions.[35] In Ricoeur's terms, illocution and perlocution are less straightforward than locution in the medium of text. Unless an inscription is timelessly true, the purpose or intention of its being produced by some particular person is more temporally anchored than the text, which continues to allow reading and interpretation. For example, something as simple as the misordering of e-mails (as sometimes happens through server error) may lead a reader to misconstrue the sequence of their writer's thoughts. An error in timing may lead to a revelation being delayed until past the time where its message would have had a salutary effect. In the *locus classicus* of this sort of confusion, Thomas Hardy's *Tess of the D'Urbervilles*, a letter from Tess Durbeyfield, detailing important revelations, is meant to reach her fiancé before their wedding day. But the letter is misplaced, and they marry while he is ignorant of a revelation that later destroys his trust in her, although she thinks that he has read the message and sees the revelation as no obstacle to their marriage. This sort of misunderstanding may occur in either synchronous or asynchronous CMC. Both types of CMC involve contributions arrayed in a *sequence*, the disorganisation of which results in participants having different grasps of the state of affairs between them.

The ambiguity of timing is compounded with the textuality of expression, in that CMC spans the possibilities of speech-like or conversational writing, common in IRC and MOOs,[36] and non-immediate modes of speech, such as are used in correspondence, and also in semi-formal discussions.[37] CMC allows both simultaneous and drawn out communication, and allows references to immediately present objects and to more context-insensitive subjects. One form of the difficulty can be stated as: e-mails give few indications of the context in which they were written, though they do have a time-specification; nothing but actually reading an e-mail will tell a reader in what context it belongs or, in many cases, who sent the message. Peter Danielson argues on this subject that clear labelling of e-mail will alleviate most of this confusion. He comments that we easily classify the print mail we receive daily, and there is usually little trauma in telling apart a newspaper, a flier and a letter from a friend. An e-mail classification system should alleviate difficulties on-line.

The problem of distinguishing different sorts of e-mail received turns, for Danielson, around ascertaining the *categories* of messages: advertising, administrative circular, student's assignment, or discussion group contribution. So long as one can tell these apart (perhaps with the aid of colour-coded buttons at the top of each message), then there will be little danger of misunderstanding the intent of the various messages one receives. Danielson identifies the sense that the user of CMCs is being engulfed by an undifferentiated wave of text, as confusion resulting solely from the identical initial appearances of different e-mails. This is indeed a general difficulty for CMC, in which nothing about a message is particular to its sender, neither the format of the message nor the presentation.

I would, however, identify a more complex difficulty resulting from the textuality and asynchronicity of CMC, particularly e-mail and discussion groups. Confusion about what sort of e-mail one is receiving stems not only from the difficulty of distinguishing the different sources of e-mail, but from the more troubling matter of not being able to expect even within a single asynchronous CMC exchange a consistent level of engagement or social environment. Compare textual com-munication with a conversation as described by Grice:[38] conventions or language-games constrain to some extent what counts as a possible move in the conversation; conversation is kept together by a temporally continuous and more or less shared sense of 'what is going on'. In correspondence the sense of 'what is going on' is attenuated, in most cases, by the distance between correspondents, and, in some cases, the time between responses. Correspondents do not normally write in ways that require immediate response, because they are quite aware that such immediacy is impossible. Correspondence is also abstract in the sense that its text cannot rely on non-verbal nuance of any sort to carry it across, nor on a shared simultaneous sense of surroundings or moods. Letter-writers evoke atmosphere, describe their surroundings and their moods, in the understanding that such aspects of their circumstances will not otherwise reach their correspondents.

But e-mail supports *both* immediate present speech-like situations, and exchanges with the pace and non-immediacy of a correspondence, without giving any clues as to which, if either, will occur. Speech-like contributions, say those that form part of a simultaneous discussion, may include spontaneous speech-like locutions prompting immediate reply and remarks relying on some shared sense of immediate context, subject-matter, mood and tone that make up a sense of 'what is going on'. CMC also allows such spontaneous conversational contributions to lie unread until after the context in which they were 'uttered' has passed, when indications of mood, tone and so on may become either indecipherable or prone to misinter-pretation. The temporal variability of e-mail often prevents the establishment of consistent ambience or shared sense of what is going on between people, simply because neither can gauge whether their contribution will be part of a virtual speech-situation or the more drawn-out exchange of a correspondence. Our expectations of the character of communicative exchanges, normally intricated with the temporality and level of immediacy characteristic of those exchanges are subject to unusual pressures though this variability.

Intimacy in CMC exchanges is potentially limited by textuality and asynchro-nicity, when nothing but texts themselves exist to establish contact between people. I say potentially here, because I do not wish to claim that intimacy is impossible in CMC, or indeed that it is always accessible outside of CMC; rather that the structure of CMC alters the possibilities for intimacy; this structure limits intimacy most particularly if we are unaware of its workings, and attribute its limitations to ourselves or our communicative partners. For established friends and new acquaintances alike, the absence of any prior social situation into which one's e-mail message might move, ignorance of whether a conversation is even possible, can destabilise one's sense of the appropriate way to 'begin talking'. Two factors work together here, as exemplified in the following example. If I want to e-mail a good friend, hoping to talk to them about something that has been troubling me, but I do not know whether they are at a computer, I cannot simply 'express myself' in text and send off the e-mail. For the more sensitive the subject, the more its presentation is something dependent on its dialogic elaboration, relating it to my friend, seeing their response on hearing it, and making sure we both understand 'what is going on' as we speak. It is important to me that my friend is willing to listen and respond, and equally important that I do not impose on her if she is busy or vulnerable herself at the time. But in CMC the only way to ascertain my friend's initial openness, and ongoing appreciation and understanding of what I am elaborating, is through a routine of question-and-answer very unlike the immediate, often non-verbal, responses I would see in a friend if we were talking.

Moreover, temporal separation of messages further upsets the extent to which either friend can presume shared experience and appreciation of the issue at hand. The ambiguity of timing in CMC thus tends to favour exchanges that do not ask for or rely on immediate feed-back and mutual responsiveness, but cover more general subjects and more enduring attitudes. That many of our emotions are temporally specific means that, once expressed in enduring text, they become rapidly less contemporary. The expression of an emotion pertaining to a particular bounded time, and intentionally related in its form of expression to the person addressed, calls for an immediate response. In asynchronous CMC relationships where no norms of immediate response can be established, expression of emotion tends to fall flat, without the spontaneous rapport of sharing and elaborating on that expression. In synchronous forms of CMC emotional expressions can be spontaneously expressed and appreciated; temporality is less untoward.

4.4 Textuality

There is, as the discussion of speech acts observed, a great deal more to expression and understanding than the meanings of words. Conversation takes place in shared spaces, during shared activities, and takes up around non-conversational activities and events.[39] Gestures and physical/emotional interactions are constitutive aspects of concrete social situations; they are generally more context-embedded than verbal communication.[40] Though they are themselves not beyond misinterpretation, they require textual *articulation* to be 'visible' in CMC. This means that crying, laughing and other bodily expressions, are invisible in CMC unless they are textually performed. Textual performance, or articulation of non-verbal aspects of com- munication transforms their social function; while their non-verbal form encourages people to think of them as spontaneous, often unconscious, their textual articulation is something artful or deliberate by comparison. Aspects of bodily comportment and non-verbal communication of which individuals are not aware may simply not appear at all.

Some non-verbal aspects of conversation, such as all the varieties and meanings of silence, or withdrawal from conversation, are *intrinsically invisible* in CMC, because their expression in text would run counter to the import of their expression in conversation. Silence is used in human communication in a variety of ways. The most obvious form of silence is the 'lull' in conversation (Goffman 1963: 65) in which people fall silent; the lull is usually figured as people having 'nothing to say'. There are many other ways in which silence signifies in conversation: it can signify, for example, a refusal to speak, a refusal to comment on a particular subject, a period of non-verbal activity, a period of silent communion, a refusal to engage with a disapproved-of person, or a deliberate pause to allow others to speak. Contextual clues are important in determining the significance of particular instances of silence. Their absence in a wholly textual environment can find no easy substitution, since a gap in someone's e-mail contributions is accompanied by no other signals. In general, then, the textual performance and reading of emotions is quite different from, and distant from, the context of simultaneous experience- and-expression of emotion that occurs when two people are together.

It is a commonplace to observe of CMC that it is lacking in non-verbal cues. And it is self-evident that textual styles cannot rely on bodily nuances of any sort. Several commentators use this observation to argue that CMC, by ruling out non- verbal aspects of social interactions, prevents emotional expression or emotional intimacy. 'Textuality', as one of the defining features of CMC in particular, is often used as a cypher for a more complex definition of the qualities of CMC, pertaining particularly to the interpersonal distancing effect of text (Culnan and Markus 1987; Walther 1996; Walther and Burgoon 1992; Kiesler, Siegel and McGuire 1984; Kerr and Hiltz 1982). In turn, CMC directs interpersonal interaction towards other types of activity, namely towards discussions abstracted from physically shared experience, and not dependent on such experience for their significance.

I shall not consider in any detail the arguments put forward for such positions, since they are usually *ad hoc* observations of aggressiveness, lack of emotion, and so on, with an attempt at an explanation. Writers discussing the absence of non-verbal cues often make the assumption of a straightforward causal connection between textual interaction and any sense of impersonality or distance experienced as part of contemporary on-line social engagements. The following argument is meant to show that textual interaction, and the consequent lack of many familiar (though not all) non-verbal aspects of conversation is not solely responsible for any sense of impersonality or disconnection that some people feel on-line, although it may be a contributory factor. I present my own position on the matter, which is that lack of non-verbal aspects of social interaction limits people's grasp of others' emotional states, of how things are going for them. This limitation, though it is not an obstacle to maintaining relationships of good-will, may be detrimental to relationships in which being able to grasp another's condition is taken to be important for the sake of that person, and for the relationship as a whole.

First, it is important to consider the categories of 'non-verbal cues', and 'non-verbal information' to the absence of which arguments about the limitations of CMC appeal. The claim that all non-verbal cues are excluded from CMC is debatable. If we accept the modified Gricean version of the argument that social context helps determine the significance of an utterance,[41] then 'social context' gives us a wider definition of non-verbal information, or non-verbal cues, than simply facial expressions, bodily gestures and intonation. An Austinian social context also includes timing of speech, social actions, place or setting of conversation, the intentional stances of interlocutors, and their attributions of intentional stances to each other. On such a reading of social context, some aspects of social context that count as non-verbal information do not depend on mutual presence, but can be conveyed in text, including CMC. CMC allows people to convey their own intentions without giving explicit voice to them; it allows people to learn about each other's implicit intentions; it shows the sequence (and sometimes the timing) of contributions; some CMC users share a sense of place derived from already existing institutions, such as places of work or of study, or from the place-like settings of MUDs and 'virtual conferences'.[42] In conclusion, not *all* kinds of non-verbal information, not all aspects of conversational social context, are missing from CMC.

Non-verbal information does take different forms in textual social interaction. Many textual styles illustrate the point that writing is not like a transcription of a conversational style, but conveys what is not written down by other means.[43] This can be seen by reading a transcript of a conversation: some of 'what went on' is not retained in the verbal traces of the language-games that occurred, and cannot be determined by them; a text-only transcript contains no compensation for absence, because it records the verbal aspects of presence. Written styles tend to compensate for the absence of physical presence, in one way or another, by narrating events, describing activities, moods, feelings, attitudes and so on; and also by conveying mood, pace, and focus.

To some extent, the intonation patterns of speech can be expressed in writing. For example, a sense of rapidity of speech is often given by punctuation, by the length of sentences, numbers of adjectives or adverbs, or by the dropping of articles.[44] Differences in importance of words and phrases can be given by emphasising particular words in a sentence (typographically or by word order). Importance can also be indicated simply by repetition of words or phrases. In some cases, netiquette conventions emerge, such as the convention, noted in Chapter One,[45] that using capital letters counts as shouting. Many people do not use capitalisation for emphasis in CMC so as not to offend; capitalisation may be taken to be rude by readers even where no offence is intended.[46]

Mood may sometimes be indicated in CMC by choice, sometimes unreflective, of vocabulary, of subject-matter or by length of sentences. For example a shortening of sentences in someone's e-mail may be an indicator of a change of mood, but is open to several interpretations, depending on our prior understandings of the style of the person writing.[47] If a shortening of sentences is accompanied by a return to more formal punctuation and capitalisation, then the combination might be read as some sort of dissatisfaction or offendedness. In other cases brevity may be characteristic of the person concerned, or of the norms of a particular discussion group; or it may indicate distraction or haste. Knowing the difference between moods indicated, however, hangs on a reader's familiarity with the writer's textual style. For example, the e-mail message 'That's great for you', will be differently interpreted (as appreciative or as sarcastic) according to readers' perceptions of its writer's temperament and current situation.

The timing of messages is also important for people using CMC, as it indicates (sometimes with less than conversational accuracy) the flow of question and answer, proposal and response. (It is for this reason that software governing the organisation of posts to discussion groups can have such a major impact on the social life of groups.) Answering a query rapidly in a discussion group, for example, may count as eagerness to help a particular person, showing off, or perhaps a sense of responsibility to the group as a whole. Since people vary in terms of how regularly they contribute to discussion groups and to e-mail exchanges, the rapidity of particular responses may also be understood in the light of other people's estimations of their usual rate of contribution.[48] Timing of messages is thus a significant non-verbal contributor to how people understand each other and how it is going for them in CMC. So, in general, CMC *can* convey some sorts of non-verbal information, if non-verbal information is taken to include the implications of written sentences, the timing of messages, or the stylistic particularities of a writer. The aspects of social context that *are* missing from CMC, facial expression, gesture, and bodily movement, are significant for their being not only non-verbal but also bodily, as I will argue below (in the section on emoticons).

Second, against the modified claim that the lack of at least the bodily non-verbal cues creates emotional distanciation, traditions of social relationships in other media of textual exchange, particularly letter-writing, suggest that textually-mediated relationships may be cordial, or passionate, sometimes intimate. Friendly relations are possible in letters despite their lacking those non-verbal cues that are related to bodily comportment. Letters afford possibilities for varieties of social interaction, albeit ones in which the people concerned evolve different mutual understandings and share different activities than in companionate relationships.[49]

CMC itself, insofar as it is textual, is comparable with other textual media as a forum for social interaction. It does not prevent people from expressing and describing emotions or conveying emotional force any more than do other forms of writing, such as letters, or fictional forms such as poetry, or novels. The lack of bodily gesture, intonation and facial expression in CMC does not rule out emotional expression and understanding, any more than textuality in exchange of letters does. Purely or largely textual communication may, however, substantially change the forms of people's social interaction and relationships, without preventing relationships from forming, by giving different norms and foci to social activity. The circumstances surrounding the use of emoticons in CMC suggest that people using CMC feel that it lacks some of the non-verbal aspects of social interaction, or at least see some advantage in supplementing words with other signs. Indeed, people describing the role of emoticons (representations of faces) often refer explicitly to them as ways of overcoming a sense of inability to convey and appreciate emotions appropriately in the textual environment of on-line interactions.[50] In other words, although a sense of lack of emotional expression, or of non-verbal communication of some sort, is experienced by many people using CMC, it cannot be put down entirely to the structural qualities of the medium.

The sense of emotional *disconnection* that is sometimes associated with textual CMC may well result in part from people's current unfamiliarity with how to write and how to read others' words as expressing themselves and how things are going for them in a synchronous textual medium.[51] Whereas some people are, through reading, capable of understanding emotions expressed in poems and novels, many people are not accustomed to such reading practices. Members of societies that are becoming decreasingly familiar with the written word and increasingly familiar with television as a vehicle for social and emotional life may, for example, have more affinity with what Walter Ong calls the forms of 'secondary orality'[52] (i.e. live and life-like television programmes) than with literacy as a way of understanding other people and how things are going for them. Affinity here includes either being more adept at interpreting speaking people (live or life-like) than people's textual expressions, or having greater confidence in interpreting speaking people than people's textual expressions.

On a more general level, as Joshua Meyrovitz has recently argued, the skills of writing and reading that together make up literacy are profoundly difficult to learn and develop. Children who begin to learn to read and write at the age of four or five are still learning to read and write, in ever more complex and sophisticated ways, when they leave school at sixteen, seventeen or eighteen, after higher education during their twenties or even later. Without such training (and for some people, even with it) self-expression and interpretation in writing are not automatic, but require attention and practice. Even for those well-versed in writing and reading, the rapidity of exchange of some conversational CMC, and its informality, may require significant adjustments both to how we read and how we write, as for example, when writing rapidly, falling into conversational mode, one forgets to mention the self-evident (to oneself). What may in some cases result from textual inarticulacy, or from unfamiliarity with the gamut of developing textual conversation styles, is often taken to be wholly the fault of a computer system that prevents people from expressing themselves.

Last, the other structural aspects of CMC that I have addressed also have distinctive effects on the social qualities of CMC. I have already described some difficulties to do with timing and computer-dependence, and will presently discuss the peculiar status of place in CMC: these may contribute in some sense to feelings of disconnection from others on-line. As I discussed under computer-dependency, the social configurations particular to CMC are not always those that would, in *any* circumstances, be conducive to amicable relationships, so that a sense of depersonalisation may be caused by genuinely difficult social situations on-line.

For example, students and staff are often together in discussion forums of up to two hundred people; workers' e-mails are automatically documented by servers in a way that would be oppressive in conversation; people in large discussion groups often have such a variety of directions that they become angered simply by the lack of unity of purpose in the group; people used to combative styles may dominate unthinkingly in groups containing people unused to or upset by combativeness.[53] People are sometimes unkind or deceptive, or use e-mail to write things that they could not say to someone's face, just as they are often unkind, deceptive or evasive in other ways. With the continuation of actually existing social difficulties among people in ordinary life into CMC, it would be naïve to assume that a sense of depersonalisation in CMC is caused solely by the absence on-line of some forms of non-verbal information.

Even if some non-verbal aspects of social interaction are available in CMC, there is nevertheless truth in the claim that CMC is significantly different from face-to-face social interaction, and that the differences that it displays may be uncomfortable, disorienting, or produce a sense of disconnection for some people. The aspects of social context, or the classes of non-verbal information, that are excluded from CMC are the bodily aspects of social interaction, which are influential in conveying emotions (even across the grain of conversations), and play important but often unnoticed parts in social interaction. I have already discussed non-verbal aspects of conversations in Chapters One and Three, concluding that familiarity with the social practices (including bodily activities) of other people and communities contributes significantly to our understandings of others. Their absence often requires greater imaginative effort to grasp the condition of a writer, and results in some particular sorts of misunderstandings.

I shall now explore the use of non-verbal signs such as emoticons (representations of faces) and conventionalised transcriptions of pauses and hesitancies as means of replacing bodily presence, and of countering any sense of disconnection, in CMC.

4.4.1 Emoticons

The role of emoticons is usually figured as a substitute for the gamut of 'non-verbal cues' or 'non-verbal information' that cannot appear in words, but which are how people understand each other in ordinary conversation. I have already noted that we cannot treat the absence of non-verbal cues as the sole cause of conflict and depersonalisation on-line. However, I now want to ask to what extent emoticons can perform even that particular task which is usually attributed to them, that is, to substitute for the absence of non-verbal communication. I will give an account of the semiotic status of emoticons, one that will distinguish them from bodily non-verbal communication ordinarily considered in face-to-face communication. The account also applies to other non-verbal signs, such as acronyms, and transcriptions of sighs, and, in a modified sense to verbal descriptions of non-verbal acts, such as describing smiles, pauses or other actions. I hope that this account will go some way towards explaining why emoticons are not a great move towards replacing bodily aspects of face-to-face communication missing in CMC.

The emoticon, in general, figures in accounts of CMC as a replacement for the absent non-verbal aspects of conversation. Since the expressive human face is missing from CMC text, argues linguist Christopher Werry, pictures of faces formed by keystrokes will go some way to substituting for it (Werry 1996). He describes the use of emoticons on-line, showing their popularity in textual contributions to chat line discussions, and states that they convey non-verbal emotional information and are a key aspect of social interaction on-line. He notes the frequency of their use in chat lines, and surmises that they function as signs of the expressive creativity of their users as well as working to express non-verbal aspects of conversation. Werry's argument is also interesting in that it illustrates that there is a wide awareness (not just a vague feeling) among CMC users that something socially valuable is missing from textual interactions in which people cannot see or hear one another. Werry undertakes no further analysis of the particular expressive and social roles played by emoticons on-line, nor of their aptness for the role assigned to them.

Nancy Baym, in a series of articles about forming on-line communities (Baym 1993, 1995a, 1995b, 1995c), argues that emoticons are 'expressively loaded innovations' that are 'created and conventionalised into unique linguistic "registers" as part of the interactive process in computer-mediated communities'. She notes that some acronyms function in a similar way to emoticons, and are also expressively loaded. She does not argue that emoticons simply stand in for facial expressions, but that they constitute alternative expressive forms *similar in function* to facial expressions. Such functions are fulfilled without emoticons or acronyms substituting, or *having* to substitute for facial expression in any straightforward way. She gives no detail about what sorts of emotional charges emoticons or acronyms might bear, whether a 'smiling' emoticon indicates a smiling face, and whether it might indicate a variety of emotions, as different sorts of smiles in different circumstances do.

Baym's position is that the particular significance of emoticons would depend on how a CMC group, or members of it, takes them up and uses them, so that she cannot be too precise about their particular use (Baym 1995a: 149–51).[54] She argues that emoticons have an important secondary function as the common social property of an on-line group, used self-consciously to signify membership of that group, and regularly circulated among old and new members of that group to enhance social solidarity (Baym 1993: 152, 1995a: 154). Members of a particular discussion group might adopt and use an acronym with particular pride, for example. Such observations provide reasons why it is difficult to associate particular 'emotional charges' with particular emoticons (or acronyms).

Uneasiness with the social conventions of emoticon-use, or indeed, other textual practices specific to CMC, extends beyond unfamiliarity with emoticons particular to CMC groups of which one is not a member, and may for some people be as broad as resistance to internet culture all together. Some people dislike emoticons and see them as part of a jargon coined by CMC users with different interests and habits, rather than as a unifying argot owned by one and all. Such people, cleaving to older or more formal textual traditions, often also dislike the poor punctuation and spelling, and the unorthodox grammar of some CMC usage. Such views are compatible with Baym's claim that use of emoticons, like other emotional behaviours, is culturally specific. They would be well explained by Cheris Kramerae's observation that emoticons evolved as part of the vocabulary of a technical white elite, and still show the traces of their styles of thought and social interaction (Kramerae 1998: 122).[55] Such claims express something important about group-membership on-line, namely the powerful sense of being excluded that unfamiliarity with an on-line group's social or linguistic practices may produce, particularly when it intersects, or is seen to intersect, with established forms of exclusion. But they need not force the conclusion that emoticons substitute for facial expressions.

Baym's model of emotional expression, whether for emoticons or for face-to-face communication, is fairly straightforward. Her descriptions treat the use of emoticons and acronyms as conveying non-verbal information about a person in CM social interaction. Non-verbal information, contributing to each person's certainty about the identity of others, is also Baym's term for the gestures, expressions, and intonation of face-to-face interaction insofar as she does not make distinctions beyond that between verbal and non-verbal (Baym 1995a: 152–6). She writes: 'Besides these emoticons, there are other ways to express non-verbal information. For instance, participants use asterisks or capital letters for emphasis … and explicit verbal descriptions of behavior. Because people being funny in CMC can't hear their audience's laughter (or lack thereof), the amused often describe themselves as "rolling on the floor laughing", sometimes abbreviated to ROFL' (Baym 1995a: 152). Like Werry's, this model treats everything outside of the spoken or written word as non-verbal information, as if there were no significant difference between someone's smile and an image of a smile.

There is a limitation, shared by Werry's and Baym's accounts, to any treatment of social interaction as information-exchange. The limitation is the division of information into two types, verbal and non-verbal, without further distinguishing types of non-verbal information, and without attending to the different value and significance attached to gestures, intonation and facial expressions in social interaction. It sounds reasonable to say that conversation is made up of a mixture of verbal and non-verbal signs and cues, of information of various sorts being sent and received.[56] And it also sounds reasonable to say that textual computer-mediated social interaction is also made up of verbal and non-verbal signs and cues. But nothing in either of these claims supports the assumption of equality of *types* of non-verbal information in each sort of social interaction, or that emoticons give the same *sort of information* as facial expressions or intonation. Without further support for the claim that we can treat bodily gestures, *and* keystroke representations of faces as non-verbal information simpliciter, it is reductive to equate them.

It is possible to make a case for a major difference between how we know others by being with them, and by interacting textually with them, by analysing the types of sign characteristic of each.[57] I shall make such a case, working in this section with the analysis of types of signs put forth by C. S. Peirce in *Transcendental Grammar*, to provide a semiotics that is broader than the purely linguistic. Simply put, the term 'non-verbal information', as it is used by Werry and Baym, covers two quite different sorts of signs: it includes both man-made conventional signs (Peirce's *legisigns*) and bodily or corporeal signs (Peirce's *sinsigns*). The non-verbal nuances of intonation, facial expression and gesture that are part of being with people are bodily sinsigns (Peirce 1974, particularly vol. 5). Sinsigns are not chosen to represent anything, although they are conventional in the sense of being part of normative human cultures. Legisigns (such as language and the codified representational grid of emoticons) are characterised by abstraction, conventionality, more or less conscious and deliberate employment.[58]

Bodily sinsigns are conventional in a weaker sense than legisigns, in that some gestures are particular to cultural groups, and have different meanings in different groups, but in that such conventions are not chosen, or deliberately modified, and in that there are significant and systematic similarities among the bodily sinsigns, *across* cultural groupings. The regularities of such forms of non-verbal communication, particularly facial expression and gesture, are strongly constrained by their physicality. Many subtleties and complexities of non-verbal aspects of social interaction are below the level of deliberate direction, while still being both affective and intentional (directed towards something). In particular, bodily sinsigns, though we usually describe and group them under verbal or conceptual categories (such as 'frowns', 'smiles', 'gentle tones', 'angry looks' and so on), are better treated as significant aspects of situations. Our senses take in whole scapes, and certain aspects thereof are recognised as significant, but this is not a matter of seeing orthographically identical signs such as words, rather of seeing recognisable aspects of situations among the mass of what our senses take in.[59] In different circumstances, different aspects will be significant to those involved, and as time passes, different aspects may become focal, or fade from significance.[60]

The various systems of signs used by human beings, such as aural, visual, haptic, or verbal systems, are interrelated in a complicated way. No single system or grid of signs is identical with the world or gives us the world in its totality. Rather, by reading the world through several grids together human beings grasp the world.[61] No single sign system, say that of sight or of logic or of language, is the master-grid; nor are different systems of signs intertranslatable. The role of hearing is not identical with that of sight; they inform me differently, at different paces. The word as idea (a legisign) is an abstract composite, composed or derived from the regularity of mutually reinforcing signs from different systems, and open to reconfiguration.

People become deeply familiar with the mass of related sign systems through years of using them. Often awareness of such signs is not a matter of explicit perception and interpretation, but a spontaneous empathetic 'reading', such as the sense that someone is hiding an unhappiness, or that they have had some expected bad news. A frown may prompt a change of one's attitude, of subject, of how one approaches another person. Complex interplays among perceptions of a social situation in which people spend time together provide a significantly different (perhaps richer) social environment, one that social writers (such as letter-writers, novelists, and including those in CMC) tend either to simulate or describe, so that readers draw on their own experience in interpreting them.

In CMC someone's typewriting invokes aspects of their condition (mood, interests, well-being and so on) that are more familiarly borne and available in their bodily presence and movement, in facial and bodily sinsigns (rather than some quantifiable barrage of signs or non-verbal information equivalent to presence). It is possible, for example, to assess whether someone is being truthful by watching their face and bodily movements; and to gauge their level of interest in a subject by attending to the animation of their face and body as they speak or hear about it.[62] It is often hard to assess the truthfulness of what another person writes on-line, even when we know that person very well, because much of how we know that person is not available to us textually. We would be wrong to say that emoticons simply replace non-verbal bodily signs such as facial expressions, gestures and intonations in CMC, because emoticons, although non-verbal, do not have the qualities of bodily signs or sinsigns.

Emoticons in particular form a fairly coarse-grained representational grid, even more limited than the emotion-words available in the English language, and far more so than the gamut of posture, gestures and tones that are part of face-to-face social interaction. Emoticons are different from bodily non-verbal expression not because they are open to greater deceptive use than facial expression, but because they provide, as a conventional and limited repertoire of representation, a fairly basic set of expressive options, significantly different in kind from the sinsigns in terms of which most people make and maintain face-to-face social relationships.

For example, facial expression cannot easily be used in an ironic or metaphorical way. Both emoticons and acronyms can be used ironically; acronyms, and third-person descriptions of what one is doing, can easily be used metaphorically. We could take Baym's example of the common CMC expression 'ROFL' which is an acronym of 'rolling on the floor laughing'. This exaggerated description of one's level of hilarity is used to express amusement, as Baym notes. Its origin is in Usenet and MUDs (multi-user dungeons). Writing 'ROFL' on-line is not equivalent to describing oneself rolling on the floor laughing, but is rather like saying 'That's a good one' as a description of one's response to a joke. In many cases the use is indirect and metaphorical, rather than a literal description of what its writer is doing. While using an expression like 'ROFL' does identify oneself with others in a group who also use that term (like using a high-five, a specialised musicological term or a shared funny laugh), the significance of the term is often as much in its being *used* (as a sign of group-membership or badge of unity), as in what it itself is taken to signify (amusement).

To take another example, the smiling emoticons :) or :-) are used frequently on-line, in a wide variety of groups, and among people who are not part of any particular group. They often appear after a sentence, and seem to be offered as a key to understanding the spirit of the inscription, as often as the mood of the writer. That is, they are not so much expressive of a mood of happiness as the proffering of a spirit of good-will or good-humour associated with the utterance to which they are attached. They are, for example, frequently found following inscriptions that could be construed as negative, ironic, sarcastic, or as intended to wound. For example, emoticons can be used in the following ways:

There's a whole lot more marking on the way :)

You just said that to get my attention :)

Isn't it about time we got off the subject? :-)

Smiling emoticons here are meant to play more or less the same role as a smile does when it accompanies someone's spoken remark, except that they represent smiles, rather than being smiles. And they are used deliberately – they are *meant* to forestall misunderstanding. In other words, emoticons are used much as assertions or sentences are used, as conceptual tools. Irony is common – a smiling emoticon may be attached to a remark that, from what I know of its writer, is unlikely to be intended so kindly. But I know much less about the writer's intent from the emoticon than I would from seeing their face. I read the emoticon much as I do the words of the message it is in.

Suspicion in interpretation may tend to limit the power of emoticons in ways that are also traceable to their status as part of a fairly coarse grid of abstract sinsigns. When emoticons are part of the CMC comportment of people we know, they are comparatively vivacious, part of the give and take of a particular social engagement. Emoticons can gather and hold significance, just as any word does, in the ways and circumstances in which they are used. They will have more meaning, and more particular meaning, for those who are familiar with their uses, and less for those who are not. An emoticon's placing is important; its situation in an ongoing conversation, particularly in relation to the contribution of the person who uses it is significant in how it is understood. And familiarity with another's style of emoticon use will give me a greater sense of what it is that they are doing in using one or another of them in an e-mail.

Without such a sense of familiarity, and particularly if I suffer from the common and general suspicion born of ignorance of the others' purposes in CMC, then I will be unable to take many smiling representations of happiness, well-meaning or kindness as genuine. I will tend instead to take them as ironic or even as deceptive, as people sometimes take the absence of the tone or gesture that would accompany a spoken remark to indicate the absence of humaneness. As with textuality in general, greater interpretative effort has to be put into 'realising' text, or, in a Ricoeurian sense, elevating the text to discourse (Ricoeur 1976: 44). But, as is well-documented on-line, and as I have already discussed, textual communication sometimes inspires a fearful or angry response. Using the above semiotic analysis of emoticons, I would hazard that fearful or angry responses occur not because anger comes across clearly in CMC, but because defensiveness leads people to read a lack of non-verbal expression as the writer's lack of good-will or common decency.[63]

To sum up, emoticons are part of a conventional sign grid. They are non-verbal in the sense of not being sets of letters of an alphabet strung together. But they are not the same sort of sign as the *bodily* and *facial* gestures, and the enunciative intonation of speech that they are sometimes seen to replace in CMC. They are not bodily, subtly various, indissociably belonging to a particular person, but few in number and typographically identical. They may well supplement verbal usage on-line, but cannot alone substitute for the ways in which the dynamic human body can express us and allow us to know other people in face-to-face conversation.

Therefore, textual representations of non-verbal aspects of mutual presence cannot go beyond textuality to give the sorts of non-verbal signs that are carried only by the physically present body. Yet CMC social interaction can allow us to come to know other people in *some way*, while nevertheless still creating many misunderstandings and, for some, a sense of impersonality or distance. Instead, as the case of emoticons suggests, we might turn to development of techniques for coping with textuality, techniques that naturalise sinsigns such as emoticons, and seek to provide a reading as evocative as possible of discourse in mutual presence.

Unadorned textuality is itself no absolute barrier to emotional expression and empathy. In general, non-verbal information characteristic of emoticons, and carried in the style of writing generally,[64] is extraordinarily useful for our understandings of others in CMC. Style, as I have described, may produce misunderstandings, particularly when textual style does duty for all the panoply of styles of a life lived practically; in some hands it may be heavy handed and less than intimate; and it does not rule out genuine differences of approach, of interest. But in CMC we must attend to the person *through* their text. Thoughtful and artful use of text is part of the mutuality of textual communication.

As I argued in Chapter Two, the attempt to be understood and the attempt to understand go together, in the sense that empathy between communicators is necessarily a reciprocal affair. To some extent, the sharing of textual conventions such as those of emoticons, or the techniques of spontaneity I have already discussed, form the basis of a common (textual) language of self-expression. This language is one that may be used to elicit and allow empathy, although, as I also noted, there is much that stands in the way of textually-mediated empathy. The nature of textuality is such that even very rapid exchange does not permit sensuous empathy.

4.5 Place and CMC

CMC allows people to communicate while they are in different places, so long as they do so in text, so that the situations from which people write are multiplied, rather than constituting a single place in which conversation goes ahead. As a formulation, this initial position simply reformulates the argument for modal and semantic opacity developed in Chapter One, and reconsidered within the varieties of textual distanciation in Chapter Three. Multiple social contexts produce complexity in the unfolding of the perlocutionary effects of writing, particularly in large groups of participants.

Like the mediated 'being together' of an exchange of letters or a telephone conversation, CMC may allow people to feel that they are *together* in some sense, despite their inhabitation of separate places, and even though there is no physical place in which they both *are* present. CMC seems to many people to constitute a place or to have place-like qualities. The sense of being in a non-physical place might, it could be argued, compensate for physical absence, by allowing a sense of place to contribute to and contextualise CMC discussion, even in physical absence. In this section I argue that such a view is problematic. The sense in which CMC constitutes a place in which people can be or feel together will be only metaphorical, sustained because a sense of togetherness has traditionally been possible only for people in the same place.[65] Instead, I argue, communicative absence and presence figure as a second pair supplementing the pair of bodily absence and presence. People in communication may feel a communicative presence, or a bodily absence. Only bodily presence engages two people in a single place.

There are several distinctions to be made here about how to understand place, before we can specify in what if any sense CMC interactions may be said to have or be in a place. The first one is the fairly well-known distinction between place and space, which corresponds roughly to a difference between *topos* (or an inhabited place or set of places), and the mathematical or scientific notion of space as undifferentiated extension. People do not inhabit space (in the same sense people are not constellations of molecules; the vocabularies of common sense and science do not intersect but run parallel). This first distinction suggests that not all physical locations will be identified by all or any people as places, as a hinterland or ocean is not a place, as the universe surrounding Earth is not a place.

Place is then different from space, in that it is inhabited, something in which people live, or imagine life to go on. People are intrinsically creatures who inhabit, whose lives unfold *within* a place or places. Social and political life unfolds in shared spaces, often ones reserved or built for just these aspects of human activity. In these cases, place is precisely an inhabited region, a region that is known under a certain *aspect* by one or more person, and is open to one or more sorts of social practice. An example of an inhabited aspectual place is a court, a place in which trials before the law are held. A court is usually a room or set of rooms in a building called a courthouse.[66] The physical existence and inhabitability of law courts contributes to the shared acceptability of the institution of the law, and of its processes and judgements, and may well be necessary for justice to be seen to be done. Insofar as different courts are, for example, assigned to particular jurisdictions, the location of any given courthouse is significant for determining the scope of the judgements handed down inside it. The ongoing existence and authority of courts is part of the mechanism by which legal precedents influence future legal decisions *within each jurisdiction*.

Jeff Malpas puts forward a similar position on place (Malpas 1994). Exploring the relationship between time, place and the constitution of persons, Malpas sees place as constituted for people through their inhabiting particular environments, through the particular practical possibilities held by those environments and taken up by their historically-located inhabitants:

> The idea of persons as constituted through landscape or place ... is suggestive of a way of seeing human beings that treats them, not as individual creatures who exist in a way independent of their surroundings, independent of the landscape, but as beings who are indeed constituted as the beings they are only within their surroundings, within a landscape, within a place. ... we might also say that in travelling we both reconstitute ourselves in terms of new places, and also carry old places with us.
>
> (Malpas 1994: 440)

This amounts to a mutually constitutive relation over time of landscape or environment and its human inhabitants.[67] The places we inhabit have significance as parts of that which constitutes us as the particular human beings we are.[68] People, events and objects are constituted in particular ways by the places within which they live, even as those places open for them a range of possibilities for the future. For example, social roles, and social place, are determined in part by those places to which one has access, or to which access is denied. A sense of a city as a place is developed through living in that city, over time, rather than in a week's visit. We inhabit new locations, make them into places, by bringing to them objects and habits from the old.[69] We set to work in new places to construct something of those places with which we are familiar, as we populate hospitals, jails and nursing homes with objects from, perhaps pictures of, the places that we have left, so that we can live in them in memory at least.[70]

Some examination of extensions to the concept of place as inhabited space might be made here, as I am arguing that CMC-as-place is an extension. First, we can imagine places that do not actually exist, whether they once did, or never did. We can *imagine* inhabiting certain places even if we *could* not; Gaston Bachelard describes, as well as the house and its cupboards, the nest, the burrow and the hole as places we imagine we might live (Bachelard 1994, particularly Chapters One and Two). If I envisage Saturn as habitable, even by animals or microbes, it becomes for me an imagined place rather than a thing. We can conjure landscapes that have never existed, by imagining them for ourselves, by seeing, hearing about, or reading those imagined by other people.[71] These places are constituted on the basis of actual (or historically) existing places (as, for example, Thomas Hardy's Wessex), and seem to present no great conundrum to the ordinary reader or viewer. In other words, we may imagine places that don't exist, and think *as if* they had a reality separate or parallel to our own, even if we do not inhabit them ourselves. In these cases, though, we are not practically formed by the places in question, since we are not party to their practices.

Second, some social practices, known as institutions, may move among physical locations, because the essentials of the institutions are defined independently of the affective relation of its members to whatever environment the institution happens to be in. The practices or institutions may thus not be practices of inhabitation, or place-making, but have integrity maintained in the cohesion and continuity of social roles and practices. Many royal courts, for example, are or have been movable, constituted within a realm larger than a single place. The essential elements of a European court, for example, are the monarch, his or her instruments of state, and whatever officiating ministers and other people are deemed necessary to the occasion. These elements of the institution of a court are transportable, and may be moved from Paris to Versailles, or from either to a battlefield, as convenient. Once the procedures for holding court have been performed, a court exists, until it is called to a close.[72] In other words, under certain circumstances, social 'places' may be established by the performance of the appropriate social practices, no matter what the physical location of the people involved. Institutions may resemble CMC places, insofar as members of these institutions also inhabit physical places whose qualities are not figured as contributing to CMC social gatherings.

The question relevant to understanding CMC is whether movable institutions actually constitute places, considered as inhabited spaces, or whether they are social exchanges the affective qualities of which are independent of physical location. My position is that movable institutions constitute organisations, rather than places, to the extent that their operation is *designed* to be independent of particular inhabited spaces. Each court or seminar is at a location; one may be palatial, full of experts and the records of cases, others provincial or rustic; but these are not essential to the social organisation of the institution. Location is internally important to movable institutions only insofar as all the people necessary to an institution must be present together (must be 'here').[73] In the case of institutions involving people physically separate, such as the 'Royal Society' as it existed in exchanges of letters, distance is considered overcome by correspondence, and place is considered to be irrelevant. The multiplication of correspondents produces a multiplication of places from which writing is addressed, considered internally unimportant, but externally multiplying contexts.

As I argue of CMC, the affect of place haunts movable and remote institutions, rather than constituting them. Insofar as particular *sites* are deemed more or less appropriate for the establishment of courts, meetings, or debates, place still contributes to the successful establishment of a temporary place such as a court. Sites' influence may be large; a court held on a battlefield will be less magnificent, less memorable than at the Palace of Versailles.[74] But while the members of institutions still perform their institutional roles in particular physical locations, and are cognisant of those locations, these locations are significant *for the institution* only as temporary placeholders for mobile persons, their knowledge and its records. In group correspondence, as in the case of the Royal Society, a group exchanged letters from numerous writers at numerous places, each of which is little more than a placeholder. The place of each writer is certainly not a shared ambience in which all participants may share; at most, others may surmise or imagine the place of other correspondents. The integrated mobile community is united by social and practical ties, such as shared activities. The remote community is integrated by exchange of messages and continuity maintained by shared interests, and empathy across distance, rather than by inhabitation of a particular place. That an institution was once linked to a particular place should not allow us to think that inhabitation extends beyond the point at which the institution becomes mobile or decentralised.[75]

To sum up, a place is constituted by the inhabitation by one or more people of a particular physical environment. A sense of place results when place and inhabitants mutually constitute one another over a period of inhabitation. Temporally-extended social practices are important in constituting and differentiating places from one another. In some circumstances, 'place' may be metaphorically extended to include environments that *have* been inhabited or which *might*, imaginatively, be inhabited. While such institutions have social integrity by virtue of the temporal continuity of social practices and ongoing conviviality among practitioners, they do not constitute places in a more than metaphorical sense.

4.5.1 Place and community in CMC

The puzzle of place in CMC seems to be twofold. There is the question of how to describe the place-like qualities of discussion groups, e-mail exchanges and chat-rooms. And there is the question of how to understand the relation between the physical places in which CMC-users are sitting, and the non-physical social space that they inhabit in CMC. As I have illustrated above, people's sharing established social practices (institutions) may give them a sense of community akin to sharing a place. In some cases, institutions disconnected from any single location can have a place-like integrity that stems from the social membership and shared practices (institutions) of a mobile or geographically dispersed group of people. This is, however, place in a highly metaphorical sense, stemming more from interpersonal familiarity, and the use of shared conventional symbolic utterances than any shared inhabitation. This we can see, for example, from the fact that contributing to a discussion group which has not recently been used by any of its regular contributors does not give the contributor a sense of being in any place at all.

But many people argue that CMC actually contains or consists of places. What is at stake in such claims can broadly be stated as 'some forms of shared social life in CMC are as legitimate as any other form'; as my argument develops, the truth of this claim can be preserved without reference to CMC place. The affirmative position appears quite often in the work of sociologists and other analysts of CMC: in Wendy Grossman's *net.wars* (Grossman 1997), Amy Bruckman's 'Finding one's own space in cyberspace' (Bruckman 1996), Rosanne Allucquere Stone's 'Will the real body please stand up?' (Stone 1991) or William Mitchell's *City of Bits* (Mitchell 1995). Amy Bruckman summarises the arguments that CMC contains social places in an article in which she compares the variety of social ambiences in CMC discussion groups with the variety of ambiences in different bars she has visited. Making an analogy between place and community, she writes:

> Each of these bars was a community and some were more comfortable for me than others. The Net is made up of hundreds of thousands of separate communities, each with its own special character … It's a lot harder to find a good virtual community than it is to find a good bar. The visual clues that let you spot the difference … are largely missing. Instead you have to 'lurk' – enter the community and quietly explore for a while, getting the feel of whether it's the kind of place you're looking for.
>
> (Bruckman 1996: 48)

Two parallel conceptual moves can be seen in Bruckman's statement that CMC interactions constitute places. One is the metaphorical association of CMC discussion groups with actually existing places: descriptions of on-line social interaction draw on the vocabulary of ordinary social interaction, including its references to place, space and environment, and particularly to community. Descriptions of using CMC may include references to 'entering', 'hanging around in' and 'leaving' a discussion group, or 'moving' from one group to another. Many descriptions of discussion groups are explicitly place-based: 'chat-rooms', 'virtual worlds', and the elaborate textual world-description of MUDs and MOOs.[76]

Such descriptions make, and do not question, a metaphorical association, between institution, or shared social practice, and place. It is to the phenomena of social presence and absence of participants in CMC that Bruckman appeals in describing CMC place. She uses the terms 'community' and 'place' interchangeably in 'Finding one's own space in cyberspace'. Yet the points at which she uses 'community' are often those at which using 'place' would strike a wrong note. For example, to claim that CMC discussions are places, she draws an analogy between CMC discussion groups and bars. In the third paragraph of the article she describes bars, not as places, but as communities. She then writes that people join communities when they use CMC, and that 'When people complain about being harassed on the Net, they've usually stumbled into the wrong on-line community'. To use 'place' here would be to beg the question about CMC discussion constituting a place.[77] These observations bolster, I think, the claim that 'place' is used metaphorically of on-line social interaction.

Rather, communities may exist *across places* without the need to describe them as inhabiting a 'virtual' place at all (Stone 1991: 84–8). Communities of letters have, in the past, existed across space, without relying on any metaphor of place to do so.[78] The loose community of humanists centred on men such as Thomas More, Desiderius Erasmus and Juan Vives did not inhabit any common single place.[79] Such communities may endure despite mutual absence for many years. They may have a great sense of each other's characters and lives; but they do not share practical life, or comport themselves together. In this sense there is no place that they share, though they may well share confidences, opinions and some (textually-mediated) activities.[80] That there is no physical location shared by users of CMC is, indeed, a reason to distinguish place, generally speaking, social understandings of a physical location, from the metaphorical 'places' of CMC.

The other move is Bruckman's treatment of the concept of place as dependent in no more than a trivial, revocable, sense on actually existing physical environments. Bruckman describes CMC as containing 'places', although the place-like qualities of CMC communities are less than wholly identifiable with place in any of its usual senses, such as I have explored above.[81] That is, contributors to CMC discussions are spread out over a multitude of places, which they inhabit in a bodily sense. To overlook this proliferation of places (and contexts) from which CMCs are sent is to risk ignoring important differences among those using CMC, such as the different fields of action open to different persons using CMC, or the range of shared actions possible for members of a CMC community, given their lack of propinquity.

People using CMC no more *leave* their physical locations than people who are asleep, daydreaming or reading, and people who use CMC from the place that each inhabits, perform in ways that are informed and affected by those places. No person spends all their time using CMC; the need to eat, sleep, keep fit, raise children, and to maintain existing relationships keep individuals tied to the places where they live or spend time. The inhabitation of homes, offices, suburbs, countries together, will continue to shape people's social practices and to constitute them as persons, even if place is not consciously thought of as constitutive of persons. For all but the most dedicated users of CMC, the places of ordinary life continue to be important. Even for these people to whom places are not considered important, the mutual constitution of inhabitant and place goes on, albeit with less awareness. Even if I consider where I live to be irrelevant to my sense of self, the physical qualities of my surroundings will still impact on how I live and think, and on the field of practical possibilities that are open to me. It will do so by confining or enabling different sorts of physical movement and activity, by encouraging different forms of social interaction, and by structuring my relationship with the natural environment.

Importantly, in its role as social context, my inhabitation of particular places is certain to separate me from correspondents who inhabit other places. Our ongoing inhabitation of particular physical places constitutes us differently from those with whom we engage in CMC, as these others inhabit other places, and do not physically live with or near us. Our physical separation from correspondents via CMC cannot fade, no matter how 'normal' using CMC feels, since we continue to inhabit and act in particular physical places. And to the extent that the contexts of each person's textual deliveries differ from the others', modal opacity and actual textual distanciation will occur. That these phenomena occur in CMC means that the sense in which a CMC 'place' is a place is not one in which the full immediacy of being in a place with someone else is possible.

Again, we can explain the neglect of the physical surroundings of CMC-users in terms that show CMC place as metaphorical. Social presence and integration are often figured in the language of place. Place may be used to describe various sorts of social inactivity or absence that are not strictly spatial in any sense. People may be physically present but socially absent: one person's engagement in profound thought is taken by others to be an 'absence'.[82] We describe death as a parting or a going away, and talk of people going off to sleep.[83] The places of sleep and death are places constituted imaginatively by reference to someone's absence from social engagement. Their constitution is simple, being nothing more, conceptually, than a non-engagement in social discourse. We may, of course, embroider on this, making it a *there* of some sort. But the basic move is the most important, since it signifies that we think of some non-spatial qualities of people as metaphorically place-related.

In other words, we do sometimes talk of place without having in mind a place that is in *any way* spatially locatable. If we consider such imaginary or fanciful 'places', they have sense only for those who are *not* in them, and no sense for those who count, for observers, as being in them at the time of ascription. It would not be possible for anyone to have a *sense* of these places that is interior to them; only an exterior sense of others being in them. The ascription of *thereness* to those who are distracted, or asleep, are ways in which a merely *social* absence is figured as *physical* inhabitation of another place. So, in using CMC we concentrate on it in a way that tends to make us socially absent from our immediate surroundings, and in touch with people in a way that is vivid and often immediate.

To summarise this argument, if place is inhabitation *of* a physical environment, then a sense of a social institution's being a place cannot produce a place that replaces the actually inhabited places from which CMC users contribute. A sense that one is *in* some place that does not exist doesn't conjure up in any more than an imaginary way the place one senses. Imagining that one is at home, or in Middle Earth doesn't produce a home, or a Middle Earth, and playing a dungeon computer game doesn't mean that you are actually *in* any dungeon.[84] The metaphorical use of 'place' for CMC exchanges conceals the fact that much about CMC relations precludes place. Terms such as 'place', 'cyberspace', 'net', 'netizen', 'forum', 'dungeon', and 'virtual frontier town', compensate metaphorically for the absence of any physical place, but no more. The social organisation of the different actually existing places from which CMC users contribute inflects CMC social relations, the economic and political results of who has access to CMC, which itself continues to depend on where one is.[85] I shall now give an alternative explanation of the sense that people using CMC are in 'places'.

4.5.2 *CMC as establishing institutions*

Via CMC, people can discuss a variety of subjects, compare computer-transmissible works and activities (texts, digital or digitised art, or computer programmes), and plan future activities together, regardless of their physical locations. The sense in which discussion alone constitutes a place rather than a communicative exchange, or perhaps a community, is unclear. A sense that one is *in the social presence of others*, or *with others*, when in mediated communication with them, is ambivalent as an indication that one shares a place with them. At the same time, using CMC, particularly synchronous CMC, demands so much concentration that its user cannot, at the time, pay much attention to the place that they physically inhabit, no matter how constitutively important that place is at other times. We might account for the sense of place felt by some users of CMC, by claiming that users of CMC share an institution, a set of practices not dependent upon its members sharing a single place. This institution would, in each case, be characterised by the ongoing *social presence* to each other of a group of other communicators who share textual social practices dissociated from communicators' locations.[86]

Mediated communication of various sorts allows communicative links without mutual presence, as well as impersonal communication. With the spread of mediated forms of communication, social exchange is decreasingly linked to any particular place. But people still associate place with social exchange, particularly since for many intimate relations nothing short of mutual presence will suffice, and mutual presence requires co-location in a single place. Thus some activities, such as communication with others, that were once linked with place, but are now possible through remote and textually-mediated social exchanges, both inter-personal and impersonal, may still suggest a place-like quality to participants. Participants' sense of disengagement from other social realms brought on by participation in a mobile or place-independent institution, continues to suggest to participants the inhabited places that were once necessary for and constitutive of such institutions.[87]

Analogous abstraction from physical place occurs when people use CMC. People can communicate together as rapidly as if they *were* together, while being physically apart. Each is socially absent from their physical surroundings, and socially present to others using CMC with them in so far as each can convey textual messages to the other or others.[88] CMC engagements would then be place-independent institutions, not physical environments constituted by inhabitation of a 'natural' world, or of the places within a city.[89] Institutions in CMC consist of social qualities such as the number and types of people involved, topics discussed (or avoided), their manners of writing, and the rapidity and length of their responses.[90]

Significantly, the pace at which messages can be exchanged, sometimes claimed to produce place (since CMC has places and letter-exchanges not), does not always encourage CMC users into having a sense of CMC as a place. E-mail is not at all associated with place, even though it supports very rapid exchanges. It was specifically designed to be letter-like, and uses place-separating terms such as 'address', 'send', 'mail', and so on. E-mail is the variety of CMC in which people write in most epistolary ways (Herring 1993a), although it tends to fall short of the complexity characteristic of letters in other historical periods.[91]

Chat environments, in which people may only partake in 'real time', would seem the most likely candidates for the status of place.[92] People's textual contributions[93] are crucially constitutive of the 'atmosphere', and people feel that they are 'entering' and 'leaving' the MOO, so powerful is the sense that one's being with others must happen *somewhere*. The MOO is constructed as a place by reference to the social whole of the group or community as they perform when sending messages to the MOO, but with no reference to the surroundings, or environment. In the same way, we might join or leave a group of people at a party, or obtain a place in a course.

But the rapidity of transmission in on-line chat discussions may also work to discourage a sense of people's being in a place together, by enabling rapid transmission of messages (one's own or others') to many further people. Such ease of transmission blurs the boundary between discussion groups, and reconstitutes individual contributions as available anywhere they might be sent, rather than *local* to a single group thought of as a place. The easy iterability of CMC messages tends to place discussion group contributions in particular in a public rather than private sphere, by allowing the ever-wider dissemination of textual contributions, often sent to groups whose membership is not strictly controlled.[94] We are then in a position to see the sense of place in CMC, an affective experience of being together with (or in contact with) others, resulting from rapid textual exchange, but where that rapidity also tends to break a group's identification as a place.

The exception to iterability is Internet Relay Chat (or IRC), in which textual contributions are not stored or iterable. This most conversational of CMC modes is also the one in which the metaphor of place is most strongly evoked and participated in, by descriptions of real and imagined places, and by the fullest immersion of participants in the conversational context required by the ongoing engagement with the social exchanges in following the scroll of singular textual contributions. Even here, many IRC exchanges do not constitute places for their participants. Even in IRC there exists a contrast between communicative presence, produced by the continuation of textual contributions at or above an expected rate of exchange, and physical presence, which is *not* produced by any amount of textual exchange. The language of IRC may often suggest mutual presence, but it draws also on the vocabulary of absence; people write in hope and anticipation of meeting, and, in some exchanges, on the memory of past encounters.

Shared communication does not always count as togetherness, particularly between intimates, and sometimes serves only to heighten the absence that is productive of textual exchange in the first place. In CMC we find ourselves with two types, rather than one, of presence/absence distinction, one associated with communicative presence, productive of the institutions of CMC, and one associated with physical presence, which even social presence cannot produce.

To conclude, CMC does not contain places like those of everyday life, in which we might live and be self-sufficient. Social presence is possible, and people may use it to establish institutions and social exchanges both broad and exclusive. People continue to inhabit their separate places and to share these with each other via description. The multiplication of places (and of contexts) from which people write means that the problems of distanciation, between physically separated correspondents, may make for stylistic misunderstandings as palpable as those Ricoeur attributes to separation of reader and writer in time.[95]

I have argued in this section that we only speak of places in CMC in a metaphorical sense. Communications technology allows pairs and groups of people to keep in touch with one another. It can also limit the membership of these groups, by preventing people who have not joined groups from gaining access to their discussions. The sequences of exchange of textual contributions among pairs or groups of people create a sense of 'togetherness' or 'mutual presence', derived from but not identical with that produced by actually being in the same physical environment with other people. It is, I argue, this sense of being together with others that suggests that we are together *in some place*. The sense that we are together is reified in metaphorical uses of 'place' in CMC; but these do not effect the creation of CMC places. Each CMC communicator always already inhabits particular places, and writes from the vantage of a *practical* life lived within them, even if that life is substantially informed by mediated communication.

Thus mutual *physical* absence of CM contributors is not counteracted by the shared inhabitation of any metaphorical, 'on-line' or 'virtual' place. Absence continues to hold the status of a structural constraint in CMC, just as it does in other epistolary exchanges, and in telephonic exchanges. The possibility of rapid communication among *groups* as well as *pairs* of people does not make the metaphor any more real, although it allows a social rather than personal sense of togetherness. It too has been possible for centuries, and can be explained as people's sharing an information sphere, rather than their sharing a physical place. This latter explanation preserves as distinct the different physical contexts of different contributors, rather than making all physical place secondary to some shared virtual place. Consequently, Ricoeur's textual problems of distanciation, which I discussed in the third chapter of this book, remain in operation in CMC.

People who use CMC also live and will continue to live in communities that exist in actual places, in which actual places continue to be important. CMC communities will continue to gain social acceptance and internal solidarity, cutting across existing communities as well as coinciding with them. We can take steps to make them coincide, and it can be socially and politically worthwhile to make the effort to do so, but the social effects of non-coincidence may well be to disrupt any sense that one belongs to and must work with and within any community at all.

4.6 Conclusions

In Chapter Two I focused on showing that empathy, necessary for the mutual understanding characteristic of intimacy, is possible in textual computer-mediated exchanges. I also argued, drawing on the discussion of personal style in the first chapter of the book, that there are particular problems with empathy in all textually-mediated communications, including CMCs. These problems, produced by the stylistic vagaries of textuality, are characteristic of CMC as well as of other epistolary exchanges, and slow rather than prevent empathy in such media. This chapter has focused on the computer medium alone, and on those structural conditions that distinguish it from other textual and remote media.

Together the above four structural constraints on CMC interact with already existing conventions of social interaction to affect the possibilities for social interaction in CMC. In particular, CMC affects the ways in which we know other persons, by providing a new, probably influential, way of interacting with them. Structural constraints will also have effects on interpersonal relationships and political decision-making. I explore these in the final chapters of this book.

5 Computer-mediated friendship

> The writing of letters ... demands an intimate knowledge the possession of which will usually prevent writing at all. The best letters are written between those who not only have sufficient talent or intellectual capacity but who also 'have eaten and drunk and lived in social intercourse' together; but that intercourse must normally be broken before letters will be written.
>
> (Grundy 1986: 220, quoting Boswell 1906: 166)

5.1 Introduction

Since CMC is increasingly part of people's social lives, extending into education, work, and home, it is important to consider the ethical possibilities that this sort of communication may sustain among people. I have already considered the constraints and possibilities of CMC in general. I now explore the implications that these constraints and possibilities have for friendships. To this end, I would like to focus in some detail on the nature of friendship, attending both to the qualities that make up good friendships, as well as those necessary for a relation to qualify as a friendship at all.

As I have argued in previous chapters, there are some distinctive constraints on social interactions in CMC. I have considered the transformation of social conduct and the limitations of context and content in textual form. I have also mentioned, without detailed discussion, the impossibility of engaging in some activities and pastimes (for example those involving physical activity, exercise, or eating) in shared virtual space. These limitations affect the range and quality of the sorts of friendship and companionship that are possible via the medium, by limiting the terms in which a CMC relationship can be conducted, and hence what ethical possibilities are available for people meeting via CMC. Some of the constraints, such as the coexistence of synchronous and asynchronous communication, are intrinsic to the medium, and will not vanish with any amount of technological innovation. Other conditions, such as the textuality of communication may be only temporary aspects of CMC, although ones central to its current constitution.

My reason for looking at computer-mediated friendship rather than, say, work-place relations, is that, as well as being an important part of most human lives, friendship is something that many people have *sought* via CMC.[1] Indeed, one of the principle reasons for which people have used CMC has been, from the early years of its development, the hope of establishing new relationships of various sorts.[2] The proliferation of interest-based discussion groups, non-topical chat groups and games-playing groups such as multi-user dungeons (MUDs and MOOs) suggests that a great number of people find enjoyment in shared CMC, as does the continued growth, in many countries, of Internet connections for personal use. Many people see the medium as providing opportunities for maintaining ongoing friendships. Some people see the medium as valuable for establishing friendships, or even partnerships, with an eye to meeting and spending time together; others consider that the sorts of relations possible via CMC do not require meetings or time spent together.[3]

In this chapter, my survey of friendship in the writings of Aristotle, Erasmus and of modern feminist philosophy is brief, put together with the aim of placing their accounts of friendship in relation to the types of communication available to people. The chapter thus approaches friendship in CMC by comparison with other accounts of friendship, both textual and companionable. In this way, I hope to illustrate why each writer values what she or he does in friendships, and to relate the understandings and oversights of each to those of the others. While there is much of importance that I cannot cover, what is included here is intended to provide an overview of the possibilities for computer-mediated friendships, taking into account the conclusions of earlier chapters of this book.

5.2 Friendship and personal relations

The realm of friendship is a broad one, with many different and unique relations counting as friendships: characteristically today, friendships exist separate from the world of institutional and professional pressures, and hence may be both less conditional and less conventional than many relations within institutional bounds. Friendships are freely chosen associations, developed and kept up through the mutual regard of each friend for the other, and through the mutual enrichment of each through the particular relation that they share. Friendships bring the inspiring and sustaining possibilities of sharing activities and histories, difficulties and achievements with a particular other person. Abiding friends may support each other in developing aspects of themselves, revealing unsuspected strengths and abilities, and doing so in a reciprocal manner.[4]

Both mutual responsibility and mutual trust are important aspects of friendships. By the same token, friendships, in which responsiveness and care for another (in whatever form it may take) is not backed up by any formal commitments or responsibilities, such as relation by blood, are vulnerable in ways that more strongly institutionalised relations are not. Relations that are freely and unconditionally entered are not bound together by conventional obligations, but may wither through extended periods of separation, as a result of differences of opinion, through simple lack of attention to one another, or through misunderstanding.

Writers on friendship have been aware that friendships do not always reach the ideals of the time, and that ideal friendships are very hard if not impossible to establish and maintain. Beginning with Aristotle at least, friendship has been seen to depend on friends having interests in common, on their having sufficient time in which to be together, and to be damaged or distorted by calculating self-interest on either part. Despite lack of time, conflicts of interest, and personal limitations, we tend to remain in our particular imperfect friendships, and the very particularity of our friends is one source of their value to us, even if they are not perfectly virtuous people. Equally, the time that friends spend coming to know one another can make each a sympathetic and perceptive critic of the other, if not a perfect model for self-improvement.

Broadly, friendship can be distinguished from other sorts of relations on a number of grounds, of which three are central to any account of friendship. (Others have different importance in different accounts.) First, friends are interested in each other at least partly for their own sakes, rather than for some good that the friend can provide. Second, friends are not under any formal obligation to one another, no matter how much they rely on one another, and no matter how disappointed they are in being let down. Third, friends come to know one another mutually well. Friendships are thus unlike star-fan relationships in which knowledge is had by only the fan, and unlike acquaintanceships, no matter how full of good-will. But there is more to be said about friendship than this. I begin with a discussion of Aristotle's account.

5.3 Companionable friendship: Aristotle

5.3.1 Friendship and the happy life

Aristotle's account of friendship (or *philia*) in books eight and nine of the *Nicomachean Ethics* is a foundational account of the practices and attitudes that constitute friendships, drawing attention to issues that have been of concern to many writers since. He enumerates varieties and elements of friendships, stressing the importance of the particularity of friends to one another, and the role of spending time together for the development of mutually enriching and fulfilling friendships. Throughout this section, it is important to keep in mind that Aristotle's is essentially an account of friendship in small societies. He invokes the importance of companionship, and of similarity of interests. It is based on a society with inefficient long-distance communication, and so comes with the qualification that it may pass over issues relevant for friendship in CMC.

The ethical importance of friendship itself is located within the larger scope of Aristotle's major ethical work, the *Nicomachean Ethics*, an investigation of ethics bent on discovering what makes for human happiness (*eudaimonia*, well-being or well-doing). As an aspect of happiness, friendship is of such importance to Aristotle that he treats it as a virtue in itself (Aristotle 1966c: 1155a4) rather than as a good (such as wealth or health, for friendship is not possessed by a single person, but exists between people) or as a beloved object (such as wine, for one cannot have a mutual relationship with wine). While goods such as wealth and health, and a sufficiency of material objects, are also deemed important for the most happy life, friendship is important at a level more fundamentally constitutive of human being than these other goods. By connecting the good of friendship with the characteristic sociality of human beings, Aristotle draws out the sense in which friendship is intrinsic to human life, and not some good that can just be added to a solitary life:

> It seems rather peculiar to give all good things to the *eudaimon* and to leave out friends, which seem to be the greatest of the external goods ... And surely it is peculiar to make the happy person a solitary for the human being is a political creature and naturally disposed to *living-with*.
> (Aristotle 1966c: 1169b8–10, 16–19 (my emphasis))

Thus friendship is a good in itself, insofar as living with others is already a valuable and essential part of human life.[5] In terms of my analysis of people as styled performers, this aspect of the *Nicomachean Ethics* tallies with the point that one becomes familiar with people's styles only by spending time with those people.[6]

Philia can be described as a relation between people who wish one another well for their own sakes (Aristotle 1966c: 1155b27–30). Its most important characteristic is reciprocity, mutual affection in which each friend recognises the other as a person with their own distinctive needs, interests and possibilities. *Philia* does not inhere in sets of virtues belonging to one or both friends, or in putting the well-being of one's friend ahead of one's own. It is the mutual and on-going well-wishing of people who are also independent of one another, that constitutes the mutual affection of friendship for Aristotle. Nor is the well-wishing of friends merely a feeling of good-will or positive appraisal of another, but includes the *embodiment* of well-wishing in an *active* concern, well-doing, for the other:

> Friendship for the sake of pleasure bears a resemblance to [friendship of those who wish each other well]; for good people too are pleasant to each other. So too does friendship for the sake of utility; for the good are also useful to each other.
> (Aristotle 1966c: 1157a1–6)

In other words, friendship is constituted not in the possession of certain sorts of fond feelings, but in the generous, pleasant, helpful actions of friends towards each other. Friendly feeling without action would not constitute a friendship, though it might count as a potential friendship.

5.3.2 *The particularity of friends*

Aristotle elaborates the importance of particularity of friends in Book Eight of *Nicomachean Ethics*. *Philia* that are based either on mutual pleasure or on advantages that each friend provides to the other are discussed first, as lesser forms of friendship. In cases of *philia* based on mutual pleasure, people become friends because they enjoy each other's company, even though they do not particularly like or value each other. In cases of *philia* based on advantage, people become friends for some gain that each can provide the other, such as access to political power, or making business contacts. These sorts of *philia* are considered inferior because they do not depend on each loving the particular qualities of another for their own sake, but only on the way these qualities are instrumental in providing pleasure or advantage. Such friendships, Aristotle argues, endure only so long as the pleasure or utility endures.[7]

The third and highest form of *philia* is that in which each friend values the other for their own particular qualities, for their own sake, *not* for the pleasures or utilities they can provide. This sort of friendship is described as being more long-lived than the others, as it is based upon aspects of the friend's character, specifically its virtues, that are more durable than the pleasures or benefits that two people might glean from one another. For Aristotle someone's personal and admirable qualities are those qualities so essential to them that their disappearance would constitute the cessation of that person.[8] For this reason, the enduring nature or the qualities of a person, the highest form of *philia* is also the most enduring form. For Aristotle, virtues are enduring qualities, and so friendships based on admirable qualities are not vulnerable to the mutability characteristic of friendships based on more fleeting ability to give pleasure or utility. For example, I may find a sharp wit very amusing, but if it is turned against me unkindly, I might not remain friendly with its possessor.

Pleasure and utility are important aspects of the greatest friendships as well as of the other kinds (Aristotle 1966c: 1157a1–6), but they are valued in relation to the virtuousness of the friend giving them, not only in terms of pleasure or utility afforded to the receiving friend. In other words, a good friendship consists of more than, say, a shared pleasure in entertaining banter or witty verbiage, and must also include knowledge of and appreciation of the particular virtues of the friend. To the extent that a friendship is good it must encompass both knowledge and appreciation of the friend as a particular, virtuous, individual.

Aristotle's insistence that friends value each other for their virtues raises the question whether Aristotelian friends do indeed value one another in their particularity, or only for their objective virtuous qualities. It is not clear whether, for Aristotle, if one loves a friend for the qualities she or he possesses, one actually loves for themselves the particular person in which those qualities appear, or whether it is only for their virtues that the love is conceived, since the objective qualities that virtuous people are meant to possess are not particular to them. Is there any significance to Aristotelian friendly relations if their mutual well wishing is guaranteed by the admirable characters of each? This problem is exacerbated by the limit of discussion in the *Nicomachean Ethics* to an appreciation of the virtues of friends, with no mention of how friends might understand and cope with those aspects of each other that are not so virtuous. Aristotle does not tell us whether friendship is possible among less than perfect people, people who are not wholly virtuous. It is not easy to know how to deal with this problem, but I believe that it can be clarified a little if we consider that, for Aristotle, part of the value of *philia* is in the way friendship itself can change people's ways of acting for the better. Moral virtues are for Aristotle habits to be practised, not dispositions or qualities (Aristotle 1966c: 1099b25–31):

> [I]t makes no small difference whether we place the chief good in possession, or in use [of virtue], in state of mind or activity. For the state of mind may exist without producing any good result, as in a man who is asleep or in some other way quite inactive, but the activity cannot; for one who has the activity will of necessity be acting, and acting well. [...] For the things we have to learn before we can do them, we learn by doing them, e.g. men become builders by building and lyre-players by playing the lyre; so too we become just by doing just acts, temperate by doing temperate acts, brave by doing brave acts.
>
> (Aristotle 1966c: 1098b31–9a1; 1105b4–8)

Philia is a good not only because it forms a bond between two people who are previously virtuous,[9] but because of the way this bond, in itself, can over time transform and enrich the ethical possibilities in the active life of friends, encouraging each to practise the virtues seen in the way of life of the other. If Aristotle sees room for self-improvement in each *philos* (Aristotle 1966c: 1172a12–14), then he must allow that people can love one another for their good qualities, *and yet* have their faults. Perfect friendships are those in which friends *become perfect*, and no person can, by Aristotelian definition, be perfect *before* being a friend (Aristotle 1966c: 1169b8–10, 16–19). His strategy of contrasting the practices of ideal friendships with those of less perfect ones based on pleasure and profit must thus leave open, even if unexplored, the possibility of friendships between less than perfect people who nevertheless care for each other for their own sake, and between whom the bond of friendship may have a mutually enriching effect.

This point does not fully resolve whether the particular qualities of someone are lovable apart from their being virtuous, but suggests that a bond of *philia* may be enriching for less than perfect friends, if each has an eye for, loves, emulates and encourages what is good in the other. The point is strongly related to Aristotle's proviso that friends should live together to develop their friendship most fully, a proviso which bears directly on friendship in CMC, and which I take up below.[10]

5.3.3 Ideals and practicalities

Ideal friendship for Aristotle involves not only love of the particularity of friends, but a measure of innate similarity: friends need to enjoy the same activities, and share the same interests, in order for a bond of *philia* to form. But the relation of *philia* is not just a matter of convenient similarity of temperament, interest or activity, but consists in the mutual well wishing and well-doing that can only come about if friends are possessed of prior similarities of outlook and virtue. The reciprocity and attention to another that are called forth by friendship are themselves virtues, and lead, for Aristotle, to the virtuous harmonisation of the rational and emotional aspects of the self that is one of the principle goals of living well (Aristotle 1966c: 1157b28–33). The love of two virtuous people for each other leads, for Aristotle, to self-betterment, to the moulding of each self in the image of the admired and virtuous other. But by linking (objective) virtue with activities and possibilities available only to the privileged elite, Aristotle, almost accidentally, limits the sharing of what he describes as ideal friendship to members of that elite.

Again, by neglecting cases of love of the particularities of imperfect others, Aristotle leaves untouched the value and possibilities of ordinary friendships for mutual improvement. But once again we can see in the Aristotelian structure of self-improvement motivated by admiration of another, the possibility that imperfect friends may also learn from and inspire one another. As I argued in Chapter One, coming to know someone results from, as well as learning about someone's beliefs, desires and attitudes, from attending to their many styled performances. Such attention, and the familiarity that it builds, combined with the good-will of friendship, tends to give friends a particular insight into each other's characters. In this way, friends may be able to learn as much from understanding each other's weaknesses (or the interplay between strengths and weaknesses), as from emulating each other's strengths. With such attention even imperfect friends will be able to guide each other in their self-development. I will return to this topic below in relation to Aristotle's specification that friends live together.

Aristotle describes the best sort of friends as those whose objective virtue can function as a mirror, by which each comes to know and to improve her or himself. Difference, and particularly inequality, in a friendship would skew its development by providing a faulty mirror (rather than by, say, providing fruitful contrasts and productive comparisons). That is, similarity, particularly similarity in virtue, is valued by Aristotle because it keeps stable the platform on which the mutually caring relation develops. His picture of the highest form of *philia* has little room for relations that may emerge despite or through differences and inequalities, or for cross-cultural pluralism of values. The panoply of friendly shared life experiences in modern society emerge within relationships in which difference may be an integral and constructive element, broadening the possibilities for mutual understanding and reciprocal caring. At the same time, differences and inequalities may endanger the stability of friendships, as we encounter disagreement or even disapproval, rather than a simple reflection of good, in the eyes of a friend. The social and political ramifications of friendship across difference are, for Aristotle, something simply to be avoided; to us they may be both desirable and necessary, for all their destabilising potential. This is one area in which Aristotle's conclusions should be qualified.

5.3.4 The importance of spending time together

Similarity of interests and activities might well be a very important aspect of friendship if friends are to spend as much time together as Aristotle expects of *philoi*. He stresses the importance of time and familiarity in the establishment of true friendships, and the value of sharing time together in producing understanding and trust (Aristotle 1966c: 1157b22; 1158a9; 1171a4; 1157b10–12). Friends cannot admit each other to friendship or be friends until each has been found lovable and been trusted by the other, a condition in which they will be 'mutually recognised as bearing goodwill and wishing well to each other' (Aristotle 1966c: 1156a3–5). Those who quickly show the marks of friendship to each other may wish to be friends, but are not friends unless they both are lovable and know the fact; for a wish for friendship may quickly arise, but friendship does not (Aristotle 1966c: 1156b29–32).

And so friendship can only be achieved through time spent together, learning to know each other, and to trust each other, all the while benefiting from each other's company. The specificity of the other is not grasped all at once; nor can his or her development as a person be foretold or meaningfully grasped in any way apart from by living life with that person.

In a vein surprising to moderns accustomed to living in family units and travelling across large distances, Aristotle argues that friends should live together, so as to have more time to share in all the activities that produce trust and intimacy.[11] When friends live together they become familiar in ways that might not come about otherwise. It is through sharing a multitude of ordinary activities such as eating, playing, discussion and politics that people come to know, understand and appreciate each other most fully as friends, for their own sakes. Conversely, Aristotle points to what may happen if friends do not see each other frequently: without companionship the possibilities for establishing or maintaining intimacy and trust are fewer, and friendships are vulnerable to lapse (Aristotle 1966c: 1157b10–12). Here again the analysis points to the importance of friendship not being simply in mutual positive evaluation of character, but the way in which the *ongoing activity* of being friends contributes to mutual well-being of the friends:

> For there is nothing so characteristic of friends as living together ... even those who are supremely happy desire to spend their days together; for solitude suits such people least of all.
>
> (Aristotle 1966c: 1157b18–22)

Partaking in the same pastimes and activities is thus an important aspect of developing and maintaining a friendship (Aristotle 1966c: 1157a14–24). A major portion of Book Eight is taken up with describing the shared practices, activities and pastimes that are important contributors to friendship; many are exalted, but others are mundane, everyday activities. Sharing in practical activities such as sports, discussion, or dining together, is an important aspect of being friends with another person, because it is in the regularity and familiarity of contact with another, as much as in majestic or exalted moral moments, that the bond of friendship and its capacity for enriching lives is developed. By emphasising friendship as something evolving through time and familiarity, through building up of a sense of togetherness in common lived experience, rather than through heroic or noble acts, Aristotle signals his awareness of the importance to friendships of sharing ordinary life, as well as great and significant moments. Shared activity provides possibilities for increasing the trust between friends, both by providing occasions for friends to trust each other, and by the gradual establishment of trustworthiness forged in common experience. Small acts of sharing and reciprocation in mundane situations also contribute by their very number to the strength of mutual trust, and by their endurance over time to the fuller understanding of a friend's character, and resulting in concernful activity for that friend's sake.

The great quantity of shared experience that builds up over time spent together may broaden understanding of the sake of the friend, of how one can best be a friend to that person, and lead to revaluation both of the self and of the possibilities for further sharing and intimacy in the friendship.[12] Such long-term bonds of intimacy through shared experience often develop today among those who spend a deal of time together, such as between close friends, lovers, and on occasion also co-workers (see for comparison, Aristotle 1966c: 1162a6–10). Their power seems to rest on the specificity of the other, the particular qualities and quirks that make up the character of a friend, and which take so long to come to know and appreciate. Bowden describes this specificity in the following evocative terms:

> Each person stands in relation to the other in a way that they stand in relation to no other person, for it is the specificity of the other for whom each is in himself that is the focus of their love. Importantly, it is this constitutive uniqueness or particularity of concern that generates the ethical possibilities of the relationship.
>
> (Bowden 1997: 72)

But such friendships are necessarily rare; nor could one life contain many such friendships. The time required would be simply beyond us.

The Aristotelian requirement that a friendship be free from the vagaries of change requires an extraordinary combination of factors for its satisfaction. The attributes and circumstances necessary for the richest *philia* is perforce remarkable, now as it would have been at the time of writing. Aristotle himself is aware that such friendship must be rare and exclusive: 'One cannot be a friend to many people in the sense of having friendship of the perfect kind with them, just as one cannot be in love with many people at once' (Aristotle 1966c: 1158a10–12). Rather than following the intrinsic vulnerability of friendship relations through their different possibilities and weaknesses, Aristotle chooses to define very narrow conditions under which friendship is most safe and stable. Instead of treating possibilities of misunderstanding, disagreement, or evolving differences between friends, as the underside of the freedom allowed between friends, he attempts to shore up the stability of politically significant aristocratic friendships by endorsing fully only the rare friendships that avoid the risk of instability.[13] However, as I have noted already, his account of friendship leaves space for mutual care for each other's sake between friends who are both different and imperfect, even though such formations may be less stable.

5.3.5 *Summary*

There is much in Aristotle's account of *philia* that meshes with and appeals to modern understandings of friendship, in particular the freedom of the relation of friends from social conventions, and the idea that lives can be enriched through participation in friendship. However, *philia* is also a partial account of the possibilities of friendship, from the explicitly normative perspective of a member of an elite for whom amity among privileged equals facilitated the stable government of the state and exemplified a political freedom not available to anyone occupied with the life roles of household maintenance or servitude.[14] Aristotelian ideal friendship, fragile by reason of existing independently of other social and institutional ties, and yet practically essential for the political stability of the nation-state, places requirements on friendship that, to be strongest and most fulfilling, make it the province only of the privileged.

The possibilities of living together with others by choice, and sharing the sorts of activities Aristotle describes (most particularly politics) would have been possible for only aristocratic male Greeks, not for slaves and women, who were not citizens, and hence unable to take part in governing a city. Insofar as friendship involved participation in politics, women, slaves and children were excluded from the possibility of the highest sort of *philia*. Furthermore, the sorts of activities that Aristotle recommends for friends are typically aristocratic activities, displaying dominance, mutual independence and personal power. Sharing emotions, particularly pain, is not seen as appropriate for friends, as it would reveal distressing and unmanly vulnerability. Thus, even though this sort of friendship is intimate, the intimacy is in the form of companionship of independent and self-sufficient individuals. It does not include mutual support through the sharing of suffering and difficulty.

Peta Bowden points out a further precondition of Aristotelian friendship, when she notes that the friendships to which Aristotle attributes the highest value are those that require equality of status, of interests, as well as mutual independence. The mother–child and family relations to which Aristotle often refers as examples of *philia* do not qualify as the highest sort, as they are not equal relationships, and involve at least one person who does not take part in all the activities of friendship, and particularly politics. Nor could relations across class very often satisfy the requirement that *philoi* have their interests and activities in common, particularly in hierarchical Greek city-states. We cannot rely on the Aristotelian solution of allotting the person with higher status to be better beloved, and the person of lower status to love in greater degree.[15] Nor can we easily accept his view that friendship is not possible between slaves, as they are merely human tools without the capacity for finer feeling; this view is in profound difference from modern understandings of the feelings and relationships of those in situations of oppression or deprivation.[16] While Aristotle does draw attention to possibilities for mutual care and love in intimate friendships, his account of friendship is addressed to an aristocratic minority and is structured already by the activities and relations of this minority.

In a more general sense apposite to the subject of this book, Aristotle's account of friendship is conditioned by Greek city life, lived on a small scale, with few opportunities to know people except by direct contact with them or through shared narratives of absent others. Aristotle's ethics concerned a society in which all lived in proximity to one another, many people neither read nor wrote, and in which letters were extremely rare. More recent technological innovations that facilitate communication and social relations permit people to keep in touch with each other, despite living apart. CMC, like other communications media, may allow extended communication between people who are physically distant from one another; again this may serve to link friends who are apart for a time, or perhaps to form the beginning of a friendship. While these observations do not mean that living together is irrelevant to friendship, they remind us that some friendships with other people are today maintained by people who meet rarely if ever, and that face-to-face friendship may be complemented by communication across distance. Aristotle's account of friendship tells us nothing about long-distance friendships, and so cannot tell us how these friendships might be valuable despite their differences from companionable friendships.

Aristotle gives us just one avowedly partial[17] view of what is important about friendship. From a modern perspective we can see clearly the connection between the difficulty in Classical times of communication at a distance and Aristotle's evaluation of living together as an essential element of friendship, and can contrast this with the social possibilities held by contemporary communications media. Nevertheless, there is much in Aristotle's account of *philia*, particularly in his account of the specificity of the relation of friendship, and the importance of valuing friends for their own sake, that is still important in modern understandings of friendship, as to other intimate relations. Some aspects of his account of friendship, notably the importance of the relational qualities of friendship, its capacity for self-affirmation, and its power to develop individual capacities for ethical care and other-relatedness, have been taken up repeatedly since, affirming the ongoing power of Aristotle's vision of friendship for contemporary ethicists (Nussbaum 1986; Blum 1980; Card 1995, particularly Chapter Five, 'Lesbian friendships: Separations and continua'). Spending time together is particularly important for Aristotle, in building familiarity and trust. This evaluation is, as I will show, repeated in other theories of friendship.

5.4 Friendship in letters: Erasmus

5.4.1 Background: Christianity, lingua franca and learning

In this section I look at friendship in letters, using a particular example to illustrate its strengths and weaknesses. I have chosen Desiderius Erasmus as the focus of this section because his views on friendship and letter-writing were immensely popular, if not wholly representative, during his lifetime.[18] I argue that the prevailing anti-corporeal doctrine of contemporary neo-Platonism and Christianity, and likewise the culture of linguistic erudition to which Erasmus belonged, served to make epistolary friendship as desirable and as worthy as companionable friendship.

By contrast with the Classical focus on companionship as an essential element of friendship, the Renaissance is characterised by a strong tradition of friendship through letters, that sees mutual understanding and enrichment to be possible without friends living together, or even spending much time in each other's company. Petrarch wrote on friendship in his *Intimate Letters*, and so did other literary friends of the period, including Marsilio Ficino, Francis Bacon and Erasmus, who was not only a prolific letter-writer but, like many of his associates, an epistolologist, or student of letters. A web of scholarship and common historical and religious interests united men (and a very few women) who rarely met face to face.[19] Friendships in letters arose within a trans-European revival of learning for which the sharing of books and knowledge over distance was of vital importance.[20]

Friendships without Aristotelian companionship sprang up. People who saw each other rarely, or who never met at all, exchanged letters on subjects known to them both, typically Biblical and theological issues, on educational techniques, and on such Classical works as were known at the time, as well as reflection on the epistolary medium, written language.[21] Learning, and respect for learning, were goods essential to such friendships, so that those who were not educated (or being educated) could not be involved in this web of friendly letter writing.[22] Shared depth of knowledge and conviction about intellectual matters under discussion sustained friendships despite infrequent meetings.

Renaissance discussions of friendship are flavoured by the views of Cicero and through him those of Aristotle.[23] Classical writers' views on friendship were used to shed light on contemporary relations of friendship and to highlight what these later writers saw as their most valuable and notable aspects. The belief in equality of all persons before Christ coloured the thought of both Protestant and Catholic humanists. And the modulation of the Aristotelian *telos* of happiness into the Christian one of virtue in conformity with the word of God served to play down bodily, social and hedonic aspects of friendship, and to emphasise the intellectual and spiritual aspects. When, for example, Erasmus echoes Cicero in writing that to be true friends, people must be united by a bond of sharing, he refers to the exchange of intellectual understanding, and to books, rather than to the sharing of activities that Cicero and Aristotle deemed essential to a full and enriching friendship. Christian doctrines of moral rectitude and impartial fondness towards all within a community supplant the supportive role Aristotle saw between particular friendships and political stability.

Desiderius Erasmus's account of friendship was inflected by contemporary social conditions. Drawing on Aristotle and Cicero, he described friendship in terms of equality and sharing of self and possessions.[24] He wrote no single work on friendship, but the entries on the subject in the *Adages* are as large as small essays, expanding on Classical themes in accordance with contemporary attitudes; and his personal correspondence is peppered with references to the subject.[25] As I shall argue, the humanist respect for learning ensured that elevated literacy was the favoured means for compensating for physical separation.

Erasmus's adaptations of Classical accounts play down the role of the specificity of the friend. For one thing, contemporary Christianity tended to limit the degree to which anyone might *require* companionship, shared activity, or devotion from a friend.[26] Erasmus, a member of an academic Christian culture that considered the body either the servant or the enemy of the soul (McConica 1991: 55),[27] held the view that we should try to love all people equally, without partiality, and should do so in a spiritual way.[28] So people may love each other for all sorts of reasons, but the best reasons are spiritual ones:

A man may love his wife because she is his wife; the pagans do as much. Or love her because she gives him pleasure; then the love is carnal. But ... if you love her above all because you perceive in her the image of Christ, for example, piety, modesty, sobriety and chastity, and you no longer love her *in herself*, but *in Christ*, or rather Christ in her, then your love is spiritual.

(Erasmus 1988: 53–4, quoted in McConica 1991: 57–8 (my emphasis))

For Erasmus, goodness and godliness of mind are paramount and objective virtues. A virtuous person is one who follows as well as possible the example of Jesus Christ, lovable not in herself, but insofar as she is a good Christian.[29] One can love another only insofar as they are objectively virtuous, and the objectively virtuous are identical in their goodness: 'A friend is one soul in two bodies' (Erasmus 1974: 19). Thus in turn character is valuable not for its personal specificity but for its possession of objective virtue. The particularity of persons cannot be valuable in itself. And particular attachments to other persons are not appropriate if they get in the way of the more primary goal of being part of a community in Christ.[30] One's activities are unimportant except insofar as they contribute to or impede the fulfilment of one's personal spiritual pact with Christ, the spiritualisation of the self.[31] The Christian view of personal virtue, and its consequent impartialist bent in regard to personal relations, then forms one justificatory slab beneath the support of friendships in letters despite their preventing shared activity.[32]

Perhaps the most marked difference between Erasmus and his classical models, forming the second justificatory slab in his defence of epistolary friendship, is his lack of emphasis on friends spending time together. There is little emphasis in his writings on shared activity and experience in producing friendship.[33] When he writes 'Friendship is equality. A friend is another self' (Erasmus 1982: 31–3), he refers to friendship in correspondence, and to a relation established through successive written expressions of learned views and opinions rather than through daily activities, shared pastimes and projects undertaken together. Christian values such as contempt for the body, and the reformatory belief in the equality of all persons before Christ, also combined to support the view that distance was no obstacle to intimate friendships. I now want to consider how Erasmus conceived of sharing between friends who lived apart.

5.4.2 *Sharing between separated correspondents*

Separation necessarily qualifies the sense in which friends may be said to share everything. Erasmus sees sharing to be possible between literary friends, despite intervening distance, and accepts Aristotle's claim that 'Between friends everything is common'.[34] The sorts of sharing available are, however, not for the most part Aristotle's shared activities, but cooperation across distance in independent endeavours. These include writing poems,[35] sharing knowledge, assistance in academic or religious promotion, moral political and religious political advice, loans and dedications of books,[36] on top of the paramount capacity of letters to allow dialogic discussion. Those aspects of friendship that engage and are concerned with bodily activities are absent from Erasmus's discussion of friendships, as shared bodily activities and projects are deemed to have no role in spiritual friendships, nor in friendships conducted at a distance.[37] Independent self-determination is exhorted as an important virtue, in conformity with the deprecation of close intimate or interdependent friendships.[38] This view tallies with the sense in which physical independence from others may provide an access to freedom in correspondence, particularly if the activities of reading and writing letters distract from dull or oppressive everyday conditions.

Characteristic of Erasmian literary friendships is the submersion of many of the mundane aspects of sharing, of the repeated shared activities that comprise Aristotelian companionable friendships and provide the opportunities for doing well, for observing the character of the friend, and for building trust so essential for Aristotle. As noted above, the sharing of ordinary activities was, for Aristotle, an important locus for the building of trust and mutual well-wishing, allowing each friend to learn more fully the character of the other, and giving many opportunities to act for their particular sake.[39]

For the Christian Erasmus, the pleasures of everyday life were unimportant by comparison with the hope of future salvation; sharing everyday activities would not contribute essentially to either the strength or the importance of a friendship in which more exalted possibilities were open. The physical separation of literary friendships, as well as the resultant absence of shared tasks and activities, may be taken to be unimportant so long as friends have shared interests and projects that can be carried on at a distance (such as discussion, and research). The broad terrain of mundane well-doing activity that was part of Aristotelian *philia* is transformed in Erasmian friendship into the literary support afforded to friends whose interests are common but whose lives are separate and largely independent. The practical dimensions of the life of each cannot be fully and mutually manifested. Thus friends' practical lives have far less bearing in a textually expressive and communicative friendship than if they were to spend their days together, as is also evinced by the longstanding literary friendships between Erasmus and people whose habits differed significantly from his own.[40]

As I have argued in previous chapters, purely textual relations are limited in that they permit only activities and projects amenable to textual performance, and only those which do not have to be *done together*. Activities such as playing a sport or music, or sharing housework and other daily activities cannot be shared. In purely epistolary friendships, friends have access only to the styled textual performances of their friends. Consequently people may lack insight both into the practical aspect of a friend's comportment and into the relation between verbal and physical performances. It is in the coincidence (or rather the disparity) of bodily and textual performances that many of a person's deceptions and self-deceptions manifest and may be apprehended. If friends' capacities to remark upon, and attempt to improve either the friend or the self rely in any measure on subliminal perceptions of unintentional aspects of styled bodily comportment, then the correspondent may lack crucial insight into the character of their friend. (For a similar argument, see Cocking and Matthews 1999: 133.) Lack of insight would thus limit someone's ability either to guide a friend or to be guided by them.

This would be particularly the case for people who have never met, since they would have no idea whatsoever of the relation between verbal and bodily performances of their interlocutor, whereas people who have met will have at least some idea of the relation. It is notable that the people we know to have been Erasmus's dearest friends, such as Willem Hermans and Thomas More,[41] spent a great deal of time with Erasmus, rather than knowing him only through letters. This observation, while it in no way negates the value of literary friendships, supports the claim that spending time together may cement a friendship in ways that letters do either less frequently or less successfully.[42]

The role of such sharing in building trust, one of the Aristotelian themes most popular among contemporary writers on friendship, is also overlooked, as will be discussed below. I will look next at how textual presence was constructed for Erasmian friends, and then to the role of rhetorical skill in Erasmian friendship, cultivated to overcome the vagaries of action and interpretation at a distance, at the cost of increased suspicion and distrust.

5.4.3 Epistolary friendship and the metaphor of absent presence

The preferred means of compensating for the absence of friends was, fairly naturally for humanists, to develop literary and rhetorical skill. Indeed, the prime importance of eloquence and the connection of eloquence with writing privileged the letter as a mode of communication for friends. Through his letters runs the trope of being together in separation. His earliest letters to friends speak often of his yearning to be with them, as in Epistle 17 to Cornelis Gerard:

> Supremely pleasant and welcome as was the whole hearted devotion to me expressed in your letter, still I felt a pang of especially acute grief at the thought that the circumstances under which we live are such that I must experience that devotion at a distance. If by any means it were possible, I should prefer to have an opportunity of conversing with you face to face and enjoying your company at close quarters, together with your embraces and most chaste kisses.
>
> (Erasmus 1974: 24)[43]

Writing is already taken to be a close second: 'But since I cannot have what I wish for I shall, like Micio in Terence, wish for what I can have and since what I most longed for has not come my way, I may improve by my skill the hand that fate has dealt me' (Erasmus 1974: 24). Erasmus already believed that learning to read and write with skill can substitute for being together. So for example he writes: 'By this means I have the illusion of circumventing the fact of our separation, and of rejoicing in your sweet presence as I converse with you in person' (Erasmus 1974: 37).

In later years Erasmus accepted the exchange of letters as on a par with conversations as a way of maintaining intimate friendships, except when it came to matters requiring secrecy or extreme care in expression.[44] Even then, when he valued friendship in letters as a form in itself, the benchmark of 'reality' against which letters were measured was the dialogue, or conversation. Throughout his life the trope for good correspondence was that of 'absent presence' or togetherness through writing (discussed in Jardine 1993: 151–3). The claim that writing summoned correspondents into an illusion of presence, or into a form of 'extended presence' is particularly common in Erasmus's later letters.

Its importance is suggested in this comment to Antonius of Luxembourg: 'But how inordinately I am drawing out my letter, while revelling in your friendship as in a delightful frenzy I am carried away and forget myself – such is the impression I have of conversing with you rather than writing a letter' (Erasmus 1975: 48). He commented in one letter that the descriptions a friend gives of his family members are as life-like to him as if he knew the family (Erasmus 1974: 31). And in consolation to a pupil whose house he had just left in 1497 he wrote: 'Any loss that did occur can be easily made up by an exchange of letters between us; indeed we can replace it by more than was lost … If you miss me, miss me only so much that none of your application to study is lost' (Erasmus 1974: 122).[45] To such friendships, in which letters provided 'absent presence', distance was no obstacle, and spending time together of no particular benefit, since the epistolary exchange was theorised as at least as rewarding and uplifting as full presence.

Contemporary understandings of writing, particularly as developed by Erasmus, took for granted writing's performative power. Far from seeing letter writing as simply descriptive or narrative, unlike the effective or motive power of words in active life, Erasmus argued that many, if not all, human activities were possible in writing. His thoughts lay in particular on the activities of persuasion and argument within a word-loving academic culture. In 'Of letter-writing' (*De Conscribendis Epistolis*), taking for granted that which Austin argued so hard to prove, he lists the actions we may perform in writing:

> In [letters] we give vent to anger, protest, flatter, complain, quarrel, declare war, are reconciled, console, consult, deter, threaten, provoke, restrain, relate, describe, praise, and blame. In them we feel hatred, love, and wonder; we discuss, bargain, revel, quibble, dream, and, in short, what do we not do?
>
> (Erasmus 1985: 71)

Erasmus thought of letters as the 'making present of absent persons in living form, the public communication of feeling and relationship, but in the language of intimacy' (Jardine 1993: 151).[46] Jardine points to several places where Erasmus argued that florid, fanciful and fictive writing was used, not to deceive, but to enliven and make vivid truths conveyed in absence (Jardine 1993: 151). As I argued in the second chapter of this book, the use of affective appeals and techniques of spontaneity[47] are integral to the vividness of textual self-presentation, aiding its primary purposes. This was certainly the case for Erasmus, who used letters above all to persuade. The importance of persuasion is evident in the observation that the rhetorical tropes referred to in the above quotation are all forms of exhortation, encouragement or discouragement. That letters allow this range of activities strengthens the case that letters allow absent presence.

As I have already explored at length, the linked questions of how people may be present to and aware of one another in writing are fraught with difficulty, not least the issues associated with separation I have discussed above. This is especially the case for friends who enjoy one another's company. In situations of writing one's own 'absent presence' for an absent correspondent the act of self-presentation is explicit, since to describe oneself or one's views in writing is already to tell a fiction, albeit a 'real' or authentic fiction, to one's reader. One's words are not an Arendtian commentary on or supplement to action, but must serve to enable the correspondent to re-present at a distance her or his situation.[48] In Erasmian literary friendships people come to know and understand each other largely through those aspects of their selves that emerge in writing, through the reciprocal expression of their attitudes, intentions and text acts. There is less possibility for cooperative harmonising of the practical activities and commitments that are constitutive of much of their lives, except insofar as each friend is engaged in projects relating to learning, reading and writing. There is also no sensuous empathy, so that imaginative projection of the friend's situation makes do for the give and take of conversation.[49] The absence of the person of the correspondent must be compensated for by the production of absent presence through styled textual self-performance.[50] The metaphor is one of supplementation.

Unintended results of limited context may affect how people read one another, as is illustrated by constant misunderstandings and calls for clarification in the correspondence of Erasmus, their effect often exacerbated by the slowness of letters in reaching their destination. The physical absence of the other, particularly the absence or invisibility of their bodily condition and their mood or emotions, common to all textual relations, is the spur to perform a written self that will be evocative for the friendly other without relying on any shared social context. Deliberate affective appeal to the other, or rhetoric, is Erasmus's avowed way of overcoming absence, and also allows action *in* absence, in the form of performative inscriptions. At the same time, the evident artifice of texts so produced may increase uncertainty about the character of the writer, particularly for one as rhetorically adept as Erasmus.

5.4.4 *Absent presence and the redemption of rhetorical skill*

This section explores the role of rhetorical learning in both developing Renaissance capacities for friendship, and in complicating the relations among friends. That text acts require different articulation from the conversational forms of speech acts, embedded in self-evident contexts, and accompanied by bodily expressions of all sorts, encouraged correspondents to develop skills in both reading and writing.

Erasmus treated learning as essential to the expression of the self in letters, in his published views on letter writing and reading in 'Of letter-writing'. At other times and places, the stylistic norms for personal letters have been conversational, informal, or colloquial.[51] In Erasmus's academic milieu, letter writing demanded both mastery of contemporary techniques of rhetoric and a memory stocked with quotations and arguments to discuss and to which to appeal. Learned and skilful writing, though it may become spontaneous, comes from the heart only after practice, of integration of thought, reading and writing. Expressive clarity and invocation of absent presence required, in this as in most literary traditions, some facility with written language.[52] Understanding and appreciating the character of another through their letters similarly depends on being able to 'read' them through their styled literary performances.[53]

Technical accomplishment was not, for most humanists, opposed to self-expression in writing, but a means to more persuasive and flexible expression of one's views and opinions.[54] Likewise the ability to quote from great classical and contemporary authorities was not mere imitation, but a positive source of personal inspiration. Rhetoric served the purpose of allowing a writer to direct a letter towards its intended recipient in ways most calculated to appeal to him or her, and to persuade him or her of whatever one had in mind. Even the simplest style could only be used effectively by those who had mastered the copious styles (for instance Erasmus 1975: xl). Skilful reading was meant, in turn, to allow readers to discern the many levels at which a letter could be taken, though this was by no means always achieved in practice.

For example, the righting of wrongs often relied on rhetorical appeals to equality between friends, and particularly to parallel virtues. Erasmian correspondence frequently attributed attitudes to friends in writing by suggesting a mutuality of feeling. Guillaume Budé, for example, replied in this vein to Erasmus about a disagreement: '… I would assert that no resentment, no touch of indignation was ever strong enough to develop into hatred. I assert this of my self, and have no hesitation in supposing it true of you' (Erasmus 1989: 79–80; also Erasmus 1975: 48). The attribution of good-will to the self and of similarity of virtue to another is designed to elicit a reciprocal affirmation from a correspondent.[55]

Another measure of the importance of skilful writing technique in friendly exchanges is in the frequency of protestations of particular authorial intention, and of attributions of intention to correspondents, not to mention eulogies of honesty and plain speaking. Much of Erasmus's correspondence is devoted to specifying his intentions, divining those of his interlocutors, or anticipating future developments in their textual performances. Frequent specification of intent was essential to maintaining trust in an environment where delivery of letters was slow and unreliable, distractions from letter-writing considerable, and the engagements and activities of correspondents between letters largely unascertainable.[56] For example, in a letter of 1498 to Willem Hermans: 'I am very vexed with you for writing such a short and careless letter. Alas for me, have things come to such a pass that it seems to you too much to lose a single night's sleep for my sake'.[57] And to Jacob Batt in the same year: 'I will not allow that you are more ardently affectionate to me than I am to you, but I am firmly of the opinion that the warmth of our affection should not become too heated' (Erasmus 1974: 161).

Erasmus pays less attention to reading skills than to writing, perhaps because the method of learning writing skills presumed an enormous amount of reading and exegetical discernment. Its importance comes out rather in the niceties of his own readings of others' works, and in the degree of care in reading presumed by his comments on writing. Many of his letters have several meanings, some intended for audiences other than the ostensible recipient. Tracy notes that sophisticated writers such as Erasmus expected readers to be attuned to the rhetorical slant of letters addressed to others and to be able to compensate for such slants. However, as the following section suggests, artful readers and writers are no more invulnerable than naïve ones.

5.4.5 Style and the side effects of artfulness

In an environment of self-conscious self-construction and separation between correspondents, the role of trust requires particular examination. As I will argue, trust is often one of the victims of a highly self-aware epistolary environment. Literary friendships, although they allow, as Erasmus argues, the *experience* of 'absent presence', give fewer opportunities than companionable friendships to spend time together, to trust and be trusted. They thus lack the wide scope of mutual experience, of opportunities for developing trust that are described in Aristotle's characterisation of friends who spend much of their time together. The establishment and maintenance of trust in Erasmian literary friendships is instead linked with the capacities of friends to share activities and appreciate each other in a textual exchange in which there are fewer opportunities for well-doing.

As James Tracy has observed in *Erasmus of the Low Countries*, trust in Erasmian friendships of letters is tenuous, undermined by the constant need for cautious and attentive interpretation, by the difficulty of verification of readings, and by the long-windedness of resolution of disputes once underway (Tracy 1996). Tracy notes, for example, the frequent occurrence of readings that confounded Erasmus's anticipations in writing (Tracy 1996: 181). Erasmus's letters show that he valued as complementary the arts of skilful self-expression and charitable interpretation, with an overall aim of civility (Tracy 1996: 159). At the same time, many of his letters were shot through with signs of distrust, such as dissimulation, or deliberate deception, of which a common example was the writing of a letter to one person in the hope that it might be read by another (Tracy 1996: 177). Likewise his readings of others' letters were often suspicious rather than charitable (Tracy 1996: 178).

Without any chance of quick resolution, disputes tended to foster bad feeling, such as a sense of being wronged or persecuted, or a sense of helplessness, and to endanger, sometimes to end friendships.[58] Ongoing uncertainty about another's views, rather than disagreement with them, constituted for Erasmus the grounds for distrustful reading and writing, and clouded many possible friendships in their early stages (Charlier 1977: 342–7). There is not sufficient room here to discuss cases in which distrust arose; Yvonne Charlier has given an excellent analysis of Erasmus's epistolary friendships and details amply the collapse of many of his friendships, such as that with Budé, through distrust or outright suspicion. Her study illustrates the extent to which epistolary friendships initially contracted with enthusiasm petered out rapidly after a few maladroit attempts at intimacy, or after an early misunderstanding (Charlier 1977: 345–7).[59] I give more attention to the role of trust in friendship in the section below on feminist accounts of friendship.

5.4.6 Summary

As with Aristotle, Erasmus's views on friendship are from a particular and partial perspective, reflecting the prevailing social and political conditions of the time, and the situation of the writer within them. Religion was both changing and losing its governing status. Social structure in the Christian world was rigidly hierarchical and women typically would have had little recognition, social, intellectual or political. The very possibility of communication via letter, historically linked with the Europe-wide spread of Christian and academic culture, allowed and sustained friendships in a way not previously possible, at the same time as limiting such friendships to those with a high degree of learning.

Erasmus's account of friendship referred to a relation that was only possible among those who were part of that network of academic and religious learning. While Erasmus, a humanist, favoured a broadened academic curriculum and wider general education, his emphasis on excellence of style and erudition of content for friendly correspondence would put the sort of activities that he saw as part of a literary friendship beyond the reach of most people, then and now. The high value placed on erudition encouraged a highly developed literary style whose mastery tended, even more clearly than Aristotle's requirements of equality in social and political activities, to tie the possibility of becoming literary friends to prior membership in a tiny educated all-male elite.[60] There was little possibility of literary friendships between intellectual and non-intellectual, for that which was shared by men of letters was not available outside of a church or university education.

In other regards, Erasmus's account of friendship both echoes and differs from Aristotle's. His own experience and expectations of friendship inflect decisively his use of Classical themes. The individual qualities of a friend are not important in their own right, but are valuable in their conformity to particular Christian virtues. Sharing, trust and mutual well-doing are considered important in friendship, but are described in terms of the sharing of knowledge and learning, or the expression of individual kindness, and lose their strength as *relational* qualities existing *between* two people. The possibilities of developing bonds through 'living through' experiences are likewise overlooked, making Erasmian friendship more wholly intellectual and less part of shared active lives than Aristotelian.

For Erasmus, important and mutually enriching friendships might be conducted by letter, without spending time together or even having regular meetings. His view of friendship is not one connected with the everyday sharing of and coping with the events of life. It discounts those aspects of life concerned with pleasure, sensuality, and particularity of persons, at the same time as it allows the sharing of views, opinions, experiences and commonalities by those who live quite separate lives, and who might otherwise never have the opportunity to share *anything*.

Erasmus values textual self-construction and persuasively affective writing, even as he endorses candid honesty, illustrating the dependence of this type of literary friendship on the mastery of rhetorical and interpretive skills, for instance in making the absent writer 'present' to the reader. His positive evaluation of epistolary friendship is enabled by the devaluation of those aspects of friendship that do not survive the physical separation of friends, and by an elevation of those that do. Even there, the finesse of highly rhetorical expression and interpretation could go over the head of readers, and result in misunderstanding. Negotiating the complexity of anticipated readings and variety of interpretations often limited trust among correspondents, forever guessing at each other's intentions, often without the opportunity for conversational dialogue. Limits on time spent together seem to have limited in turn these friends' capacities to judge one another's characters, to trust one another, and to develop in each other's light.

The Erasmian theory and practice of friendship are together suggestive for CMC. Hermeneutic problems may result from separation between friends, and, while careful reading may resolve some of these, rhetorical skill and analytic ability will not necessarily do so. These findings for epistolary friendship will also be qualified with regard to CMC. The two media differ markedly as to timing. Letters are intrinsically slower than CMC; in the time of Erasmus they might take months or years to reach their destination. Thus the exchange that occurs in CMC is more like conversational dialogue than the slower dialogue of letters. For this reason, misunderstandings and confusions may be resolved more rapidly in CMC than via letters.

5.5 Contemporary feminist accounts of friendship

5.5.1 Aristotelian friendship reconsidered: particularity, difference and trust

In recent years there has been an influx of new philosophical publications about aspects of friendship, following a period of comparative neglect of the subject. Notably, many books on women's friendships, both general and based around the lives of particular women (Raymond 1986; Faderman 1981; Myers 1990; Nestor 1985: Fitzgerald 1985), have been published in the last two decades, as have works revaluing the importance of friendship in general (Friedman 1989a, 1989b, 1993; Rubin 1985). This return to discussion of friendship is coincident with a renewed emphasis on virtue ethics (both Aristotelian[61] and non-Aristotelian[62]). Many accounts, prominently those of women and other subordinate groups, also show greater awareness of the structuring effect of the communities within which friendships exist (for example Faderman 1981, Nestor 1985), by comparison with earlier accounts of friendship that are keener to describe the exalted qualities of friendship and ways to develop it.[63] With their emphasis on particularity, and their situatedness within contemporary Western societies, with affordable travel and mediated communication, the findings of these books should be able to shed further light on possibilities for friendship in CMC.

Contemporary feminist accounts of friendship balance the Aristotelian and Erasmian accounts given above, both of which neglect both women's friendships and their views on the subject.[64] Such analyses tend to taken into account, for example, the complexities of friendship across differences, such as those of gender and race. They are often attuned to the structural pressures that other social relations, particularly exploitative and hierarchical ones, place on friendships. Sandra Bartky and Annette Baier attend to systematic lopsidedness in male–female friendships, in which women characteristically provide more emotional support while having less personal autonomy.[65] Peta Bowden gives insightful and wide-ranging discussions of types of caring in friendship, examining different practices of care between friends, and attending to the variety of friendships as well as to similarities (Bowden 1993, 1997).

I shall focus mainly on Bowden's account since it comprehends many other accounts, and acknowledges the variety among them; my analysis is supplemented by references to other accounts where necessary or illuminating. By using a survey form to show the possibilities for ethical caring in different accounts of friendship, Bowden's own account shows that many different forms of social structure have the capacity to support different sorts of caring friendships, some intimate, others reserved, some valuing personal similarity, others difference. The value of particularity and partiality in friendship is occluded by approaches that exalt independence and self-containment, of which Aristotle's account is an example; particularity and partiality are largely neglected and even denigrated in Erasmus's account, for all his strong personal attachments to his friends in practice. And it is with the importance of particularity of friends in mind that Bowden elaborates the role and importance of caring in the theories of friendship that she covers.

A strength of many feminist accounts of friendship is in their explicit assertion that coming to an understanding of friendship involves the integration of theory and life practices.[66] A grasp of friendship shows not (or not only) in the theory that one puts forward, but in the concernful ways in which one encounters actual other people, and in which one acts when not around them.[67] Such accounts, generally speaking, acknowledge the cultural variability of practices of friendship, and the consequent variety among theories. Feminist accounts of friendship are, indeed, many and various, best understood in relation to one another and the context of social practices and values in which they arise. For example, Lillian Rubin's account of friendship is sustained and bounded by a body of research into the understandings and activities of friendship among contemporary men and women (Rubin 1985). Work such as that of Nel Noddings (Noddings 1984) shows that some contemporary female friends often value female caring patterns as inevitable, if not wholly pleasant, aspects of contemporary life for women.

Friendship emerges in the work of Rubin, Bowden, Friedman, and Noddings, among others, as being a relationship with great possibilities for moral and personal development, free to a great degree from the institutional constraints that surround most other relationships. At the same time, it is shown as an especially vulnerable relationship, fragile because of its lack of institutionally recognised conditions, and through the non-conditionality of the love that each friend has for the other. Since the ties that bind friends and allow them to act voluntarily for each other's sake are not legal or institutional, they can also be broken off without recourse. Nor do friends have rights with respect to what they can ask of each other, despite the importance within friendship of being able to count on one another. In other words, the freedom and peculiar joy of friendship with a particular other person comes with the relinquishment of 'terms of dealing' or 'control' that structure many other sorts of relation.[68] Many feminist perspectives on the value of friendship base that value both on friendship's freedom from the more rigid expectations of social roles, and also on its requirement of honest and reciprocal self-disclosure in order for each friend to know and care for the particular other (Bowden 1997: 80–4; also Raymond 1986).

Although feminist writers also value the Aristotelian specificity of the friend, the particularity of the self emerges, in modern feminist writing, in ways unlike those canvassed by Aristotle. For Bowden, for example, self-disclosure takes a more prominent form than in the Erasmian account of friendship or in the *Nicomachean Ethics*. Aristotle saw in friendship the benefits of mutual self-affirmation and improvement through association with other exalted and confident individuals. Negligent of the importance of friendship between ordinary imperfect people, Aristotelian ethics had little place for honesty in regard to personal defect or weakness, the disclosure of which would tend to undermine the worthiness of someone as an Aristotelian friend. Bowden sees in friendship a space in which people may come to understand and develop themselves by disclosing and facing their weaknesses as well as their strengths. This occurs through shared activities and opportunities for discussion and mutual understanding and aid that arise when friends spend time together.[69]

Feminist accounts of friendship tend to place importance on friends spending time together. Spending time together allows friends to 'live through' each other's experiences, and share their stories, disclosed in an atmosphere of trust and reciprocity. It allows friends to appreciate each other's perspectives, and become more aware of their own perspectives.[70] In turn, the new perspectives afforded by living through another's experience after them may allow moral transformation, granting new moral understanding of others' life situations and choices, and of how one's own attitudes and choices affect the lives of others. Hearing a friend's responses to one's decision gives one further insight into the significance of that decision. Sometimes that response may be an affirmation of the decision, sometimes it may be critical of it; and sometimes it may be a consideration of the role or importance of the decision itself in one's life. All these responses are part of experiencing one's life as entwined with the life of the friend.

In other terms, living through each other's experiences permits an increased (and increasing) degree of empathy between friends. The reciprocal appreciation of another's view grants friends the possibility of re-thinking themselves. It allows, in Iris Murdoch's words, a reciprocal form of the self-realising human activity in which one 'makes pictures of himself [sic.] and then comes to resemble the picture' (Murdoch 1962: 122). It does so by allowing friends to appreciate each other's moral stories, or moral pictures, not as 'cautionary tales' or homilies on goodness, but as recountings of the ethical experiences, values and choices of particular others, and as concrete practical possibilities for oneself. That the details of another's account emerge most fully in minute and attentive living together of each other's experience means that friendship takes time to develop, and requires time spent together; in no other way can the details of someone's particular life stories and perspective emerge as theirs.[71]

The process of self-disclosure in telling stories and giving perspectives is matched by the act of making space for the friend's self to emerge in all its particularity. As such it requires attentiveness and responsiveness to the other, to enable them to disclose themselves in an atmosphere of trust and support. Without an atmosphere of trust and a committed affirmation of their value for their own sake, friends may be reluctant or unable to take the risk of disclosing themselves in their own terms (Bowden 1997: 83). It is within the bonds of friendly trust, esteem and affection that people may feel free to step away from obligations to behave in conformity with social roles. In contexts dominated by institutionalised role-behaviour, such stepping away is not easy, since it may count as repudiation of the role, as selfishness, or as irresponsibility. The constraints in friendships are somewhat different, requiring understanding and attention to aspects of another that may be unconventional or odd.

Indeed being there for a friend may often require attending to a self that is less than perfect, to a self that is facing but has not yet overcome personal or moral weaknesses. We may be called upon to attend to a friend struggling to deal with actions or thoughts that are morally repugnant to us, for all that we love that friend. Attentiveness to a particular imperfect other self, the creation and maintenance of an atmosphere in which they feel able to become themselves, may thus require of friends great effort as well as much time. Margaret Walker notes that it may take immense effort to read souls in bodies (Walker 1998: 177–98). Maria Lugonès argues that the empathic immersion required to appreciate the situations and perspectives of those whose lives are very different or distorted in our understandings, takes even longer and requires even more effort; it may require that we give up our own hard-held perspective in order to appreciate the situation of another (Lugonès 1987).

These feminist theorists of friendship value the sharing of personal vulnerabilities and weaknesses in friendship as a path to self-improvement as valid as Aristotle's emulation of noble friends without any confession of personal weakness. Feminist valuing of the particularity of friends can thus embrace not only the virtues of friends, but also make room for the faults and limitations that are part of that person. Friendship, conducted outside of institutional bounds, can allow self-disclosure a space in which there are fewer and less rigid expectations, greater tolerance of weaknesses, vulnerabilities and imperfections. A friend's self can emerge without having to be defensive about that self. Limitations and imperfections can be faced in an environment of understanding and desire to help. Mutual support and careful attention can allow friends to move towards self-improvement and fulfilment in ways that would be too risky in less intimate relations. In the tolerance of and help for weaknesses and flaws in friends lie possibilities that would not be open if we were, like Aristotle, to reject 'ordinary', imperfect people as possible friends. It also allows us to love a friend for their particular self, for their own sake, even if they are not perfect; since, for one thing, we may learn from and support those who are not perfect at least as much as those who are.[72]

The need for attention and caring towards friends in order for them to be and become more fully themselves shows that a lack of institutional bounds does not yet give complete freedom to friends. The value of being able to admit weaknesses and limitations, and of maintaining an atmosphere of trust for such revelations encourages restraint in the behaviour of friends, in the forms of attentive care, honesty rather than deceptiveness,[73] and consistency rather than variability. These are, at times, difficult tasks; I have already considered the value of attentive care in allowing the friend's self to emerge fully and to negotiate self-improvement and self-fulfilment for ordinary, less-than-perfect people. Allowing a friend to develop also requires, as does developing with the assistance of a friend, a measure of trust.

Trust is an essential part of friendship, particularly of intimate friendship; it has figured in Aristotle's account, and it had a place in the mediaeval and Renaissance traditions of epistolary friendship. Since trust is a relational virtue (at its strongest when it is shared between people), trusting is an issue that involves attending to, being familiar with, the particularity of persons. Annette Baier, who has written comprehensively about trust from a feminist perspective, links it with discretion: she argues that trusting someone is equivalent to giving them discretion in how they comport themselves in relation to us, and to *not demanding* that they always account to us for what they do. I trust someone when I give them discretion in how they care for things that matter to me, confident in their good-will towards me. I am not trusting a friend if I must constantly be asking for their reassurance, or asking them to account to me for what they have done in relation to things that matter to me. At the same time, my trust is only ethical if its grounds could be revealed without destroying the trust. If, for example, my reason for trusting someone were that I thought them too frightened to betray me, our relationship could not survive the revelation of these reasons (Baier 1986: 258). Mutual honesty is thus one of the primary conditions for the development of ethical trust between friends.[74]

Baier's analysis also injects an element of temporality into the existence of trust between people. Since evidence of trustworthiness cannot come at a single meeting, it will put down roots only after people have known each other for some time. She points to the importance of people's experience of each other for the establishment of trust, including experience of the other's ways, of their trustworthiness in the past, and the testimony of others who know that person, such as friends and family, as contributors to mutual trust. These two elements of her account of trust together suggest that the intimacy of a friendship of mutual support and improvement ripens slowly rather than springing alive fully formed.[75]

Trust may in certain cases place limits on honesty, as is suggested by the action of the truster granting discretion to the trusted to take what the trusted thinks is the best course of action on behalf of the truster. On occasion, I may feel that it would be for the best to conceal something from a friend, be it about myself, about them, or about some separate matter. I may even lie directly to them. I may feel that the time is not right for a particular painful revelation; or I may feel that the friend need never know what it is that I am concealing. Whether such deception destroys trust or not depends on whether the deception is, once discovered, taken by the truster to be performed with their best interest at heart. Not all discovered deceptions break trust, though if such deceptions cause significant ill effects, even the best intentions may not be enough to maintain trust.

5.5.2 *The power of conversation*

Feminist theorists of friendship recognise, along with Aristotle and Erasmus, the importance of discussion in friendships. The value of talking emerges in all accounts, and is explicitly discussed by some, such as Bowden. Bowden is quick to acknowledge that verbal discussion is important but not solely constitutive of friendships, in which discussion is part of caring practices broader than the use of words alone (Bowden 1997: 82–3). She shares with writers such as Lillian Rubin and Marilyn Friedman the view that it is in discussion that trusting intimacy is forged and caring support is shared. While spending time together would require regular meeting, conversation and discussion are integral to making that time together valuable, and may also be shared through various communication media.

The importance of discussion certainly allows for mediated friendships as well as companionable friendships. But most points in Bowden's analysis suggests that friendship develops most fully in circumstances of long-term companionship, which offer the greatest opportunities for knowing and doing well for a friend. Coming to know a friend's sake is not possible without knowing something of their own self-understanding, and the practical ways in which they negotiate the world. Equally, the shared pleasures of spending time together, of talking and eating with friends are important simply in building a sense of togetherness. Feminist views in which the particular person is valuable in themselves, not solely because of their virtuousness, expand on Aristotle's perfection-oriented account of friendship to allow valuable friendships between ordinary, imperfect people, and contrast with Erasmus's treatment of personal particularity as subordinate in value to the possession of objective virtues.

5.5.3 *Summary*

Generally, the accounts of friendship of writers such as Peta Bowden, Marilyn Friedman, Lillian Rubin and Sandra Lee Bartky all share preoccupations with the great importance of partiality in the friendly relation. As an ethical stance, this runs against impersonalist and obligation-oriented ethics such as Kant's. In addition, against Aristotle, Cicero and Erasmus, they value friendship as a personal and intimate relation, rather than one in which each friend's problems remain unshared. Such valuations are given a great deal of support by the wider feminist literature on caring,[76] although they are by no means universally accepted. Certainly, their status as part of the best and fullest friendships is compatible with our seeing value in other less personal and less intimate friendships.

These feminist accounts of friendship are significant in relation to CMC friendship, since they emphasise aspects of friendship characteristic of contemporary Western life, namely the association of friendship with intimacy or privacy, and the treatment of imperfect friendships as nevertheless valuable in themselves. These accounts extend and, in some places, correct the earlier accounts of friendship considered in this chapter. The first two accounts, defending the independence of each friend, did not leave room for the intimacy or mutual support and discovery that are both practised by female friends and theorised by women writing about friendship. Feminist accounts reveal how large a part intimacy may be of contemporary friendships, particularly those between women. Further, both Aristotle and Erasmus, with a fixed ideal of human excellence in mind, treated differences between friends as indicative of imperfections, and as a risk to the stability of the friendship.

5.6 CMC friendship

5.6.1 Drawing threads together

I have described in earlier chapters the role of styled performance, along with beliefs and desires, as expressive of individual character. I have also argued for the importance of attending to the performative styles of other people in our understanding them as other selves. Textual performances, I argued, are just one aspect of the totality of a person's styled performances, and less than wholly indicative of another's self. The extent to which performative inscriptions are circumscribed by physical absence further supported this view.

On the interpretive side of personal social relations, I have detailed the importance and the difficulties of attending to people through their writing. Styled textual performances tend, as well as enabling imaginative, expressive and communicative possibilities, to obscure the embodied whole of personal comportment. Textually-mediated empathy with others' described, alluded to or enacted experiences, the means by which we might experience the experiences of others in text, was, I argued, somewhat limited by the lack of sensuous empathy characteristic of textual communication.

In my discussions of friendship, including friendships through letters, I have tried to show the variety and range of possibilities of attention to style in friendships, and the different aspects of persons that are focal for different varieties of friendship, as well as overlaps and commonalities among the accounts. By showing how literary friendships encourage people to construct 'true fictions' of self, in order to emulate bodily presence and context or circumstance, this last section has provided some suggestive material for considering friendships in CMC.

The Aristotelian conception of friendship develops the theme of the constitutive importance of friendship for human well-being. Friendship is taken to be a relation between people wishing each other well for their own sake (although many friendships contain some component of self-interest). Friendship is also an activity, necessarily involving active care for the friend as well as friendly feelings towards them. Friends, ideally, develop their selves by each other's light, and come to be perceptive and sensitive critics of each other's faults. For this sort of mutual improvement to be possible, friends need to spend time together, and preferably to live together, so as to share in activities, and to allow both trust and understanding to develop between them. While Aristotle lived at a time when CMC was inconceivable, that he linked trust and mutual understanding to friends spending time together suggests that computer-mediated friendships may lack crucial resources for building trust and mutuality.

Erasmus's work, supported by and appealing to sustained and rewarding literary friendships, shows that friendships across distance were sustainable in his day (as they were not in Aristotle's time), although they seem to be premised on the shared engagement and facility of both friends with letters and learning. Such friendships may involve the total engagement of both friends, with great care and respect by each for each, but they do not enable the degree of familiarity and mutual knowledge possible through sharing time together, and through sharing and discussing the mundane tasks and activities that are their lot. The intensity of literary friendships, enabled by great skill, erudition, and embedded within lives already devoted to matters conceptual and linguistic, were the province of very few. Interestingly, as in the case of CMC, the development of epistolary friendships encouraged the formation of an educated trans-geographic social 'world' separate from those constituted by association within geographic or national boundaries.

The possibilities of friendship for self-improvement and mutual regard are juxtaposed with other possibilities raised by contemporary feminist accounts of friendship, such as moral growth (Murdoch 1962; Walker 1998) or overcoming gender and race prejudices (Walker 1998; Lugonès 1987). Many feminist writers on friendship point to systematic distortions and exploitations within friendships that may occur when one friend's caring remains less than fully reciprocated by the other, and to the non-reciprocity that is linked with deception of a friend. Bowden's analysis in particular reveals the variety and complexity of the possibilities for caring in many different relations of friendship, illustrating that reciprocity, intimacy and particularity of friendship are strands running through almost all accounts of friendship, though described with differing emphases by different writers. This variety and complexity must be kept in mind during the following account of friendship in CMC, which cannot hope by any means to be comprehensive, but at best partially representative.

By highlighting the degree to which friendship is based on sharing and appreciating each other's experiences, and strengthened by 'going through' life together, Aristotelian and feminist accounts of friendship together signal an area in which CMC, like Erasmian epistolary friendships, so often waylaid by interpretive difficulties in 'situating' the writing of each friend, might impede the establishment of relations of intimacy and trust. Without the possibility of sharing time together, and of sharing many of the *activities* of life, and without the opportunities for mutual assistance through such sharing, CMC friendships may develop more slowly than companionable friendships. Difficulties of interpretation, and lack of knowledge about others' life circumstances, may tend to lower the pace at which people meeting in CMC come to trust one another.

The various emphases and occlusions of the accounts of friendships given above suggest that differences in communicative structures and possibilities tend in turn to produce different goals and possibilities for friendships, in which spending time together has varying importance, and in which self-expression, shared activity and discussion are differently accented. We should certainly be careful about judging CMC friendships by the benchmark of a single account of friendship, considering that this particular communicative structure is novel and unique, and that it may provide for configurations of friendship not previously available.

The point stands, though, that all the above accounts of friendship *value* friends, for themselves or at least for their (virtuous) qualities. People, including users of CMC, will have a variety of approaches to and understandings of friendship, but all of these will involve varieties of active love and caring for a friend, whether this is abetted or thwarted by the lines of communication between them. I shall focus here on ways in which CMC structures the sorts of friendship that are possible, and consider how people engage in and understand CMC friendship as well.

5.6.2 Spontaneous coping in on-line social practices

Note should be taken first of all of the spontaneous adaptations people make to CMC, seeking out or avoiding some sorts of formats; playing at self or avoiding such play. People rarely try to figure out complete and principled strategies for using CMC, any more than they do for writing letters. Different people encounter and negotiate the medium with different degrees of reflection. Many of the conditions for communication of CMC are so obvious that people take them in their stride, as earlier people appropriated the media of letter, telegraph and telephone without pondering or criticising their transformation of human relations (see for discussion Standage 1998). Uses such as specifications of context and circumstances of writing, elimination of indexical expressions whose appearance outside the context of writing might easily be misinterpreted, and avowals of intention come easily to many CMC users.

Equally, the novelty of the medium has provoked a large amount of reflection on the means available to people for their on-line relations, as studies of discussion groups have made amply clear.[77] For example, some CMC-users identify usages such as emoticons and signatures as being unique to CMC, and hence as badges of 'experience' or belonging to a computer-mediated social group. Sometimes such adaptations to textual environments are self-consciously adopted and shared by on-line groups, as signs of belonging. Lists of emoticons, common abbreviations, and of appropriate ways to behave, are frequently circulated among discussion group members or in less formal networks, and are treated as the common property of these networks.

Such adaptations are, as I have already argued, spontaneous responses to a sense of absence of the face and of gesture of other persons in CMC, and the concomitant limitations on emotional expression. The descriptions of emoticons within discussion groups and chat groups as a common language suggest that emoticon users employ representations of the absent emotional face to overcome felt limitations of textual expression, and take these representations up as their own. Similarly, conventions of expression, such as Baym describes, can be seen as measures taken more or less spontaneously to prevent misunderstandings, strife, or breakdowns of communication in CMC (Baym 1993).[78] As I argued in Chapter Four, emoticons, as they signal patterns of group-belonging as well as emotional states, do not always resolve misunderstanding; they too have a grammar of use that may be misinterpreted.[79]

We would expect friendships in CMC to have a lot in common with friendships of letters, as they share the conditions of mutual physical absence and textuality. The varieties of friendship that appear and thrive in CMC will be bounded by the conditions of absence and textuality, as friendships of letters have been in the past. In addition, there is a major qualification of the tyranny of distance for CMC, in that it does not necessarily translate into temporal separation between contributions. CMC allows almost synchronous textual communication. Structural conditions obtaining in CMC, such as I have noted in Chapter Four, will also affect the forms of friendship possible. Where these conditions apply only to some sorts of CMC interaction, as synchronicity is necessary in on-line dungeon environments and chat groups, but not to e-mail or discussion groups and lists, different inflections in the possibilities for friendship are also to be expected.

5.6.3 Three aspects of CMC friendship

To understand the dynamic of friendly relations in CMC I want to return to the account of empathy that was given in Chapter Two.[80] In empathising with someone else, I co-experience the experience that is theirs, *as if* it were mine. Another's experience, however I apprehend it, is at once like what I have experienced myself, and not my own. I must apprehend it with faithfulness and with care, because, in being the experience of another, it may be unlike anything I have myself known, and also because a styled textual contribution is less than self-evidently the expression of a particular person. I am always at risk of not grasping it in its ipseity; yet I must be faithful to that experience as the experience of another self.

Empathy does not occur simply on occasions on which I apprehend, say, sadness or joy, in the face or the descriptions of another; it is fundamentally part of my apprehension of the whole of a person as an acting individual like me. When someone speaks or writes, they give of themselves, more or less generously, more or less cautiously. They disclose themselves even in speaking the most familiar truths, or the most banal pleasantries, even in lying. But without the physical presence of their writer, printed, textually presented truths and banalities have less of a place as part of a person. Speech, the speech of a person, is irreducibly theirs; writing, separated from the person is not intrinsically theirs, but must be identified as theirs by a reader.[81]

My account of empathy suggests that textuality, by virtue both of its nature as linguistic abstraction, and of the separation of textual language from the self to which language is normally only the *articulation*, presupposes empathy, but privileges the linguistic expression, as text, over the person. Textual communication does not allow the sharing, in a single moment, of simultaneous feelings, be they of mutual recognition in difference, or of togetherness. It allows at most the simultaneous experience of the mediating text, unsupported by any form of sensuous empathy. In CMC I may be here, now, with another, but I am also not with them; I might at any moment find out that I am, or they are, an impostor, or that I have been quite deceived about their character. Faithfulness to the other would be an extreme exposure if I cannot know whether they speak in good faith, or know who they are; my ability to appraise the other's faith is limited by the absence of the sensuous empathy with which much of my assessment of others' characters is performed. And my faithfulness to the other is a sham if the self whom I reveal in conversation is not my own self.

This faithfulness characteristic of human relations in presence is thus transported into the CMC textual relation in a unique form, with its own particular forms of understanding, and misunderstanding. Without the temporal boundness of being with another person, all ways of being oneself must include and be based on the textual activities of reading and writing. The reading of the other as another self, in the absence of that other's physical self, complementarily, necessarily requires interpretation effecting an elevation from written style to personal substance that is substantially unlike interpretation in full presence. As I have already argued, in this activity we are constantly at risk of mistaking textual style for personal style, where personal style is taken to apply to the gamut of a person's performances, not simply their inscriptions.

Thus, to generalise with Nancy Baym that 'participants' communication styles are oriented around common social practices before they even enter into CMC, practices that are unlikely to be supplanted by computer mediation' (Baym 1993) is already to neglect the differences between the possibilities of face-to-face conversation and those of computer-mediated conversation. Baym's argument is that people coming to CMC will usually already belong to a common subculture, such as that of a university, a workplace, or a fan club, whose practices will inform and construct on-line interaction. The purposes and practices of the CMC group will then evolve through the appropriation by group members of influential cultural practices. But without a consideration of how CMC communicative possibilities differ from face-to-face communicative possibilities, systematic slants in appropriation cannot be made manifest. Certainly not all on-line groups are drawn from such homogenous backgrounds as Baym suggests.

Likewise, the sensuous empathy remarked on in Chapter Two is absent from CMC. The familiar facial and bodily indicators of temperament and character are not present, or are transformed in textuality – manners of speaking, forms of address are all specifically textual. Textual creation, in descriptions and evocations of mood, tone, context and nuance (which can all be conventionalised) must supplement for those aspects of mood, tone, nuance and context that are not part of the semantic content of social exchanges. As Erasmus specified for epistolary exchanges, the creation of 'true fictions' to evoke the absent self to a reader is then an originally textual expression. Such uses of words are not transcriptions of oral locutions, but specifically and originally textual. They do without and compensate for bodily nuance and tone of voice; they do without and compensate for the on-going flood of response that the absent reader would be giving if engaged in conversation with the writer.[82] As in the case of Erasmus, the true textual fiction transforms the empathic act of the faithful reader, by requiring faith to the writer through their text. And this faith must be maintained even in the absence of much of what the reader would know of the writer were they to spend time together.

I have already described some of the ways in which self is styled in writing, by a combination of assertoric and affective expression, techniques of spontaneity, and descriptive evocation of self and other in textual performances. Such more or less deliberate self-styling is necessitated by the opacity of writing, particularly the opacity of affect that limits textual empathy. Thus writing the self in CMC will be a more or less deliberate creative process, especially when interlocutors are completely unknown to one another. However, CMC self-creation will be significantly more a mutual creation in CMC than in published writing and letter-writing, because friends will be able to contribute to and modify self-descriptions in a reciprocal manner, rather than in the slower alternation of epistolary exchanges. Such creation will be particularly a mutual activity if the pace of communication is rapid enough for people to contribute a conversational flood of immediate responses to each other.

As more rapid correspondence makes CMC more like mutual presence than (slower) epistolary relations, so it tends to allow more cooperative activity at a distance. Coordination may be closer, queries answered more quickly (in some cases at least). The (symbolic) text acts that I have argued are possible in CMC may take more immediate effect, be debated more rapidly and thoroughly, and may be more fully part of a dialogue between friends. In this sense, distance bridged by CMC is less of a separation than distance bridged by letters. Sharing of practical activities may not be possible, even if close coordination of activities is possible.

CMC does allow of sharing of some sorts of activities. Those activities performed via computer, such as modifying web-sites, working on computer-based projects, and so on, can be performed together.[83] The involvement of computer-mediated friends in common projects of understanding will, as with epistolary friendships, be one excellent way of maintaining friendships, given that these friends come and continue to understand one another. Indeed, the engagement in activities with a common interest may well be the best way to give a CM friendship time to develop. It would allow each friend to work with and for the other, and the constant textual dialogue in which they could engage is the surest way to an eventual grasp via CMC of each friend's self by the other.

5.7 Conclusions

This chapter has covered the territory of theories of friendship. It has also looked at the relation between theories of friendship and the practical terrain of friendship for those professing such theories. I have paid attention to friendships in letters, since CMC shares some structural qualities with the epistolary medium more broadly. This chapter has examined theories of friendship to see how they shed light on the nature of CM friendships.

First there may be difficulty in interpreting CMC contributions, such as lack of clues about the nature and quality of the writer, particularly as regards his or her practical performances and the relation between verbal and non-verbal perform- ances. Consequently, there is risk of misunderstanding by the reader, the develop- ment of cross-purposes, and the lengthy entanglement of mutual explanations. Difficulty in interpreting a friend's textual performances (or in the case of silence, non-performance) may also damage trust in the CM friendship, since silence is particularly hard to interpret in textual media. For example, in CM friendships there may be difficulty in interpreting the inarticulacy of surprise or sorrow, and in understanding the varieties of silence.

As we learned in the case of Erasmian friendships, rhetorical errors may also be performed by friends who presume that the interpretive limits of textually- mediated communication can be surmounted by noticing and taking into account their existence. Textual performances may still be misinterpreted, no matter how carefully writers use the means of textual self-presentation available to them. For example, we cannot always know and express all relevant aspects of background or translate the nuances of our bodily performances into our textual performances. Even the use of CMC-specific verbal (textual description of one's present activity, real or quasi-fictive) and 'non-verbal' tropes (emoticons) do not glean from their novelty or specificity the power to convey non-verbal states in the same way that facial expressions do (though of course any writing may unintentionally give away things about the writer). An icon representing a smile is as generic as the words 'I'm smiling'; the inscription 'Geri's laughs' is more generic than Geri's laugh.

There are further risks to be found in the interpretive virtuosity sometimes employed in overcoming these limits. Over-interpretation may result from attempts to overcome the hermeneutic problems of textual CMC. In turn, as I have argued for the case of epistolary relations, suspicion may result from generalised uncertainty about the character of a correspondent, even when there are no particular grounds for such suspicion. Clearly, this is the sort of suspicion that we would hope on- going communication might lessen; indeed most empirical studies of CMC relations suggest that nothing about CMC intrinsically destroys or prevents trust. The case of Erasmus suggests that distrust is prevalent in epistolary relations, although it is far less in the case of established friends than in the case of those who are trying to make new friends in the textual medium.

The increased risk of distrust and miscommunication in textual media, which risk is particularly great for people encountering one another for the first time, may be explained by the peculiarities of how the self is disclosed in wholly textual performances. Since one popular compensatory means of textual self-presentation in CMC is to tell 'true fictions' of the self, in some cases to embroider substantially and even to create fictive personae, the notion of self-expression as authentic self- disclosure may be subordinate to self-expression as a playful form of independence. In keeping with the value of honesty and self-disclosure to friendships in general, discussed above, it can be imagined that as the degree of truth in fictions of the self decreases, so the possibility of friendship also decreases.

In any case, even for the closest and most intimate friendships in CMC the textually-performed self is not a unity of experience and expression holistically perceived by other selves in the flow of life, but an expressive construction whose psychic condition must be inferred from written material alone. One of the challenges for maintaining friendships in CMC is allowing self-disclosure at the same time as creativity of expression. Care is also needed for friends to use the medium to develop confidence and trust, since by all accounts textually-mediated communications of all sorts encourage a hermeneutic intensity that often breeds suspicion, even where none is warranted.

6 Politics and CMC

[W]e failed to realise the democratising potential of television, and risk the same failure with CMC, because we have focused literacy education too narrowly on the encoding and decoding of written text.

(Lanham 1974: 7)

6.1 Introduction

This chapter discusses the possibilities of CMC for political activity. The focus shifts away from personal relations, as I turn to the issue of computer-mediated political relations. This is primarily because political relations do not positively require those involved to be engaged in ethically engaged communication, that is communication directed towards establishing mutual understandings. To this extent, political CMCs will not involve the same degree of interpretive trouble as do personal relations in CMC. Nevertheless, as I argue, political CMCs do involve interpretive difficulties. The overlaps and continuities between personal and political relations suggest that, while computer-mediation has some impact on the practice of politics in CMC, the comparative instrumentality of political relations reduces that impact to some extent by comparison with CMC friendships.

This impact is well worth considering, given the global scope of political relations in CMC. Already CMC (like other communication technologies) sustains webs of relations that support generalised political discussion, and facilitate informed political action at national and global levels. Certainly, much political activity still continues to be located at the national or state level. But trans-national or global political organisations are emerging, some part of a growing system of international governance (such as the United Nations bodies), and civic society organisations (or CSOs). Examples of CSOs are Oxfam, Amnesty International, Greenpeace, and Transparency International.[1] We might also want to include social movements of a broader scope, such as the affiliation of individuals and interested organisations in series of globally coordinated protests against the World Trade Organisation, although reference to institutional boundaries is of limited use in describing such movements.[2] The influence of such groups and movements is often quite tangible, as in the case of closing down of the WTO conference in Seattle in 1999, and the inclusion of civic society organisations at the WTO Ministerial Conference in Doha in 2001. It is within this global scope that the strengths and weaknesses of CMC for political activity are played out.

This chapter falls into three main parts. In the first part I discuss the nature of political relations generally. I argue that political relations, while in some sense distinct from personal relations, cannot be wholly separated from them. Political relations cannot be clearly separated from personal relations because of the general dependence of all politically involved persons on networks of personal relations, which sustain and support the more abstract ideals associated with political roles, activities and goals. To the extent that political relations are also personal, the interpretive difficulties of CMC, discussed in the first four chapters of this book, will also apply to political CMCs.

The second part focuses on the scope of political relations in CMC. I consider the conceptual possibilities for political relations in CMC, asking whether the ideal of a global participatory democracy is feasible, conceptually or practically. I do this by exploring the political possibilities of Habermas's account of discourse ethics, a popular model for CMC democracy, and ask whether his 'ideal speech situation' might be an appropriate ideal for a global political community. I conclude that the theory has flaws that will not be eradicated by importing it into CMC.

In the third part I explore the avenues that CMC opens up for political activity, even if Habermasian discourse ethics cannot be realised in CMC. Political activity in CMC is burgeoning, and the medium offers many positive possibilities for political engagement and participation, and for concerted political action.[3] The transnational quality of much political CMC has encouraged some political philosophers to talk of the emergence of a global public sphere[4] (Ess 1996: 216–19) or global civil society (Frederick 1993; Hamelink 1991a, 1991b). However, the currently fragmented nature of CMC political activity suggests that, rather than there being a single global public sphere, there is a collection of public spheres, some of them with global reach, none of them accessible to all inhabitants of the globe. I conclude that CMC is a promising resource for political activity, providing a wider variety of views than traditional mass media, and access to international- or global- rather than national-level participation for political discussion.

6.2 Political and personal relations

6.2.1 Traditions and distinctions

In light of the interpretive difficulties that CMC poses for personal relations, I explore in this section the interconnections between personal and political relations generally. I argue that, almost no relations are purely political, although we can distinguish personal and political aspects of relations. The significance of this partial interconnection of personal and political is that, within CMC, hermeneutic difficulties characteristic of personal relations may sometimes crop up in political CMC.

By political relation I mean a relation in which political goals and activities have primacy. In such relations developing mutual understanding with the other people involved becomes either irrelevant, or a goal instrumental to political goals and activities. Within political relations, mutual understanding is teleologically subordinate to political goals and activities. By political activity I mean, broadly, the range of activities associated with or contributing to the governance and organisation of a society. This extends both below and above formal national (and state) government. It includes, first, those activities associated with local government. It also includes activities associated with community self-government, where communities might include formal or informal associations within a neighbourhood, and activities associated with self-adjudicating communities, that is cultural and interest groups such as 'the green community' or the 'Baha'i community'.

Because political relations are maintained between people and organisations functioning at local as well as national or global levels, it is impossible to claim that politics is *essentially* located at any *one* of these levels. All those involved in the political process, at any level, even if it is just as participants in coffee shop discussions, or on CMC discussion groups, are engaged in political discourse.[5] But I want to put forward a different claim: that because those involved in political activity of any sort are also constituted in webs of social relations, many of which are personal, we cannot separate personal and political realms with any precision. Nancy Fraser articulates this idea when she describes the public sphere as 'a theater in modern societies in which political participation is enacted through the medium of talk' (Fraser 1997: 92). She treats the public sphere in contemporary Western societies as consisting in a multiplicity of overlapping public spheres, differentially empowered (Fraser 1997: 92). This cuts across an older tradition in which a single official public sphere is conceptually and practically privileged over all private domains.

This tradition is explored by Kymlicka and Nelson (Kymlicka and Nelson 1996). They argue that modern citizenship (that part of one's life associated with the public sphere), is traditionally aligned with a raft of abstract concepts such as duty, responsibility and right, which are impartial, impersonal and apply to persons conceived atomistically as independent individuals. It is aligned *against* such concepts as care, undertaking, responsiveness, which are particularist, often partial, and apply to persons as persons in relations.

The sphere of political relations has, historically, been cordoned off from that of personal relations. The separation has taken a number of different configurations. Classical cultures, broadly, considered the sphere of political relations as an area of comparatively free self-determination, unlike the realms of compulsory filial and parental associations. Citizens had the opportunity to contribute to the determination of the city or state. However, politics was an activity only open to free male citizens. Women, along with slaves, and resident aliens were completely excluded from the Classical public realm (see for example Okin 1989).

Enlightenment ideals separate private and public rather differently. Broadly, they treat the private realm as that of particular, partial relations with others, and as associated with emotions rather than reason. The public realm is thought of as that in which impartiality and duty are paramount, and in which reason is appropriate. The Enlightenment model is the one on which most contemporary democracies are still modelled. So, while the political and personal have usually been seen as in opposition, the two opposites have been seen rather differently across time.

There are some practical reasons for the conceptual separation of political and personal relations. First of all, political activity and organisation involve what I characterised in Chapter Two as communications whose success is assessed in terms of the transmission of information, rather than in terms of the ethical value of the communication *qua* communication between two people coming to understand one another. That is, many political communications constitute instrumental communications, part of a discourse ordered to the achievement of a larger (political) goal such as the satisfactory resolution of a debate, or the smooth operation of an organisation.[6] Many political communications perform their *political* role well *regardless* of the quality of the personal understanding embodied in such communications, or of the ethical content of the communications in question.[7]

Second, a barrier is placed in the way of widespread personal discourse, in most political systems, by the employment of some form of representation.[8] Representation figures in democracy as a practical alternative to universal participation in decision-making. Debate among representatives replaces debate among all those affected by political decisions. The view put forward by a representative is a composite, not agreed to on all points by all concerned, and so representative in only a broad sense.[9] Consequently, from the traditional perspective, it is not obvious that political CMCs could be required to be ethically valuable in the sense defined in Chapter Two of this book, that is, that each party must make a sincere effort to understand the other as a person.[10] Third, the demands that political involvement makes on people, particularly those involved in formal political activity, are onerous.[11] Political activity, associated with the governing of a society as a whole, raises questions about the ordering and the fairness of whole societies in ways that require more of participators in politics than attention and responsiveness to those individuals they know personally.[12]

These three practical considerations have, particularly in large and populous democracies, both emerged from and sustained a political tradition in which the private and public realms are separated, not only physically, but also conceptually. In contemporary Western societies at least, typical pictures of political activity tend to reinforce the separation of public and private realms by focusing on and idealising those aspects of politics that *are* largely impersonal, impartial and based on duty. The private realm is conversely identified with those values that find no easy expression in the political realm, even at the cost of paradox or contradiction.[13]

Contemporary discussions of politics via CMC tend to mirror the 'traditional view' of political participation, and to stress the impersonal uses of CMC for politics, while overlooking the personal. For example, James Rosenau treats networks as political communities independent of personal affiliations (Rosenau 1998). David Held and Damian Tambini treat networks as fora for debate between dispassionate individuals (see Held 1998; Tambini 1998).[14] A partial exception, Charles Ess moves some distance from the traditional view, specifically by acknowledging the roles of reciprocal perspective-taking and solidarity in political participation (Ess, 1996). I discuss his approach below.

6.2.2 *Intertwining of personal and political relations*

It is my concern here to question the separation of public and private realms, and their associated conceptual paraphernalia, that is characteristic of the 'traditional perspective'. I do not wish to argue that personal relations are the ideal towards which people engaged in political action *should* work, nor that *all* political action is already personal. Rather I want to draw on recent feminist discussions of politics to argue that there is a complex intertwining, in the activities of politics, between more personal relations and relations that are less personal. My goal in doing this is to illustrate that, while CMC may widen the possibilities for political activity, the overlap between political and personal relations means that political CMCs are not free of stylistic misunderstandings. Stylistic misunderstandings will occur in political CMCs just because political CMCs are the styled performances of particular persons.

First, the interrelation of personal and political relations is obscured from within orthodox party politics by the perceived opposition between private and public realms. The interrelation is consequently more clearly visible outside of the structures of orthodox party politics, both in informal political activity, and also in the gendered interconnections between those involved in formal politics and those who care for them. Smaller, politically active groups, such as civic society organisations (for example, environmental groups, community groups in liaison with local government, pressure groups and so on) are often more tightly knit, involve more personal relations, and often explicitly acknowledge the sorts of partiality that such webs of personal relations within politics bespeak. In the public sphere generally, including political discussion outside of particular deliberative or decision-making fora, personal relations evidently count for a great deal. In many cases personal relations are the context within which political opinions are debated and decided, political news is disseminated and discussed, and the impacts of political decisions on individuals and communities are considered and assessed. So, in these cases it is difficult to say whether relations belong in the private or the public spheres defined and separated by the 'traditional view'.

Indeed, one of the strengths of political participation in CMC has been that those involved often have personal ties as well as political ties to bind them. People find themselves in new public spheres, such as discussion groups devoted to political issues, or discussion groups devoted to other issues, but in which political discussion arises. (In both cases, while groups might have global reach, they would still be only partial public spheres, not having universal membership.) This access to new fora for political discussion and activity opens up, not only possibilities for discussion, but for a range of political activities. An example familiar to many users of CMC would be the e-mail petition, which can be distributed globally via networks of personal relations. Personal connections have helped to sustain major political activities, such as protests against the World Trade Organisation in Seattle in 1999, Gothenburg in 2000 and Genoa in 2001.

Further, the 'traditional view' obscures just those sorts of political activities in which personal and political aspects of relations intertwine most closely. Within undervalued areas of political participation, those that fall outside of formal politics, political relations are likely to be, at the same time, personal. For instance, even if women do not match men in numbers in the higher echelons of politics, they are present in substantial numbers in those areas of politics not traditionally lauded or credited with being of importance.[15] Ruth Lister's perceptive analysis of contemporary citizenship treats types of activity such as informal politics[16] (Lister 1997) as distinct from the formal politics of elected government. She argues that informal political activity (in which women play a large role) is at least as important as formal. Informal politics take place at the kitchen table, or at home computers as often as in public places.[17]

At a subsidiary level, the 'traditional view' obscures the intertwining of personal and political relations and aspects of relations by overlooking the origin of political sensibilities and activities at home. It separates political relations from those personal relations in which all people, politicians or no, are involved, and thereby ignores the cultural heritage of politicians as members of families and participants in other personal relations. Political activity arises within societies that are constituted by manifold caring relations, both within families and between citizens who know each other personally. Contractual relations of the sort characteristically associated with political and other public-sphere activities cannot be seen as freestanding, although this is how many contract theories have pictured them. The ability to make and maintain contracts, involving being able to trust those others with whom one contracts, and to sustain cooperation within contracts, are dependent on citizens having social skills and ethical capacities that are learned independently of any contract.[18]

These observations about the intertwining of personal and political (aspects of) relations lead to a further conclusion. Since political relations are sometimes, if not always, also personal relations, the interrelation of the personal and political is best characterised as a matter of interpersonal relations that have personal and political aspects. A division into personal or political relations cannot capture the complexity of citizens' engagements with each other. Many political associations are sustained by personal relations among, say, party members, or affiliates. Many people engaged in political activities together *do* have a personal relation with each other, although the personal may be instrumentally subordinated to political activities or goals that are more important to each than the particularity of the other.

This conclusion has the added strength of allowing us to accept certain facets of the distinction between private and public spheres that continue to be both necessary and valuable to the practice of politics in contemporary mass societies, of which two stand out.[19] It recognises the need for greater instrumentality and efficiency in political communications, the unreasonableness of the demand that all political relations also be oriented towards mutual understanding. It also recognises the comparative freedom of political communications from the requirement of attending to the particularity of the other, in that political relations or aspects of relations may, in teleological terms, subordinate personal understanding to political goals.

In summary, political relations (and aspects of relations) are threaded through with and dependent upon personal relations or aspects of relations. Even though personal relations are denigrated within the 'traditional view' of political activity, and the informal political activities of those people associated with the private sphere remain unrecognised, personal relations contribute essentially to the maintenance of respect and trust necessary for political coordination. Personal aspects of relations (such as friendships among political allies and combatants) contribute substantially to the contemporary practices of politics, even if those contributions are indirect or overlooked.

6.2.3 Style and political relations in CMC

In this section I argue that stylistic misunderstandings of the types discussed earlier also occur in political CMC, although their effects on relations are less serious than in personal CMC. Contextual opacity, that is, the obscuring of the mood or intention of a writer of CMCs, occurs in political CMC exchanges as well as in exchanges that are part of purely personal relations.[20] To the extent that political CMC relations (or aspects of relations) are intertwined with and dependent on personal relations (or aspects of relations), they will, according to the argument in Chapters One to Four, suffer from the stylistic confusions characteristic of CMC. But the nature of political relations and political aspects of relations, particularly how they differ from personal relations and aspects of relations, is such as to render stylistic misunderstandings less serious in effect.

The description of political relations or aspects of relations discussed above gives some sense of when political CMC are likely be subject to hermeneutic misunderstandings, and when they are likely to be free of them. I noted that political relations (or aspects of relations) are those in which political activities and goals are ostensively teleologically prior, and personal particularity and understanding subordinate. By inference, political communications (communications that are part of political aspects of relations) are also marked by the teleological priority of political goals.

The teleological priority of political over personal goals within political relations (or aspects of relations) by no means prevents, in and of itself, stylistic misunderstandings of the sorts I have discussed in earlier chapters. In terms of the importance of styled performance, argued for in the first chapter, textual misunderstandings may still occur between those who have not established a relationship oriented towards mutual understanding. Temporal misalignments and other incongruities may lead to confusion among strangers. Character may be misread in significant ways by those in political competition as well as by acquaintances hoping to become friends.

I noted empirical findings that misunderstandings in CMC often provoked a good deal of anger, as exemplified in the frequency of flaming and other forms of textual abuse.[21] Empirical studies of interaction in CMC fora expressly set up for political purposes evince patterns of flaming and abuse similar to those earlier charted in social CMC (in places such as Usenet). Such problems figure in recent empirical studies of communities that instituted networks with political functions. Roza Tsagarousianou, for example, studied the Pericles network in Athens, and found that there was a substantial amount of flaming, and that this made political cooperation a difficult and often-interrupted task (Tsagarousianou 1998a, 1998b particularly 52–7). Sharon Docter and William Dutton's study of Santa Monica's PEN network made a similar observation, citing organisation theory research about the 'stark and less civil' qualities of on-line discussion (Docter and Dutton 1998: 145). Docter and Dutton also noted that at least one city councillor involved with PEN had come to avoid using the network, because he had become the target of aggressive flaming (Docter and Dutton 1998: 145–6).

In other words, it is not safe to assume that even impersonal political relations in CMC will be devoid of style, and hence of stylistic misunderstandings. Lack of a personal relation between people does not preclude emotional engagement, at least of some varieties. Admiration or anger, trust or distrust, good or ill will, may predominate in impersonal and in instrumental relations.[22] In other words, even if there is no personal relation between those who are engaged in political debate or activity in CMC, stylistic misunderstandings may still occur. Indeed, they may occur more often, precisely through interlocutors' mutual unfamiliarity with each other's performative styles.

Besides, even if political CMCs do not aim primarily at mutual understanding between the particular people involved, they are still exchanges among particular people. These people's styled textual performances, including text acts, will perform in each instance in particular modalities, and will be expressive of aspects of that person's character that require our attention to be understood. Understanding the meaning of a person's sentences is often, though not always, dependent on grasping the modality and character expressed in their styled textual performances, whether or not that person matters as a person to their interlocutor. Failure to attend ethically to a person's particularity in an instrumental relation does not dissolve that person's particularity, nor cut through the style of their textual performances to some unstyled 'truth' below. Indeed, since political (aspects of) relations intertwine with personal (aspects of) relations, the path to coordinated political action will often lie *through* rather than alongside engagement in personal CMC oriented towards mutual understanding.

Thus, the teleological priority, within political CMC, of political goals over personal particularity or sustaining relationships, taken on its own, does not suggest that stylistic misunderstandings are less prevalent or that their effects may be less serious than for personal CMC. However, other characteristics of political relations and aspects of relations *do* lead to the comparative insignificance of stylistic mis-understandings in political CMC. These characteristics are the relative unim-portance of personal particularity within political relations and aspects of relations, and the marginal status given to attempting to understand persons in their own terms, within political relations and aspects of relations.

First, the unimportance of personal particularity in political relations in CMC means that less effort need be put into attending and understanding persons with whom one exchanges political CMC. Consequently, a diminished focus on empathic attending will tend to be normative for those relations. Certainly, the stylistic particularity of participants in a political debate may matter strategically for those taking part (that is as indicative of character, or as a clue to future actions). It is less likely to be of *intrinsic* value for those taking part in political CMC, except for some communications for those who share a relation that has both personal and political aspects.

Second, the marginal status of the attempt to understand others in their own terms makes contestation over meanings less problematic in political CMCs. Negotiation of meanings will be part of political CMCs, and of political relations generally, and there may well be instrumental benefits in understanding others' terms, as part of that negotiation of meanings. But there is no sense in which the terms in which another understands themselves are *essential* to political CMC, or indeed to political relations or aspects of relations generally.

The lowered stakes for interpersonal understanding in political CMCs are played out in the normativity of treating the political CMCs as texts. Political CMCs, as I noted above, are not generally treated as being styled in ways that are expressive of character. Rather, as per my distinction in Chapter One, political CMCs are understood as having styles that are ornamental properties of texts designed primarily to convey information, or rhetorical properties of texts designed primarily to convince or persuade.[23] While affective and particular relations remain important for common political endeavour and cohesion, the sheer bulk of communication that must be done requires that political communications be more instrumental than personal ones.

Likewise, attending to the attitudes and character of those communicating is not intrinsically important for the success of much political CMC, although this is not to say that it might not be of some benefit in aiding cooperative endeavours. Hence there will probably be less focus on style as expressive of character in political CMC than in personal CMC. So long as a political CMC is treated as something providing information, rather than as something expressive of character, people will be less attentive to or concerned about what styled texts reveal of character, and less prone to be offended if the details are anomalous or disagreeable.

Third, stylistic misunderstanding in political CMC tends to be less common. Both the characteristic subject matter and existing political conventions make political discussion less prone to stylistic variety. Although political discussion inevitably involves styled performances, its style is comparatively formalised and regular.[24] People engaging in political CMC will tend to follow familiar descriptions of relevant entities and events, or to cite previous descriptions of them, rather than drawing on novel descriptions. They will also tend to avoid verbal uses prone to semantic opacity (such as neologism, live metaphor, or fanciful phrasing). This comparative regularity works to reduce the likelihood of stylistic misunderstandings.

To summarise, there is less at stake in the style of political CMCs than there is in the style of personal CMCs. Style in political CMCs is not usually intended or taken as expressive of self. Further, less hangs in political (aspects of) relations on the maintenance of close personal understandings. Consequently, misunderstandings are often of less significance, for reasons that I have already alluded to in

Chapter Five. That is, misunderstandings in political CMC, particularly between people who do not have great and specific expectations of each other as persons, are less likely to have negative repercussions for the relation in question.

I specified at the beginning of this section that political activity is that range of activities associated with or contributing to the governance and organisation of any society up to and including the global polity. Political activity involves political relations, or aspects of relations. However, as I have argued in this section, relations that have a political aspect often also have a personal aspect. Indeed, the political aspect of relations is often sustained by the personal aspect (just as political activity generally involves webs of informal politics closely connected with webs of personal relations). In this sense, any account of political activity in CMC must also take into account the webs of personal relations that background that political activity, and must acknowledge the potential for serious stylistic misunderstanding characteristic of personal CMCs.

In such an account of political activity ways of dealing with styled political discourse must be addressed not only for national-level politics, but for politics at every level. The immense variety of types of communication that come under the rubric 'political discourse' once we move beyond the 'traditional view' of the public sphere necessitates some broadening of the terrain of political relations. In the next section I consider Jürgen Habermas's account of discourse ethics as one possible model for political relations in CMC, and assess to what degree he addresses the issue of style as constitutive of selves in social relations.

6.3 Habermas's ideal speech situation and on-line politics

6.3.1 The potential of CMC for global political discourse

In this section I want to explore the possibility of using Jürgen Habermas's discourse ethics as an ideal for political CMCs. Habermas's account of discourse ethics is, I claim, promising for political CMC, for two reasons. First, discourse ethics is discursive; it takes decisions about normative matters as ones that should be determined by discussion among all those affected by them, rather than by solitary debaters or by political representatives. Second, discourse ethics treats participants in political communication as engaged in a giving and consideration of reasons for claims that is capable of transforming participants' understanding of their shared moral terrain. Given the pluralism of contemporary societies, a politics that recognises and endorses transformative debate seems like a promising model for CMC.

However, Habermas's position is open to criticism at a number of points. His highly abstract account of the role of discourse overlooks many of the concrete particularities of discursive situations. It cannot, for one thing, be made to discriminate the qualities of CMC that militate against reasoned debate of all with all; it must treat them as of a piece with other 'distortions' of discourse. That many people can engage together in discussion via CMC is, I think, the main reason why CMC seems a fertile ground for the concrete application of discourse ethics. But other qualities of the medium cannot be said to be especially suited to discourse ethics. In particular its limitation to text does not make CMC political discussion more impartial, or more like a reasoned debate, than other forms of political discussion. The discursive dice may be loaded against certain sorts of people (and, by implication, against the interests and needs that these people have) by virtue of norms of styled self-expression that are taken for granted in abstract discourse ethics. This difficulty is not eliminated in CMC. I conclude that discourse ethics may be a valuable model for how to use political CMCs, but only in the same sense that it is useful elsewhere, as one guide to the ideals that we seek in using discursive media for political activity.

The impact of CMC on the scope and nature of political activity is widespread, and certain to increase with time, since almost everywhere that CMC networks exist, people and organisations are using them for political purposes. It is worth stating the advantages that, at least for those who have access to it, CMC holds out for political activity, particularly for coordination of political activities and campaigns. CMC is immensely more efficient than letter, or telephone, for coordinating national or global political activities. Once set up, a computer network allows comparatively cheap communication at a distance, and can be used to coordinate with large numbers of people far more easily, cheaply and rapidly, than a letter-network would do.[25]

Further, CMC allows many-to-many communication, both synchronous and asynchronous. Unlike letters and telephones, anyone who speaks on a discussion group oriented towards public political debate may be taken to be speaking to, and to be heard by (potentially) all those others involved in the group, and through them, by others again. In other words, CMC opens up new fora for political discussion. It may do this for those organisations (companies, CSOs, governments) that want to have a political say. And it does it also for those organisations that want to allow their constituents to participate in debate on political matters.

It is this second possibility that has captured the imagination of many users of CMC. The notion of 'global participatory democracy' is enticing, and, in principle at least, possible if all the people in the world were in contact via CMC.[26] The coordination of a population of millions in a participatory democracy would be far more easily managed if they could debate and vote via computer. Participatory democracy at a local or regional level seems not only enticing but also increasingly practicable, and affordable. Since 1980, many participatory-democracy projects have been conceived, and some put into action, using CMC to allow more participatory forms of democracy in various cities and states. Such forms of political activity are, given the current (technological and financial) limits of CMC, overwhelmingly textual.[27]

6.3.2 A characterisation of discourse ethics

The ideal speech situation (or ISS) is a notion used by Jürgen Habermas, partly to underwrite the possibility of maintenance of social cohesion (which he characterises as 'Lifeworlds' shared by groups of people)[28] and partly to provide understanding of what may have gone wrong where social cohesion has been damaged or destroyed.[29] It reflects Habermas's use of theories of language and communication[30] as the ground of his critical theory and social analysis. Because of its focus on communicative social solutions to ethical problems, and because of the nature of CMC as a widely distributed medium supporting discussion, Habermas's ISS is worth considering as a model of ethical standards for political debate in CMC.[31]

An ISS is a procedural ideal. Described roughly, it is a situation in which people talk together about the moral norms that affect them all, and arrive, by process of rational argument, at a conclusion about which moral norms they should, together, accept. They debate by advancing claims for which they are prepared, if necessary, to give reasoned justification. All who are affected by the decision[32] participate in the discussion. No participant conceals their intended outcomes from other participants. There is no coercion,[33] anyone may raise any claim, and debate does not end until consensus is reached. All these conditions must be met for a speech situation to be ideal.[34]

After discussion and argument, all those involved in the ISS apply the moral norms they have accepted to the problem that sparked the debate, and agree on a course of action which is satisfactory to them all, and which they then proceed to carry out. Both the moral norms accepted and the course of action arrived at result from the sharing of rational arguments, and are not just an aggregation of the views of each individual.[35] Consensus is reached not, strictly, by people providing reasoned justification for claims, but through the 'transformative' effects of reasoned debate on the views of those who participate. Given that all those concerned with a particular decision participate, the 'transformative effect' may include not only people changing their minds, but a greater transformation, of 'the totality in which these moments are related to each other' (Habermas 1985: 202–3, quoted in Warnke 1995: 256).

The ISS's primary function is as a transcendental condition of the possibility of interpersonal communication. Habermas's contention is that we presuppose the possibility of untrammelled communication and reasoned accord when we open our mouths to speak. As noted by William Outhwaite, the ISS performs a function similar to Kant's transcendental illusion, 'involving the extension of the categories of the understanding beyond the limits of experience, but with the difference that this illusion is also "a constitutive condition of the possibility of speech" ' (Outhwaite 1994: 43). That is, the ISS is for Habermas not just a regulative ideal but a possibility that is necessarily assumed by us in the very fact that we do engage in consensus-oriented discussions with other people.[36]

As James Tully notes, Habermas's ISS merely makes explicit the assumptions shared by any moral theory that makes use of concepts of public and reasonable agreement in order to establish and maintain social cohesion (Tully 1989). The ISS is only secondarily a guide for improving real speech situations, and for assessing how and why an ethical debate about how to proceed may have gone awry. Criticisms of the ISS directed at its practical unattainability leave out of question the desirability of the goal of justification-based consensus, and leave unexamined the presupposition that speech is fundamentally directed towards reasons-based production of consensus.[37]

Before I talk about reasons-based attempts to reach consensus, it is worth noting the limited range of claims on which consensus can be reached. Habermas is not claiming that the whole of ethics is discursive, since he recognises that ethics is largely a matter of comportment, or behaviour. What he *is* claiming is that the resolution to ethical difficulties lies in debate about the moral norms within which ethical behaviour fits. Consequently, these norms, which today must hold for the whole of pluralist societies, tend to be very abstract indeed; for instance, debates about substantive value differences are not amenable to debate in the ISS.

In *Moral Consciousness and Communicative Action* (particularly in 'Discourse ethics', and again in 'Morality and ethical life') Habermas makes several claims that suggest how very limited the role of redemptive discourse is in modern society. The more pluralistic the society, indeed, the more abstract the sorts of issues that can be dealt with. Questions below this in terms of generality are not so straightforwardly amenable to redemption of claims in a discourse, since there will be insufficient commonality on substantive ethical issues for normative commonality to emerge:

> As interests and value orientations become more differentiated in modern societies, the morally justified norms that control the individual's scope of action in the interest of the whole become ever more general and abstract.
>
> (Habermas 1990b: 200)

Such a claim suggests that the power of the ISS to coordinate debate and produce consensus are indeed limited.[38] Even if, as Seyla Benhabib has argued, discourse ethics cannot exclude in principle the discussion of questions concerning the good life (Benhabib 1990b: 15–16), consensus on these questions is unlikely.[39]

Given what I have said so far about the breadth of political activity and engagement in CMC, not to mention the diversity of backgrounds and outlooks of those using CMC together, it seems reasonable to deny that all those involved in CMC share common conceptions about the good life. Thus the range of moral norms on which CMC participants can agree using the discourse ethics will be highly abstract ones, such as the existence of universal human rights. Meanwhile, the problem of application of these ever more abstract norms to particular situations grows ever more intractable.

6.3.3 Taking rational consensus as the goal of moral debate

The first thing to be said about discourse ethics in relation to political CMC is that it is an ethical theory that sees moral issues resolved through a process of reasoned argument by all concerned. All those people affected by a decision must be involved. This is because moral justification is not, for Habermas, a following-through of impersonal reasoning about moral matters, a procedure that any competent reasoner could perform. Rather, it is a matter of all those involved giving *each other* reasoned justification; and consensus is conditional on all those involved accepting the reasons given. Thus the actual involvement of all in the process of giving and assessing reasons, oriented to reaching consensus, is essential to the ideal status of a speech situation.

Habermas follows Kant in holding that the possession of rationality is universal among human beings, and is precisely what keeps open the possibility of ethical behaviour. And both argue that reason is the fundamental defining characteristic of humanity, for two reasons. First, the capacity to reason confers autonomy and responsibility upon all persons, and second, the exercise of reason grants individuals the possibility of significant self-determination.[40]

Habermas defines rationality in more social terms than Kant. He adds a fourth category of reasoning, communicative rationality, to those mapped out by Kant. This type of rationality is the basis on which other forms of rationality rest. For him, rationality is intrinsically bound up with a quite particular use of language, that is, its capacity to coordinate human action.[41] Consequently, moral consensus (in a more or less ideal speech situation) becomes the *criterion* for the validity of moral norms. If we accept this account of rationality, and its implications, then we will find that CMC is an admirable medium for moral and political debate and activity.

The move from Kantian subjectivity to a more intersubjective approach to rationality is reflected in Habermas's modification of Kant's principle of universalisability, described here by Seyla Benhabib:

> Instead of asking what an individual moral agent could or would will, without contradiction, to be a universal maxim for all, one asks: what norms or institutions would the members of an ideal or real communication community agree to as representing their common interests after engaging in a special kind of argumentation or conversation? The procedural model of an argumentative praxis replaces the silent thought-experiment enjoined by the Kantian universalisability test.
>
> (Benhabib 1990a: 331)

Further emphasising the move away from Kantian 'monological' decision-making, Habermas defines the deliberate non-disclosure of one's aims and intentions within communicative rationality as deceptive or manipulative.[42]

The social nature of Habermas's moral theory makes CMC seem ideal for realising ISSs. Political CMC would allow not only those who share the same educational institution or neighbourhood, but all those with access to CMC within a given political nexus (say a nation), to partake in speech situations with at least the potential to be ideal. Political CMC involving all affected, if used in actual political decision-making processes, also represents an advance on representative democracy, in which people vote once every few years. CMC would, if used to allow, say, nation-wide debate, allow all affected by political decisions to debate and contribute to those decisions.[43] Wider still, CMC might allow ISSs to emerge for citizens of all countries of the world, in relation to matters of international concern, such as global trade regulation and global poverty reduction.

But is reason-giving the best way to achieve transformation of understanding, and thereby a mutually acceptable consensus? Habermas's focus on rational debate and orientation towards consensus risks, not simply idealising the conditions necessary to ethical political debate, but distorting them, and neglecting non-argumentative means important to achieving consensus and coordinated action. To accept discourse ethics, we must agree that what CMC is good for, in ethical terms, is conflict-resolving consensus-oriented debate on moral norms. We must also accept that consensus on a moral norm is necessary for the validity of that moral norm. And critics of Habermas have noted that in pluralist societies the focus of participants on consensus is less likely, as the possibility of consensus itself fades (for instance, Moon 1995).

Responding to this criticism, supporters of Habermas claim that consensus, like some other ideals, nevertheless remains worthy of pursuit as the goal of discourse. Charles Ess, for example, reorients discourse ethics towards pluralism. He agrees that consensus on moral questions is essential for on-going practical cooperation in pluralist societies, and should be established to the greatest degree possible (Ess 1996: 206–9). But, holding that a plebiscite, or single forum with contributions from one and all is easily subverted, he argues for a 'pluralist democracy' of multiple public spheres (identified with discussion groups). Ess sees rational consensus-oriented CMC debate within these smaller groups as preferable to a CMC plebiscite as a way of ensuring on-going practical cooperation (Ess 1996: 220).[44] Elisabeth Lawley argues that CMC is ideal for the discourse ethics of an ISS, although the technical constraints of the medium, such as the capacity for technological obfuscation and surveillance, are seen as obstacles to achieving an ISS (Lawley 1992). In other words, supporters of Habermas hold that the ideal of the ISS is substantial and desirable, even if it is not fully attainable in pluralist societies. It may still be a valuable ideal for criticising speech situations that are less than ideal, for detecting cases of exclusion of those concerned, and uses of distorting or coercive speech.

Yet the giving of reasons is not the only available means of transforming people's moral positions, and while it is a good means, it may not be the only good means. While it would be foolish to assert that people should accept moral norms on the basis of poor reasons, it is not inconsistent with this view to hold that the means by which people come to accept moral norms for which excellent reasons exist are not, and should not be, limited to the giving of reasons alone. Discourse ethics focuses on consensus and rational argument at the expense of other important functions of communication, particularly those aspects of communication that establish and maintain understandings, yet without being oriented towards consensus. One such function is encapsulated in the dimension of style, instantiated in the capacity of styled verbal and non-verbal performances to express aspects of self, and to establish and maintain understandings. In the next section I consider the explicitly discursive aspects of discourse ethics in more detail, arguing that some communicative functions that are *not* oriented towards producing consensus through rational argumentation are important to political discussion, in CMC as elsewhere.

6.3.4 Communicative action and style

Habermas's account of communicative action allows that action may be coord-inated discursively through reasoned debate among all concerned. Speech constitutes action in some cases. This possibility, which I have established for textual communication in Chapter Three of this book, is one of the great strengths of political CMC. That we can perform actions in words, and also coordinate actions through words means that discursive activity has a comparatively wide moral breadth.[45] The significance of speech acts lies not in their descriptive truth, but in the actions that they bespeak. Habermas would say that some sorts of speech (speech acts) contain claims not only to descriptive truth but also to sincerity, which can only be tested by examining subsequent actions (Habermas 1984: 113).[46]

Communication has the capacity to coordinate action because, according to the transcendental arguments of *The Theory of Communicative Action*, the very condition of human speech is the possibility of intersubjective consensus. It is within language, and uniquely within language, that people may coordinate their actions, question one another's beliefs and intentions and affirm consensual action: 'the linguistic domain … is the only place where the validity claims of speech acts can be verified' (Habermas 1984: 256). The procedure of reaching rationally-motivated consensus, including discussion of the validity of claims, requires and *presumes* a universal informal logic of argumentation.[47]

Given the number and variety of people who may be involved in a speech situation (let alone in a CMC political debate), the clearest way Habermas sees to providing common ground for reasoned testing and defence of claims to normative rightness is to argue that all claims to normative rightness vouch for their own universal validity, in that they abide by the informal logic of argumentation. That is, anyone who is sufficiently rational to take part in debate ought to be able to tell when she or he is engaging in bad argumentation, or manipulative argumentation, because these will stand out either as logical flaws or as contradictions. Cases where people do not carry through with actions as consensually agreed are, Habermas argues, both in the minority, and involve a particular intentional disruption to the process of reaching consensus, i.e. the deliberately misleading communication of one interested in their own satisfaction regardless of that of the larger group.[48]

Habermas thus accepts that truth-telling is the primary use of language. And, in doing so, he grants no role in moral discourse to fictive, expressive, or playful language. He does assert that discourse may effect a transformation of our understanding. But this is meant to occur through the giving of arguments whose transformative power inheres in their logical validity. He grants no role to other functions of language, such as phatic communion, expression of emotion or playfulness. And he neglects the capacity of discussion not oriented to consensus to produce insight, understanding and cooperation. These are serious oversights, since the value of consensus-oriented debate, and the validity of consensus itself, are established only at the cost of ruling out as illegitimate many discursive practices that may be genuinely encouraging of finding common ground, and of producing insights and understandings that advance political debate.

This criticism of Habermas has already been elaborated by Georgia Warnke. She starts from the observation that Habermas's claim that moral debate has the capacity to transform our moral understandings,[49] and argues that Habermas underestimates the value of debate even if it does not consist of competitive reason-giving oriented towards consensus. Moral transformation occurs not so much in our hearing others' arguments as in the ways in which those arguments can 'provide a balance to our possible moral and political insensitivities and blindnesses' (Warnke 1995: 256).

Warnke spells out the possibility of moral insight through debate aimed *not* at consensus, but rather at practical compromise and understandings of difference, in terms of debates in aesthetics. One key example she uses is that of recognising different interpretations of a single novel. If someone reads a novel and interprets it in reading, then she may stand by her interpretation even if she finds that others have understood it quite differently. She might come to see that these other under-standings provide different, perhaps deeper, insights into aspects of the novel, than her own understanding. And her own understanding may be enriched by seeing that there are other meaningful interpretations. Warnke concludes from her analogy that 'the fruitfulness of our discussions are less dependent on the force of the better argument than on the insights into meaning we gain from one another' (Warnke 1995: 256).

I would elaborate this claim, which Warnke makes in terms of aesthetics, in other terms, more closely related to my earlier discussion of the interrelation of personal and political relations (and aspects of relations). Her account of trans-formation makes an implicit association between aesthetic understandings and interpersonal understandings, that are more like acts of attending ethically to the styled expressions of other persons than like assessments of the validity of argu-ments. Warnke describes aesthetic debate as going on between particular persons, where each is attending to the views of others. Such debate is not simply a matter of hearing the logic of an argument, but also involves attending to the views and situation of the speaker in order to make sense of the argument. Understanding comes from attending not only to the arguments, but also to the feelings and the circumstances of people who express them. To extend this point by reference to Chapter Two, discourse designed to reach consensus about which moral norms will be accepted will benefit from empathy among participants as well as from logic.[50]

Warnke's account of political debate acknowledges, unlike Habermas's, the mutual embeddedness of style and content, including the possibility that stylistic differences may impede understanding. Stylistic misunderstanding might, for example, result in one or more parties to political debate failing to carry through with actions discursively agreed upon. Such misunderstandings are common enough in agreements in ordinary language, if for example an agreement rests upon undetected equivocation. Habermas could himself recognise such a contin-gency, but would probably treat it as a distortion of the speech situation in question.[51] And while an explanation appealing to distortions may be satisfactory in accounting for misunderstandings, it cannot account for the possibility that the style of a contribution to an ISS, rather than the argument alone, can make a beneficial contribution to the transformation of understandings and the production of a consensus.

The particular ways in which styled performances are productive or inhibitory of mutual understandings are not addressed, and indeed cannot be addressed so long as persuasion by rational argument is the avowed goal of an ideal speech situation. Styled performances (both discursive and non-discursive) might further mutual understandings and create further possibilities for compromise and cooperation, in CMC as outside it, in ways that idealised rational debate cannot. Equally, that stylistic misunderstandings may impede coordination of action does not appear as a possibility in Habermas's discourse ethics. Communicative action cannot then account for ways in which styles of performance may systematically upset or distort communication among people, despite good intentions, even while they are in the process of trying to spell out just what stylistic differences obtain among them.[52]

6.3.5 Other limitations of discourse ethics as an ideal for CMC

I have set out above two limitations of Habermas's discourse ethics, both of which tell against any attempt to apply the theory to political CMCs, the problems facing ISSs in pluralistic societies, and the role of communication functions besides competitive reason-giving in furthering political discussion. I now want to focus on two further important limitations to discourse ethics, which also prompt moves towards taking working compromise and understanding, rather than consensus and justification, as the goals of ethical or political debate.[53] First, Habermas's use of the transcendental argument for universal pragmatics means that, for him, there do indeed exist universally accepted rules of argumentation and validation. He must thereby assume that performative style does not affect others' judgements of the cogency of claims. Given the view that style is an irredeemably significant aspect of interpersonal communications, this assumption is not acceptable.

The problem has been raised most urgently by Iris Marion Young, who argues against Habermas that his supposedly impartial procedural model has exclusionary implications. It privileges 'the dispassionate', 'the educated', and those who feel that they have a right to speak (Young 1997b: 64):

> Norms of assertiveness, combativeness and speaking by the contest rules are powerful evaluators or silencers of speech in many actual speaking situations where culturally differentiated and social unequal groups live together.
>
> (Young 1997b: 124)

Young also argues that discourse ethics encourages an agonistic model of deliberation, which values competition and victory. She cites particular social groups (Hispanics, women, the less well-educated and the less confident and competitive members of a culture) who would not benefit from a procedural model of the sort which Habermas proposes.

In Young's terms, the conditions of debate in political CMC particularly favour certain political groups. Depending on the forum, these might be English-speakers, men, people who have access to CMC, those with higher education, and so on. In Roza Tsagarousianou's study of the Pericles network in Athens, for example, it was shown that those in management positions in the public service made vastly more use of CMC democratic fora than did any other group (accounting for about 40 per cent of all uses of the fora). The majority of these workers (65 per cent) were male (Tsagarousianou 1998a: 44). Certain groups, such as homeless people and the aged were specifically encouraged to participate in Network Pericles and did so, with some degree of success.[54]

These objections highlight a difficulty for Habermas's supposedly universal procedural model. The question here is whether some of its key requirements, such as universality of claims to normative rightness, can themselves avoid attracting the status of non-universal cultural norms. Young's version of this difficulty assumes that ideals of clarity, generality and so on are, in effect, 'arbitrary cultural norms', in that they serve no purpose other than to reinforce the privilege of a select group of 'white middle-class males'.

Habermas goes to some lengths to avoid this criticism. For one thing, he has frequently stated that the ISS is indeed an ideal situation. Almost no ordinary case of discourse will live up to the ideal. And the sorts of cases that Young describes, where some groups are precluded from expressing their needs and interests, do not satisfy Habermas's criteria for an ISS either. They fail as examples of ideal speech situations, because some groups' views are not considered from their own perspectives.[55] Habermas can, I think, avoid this version of the problem of difference.

There is a second form that the problem of difference, pointed to by Young, might take, relating specifically to the range of performative styles of participants in speech situations. We can agree with Habermas on the importance of adherence to a canon of informal logic in discourse, and yet still hold that there is more than one style of presenting claims and arguing for them. The second form of the difficulty of difference occurs when one particular style of presenting and arguing for claims, out of the many that exist, is privileged in debate over the others by those who already have positions of power and authority.

This version of the difficulty does not tell directly against the codes of informal logic to which Habermas believes participants in discourse should hold themselves, since it accepts that privileging of one style of presenting and arguing for claims over others is indeed a distortion of the speech situation. Rather, it shows a practical weakness in Habermasian proceduralism, in that there is no remedy within the ideal speech situation for a distortion such as this. Those whose style of presenting and arguing for claims is undervalued will, by virtue of this undervaluation, have difficulty in pointing out that their styles (and hence their arguments) are undervalued.

Interesting support for this version of the difficulty of difference can be found in work on discourse analysis, by Deborah Tannen and others (Tannen 1984b). Tannen's findings suggest that what are essentially different styles of conversation are often interpreted instead as unreasonableness. For example, rapid speech may be interpreted by someone accustomed to slow speech as expressing a high level of emotion in the speaker; voluble disagreement may be interpreted by a timid or easily-inflamed participant as verbal violence or coercion. While such variations do not necessarily require us to reject Habermas's discourse ethics as unworkable, they certainly complicate the claim that a consensual conclusion can be brought about in any simple way by the 'justification of claims to normative rightness with reasons', because it brings home the breadth of what might, to different styles of reasoners, count as a justification.

Deborah Tannen's conclusions suggest that Young's criticism of Habermas on the grounds that his procedure privileges the privileged is one that can be levelled at any procedural model of ethics (including those which stipulate that no dis-privileged person be discriminated against). So, for example, a procedural ethics that attempted to overcome privilege by allowing women or minority groups longer time to speak, cannot be guaranteed of achieving its aim. It might, instead, work against these disprivileged groups by singling them out as in some way 'incompetent'. We are led to the conclusion that, regardless of the procedures used, those who are in a position of greater power in a relation may, if they choose, and often without conscious choice, have the better end of bargains. Inequalities may be perpetuated whatever procedure is used, and may occur even when deliberate and concerted efforts are made to compensate for the effects of uneven distribution of privileges.

Thus, awareness of the ways in which particular procedures may tend to reproduce particular inequalities is essential to any attempt to minimise such inequalities. It can, for example, highlight the way in which assumptions of *particular* similarities tend to normalise characteristics and ideals that are not representative. Unfortunately, Habermas's account of persons focuses, as I have described above, on persons' common status as rational deliberators seeking consensus through argumentation, so obscuring the possibility of there being other, productive, ways in which individuals may engage in political discussion. This focus on a *particular* commonality leaves out significant differences among persons and groups of persons, for instance in the ways they engage in discussion and present arguments. This in turn leads to neglect of the ways in which some differences tend to mirror and reproduce inequalities. Accounts of political CMC that accept Habermas's account of the ISS are consequently at risk of overlooking both stylistic differences in political negotiation generally, and the particular role of styles in enabling and inhibiting CMC political deliberation.

For example, Habermas makes the optimistic presupposition that it is straightforward for a spectator to separate logic (convincing) and rhetoric (persuading), and for debaters in an ISS to detect instances of the latter. Under a theory that treats the style of performances as inseparable from aspects of interpersonal understanding, no such distinction between logic and rhetoric can be made. Rhetoric must be identified with styled performance, whether that performance is intended to deceive, or persuade, or not intended to do either, is constitutive of people's selves. No verbal presentation of an argument to an audience is unstyled.

In *Moral Consciousness and Communicative Action*, discourse in an ISS is not taken to be hermeneutic in the sense specified by earlier works such as *Knowledge and Human Interests*. In *Moral Consciousness and Communicative Action*, Habermas employs the informal logic of argumentation, wherein the sincerity of someone's claims is assessed by reference to their subsequent behaviour. In his view, the logical 'core' of a claim is overlaid by what might be described as stylistic 'ornament'. If such ornament introduces confusion into debate, this can be clarified by further questioning. Such a model, by privileging the universal-reasoning component of someone's expressions over stylistic components, must treat non-verbal and stylistic expressive phenomena, not only as 'linked to the responses of the human body', but also as irrelevant to the universal-reasoning component. Given that, as I have argued, style is intrinsic to persons' performances, and indeed constitutes one of the levels on which people come to understand one another, Habermas's narrow focus on persons as constituted by the commonality of reasoning capacities must be seen as a limitation of discourse ethics.

This limitation is particularly significant for the value of discourse ethics as an ideal for CMC. Many Habermasian CMC theorists, notably Charles Ess, adopt Habermas's account largely unmodulated and as such import it into the environment of CMC largely unchanged. Such accounts of political CMC will already presuppose a Habermasian 'thin' understanding of human beings as oriented towards consensus through competitive giving of reasons. Habermas's focus on argumentation, his later focus on the linguistic requirements for communication rather than on the hermeneutic account of communicative action employed in *Knowledge and Human Interests*, and his exclusive focus on deontological and justificatory aspects of ethics have meshed firmly with certain obvious characteristics of CMC. I identified some of these characteristics as technical constraints of the medium in Chapter Four. Notably in the context of this chapter, CMC is (at least currently) text-based, excluding communication through nuances of bodily communication, intonation, and enunciation.

Habermasian discussions of political CMC identify the linguistic focus of CMC as making the possibility of achieving an ISS more realistic in CMC than elsewhere. Two main arguments are given. The first is that the bodily absence brings with it the absence of non-verbal interference or 'noise' from the scene of debate, and thereby focuses participants' attention more firmly on the matter of reaching consensus over norms; the second is the argument that the types of discrimination that distort speech situations, based on personal attributes more easily detectable in face-to-face conversation (such as gender or race), occur less frequently in CMC.

But, to the first argument, it is not clear that bodily absence rules out all types of interference, although it may rule out some. Stylistic misunderstandings, as I have argued, characterise CMC as much as they do other forms of social interaction, and can certainly interfere with the reaching of consensus. In the case of some text acts, whose form in face-to-face interaction involves non-verbal performances that are conditions for the felicity of the act, or that add to the solemnity and significance of the act, bodily absence may increase interference.

To the second argument, while there is indeed substantial evidence that use of

CMC can allow the normally less confident to contribute more confidently (Korenman and Wyatt 1996, Colomb and Simutis 1996), the matter is a complex one, and one that requires on-going empirical investigation rather than resolution a priori. Against the claims of Habermasians such as Ess, it is the case that text-only political CMC is perfectly compatible with a Youngian 'tyranny of style' of the kind discussed above; deliberate and unwitting uses of power can both distort a CMC speech situation. Ess indeed acknowledges the dominance of 'overt sexism' and the predominance of 'the covert privileging of male discourse' in CMC. So it is not clear that CMC *is* more likely to produce an ISS than other political fora.

Ess has a further argument. He holds that power imbalances (not specifically stylistic ones) are only produced if such dominance occurs in a CMC plebiscite, in which libertarian norms are held:

> Briefly, the plebiscite conception seems to entail a problematic information flood and tolerance for all forms of communicative behaviour, and hence cannot justify efforts to curb certain kinds of discourse in the name of democratising communications. By contrast, the framework of the discourse ethic and its more communitarian and pluralist conception of democracy would moderate the information flood in ways reflecting current practice.
> (Ess 1996: 216)

The plebiscite, *unlike* smaller groups, is 'potentially *anti*democratic, as it allows for individual voices to be overridden by power, whether in the form of aggression by a few or in the form of the "tyranny of the majority" ' (Ess 1996: 218). In pluralist CMC, by contrast, Ess holds that political CMC occurs among smaller and self-selecting communities, which thereby may institute netiquette and avoid power differentials.

I agree with Ess that a plebiscite characterised by robust freedom of speech faces the difficulties that Ess describes. I would also agree with the empirical claim that political CMC currently consists of something very close to Nancy Fraser's account of contemporary public political discourse as a number of (sometimes) overlapping public spheres, some with more power than others (Fraser 1994a).[56] However, I do not agree that pluralistic CMC made up of small groups will avoid the problems of power and aggression characteristic of large groups.

Ess cites Susan Herring's studies of CMC in defence of his position. But nothing in Herring's work suggests that CMC groups smaller than a plebiscite are *less* prey to power imbalances. Herring's discussion is of precisely the sort of CMC group (small, self-selecting, characterised by an emergent self-regulating netiquette) (Herring 1996b: 115–20) that Ess describes as part of a 'pluralist democracy', and shows that power imbalances are typical of such groups. Other quantitative studies of feminist discussion groups, such as that of Kira Hall, also suggest that even small self-selecting discussion groups may perpetuate power imbalances, despite their employment of netiquette (for instance Hall 1996: 156–8). Ess's account of the role of discourse ethics, then, displaces power imbalances and stylistic differences into large political CMC fora, although they are characteristic of small and large fora alike.

The overlap between Habermas's 'thin' account of persons and the technical constraints, such as textuality, imposed by CMC have, I think, conspired to hide the difficulties characteristic of interpersonal communication in CMCs. I argued earlier that Habermas's focus on logical argumentation oriented to consensus as a way of resolving normative disagreements overlooks the ethical possibilities and benefits of types of speech that are not logic-based reasons for claims (such as narrative or agonistic discussion without consensus). In this section, I have argued that a focus on persons as logical arguers overlooks the significance of stylistic differences, be they productive of cooperation or of misunderstandings.

These concerns can be fruitfully linked with the analysis in the first part of this chapter, of the connections between personal relations (and aspects of relations) in CMC, and political relations (and aspects of relations) in CMC. I observed there that stylistic misunderstandings will be somewhat less prevalent in political CMC relations (or aspects of relations). Since political relations are ones in which there is comparatively little focus on understanding others' selves through their expressive styles, there is also likely to be less at stake in stylistic misunderstandings. This is a promising start for discourse ethics and its focus on consensus rather than understanding. However, if we recognise that Habermas's account of discourse overlooks important aspects of selves and the role of interpersonal communication, then it becomes clear that Habermas overlooks just that level of communication (the stylistic) in which understanding and misunderstanding are crucially determining of ethical and political cooperation.

In short, the textuality of CMC does not make it a medium *more* suitable to Habermasian discourse ethics than face to face or representative political debate. Stylistic misunderstandings may occur in political discussion in CMC as in personal relations in that medium, and will not be ruled out by small fora with netiquette any more than they would be by small sized social gatherings. Further, as noted above, the aim of discourse ethics to produce consensus on moral norms among all those affected, produces, in pluralistic societies and intercultural debate, highly abstract moral norms. The continued existence of multiple 'thick' conceptions of the good means that, in some cases at least, the development of highly abstract moral norms achieves only half the work of finding mutually acceptable solutions to practical ethical problems.

6.4 CMC politics: strengths and uses

6.4.1 Taking up CMC for political activities

In previous sections I have argued that political relations (and aspects of relations) place teleological priority on political goals and activities, in which communication is comparatively instrumental, and in which less is at stake in terms of ethical aspects of relations. Given this proviso, CMC may, by virtue of its comparative speed and reach, further political relations and immensely increase the scope of political activity, both formal and informal. However, to the extent that political relations also involve interpersonal relations (or aspects of relations), the constraints of CMC on friendships explored in Chapter Five may also work against the maintenance of political community and the sustaining of political action, whether at the national, trans-national, or international level. My analysis of Habermas's discourse ethics tends to support this conclusion, although it also highlights the capacity of styled textual performances to further mutual understanding in CMC.

I now want to move on to a more positive appreciation of the political possibilities of CMC. I have explored the risks of stylistic misinterpretation, and the workings of power in large and small CMC fora alike. But we still have good reason to value political discussion, even with its attendant risks. I want in particular to draw attention to the political potential of CMC to produce, not an ISS, but a proliferation of smaller political discussions, some global in their reach, all less than comprehensive in their membership. These discussions, which are easily accessible, are ones in which large numbers of people may become accustomed to thinking about political aims, and engaging in political activity.

I first consider the sorts of political uses to which CMC is characteristically put, so as to show how CMC is supportive of political engagements and activities. The variety of takings-up can be shown in a quick comparison of different political organisations' uses of CMC. I follow the general scheme of James Rosenau and David Held, articulated in Held 1995 and Rosenau 1998.[57] I then explore the capacity of CMC to lead people *into* political engagement and participation, at both national- and global-levels.

At present many large state-based political parties use CMC extensively. It is employed as an administrative tool, for newsletters, fund-raising, and so on.[58] But large political parties also continue to conduct a fair amount of discussion and activity at a local and face-to-face level, and they continue to use other media, particularly print and television for their campaigns and press releases. The degree of uptake varies tremendously from country to country, in line with the degree of technological diffusion, and varieties of assimilation characteristic of each.[59] For example, in the US major political parties have large interactive web-sites. Occasionally, political figures conduct public on-line fora.

Civic society organisations (CSOs) with a political focus make use of CMCs in various ways, and to various extents. For example, political groups whose focus is primarily on a single state or country may use CMC as part of their coordination and information-sharing strategies (saving time, photocopying and travel). Many groups use CMC simply to keep in touch, and to share information and coordinate their activities within the organisation. Some use it to make decisions about policy and strategy. Many use web-sites as a form of public presence, as an addition to newsletters. Many CSOs are now able to coordinate with each other in global campaigns in ways that have previously been impossible.

Individuals, whether or not they belong to mainstream political organisations or CSOs, use CMC to present their positions to others, to share political views, and argue about politics. Such debate occurs in the informal public sphere, although many of the small group debates that are conducted in this manner in CMC are among groups who never contact one another; so in a sense, there is no *single* public sphere but rather a multiplicity of smaller public spheres.[60] However, in line with what I have argued about connections between 'public' and 'private' spheres,

I would like to emphasise the degree to which debate in the informal public sphere *is expressive of and belongs to individuals.* CMC political debate in informal public spheres is debate among people who are not constrained by any explicit set of procedural or teleological guidelines, and who are engaging in discussion with particular others. Such engagements may be between persons who perform textually as themselves, or persons performing quasi-fictive selves, between persons who are anonymous, deonymous, or going under their usual name. Further, personal relations and aspects of relations are not ruled out in informal public spheres, and are not usually considered to prejudice the debate that goes on, as the 'traditional model' described above would have it. Such debates more closely resemble Georgia Warnke's aesthetic-political appreciation than Habermas's discourse, and require of political participants some degree of insight into the selves of other debaters in order to unpack the significance of others' expressions, even when those expressions relate to political issues or moral norms.

Drawing on this brief list, there are several types of activity that are characteristic of CMCs as used for political communication. First, there is a range of political CMCs that belongs more precisely to formal politics, or the sort of political activity in which political organisations engage as united bodies. CMC is useful within organisations for policy formation and strategic planning, both of which are varieties of decision-making that go on in all political organisations, from the most local to the most global. The difference with CMC is that, of course, participants can engage in synchronous political debate and comparatively rapid decision-making despite physical separation, and can coordinate activities at a global level. While such coordination has been possible before now in formal politics, CMC makes it comparatively more affordable and comparatively more inclusive.

CMC can be used by members of a political organisation to raise citizens' awareness of an issue or an organisation. This is common both for formal political entities and for CSOs. For example, the Republican Party in the United States maintains a range of web-sites using advanced programming to attract the attention of politically apathetic US citizens, in what amounts to an attempt to woo them through technology rather than policy.[61] Greenpeace has also tried such tactics, and in ways that are far distant from the rational argument characteristic of the Habermasian ISS. (See the discussion of Greenpeace tactics in Prins and Sellwood 1998.) The Sandanistas in Nicaragua used a web-site as a means of alerting those outside their own country to the oppression and censorship they were facing. Political CMC as part of an organisation might also include attempts to garner support for an organisation, or for an issue, by soliciting donations, cooperative help or membership.

Second, political CMC can be used by political organisations to disseminate their own reports to media, so as to avoid 'media filtering'. This sort of use is avowed by members of both Republican and Democrat political parties in Rash's study. The cases of the Sandanistas, and of minority groups such as women in Afghanistan, are similar, in that without CMC their circumstances and cause would be almost unheard of outside their country. There remains in such cases the question of the relation of political communication and subsequent action, but the types of political performative inscription that I have already mentioned, such as petitions, pleas and promises may have some effect. For example, numerous petitions were circulated concerning the effects of US armed intervention in Afghanistan following terrorist attacks in the US in September 2001.[62] Many CSOs have web-sites that allow people to sponsor children or to contribute aid to countries in need;[63] even some commercial web-sites contribute a portion of advertising revenue to charitable causes.[64] In other words, the uses of CMC as a medium of communication open the way for many more citizens to become politically aware, and to participate in political action, alone or jointly, textually-mediated or in other fora.

Third, CMC can be used for general discussion of political issues. In Habermasian terms, CMC enables, not an ideal speech situation with participants oriented to consensus, but a public sphere in which political (as well as more broadly ethical) issues are discussed. CMC contains, to employ Ruth Lister's distinction, both formal and informal politics. Many discussion groups, for example, are interlinked by common membership. Formal public spheres are those fora set up for official opinion gathering, used by people involved in political activity through political parties. The textual performances of informal public spheres would include opinion sharing, opinion gathering, opinion formation, as well as information gathering and sharing. It might include informal discussions of all sorts, and discussion of peripheral (perhaps non-political) subjects, from theoretical or utopian perspectives.

Finally, CMC allows people who are not part of any formal political organisation or movement to engage in and coordinate political actions, in ways that have not been so accessible in the past.[65] This can be done very rapidly, and at a distance at a cost affordable to many political organisations. For example, Greenpeace uses CMC to coordinate people who are far apart to act in concert. Greenpeace is thereby able to organise elaborate international campaigns against multi-national organisations who would otherwise face no concerted opposition (Prins and Sellwood 1998). CMCs are also used to coordinate action among political organisations. In various campaigns to halt World Trade Organisation meetings in recent years, CSOs and unaffiliated individuals communicated via CMC to coordinate the action. Individual members of these CSOs, dispersed around the world, were able to coordinate global action without undue cost, by using CMC mailing lists, discussion groups and e-mail (Cohen 2001).

Examples such as these suggest that CMC, by providing fora for discussing information and means of expanding networks of coordinated action, provides easy opportunities to become engaged in political activity. For example, people who are concerned for the state of the environment may find in CMC possibilities for engaging in political action in the pursuit of the preservation of the environment. I want to expand on this idea. The political possibilities of CMC are more than simply a continuation of political activity by other means. CMC allows even those not engaged in formal or informal politics chances to raise their political awareness and to develop political skills such as the capacity to negotiate. I explore these possibilities below.

6.4.2 *Political benefits of CMC participation*

In terms of the benefits of political participation on-line, to follow an argument made by Carole Pateman in *Democracy and Participation* (Pateman 1970), there are many opportunities even in non-political CMC to engage in discussions that are *de facto* political. Drawing on Rousseau, Mill and Cole, Pateman argues that self-organisation in workplaces is a valuable way for citizens to become politically competent. Pateman begins from the position that political participation is essential to the maintenance of democracy.[66] It is by engaging in politics that people become capable of political action and coordination. However, Mill and Cole move away from Rousseau's position that engagement in formal politics is the only way for persons to develop political skills and capacities. Mill and Cole both stress the opportunities afforded by workplaces, in which people gather together and engage in coordinated action, for collective decision-making and self-governance, and hence for the development of political skills, even in those who have no contact with formal politics.

Many CMC discussions, even those that are not political in their focus, afford possibilities for developing political skills and capacities, in that they are concerned with procedural issues of how persons comport themselves in CMC. I will take up Pateman's argument to suggest that even the informal public spheres of CMC discussion groups that do *not* specifically embrace political subjects or activities may still generate possibilities for citizens to engage in and gain practice at political engagement.

Given that the goals of political CMC are many and dispersed, and that the fora in which these goals are debated, formulated and (sometimes) implemented are many and difficult to assess, I want to focus on an important use for political CMC, that is the building of political awareness and skills through engaging in the practice of politics via CMC. Under the category of political skills I include skills such as negotiation, consideration of the relation of one's own desires and those of others in a political organisation or entity, and the capacity to cooperate without consensus. I have chosen this issue because it suggests a sense in which CMC opens up possibilities for politics that were not previously available. Certainly CMC political activity covers similar areas to those covered by conventional politics, namely general discussion of goals and values, policy formation, canvassing, communication of information and advertising, and some forms of actions, such as performative inscriptions. But if CMC discussion groups, through their various technical constraints and limitations on mutual understanding, prompt participants into negotiation leading to collective self-determination, then the political capacities of CMC are both unique and valuable.

I want to specify that political CMC is something that is *accessible* to anyone who has a computer and internet connection. This means that, after the initial outlay on the equipment, political CMC may be easier to engage in than other forms of political activity, that require travel, scheduling of meetings at particular times, and physical presence. CMC allows those who are otherwise too tired or too busy, physically incapacitated, or too intimidated, to engage in political discussion and activity. Further, CMC has the potential to enable participation in political activity on two levels, one fairly obvious, the other less obvious. I have already referred to the level at which those who have a stake in those issues not already firmly on political agendas, do not have the same ease of access as the educated and (comparatively) wealthy do to formal politics. By increasing the accessibility of political activity in the informal political sphere, CMC allows those without easy access to formal politics the opportunity to engage in political activity and to learn the skills involved. The other level of the problem of participation that CMC addresses, elaborated by some recent feminist writers on behalf of women and minorities, is that the whole range of activities that people learn by becoming involved in politics are less accessible for women and for many minority groups. For example, women tend to attain the higher levels in political associations in smaller numbers than men, because, taken collectively, they have fewer chances than men to develop their abilities. Such arguments can also be made, as Young, Fraser and Lister do, in the cases of minority groups such as immigrant groups, the disabled and those in poverty (Young 1990a, 1990b, 1997b; Fraser 1997; Lister 1997).

The capacity of CMC to allow many to participate in political activity and engage in political relations may be at least one new avenue for allowing those who have traditionally under-engaged in political activity, such as women, minority groups and the poor, to engage in it now, if they so desire. Furthermore, given the capacity of CMC to support performative inscriptions, and thereby various forms of direct political action (such as petitions, promises and other commitments) as well as debate and resolution of dispute, the range of computer-mediated political activities open to women and minority groups is substantial. These capacities will be realised, of course, only within the on-going constraints that many of the global poor and disadvantaged are still illiterate, and that many poor people even within wealthy nations have few prospects of regular and affordable access to CMC in the near future.

With reference specifically to political activism, while physical forms of political activism such as marching and blockading are all but impossible via CMC, the medium gives citizens enormous resources for *organising* various forms of civil disobedience, at national- and global-levels. It also provides a range of *alternatives* to physical forms of activism, including on-line petitions and e-mails to political candidates and office-holders at national- and international-levels, that are less likely to cause harm to persons or damage to property.

To sum up this section, CMC offers many possibilities for collective political action, and its support for performative inscriptions means that the medium is far more than an area for discussion. However, as I have emphasised above, there are political possibilities open to participants in CMC even if they are not engaging in CMC for the sake of political ends. Conflicts and stylistic misunderstandings often result in debate about processual issues, and often elicit negotiation and collective self-determination by those participants involved in such debate.

If we agree with Pateman that political abilities such as the capacity to negotiate, and the development of a sense of political involvement are important for citizens' ability to participate in formal or informal politics, then CMC's tendency to produce debates about procedure may be considered valuable, even if it does spring from misunderstanding or disagreement. We can, I think, conclude that CMC discussion can contribute to the development of citizens' political capacities, and to their readiness to engage in formal or informal political activity themselves. The uses of the medium cannot be overstressed.

6.5 Conclusions

Political possibilities for CMC are at once tantalising and indefinite. As participatory democracy becomes feasible at local- or even national-level, the global communicative possibilities of CMC (not only the political ones) have already been taken up by many people, and are, in some cases, fragmenting national culture as much as supporting or contributing to it. (See for instance Hall 1991.)

CMC offers its users a means of keeping in touch that is faster and more efficient than letters, cheaper and more inclusive than telephones. As such, it has allowed people to become politically engaged and organised. It has been used by some local and state governments who value political participation by constituents, to further political engagement, as well as to provide a cheap and accessible method of publishing government documents. The openness of early CMC culture has opened up new fora for political debate among citizens (and across cultures).

To some extent CMC political relations are supported by personal relations conducted in CMC as well as off-line. I have highlighted the importance of personal relations, both for forming and maintaining the values of the society in which political activity is to go forward. Nevertheless, as I have argued in previous chapters, personal relations are limited in important ways in CMC, by textuality, temporal peculiarities of the medium, and by the physical (and often cultural) distance between participants. So, to the extent that political relations are intertwined with and dependent on personal relations, political relations in CMC will be affected by the limitations on interpersonal possibilities in CMC.

This limitation becomes more serious once we observe the importance of styled performances in political relations as well as in personal relations. I make this point generally, and then in relation to Habermas's ideal speech situation, which has been taken by some theorists to be a model for CMC political discourse.

In the fourth section of this chapter I looked at the strengths of CMC for engaging people in political activity. I have not argued specifically that capacity for political organisation and self-determination are essential to the maintenance of democracy, but I accepted such arguments as put by others, as the background for discussion of political CMC and political aspects of non-political CMC. I have explored the capacity of the forms of political relations common even in non-political CMC to develop participants' capacities for political activity, cooperation and organisation. Even in the absence of a single public sphere in which all voices can be heard, CMC's tendency to encourage political engagement and activity is likely to make increasing numbers of CMC-using citizens competent in political activity. Those forms of CMC that are explicitly focused around political subjects have, in addition, the capacity to encourage political participation through the comparative ease of coordination and of some performative inscriptions, such as petitions and use of political web-sites.

Conclusion

In discussing ethical issues in CMC my project has been to provide a theoretical framework for considering how people express themselves and are understood in textual CMC. Rather than focusing on the larger patterns of social engagements in CMC, as do many utopian and dystopian accounts of social worlds affected by new media, I considered CMC largely as a medium of exchange between particular persons. I looked at it through the framework of a theory of style. Understanding the styles in which persons perform (both verbally and non-verbally) is an integral aspect of our understanding of those persons, another way in which we learn about them. We may learn of others' beliefs and desires from what they say about those beliefs and desires. These aspects of others' selves are verbally accessible, articulable, and broadly reproducible. Less articulable, less reproducible and less neatly correlated with our usual attributions of character or personal identity, style gives no direct window onto a person's thoughts, or beliefs or desires. Instead style shows rather than telling. And what it shows of a person's self often cannot easily be told, although it may be quite perspicuous in itself. What florid speech tells us about a person cannot easily be specified; what Samuel Johnson's spoken style said about his character is hard to pin down; what a woman's decision to describe herself as a man, in an on-line interaction, tells us about her is equally hard to specify. And yet there is significance in style. As I have argued, there is moral value in attending to others' styles, insofar as style may be expressive of the self in ways more subtle than verbally expressed beliefs and desires.

In textual CMC, therefore, the expressive capacities of styled text are immediately marked out as being of moral interest. Style, of both verbal and non-verbal performances, is expressive of self. But CMC is textual, and does not convey the corporeal aspect of dialogue in full presence. Hence my case that textuality, whether in CMC or elsewhere, limits the expressive range of the self. This is not to say that textuality does not have immense expressive capacities; I illustrated some of these in Chapters Two and Five, in discussions of 'techniques of spontaneity' and of Erasmian absent presence. I did not argue that all CMC expressions, being textual, are deliberately voiced, or that undeliberate intentional stances are undetectable in CMC. It would be a grotesque mistake to identify language with deliberate expression, or to treat non-verbal performance as entirely undeliberated expression. My point was, rather, that styled non-verbal performances are part of a person's lifestyle as a whole. They have expressive capacities independent of expressive styled verbal performances. Understanding of styled non-verbal performances may indeed contribute to our understanding of another's self as a whole. Hence their absence from CMC constitutes a limit on stylistic expressiveness on-line, and on understanding others' lifestyles in that medium.

In Chapters Two and Three I explored the ramifications of these limitations for various ethical and social aspects of communication. In Chapter Two I discussed the nature of empathy and its role in CMC. Edith Stein's account of empathy provided me with the groundwork necessary for spelling out the workings of empathy. I also extended Stein's account to deal with the experience of empathy through text. I examined first the role of language in specifying the objects of a person's experience, and giving more particular detail about the nature of that experience than could be gleaned by observation alone. Empathy without an understanding of the object of its experience would, I argued, be limited indeed. Study of textual expression also indicates that texts can move their readers to empathy with the absent writer, although some degree of abstraction, and a degree of trust in the honesty of the writer are required for this empathy to be ethically valuable.

Chapter Three approached the question of what sort of activities are possible in textual exchanges such as CMC, considering first dialogue in text, and then what I called 'text acts' or changes in worldly conditions effected by the use of words. I considered Paul Ricoeur's account of textual distanciation, in which he claimed that textuality precludes dialogue. I agreed that texts may be affected by distanciation, but that its effects were contingent, rather than essential to texts. I located the possibility of dialogue in text in the exchange of multiple texts, rather than, as Ricoeur does, in the relation of reader to a single text. This conclusion was reached without the need to engage with the more complex question of dialogicity within single texts. I concluded that text acts are, likewise, possible social acts, although the degree to which we can accept them to be felicitous depends on the degree to which we believe performatives generally to be constituted by conventions. If, as I accepted, most performatives are recognisable social practices (if not conventions in the stronger Austinian sense), then on-line textuality may in some cases work against the felicity of text acts. Insofar as textuality limits stylistic expressiveness, and consequently limits or distorts interpersonal understandings, the conditions for mutual trust will be eroded in CMC. Our capacity to recognise inscriptions as examples of types of performatives may also be eroded. These limitations are, however, comparatively small given the immense social possibilities available in CMC if indeed it allows both full dialogue and the many varieties of social action embodied in text acts.

In Chapter Four I turned aside from the question of the moral possibilities of CMC and instead considered the technical constraints of the medium. To some extent this chapter brought together themes and issues raised indirectly in earlier chapters. I considered the technical qualities of CMC under four main headings, those of machine-dependency, variable temporality, textuality, and the multiplication of inhabited places. I took all four of these constraints to be at once limiting and enabling, though the implications of the last remain profoundly ambiguous.

It remained then to consider particular types of relationships and their configurations in CMC. I first considered friendship and other intimate relations, in Chapter Five, and then political relations, in Chapter Six. Friendships and intimate relations I considered to be strongly affected by their instauration in CMC. Certain aspects of friendship, such as the value of mutual analysis, and perceptive criticism, and that of spending time in each other's company, are limited in a textual environment, although, as the case of Erasmian friendships in letters indicated, textually-mediated friendships can be mutually sustaining in a variety of circumstances. I noted that the strength of CMC for friendships could be best described as giving absent friends another way of keeping in touch, but that friendship itself was best and most fully developed in companionable relations.

Political relations are, I argued, less affected by the technical constraints of CMC. Style is still an important consideration in political relations (and aspects of relations), but less as the expression of a self valuable entirely for its own sake, and more as the expression of a self performing a role in a political enterprise. Certainly, understanding someone's style, like knowing them personally, may be valuable within political relations (and not just morally valuable, since we may also value insights into the character and intentionality of those whom we do not like or admire). Yet there is less at stake in stylistic misunderstandings in political relations (and aspects of relations), because the understanding of the person as another self does not have teleological priority in such circumstances.

One of the points that I developed in Chapter Six is that, in terms of its political possibilities, the reach of CMC more than compensates for its limited expressive capacity. In political relations (and aspects of relations), understanding other persons' selves may yet retain some intrinsic value, and it certainly has instrumental value. This much is indicated by the intertwining of personal and political aspects of relations that I noted as characteristic of sociality generally. But the political goals served by understanding others' selves through attention to their styled performances, such as the coordination of many people organised towards a generally accepted goal or goals, are themselves extremely well served by the medium. CMC allows large numbers of people to discuss political issues, and to coordinate actions at a distance in ways that are of immense political significance.

I discussed some ways in which CMC is important in achieving political goals, such as the coordinated campaigns by CSOs and individuals against actions by trans-national corporations and international bodies that are not, effectively, accountable to the people of any single nation. In such cases stylistic confusion still leads to misinterpretations, but there tends to be less at stake in stylistic misunderstandings within political relations (and aspects of CMC relations) than personal, because understanding persons was not taken to be a good in itself in political relations (and aspects of relations). Thus CMC affords, I concluded, significant opportunities for establishing and maintaining political relations (and aspects of relations).

It is in relation to the political capacities of CMC, I believe, that further research into style in CMC will be of most value. Once users of CMC recognise the extent to which understandings are established, maintained and influenced by persons' styles, we will be in a better position to take into account the workings of style. We will be able to make the most of the insight that others' styles give us into the intentional structure of their performances. We will also have a means of understanding others' performances (both verbal and non-verbal) in ways more subtle than as fully deliberate expressions of consciously deliberated beliefs, intentions or desires. This will allow, for instance, greater tolerance of others' expressions than is currently characteristic of CMC exchanges, in which even offhand remarks, even remarks modified by some chance technical failure, are easily taken to be deliberate insults. In view of the possibility of text acts, we are in a position to take seriously the transformative powers of communication on-line.

Style is, of course, only one aspect of the myriad problems and possibilities raised by global political action. Other issues to be considered are those of governance, of the value and practicability of global participatory politics. The question of equity of access to CMC as a political medium is also an immensely important issue, nowhere less than in terms of global political activity. Numerous organisations, including many CSOs and the World Bank, are currently attempting to address the lack of access to CMC in developing countries, under the rubric of 'bridging the digital divide'. The potential of such projects for encouraging political participation, while sometimes overlooked by their developers, is substantial in developing countries. Questions of the capacity of CMC to facilitate certain types of negative discrimination also need a more thorough treatment than I have been able to give them.

Questions such as these are already engaging a large number of scholars and political analysts, as well as people participating in more general political discussion, and are likely to do so for some time. The pace of technological change continues to be rapid, and political struggles involving CMC continue to multiply. In conclusion, I hope that empirical and conceptual forms of research into CMC will continue to be conducted side by side, and to shed light on each other. And I hope that awareness of the role played by style in interpersonal understanding can contribute to a lessening of confusion and misinterpretation in all forms of CMC.

Notes

Introduction

1   See for instance Castells 1996; or see Austerlic 1999 for an argument that the Internet allows for the establishment of new or hybrid cultures, to the enrichment of all involved.

2   The basis for these preconditions, which I can only foreshadow at this point, will be developed and argued for in Chapter Five.

3   The most thorough analysis of this subject is in Castells 1996. Castells' view is characteristically information-oriented, in that he discusses the flow of information rather than the comportment expressed in such flows. Indeed, he grants explicit priority to information-flow since he sees it as taking on a life almost entirely independent of human concerns. I do not share his views on the effect of increased computerised information flow when it is taken as relevant to the still social and sociable world of e-mail and other electronic forms of interaction.

4   A number of recent large-scale studies confirm this position. The most recent is that of the Virtual Society Research Group, headed by Steve Woolgar (Ward 2000).

5   Bell, Philip and Bell, Roger *Implicated: The United States in Australia*, 1993.

6   Some children, notably the deaf and the mute, do not learn speech as their first language, as they are incapable of doing so. The one cannot apprehend particular spoken words, the other cannot voice words, though she or he may come to understand them. It is significant, however, that these children, if they learn a first language at all, do not learn a written language first, but master either sign-language or lip-reading. Both of these learning experiences, like learning speech, involve being with others and sharing experience of the world with them as a crucial part of learning the language. Neither suggests that text can be a first language for children (Cavell 1979, particularly Chapters Four, 'What a thing is (called)', and Seven, 'Excursus on Wittgenstein's vision of language').

7   Similarly, the televisual media have not always been seen as a desirable presence in the raising of children. Claims that television viewing somehow corrupts or alienates children from the societies in which they live attest to the strongly felt sense of many adults that mediated communication is a poor second to unmediated social activities.

8   http://www.consult.com is a US-based researcher into Internet usage in Australia. They find that, while home internet use is currently increasing by between 20 per cent and 40 per cent a year (in estimate), most people who have Internet access first obtained it through work. Most who have Internet access both at home and at work prefer to use their work connection, because it is faster. It is also worth noting that Internet use distribution is largely limited to those who are either wealthy or working in information industries.

9   Typically it is in Multi-User Dungeons (or MUDs) that orthographic facility is essential. I discuss this issue in some more detail in Chapter Two.

10 Some cultures, more aware of the expressive and communicative role played in social exchanges by non-verbal performance, already show a strong preference for non-textual forms of CMC. On this issue, see Heaton, L. (2001) 'Preserving communication context: virtual workspace and interpersonal space in Japanese CSCW', in C. Ess (ed.) *Culture, Technology, Communication: Towards an Intercultural Global Village*, Albany NY: State University of New York Press: 213–40.
11 People who already know each other before they use CMC clearly have some advantage, in this respect, over those who meet on-line.

Chapter 1: Style and ethics

1 Specifically, relationships in which textually-mediated communication is the only form of contact.
2 Cicero's *De oratore* is perhaps the most famous of such works of rhetoric (Cicero 1948). Others were written by Aristotle, both Senecas, Horace, and Quintillian.
3 See, for instance, Gleason 1995. An enormous number of Classical rhetorical texts survive.
4 Erasmus' *De conscribendis epistolis* [*On writing letters*] treats copiousness as virtuous, as full an expression as possible of one's concern for correspondents. Erasmus 1985. See also Jardine 1993, which contains discussion of the importance of letter-writing for maintaining the social relations that constituted international literary communities, and of the importance of style, as both demonstration of literary mastery and of social sensitivity.
5 This transformation is covered in many works on the history of literary style, such as McIntosh 1998.
6 For a detailed analysis of literary and stylistic techniques used in these novels, see Altman 1982.
7 See, variously, Derrida 1979; Ulmer 1985; Conley 1982: 74–92; McLuhan 1962; Bolter 1991; Lanham, 1993.
8 Lanham is understandably sceptical about the possibility of any definitive account of what constitutes good literary style.
9 He focuses on this topic particularly in the fourth chapter of Lanham 1993, 'The "Q" question'.
10 See for instance, Lang 1990, Chapters One and Two, which discuss genre as an important stylistic aspect of philosophical writing. Chapter Four of the same book gives an analysis of Descartes' *On Method* in the terms set out in Chapters One and Two.
11 This vulnerability of the pure expressive theory of style is already hinted at in Robinson's need to attribute attitudes and emotions *either* to the author of a text, *or* to an authorial voice. That both might appear in a single text immediately endangers the idea of a simple expressivism.
12 Reader-reception theorists, such as Hans Robert Jauss, develop these themes explicitly. See for instance, Jauss 1982.
13 Although this variety may well be understood in terms of the overall style of an expressive individual, it may also be understood in social terms, as expressive of class-membership, role-inhabitation or cultural belonging.
14 This point is made in Goodman 1975.
15 In 'The status of style' Goodman distinguishes style from signature, which includes any aspect of a work that distinguishes it from other works, and may include qualities that are not stylistic, such as the presence of a literal signature. He argues that style is exclusively concerned with the symbolic functioning of a work, or the socially significant aspects of a work, whether these be expressions of emotion, of abstract qualities, or not expressions at all (as in the case of musical style). As symbolic functioning concerns those aspects of a performance or object that are significant

to an audience, the difference between Robinson's individual-expressive account and Goodman's position is the difference between a broadly subjectivist account and a more intersubjective one.

16   Goodman 1975: 810. Note that it is in keeping with his objectivist approach that Goodman does not here treat the variety of possible attributions and perceptions of style as a positive quality. Styles are treated as available to be sought out and identified: 'Styles are normally accessible only to the knowing eye or ear, the tuned sensibility, the informed and inquisitive mind … What we find is heavily dependent on how and what we seek. We fail to see the face in the woods in a child's picture puzzle. We may miss form and feeling as we focus on what is said, or miss what is said as we listen to rhyme and rhythm' (Goodman 1975: 810).

17   If in style there is to be no reference to the expressive intentions of the creator of a work or performance (or indeed to any 'historical biographical, psychological and sociological factors') then Goodman's account prevents us from being able to say anything about why a performer (writer, speaker and so on) does or makes just that performance or object. This approach, the main goal of which is to avoid the simple identification of artistic expression with the picture of an 'artist' deliberately picking styles from a list to express his or her current feelings, thereby prevents us attributing any significance to the intentional (or unintentional) actions of performer or artist. The importance of expressive attitudes can be retained in an account of style, by allowing that they may be less than wholly deliberate, including for example 'expressive' in the sense that someone may give an 'expressive' wave of their hand, without having or being able to say just what that wave expresses.

18   Goodman himself locates the study of style within the larger project of understanding 'the work of art', a matter of gaining 'insight' and 'comprehension of the work', and of works of art in general. As I shall argue presently, this broadly aesthetic project is significantly different from that of understanding style as part of people's comportment, which is both an aspect of engaging in social interaction generally, and of understanding individual people. It is not such a surprise after all that in artistic matters the style of the artist should accede to that of her or his creation.

19   Throughout Chapter One I shall have little to say about structural or poststructural approaches to literature and to style in general. Structuralists hold that authorial intention is irrelevant to the significance of a text. They are concerned with the literary text as closed systems of signifiers, 'a machine producing meaning rather than a vehicle of meaning' (Paulson 1988: 20). I hold, against structuralism, that the dependence of individual verbal productions on a social system of language is compatible with the attribution of those verbal productions to individual performers and writers, and that much of what people see as significant about verbal productions hangs on their belonging to just that performer or writer.

20   The distinction between intended audience and unintended audience is of great importance in a consideration of styled performances within the realm of social interaction. While the possibility of further audiences for a performance or text cannot be ruled out, and while many performances and texts are intended for an audience only very generally conceived, many social interactions, and most correspondences are marked by the performer intending their performance for particular people, and by the audience knowing that this is the case. (For sophisticated examples of such intending, see the discussion of friendships in letters in Chapter Five.)

21   Herder uses the word *Volk*, a term that comprises a people, and is less concerned with geographical boundaries. However, Herder's work does not preclude the existence of groups whose coherence rests at a less than national level, as he supported the preservation of minority and endangered cultural groups. See Herder 1967, or Spencer 1996, for a commentary.

22   See Chapter Two for more detailed discussion.

23   For similar distinctions, see Goodman 1975 and Robinson 1984.

24   The notion of a self-adjudicating community is developed by Robert Brandom (Brandom 1984).

25   This variety, which might be considered as stylistic, is also addressed in Chapter Three, section 3.3.

26   This point has been made famously by Nelson Goodman. His observation is that 'we need not have worried about the difficulty of distinguishing form from content: for that distinction, insofar as it is clear, does not coincide with but cuts across the distinction between what is style and what is not. Style comprises certain characteristic features both of what is said and of how it is said, both of subject and of wording, both of content and of form' (Goodman 1975: 802).

27   The what–how distinction gains its particular plausibility from the assumption of a sharp distinction between matter and manner in writing.

28   So, to illustrate, much of the groundwork of current stylistic analysis has come from aesthetics, particularly literary studies, in which frames of reference are fairly clearly set by the existence of autonomous art objects and quasi-autonomous staged performances.

29   An example is that of mediaeval painting 'in the round' showing several perspectives at once; this style was not remarked on at the time, but was seen during the Renaissance as naive and unrealistic, as it did not show the perspective of a single person; in the 1950s, Mediaeval European painting was given a further interpretation by Heinrich Wolfflin as indicating a different understanding of time.

30   Nicholas Hudson's discussion of the transformation of written English in eighteenth-century England gives vivid examples of the development of written (cultured or formal) styles away from more oral (colloquial or informal) styles during that century. (See Hudson 1994, particularly Chapters Five and Six.)

31   An analogy might be drawn here with the theory of underdetermination of theory by facts, in disciplines such as sociology, in which personality and character types are assigned, and where these classifications identify as salient only certain behaviours and attitudes.

32   Indeed, just as only some of the many frequently occurring nexus of practices crystal-lise into roles or institutions (MacIntyre 1984: 194–7), other, perhaps less obtrusive, stylistic regularities may remain unobserved and untheorised, as in our appreciation of people's styled artistic productions we often pay little or no attention to their personal or lifestyle.

33   That is, a version of expressivism that does not insist that all performances straight-forwardly express the attitudes and emotions of a single individual, or that what people are invariably doing in speaking, writing and performing is intentionally and single-mindedly expressing their attitudes and emotions.

34   See, for example, the discussions of character-attribution in Campbell 1989.

35   So while individual styled performances may shed light on a person's character as a whole, it will be through seeing many such performances that I come to know that person well. The development of character over time likewise cannot be fore-grasped from seeing a single styled performance.

36   And, as might be expected, it is easier to attribute certain styles to animals, than it is to plants, and more difficult again to imagine rocks, or other inanimate objects having a style. In the case of animals, descriptions of cats as possessing particular styles, or the ascription of different styles to dolphins and chimpanzees usually result from a period of living with and 'getting to know' those animals, and learning to differentiate among their various ways of acting. Our tendency, even then, is to treat the behaviour of animals as indicative rather of unreflected-upon biological functions (hunger, the urge to reproduce) rather than as expressive of choices.

37   The treatment of style as rhetorical means of persuasion or affect sees it as something deliberately added to content for effect. Rhetorical treatises of the Renaissance focus on achieving particular effects; Richard Lanham's recent revision of Classical

and later rhetoric (Lanham 1993) substitutes cooperative for persuasive rhetoric but without questioning the identification of style as a chosen means to an affective end. This is not a treatment that I support, particularly because it reaffirms a content-style dichotomy.

38   The connection between style and choice may also be seen in how people understand one another, treating those whom they cannot easily differentiate, or in some cases do not try to differentiate, as lacking both style and autonomy. Whole cultures may be dismissed as having no unique style if little attention is paid to them and their ways of acting. If I perceive a person to be so mentally impaired that they are incapable of reasoned choice, then I am less likely to see their behaviour as styled. Even if they manifest complex behavioural regularities, I am likely to take these as biologically conditioned rather than as manifestations of a individual style, although ongoing familiarity with such a person may change my mind.

39   We may, for example, appeal to a difference of style when we don't wish to attribute responsibility in a disagreement or conflict to either party.

40   While many artefacts are not art objects, I have chosen aesthetics as the focus of this section because style has often been elaborated as a specifically aesthetic concept, often with reference to the artefact as an expressive object.

41   In historical terms, style words were applied to works of art first, and to persons second.

42   Likewise, although style is an aspect of linguistic activity, and is often considered solely in the linguistic domain, it is, I think, better not treated as solely a linguistic phenomenon. Language-use consists of verbal expressions used within the constructions and constraints of overlapping differentiated social practices of the many communities in which each of us lives. Consequently, styled language is best seen as part of styled social activity more generally. This issue is dealt with in more detail below.

43   Most recent theorists of style take this, or a similar definition, as a starting place for discussions of style. The theorists that I have discussed in some detail (Robinson, Goodman, Altieri), target it as a straw-man. As Wollheim points out, while many people would accept such a definition, most do not act as if it were uniformly true.

44   A simple stylistic feature with which to demonstrate this form of variability is silence. The use of silence in plays, as in conversation, may not be stylistically significant, that is not consistently expressive or symbolic. But, when it is, silence may have an immense array of imports, from fear to delight, from nervousness to confidence, from the passing of time to time's absence.

45   Indeed, stylistic characteristics of the works of artists or schools may become very well known, perhaps better known than individual works or artists.

46   For example, John Donne stands out as an individual writer against the proliferation of works in what is called a 'metaphysical' style. The category 'metaphysical' captures only the broader commonalities of a certain variety of poem, but not the individual qualities of the greatest exemplars of this variety.

47   It is comparable with habit, which by definition involves repetitions of an action. I cannot exhibit a habit on only a single occasion (though you may well only notice me engaged in it once). As Theodore Schatzki emphasises, 'practice' may connote effort and diligent application, or a less deliberate, yet still iterative, activity (Schatzki 1996: 88–110).

48   So that, as Jenefer Robinson observes, there are no instances of works conforming perfectly to a generic style.

49   Berel Lang makes this point elegantly about philosophical writing in 'Plots and acts of philosophical genre': '[B]eyond ... qualifications ... is the textual (and generic) intention – the sense of what the philosophical text is meant to *do*, as that shapes and is shaped by, the genre' (Lang 1990: 38).

50   Perhaps the most we can say is, with John Richetti, that style is 'not simply a number

of qualities a text possesses but an author's activity *visible in a text* (Richetti 1983: 14, my emphasis). Richetti's formulation is a significant move away from a formalist view of style, and towards a recognition of the importance of understanding the performance of the artist for understanding the significance of a work of art.

51 Even in this case, performance is significantly different from ordinary social action, in that there is little or no scope for audience to interact with or affect the performer. The experiences of performer and audience of a performed work of art are profoundly different.

52 Goodman 1975: 806. In collaborative projects, plays, musical performances and so on, there may be so many lives involved that the style of the finished work cannot be associated with one person or their life.

53 Indeed, the appeal of some genres is the formal 'purity' that they allow.

54 Ruquaiya Hasan argues, in this vein, that style is a matter of rhetorical intention, rather than expressive intention (Hasan 1971: 299–329). While her approach can account for works of art that do not appear to (intend to) express anything about their creators, it leaves little room for the less-than-deliberately expressive styles of performance for which I have argued above.

55 The life of an artist is typically studied, if it is studied, only as it contributes to the audience's appreciation of their oeuvre.

56 That such inaccessibility is not necessarily the result of separation between one person and another is illustrated by the success of dialogue of sorts in letter; but conversational dialogue cannot survive unaltered in mediated communication, as I shall elaborate in the following sections.

57 See, for instance, the discussion of the horizonality of interpretation discussed in section 1.3.

58 The degree of openness of an artefact to interpretation has been the subject of intense debate in recent years. I can only note at this point that expressivism denies the possibility of infinite reinterpretation of artefacts, by arguing that style cannot be understood except as expressive, even if that expression is less than fully deliberated.

59 That is, unless the work of art is actually the living self, as a few people, including Oscar Wilde and Quentin Crisp have claimed (Crisp 1979: 55).

60 Understanding the style of a work from a different period or culture, in which different associations are made between formal characteristics or properties and emotional or psychological states, may push an audience to attend as much to a generic style belonging to another culture or period, as to the individual styles of particular practitioners.

61 See, for example, Karg-Elert 1931.

62 There are many ways of trying to associate natural language words with musical signs, such as the 'word painting' common in Burgundian music of the fourteenth century. A typical example of word painting would be to notate the word '*occhi*' ('eyes') with two semibreves, which look like eyes in musical notation.

63 Employment of a particular schema with particular intent, or even spontaneously, given an artist's prior intuitive grasp of a schema, may have limited or contrary impacts on audiences differently educated.

64 Herder and Schleiermacher held that all aspects of a life are styled, and indicate both personal temperament and group belonging. As such, while artistic objects perform these symbolic functions, they are not alone the key to either individual or group.

65 There is a good case to be made that artistic style is itself often employed less than deliberately.

66 For more on this subject, see section 3.3.3.

67 When people converse, their style of language, like their manners, is not usually a subject of conversation, but a performative substrate to it, part of expression but

not of enunciation. Someone's style of speech is averted to, in ordinary parlance, only when it is remarkable for some reason, for example, an unusual or offensive style of speech, beauty of expression and so on.

68 See, for instance, Tannen 1984a; Tannen and Lakoff 1994.

69 I shall not address at this point the question of there being any innate superiority to face-to-face communication, and shall leave entirely alone the much larger question of the superiority of face-to-face cultures. There is evidence that at least some face-to-face cultures (i.e. cultures in which no mediated communication is used) are marked by greater degrees of distrust and competitiveness than literate cultures in which much interaction is mediated (Saunders 1985: 35–68; Gleason 1995: 55–6).

70 It is also partly a function of the gap between persons in light of differences of character is shown by the existence of misunderstandings caused by stylistic differences in conversation as well as in writing.

71 The very choice to use e-mail rather than, say, initiate a conversation may, on occasion, count as stylistic.

72 It is thus not surprising that self-descriptions in MUDs tend to be less than informative about most aspects of individual identity. For an argument to this effect, see Bassett 1997.

73 Berel Lang considers the problem of creative self-deception in a discussion of style in fiction and in autobiography. He argues that autobiography is a literary genre very close to fiction in that the start and close of the narrative do not necessarily coincide with the start and close of the narrator's life, and in that the narrator has the liberty to invent any or all aspects of her or his life. This liberty is, Lang argues, almost identical with that granted to authors of fictional texts, which in any case, share with non-fiction most commonplace assumptions about 'matters of fact'. The only difference is that the world of the autobiography is shared by the reader, who may then make interpretive judgements about the accuracy of the autobiographer's self-perception, and of her or his self-description (Lang 1990, particularly Chapter Nine, 'Autobiography as literary fact').

74 Some people will find this effort greater than others, depending on their facility with writing, and with interpreting others' textual expression.

75 I owe this point to Peta Bowden.

76 Sherry Turkle gives examples of children who did not learn to read or write until they could relate these activities to their everyday forms of communication (Turkle 1994; see also Kersenboom 1996).

77 Speaking with varied tongues, far from being the province of liars and novelists, is a part of ordinary conversation (Tannen 1989).

78 On the significance of silence in CMC, see section 4.3.

Chapter 2: Empathy in computer-mediated communication

1 It is also worth noting at this point that I have taken a virtue-theoretical approach to empathy, and to ethics more generally, because I hold that this is more appropriate for understanding the quality of interpersonal relationships than other approaches to ethics.

2 I have already remarked on the difficulties of knowing all people well, and clearly there is no possibility of attending to the mass of styled performances of all people.

3 Or at least the attempt at empathy, since, as I argue, empathy is a practice (rather than an unwilled or spontaneous experience), and, as I also argue below, the practice of empathy may be thwarted by one's having a mistaken grasp of another's experience, or by the reticence or deception of another. See section 2.4.

4   It is not essential to all interpersonal relationships, for reasons that I address in this chapter. It is however, as I shall argue, essential to ethically engaged interpersonal relationships. I return to this subject again in Chapter Six of this book, where I discuss ethical issues related to non-intimate interpersonal relationships.

5   This account of mutual understanding, embedded in coordinated social action stands as an alternative to rational-choice theoretical accounts of social action, which treat empathy, mutual understanding and trust as spin-offs from competition, as for example in the illuminating work by Martin Hollis in this field. See Hollis, *The Cunning of Reason*, 1987. An approach to ethics drawing on the expressivist–interpretive axis that I have been delineating perforce places much emphasis on understanding others as other selves as a primary activity, one that constitutes self as much as it interprets others. The prisoners' dilemma and more sophisticated rational-choice theory accounts of self-interest-breeding-cooperation ignore the importance of trust, care, other-directedness and interdependence in the lives of actual ordinary humans. Even sophisticated rational-choice theorists such as Hollis tend to treat trust and interdependence as adaptive mechanisms, overlying a basic self-interest inherent in human nature. There is little space here in which to critique such approaches, which assume as much as they argue. Suffice to say that the inter-subjective approach to empathy taken here suggests that self-consciousness (and by implication rationality) is not possible without an awareness of others as selves, which as such requires cooperation and trust, at least of the varieties exhibited in the relationship between parent and child.

6   Its significance has been developed by philosophers such as Peta Bowden, Maria Lugonès, Iris Murdoch, and Iris Marion Young.

7   In keeping with this position, I argue that empathy can be developed and adopted as a stance.

8   For a discussion of the ethical limitations of empathy, see section 2.4.

9   Regular (that is non-computer-mediated) friendships and relationships, such as mothering and partnerships, have been the usual sites for theoretical elaborations of ethical attention.

10 The position that two people may have the same feeling, mood or sensuous experience, and indeed that experiences are inherently shared rather than individual is famously expounded by Max Scheler using the concepts of *Mitwelt* (shared world) and *Mitgefühl* (fellow-feeling), in *Wesen und Formen der Sympathie* (Scheler 1971).

11 These points are defended in more detail in section 2.3.3.

12 I hold that comprehensive objectification of singular experiences in reflection is neither possible nor necessary for a nuanced reflective understanding of the experiences of others (and, equally, of the non-human world). Rather, objectivity can be had in a *weak* sense, as having a conceptual grip on something without that grip being one of transcendental access to a single true reality.

13 This description emphasises my support for the view of projects of understanding as ongoing. It is perhaps appropriate to point out that from our everyday perspectives, projects of understanding often move so slowly as to seem stationary (as for example the meanings of words are rarely held to be 'in progress' at the moments of their employment). There are also strong pragmatic reasons for settling on fairly fixed and unchanging understandings in certain circumstances. For example, my understanding of a person's character is not completely altered or destroyed if they once do something that I consider to be 'out of character' for them.

14 Of course, I may see a face and not see it as one in pain, if I am distracted, or selfish, or simply do not recognise the pain; I may even, if sceptical or cynical, come to think of faces in pain as something separable from being in pain. But these possibilities do not rule out the experience of empathy; rather they delimit it. The first three are examples of failure of empathy through mistaken observation, and

are all quite common. They involve a failure to orient oneself towards another as a person, or a limitation in one's experience of how pained faces look, that can be overcome. The final case is one in which reflection on the relation between pains and faces has given a person insight into the possibility of deception present in the fact that the pained face can exist without pain. It is thus again a reluctance to orient oneself empathically towards another, but this time located in a suspicion of the other's intent, not in unawareness of them.

15   The clearest case I can think of is that of wincing when we see someone else hit, which is a response so spontaneous that it is often difficult to avoid.

16   Erving Goffman argues that this claim is, in western culture at least, a platitude brought out to provide legal indemnity to non-verbal aspects of comportment, and that much of our bodily movement is as deliberate as our speech (Goffman 1963). Analyses of performative aspects of human comportment also illustrate that at least some aspects of bodily movement may be closely controlled and monitored (see, for example, Gleason 1995 or Foucault 1986). However, such arguments are usually aimed at 'verbal reductionists' who limit *all* meaning and communication to the linguistic sphere. They rarely seek to prove that non-verbal communication is either as explicit or as consciously controlled as verbal communication, and thus run past the arguments presented here.

17   See section 2.5.

18   We could thus compare the empathic awareness of another's experience with appreciating their self *through* their styled performances, but not so easily with appreciating the beauty or significance of an art object or performance.

19   Stein's example of ideation is appreciating the beauty of a mathematical axiom.

20   At this point Stein's analysis is brief, giving no further clarification of how intellection can, as a primordial experience, be independent of sensuous experience, given that the self is necessarily embodied.

21   Stein's term is *Vorstellung*.

22   A great deal more could be said about how such imaginative co-seeing functions, as co-seeing is one of the important and unique aspects of Husserlian phenomenology, spelled out in a variety of ways by him and those who followed him. I shall only touch here on those aspects of co-seeing most relevant to an account of empathy.

23   It is worth noting that this is not meant to be a full account of the workings of memory, but a discussion of non-primordiality designed to shed light on the role of imagination in empathy. A fuller phenomenological account of memory would also describe the relation between past experiences and present. The following discussions of anticipation and fantasy are sketchy for the same reason.

24   Insofar as surmises are not remembered but inferred, they are not strictly sensuous experience at all, but mental placeholders for experiences I remember having forgotten.

25   As suggested in the foregoing remarks about how understandings of the past change over time, there is no singular fixity of meaning to be found in the past so long as our present continues to evolve. However, the variety characteristic of the future is not simply that of different *understandings* of past happenings, but a range of possible *happenings*, and is thus a different order of variety.

26   Note, though, that fantasy can be experienced in the mode of actuality, as well as that of possibility. If I fantasised in the mode of (non-primordial) actuality that I was out flying or happy in a job I had always disliked, I would not be fantasising that I was doing the impossible (which would entail that I knew myself to be fantasising); rather I would be experiencing as possible that which I would otherwise have taken to be impossible.

27   Though, as I have noted, I live the other's experience through, not as mine, but 'as if' mine, drawing on my own experience to do so. I am constrained by my own experience even as I am led to imagine the other's experience for myself.

28   Indeed, Stein's own use of objective is probably a weaker sense than that of indubitable or incorrigible knowledge of an experience. Throughout her work, as in theological phenomenology generally, objectivity is simply awareness through reflection on oneself as a subject, and does not refer to any total divorce from the experiential locus of one's own embodied self. I would certainly agree that reflective consideration of experience in representation is not a necessary step in representation, and that people ordinarily do not go further than the second stage of exploring the tendencies of the experience.

29   Stein calls this fusion. Thomas Aquinas calls it 'self-consciousness' (Copleston 1955: 27), and Karol Wojtyla 'cross-referencing' (Wojtyla 1979). Husserl describes something very similar in his fifth *Cartesian Meditation* without naming it.

30   Intersubjectivity as a phenomenological position is developed in detail by Maurice Merleau-Ponty (Merleau-Ponty 1962 and 1964).

31   More detailed discussion, in terms of dialogue rather than of experience more broadly, is contained in Chapter Three, section 3.2.

32   She also explains the limitation of our empathy with animals and plants as being determined by our perceptions of their bodily similarity to us; the more they resemble us bodily, the greater our capacity to empathise (Stein 1989: 45). More recent work on the high visual appeal of small children's and animals' physical appearances adds nuance to this view, as does the observation that people who have no control over their facial expression are not empathic to others.

33   This point holds whether or not one believes, as Stein does, that there is a single most virtuous form of human being, since what is at stake in limiting psychic empathy is there being cultural difference, whether those cultural differences are described as being habituated moral failings rather than habituated social practices.

34   The phrase is Wittgenstein's (Wittgenstein 1958: remark 281). Walker's discussion of it draws as much on Stanley Cavell's discussion of the phrase (Cavell 1979: 367–72), and on Wittgenstein's more 'generic' account of human souls (Walker 1998: 185).

35   Of course, I may empathise with the trauma of each person while also retaining a sense that one of the experiences in question is generally more traumatic than the other.

36   The intelligibility of others' experiences as in unity with their actions is discussed briefly by Stein; she comments that we may consider a dog's wagging its tail as an expression of joy, 'if its appearance and its behaviour otherwise disclose such feelings and its situation warrants them' (Stein 1989: 86). Once again, however, her approach is transcendental, assuming that there is an objective structure of mind accessible through phenomenological contemplation; I would prefer to maintain that intelligibility is something learned through practical immersion in a world intelligible in many possible ways, rather than given to us in a singular form.

37   The ethical possibilities of empathy have been explored thoroughly by Diana Meyers, who addresses this limitation in part (Meyers 1993). Daryl Koehn has put forward criticisms of empathy as the basis of an ethics, rather than as an important aspect of ethics (Koehn 1998: 53–79). Her discussion of the limits of empathy as an ethics helped me to formulate this section.

38   Stein calls them, after Husserl, *Erinnerungsabrégés* [abridged memories] (Stein 1989: 30).

39   It is perhaps indicative of a Husserlian fealty that Stein does not make more of the phenomenological variety of experience, but instead tends to treat sadness, joy and surprise as if they were phenomenological simples. Yet it is possible to discern in her work an attention to the peculiarly aspectual nature of experience, an attention that has more in common with a Wittgensteinian than a Husserlian approach to the human apprehension of the world.

40   Arendt refers to the possibility of understanding words by reference to the circum-stance of their utterance, and likewise to the possibility of understanding someone's blush *as* either anger or shame only through finding out more about the object of their experience.

41   This developmental position is argued for by cognitive scientists including Dianne Ackerman, Mark Johnson, Ronald Finke, and Mark Turner. For a discussion of this position, see Ruthrof 2000, particularly Chapter One.

42   That is, as capable of affording, not just perspective on, but objectivity about experiences.

43   See, for instance, Stein 1989: 81, where she refers to the possibility of getting to meaning 'through the pure type of the word'. She sharply distinguishes the form of writing from the content: 'The form can be unnoticed; but it can also push itself forward (for example, if it does not clearly reproduce the contour of the words)'. She says of what we might call performative utterance: 'Now [the words] are no longer merely the expression of something objective [i.e. a statement of how someone feels or what they experience], but at the same time are the externalisation or the announcement of the person's meaningful act as well as of the experiences behind it, such as perception'.

44   Husserl, like Stein, treats language as signs going proxy for things or phenomena (see for example Husserl 1931: 210). He distinguishes a universal semantic function of language from an indicative function of language-use in particular contexts. See also Husserl 1973: 108.

45   Compare also with Husserl on understanding the propositions that make up ordinary scientific writing: 'In the first place, all 'logical' acts (those of signifying [i.e. writing]), in so far as they were still effected in the mode of confusion, are to be converted into the mode of originary, spontaneous actionality; thus perfect logical distinctness is to be established. But now the analogue is to be produced in the grounding substratum, everywhere unliving is to be converted into living, all confusion into distinctness, but also all non-intuitiveness into intuitiveness' (Husserl 1931: 260). The peculiar difficulty of Husserl's terminology here would tend to support his point, that under-standing a sentence requires us to recreate, as well as we may, the experiences [or substrate] that ground them.

46   Think of how difficult it is to understand people speaking another language when one first arrives in a country equipped with a few years of school-learning of that language – familiarity with the words as equivalents to English words does not make up for familiarity with the usages in the context of the social practices of that country, which are comprised of mutual understandings that cover both verbal and non-verbal usage.

47   The extent to which expressly individualist theories of action, such as game theory, presume a measure of empathy between people is convincingly demonstrated by Martin Hollis (Hollis 1987). Some game theorists themselves remark upon the importance of empathy as a container and boundary for competitive antipathy; see for example the more recent strain of game theory, following work by Robert Axelrod, has trumpeted the role of empathy in competition as an entirely new discovery. None of these views gives any conceptual explication of the nature or forms of empathy, most presuming it to be a form of mutual recognition of selfhood. See Axelrod 1997.

48   A fuller discussion of this subject must wait until Chapter Four, since the temporality of CMC has implications that impact on more than the capacity of CM communi-cators to empathise with one another.

49   Notably, in many cases it is not. As I have described, and as is also documented elsewhere, temporality in CMC exchanges varies widely. See, for instance, Baron 1984; or Baym 1993. Exchanges may be almost instantaneous, or involve separation of days or weeks between contributions. Different social groups and intimate exchanges often normalise temporal regularities (Baym 1993: 143–4).

50   Of course it might have, as for example it does in anomalous claims such as 'It is raining but I don't believe it is'. In adopting Stein's example I am also accepting her generic contextual assumptions about utterances of 'It is raining', rather than complicating the field by considering playful, fictional and deceptive uses of the sentence. For more on these issues, see Chapter Three.

51   And indeed, the speaker or writer may him- or herself be quoting the weather report, or the words of a third person.

52   The role of such verbalisations in ordinary conversations is discussed in Chapter Three.

53   As I argued in Chapter One, appreciation of textual style, in our understanding of others in CMC, tends to formalism and impersonality, and may undermine the appreciation of style as performance relative to the lives of particular people.

54   The epigraph to this chapter, a letter from John Keats to his brother and sister-in-law on the death of another brother, is one striking example (Keats in Forman 1935: 246).

55   We could equally figure some form of intelligibility as an epistemic responsibility of writers. However, throughout this book I have tried to emphasise the ways in which purely epistemic interpretation (understanding of what someone means) is tied up with both what someone is going through and, particularly, with who someone is.

56   I take up these subjects in Chapter Four in more detail. See section 4.4.

57   The history of letters is a rich source of insights into the limitations and possibilities of textual exchange, between friends and strangers and also among groups (since many letters were circulated).

58   That many forms of textual performance earn the name 'technique' rather than, say, habit, is testament to the effort involved in producing limpid, vivid and personal writing. Certainly the use of the term technique does not signify that these techniques are tropes whose employment automatically engenders a certain empathic readerly response.

59   One evocative phrase is addressed in a short letter to the woman who cared for his mother: 'You frighted me, you little Gipsy, with your black wafer …' (Letter to Lucy Porter, July 1749, quoted in Grundy 1986: 216).

60   Of course, many on-line fora are designed for discussion of particular topics, and participants in such fora may tend, spontaneously or by design, to eschew discussion of everyday events, or any subject not directly relevant to the topic of the forum. Some fora, such as www.slashdot.org, and other computing sites, actively discourage 'extraneous' discussion by charging for membership, charging for each contribution to discussion, or by rating contributions according to their relevance to appointed topics of discussion. I have already specified that I am concerned with *ethically* successful communications, and not those communications whose terms of success are conceived solely in terms of information transmission.

61   Many studies now show that the contrast between orality and literacy is often contingent, and that there are few necessary qualities to either. Nicholas Hudson argues that writing has been becoming less 'textual' and more 'oral' for at least the last three hundred years (Hudson 1984). McIntosh argues that the formality of both speech and writing varies over time (McIntosh 1998).

62   Sophisticated techniques for textual self-performance are also described in more detail, in terms of text acts, in section 3.4.

63   Here the paradox of 'techniques of spontaneity' emerges clearly: we may have to work very hard to write in ways that elicit empathy as well as our conversational presence would do. To the extent that they require effort to produce effects that will be realised *elsewhere*, techniques of spontaneity may emphasise the separation, the one-sidedness of writing, particularly for the writer. Oliver Ferguson gives a discussion of this issue in his 'Nature and friendship: the personal letters of Jonathon Swift' (Ferguson 1966), noting that heightened authenticity of expression may be achieved through learning techniques of self-expression.

64   It should be possible to tell apart writing made in haste from a letter suggesting that its writer is offended, both by style and by subject matter. 'just in … phew thanks for the mail, will get back to you when I've got thru that paperwork', is more characteristic of haste. 'Yes your message came through. I've read it', perhaps more characteristic of someone upset or offended.

65   Feigned dialogue is a regular part of epistolary exchanges; Jonathon Swift's most personal letters, published as *Journal to Stella*, contain several episodes of feigned conversational banter (Swift 1948).

66   The distinction is between narration of recent events and narrative descriptions of 'the present moment'.

67   See Janet Gurkin Altman's discussion of suspense in *Clarissa* (Altman 1982: 126–7).

68   I discuss these performances further in Chapter Three.

69   The 'threading' system in discussion groups links contributions to previous contributions, and so makes repetition, and paraphrase seem verbose or presumptuous. Many e-mail programmes also employ quoting; they can be employed with humour, one separate from the construction of imaginary dialogue.

70   Johnson's responses sometimes seem to come close to 'arguing for the sake of arguing', or what we might call playing the devil's advocate; and such arguments are also characteristic of CMC exchange.

71   Narrative is one of the four mainstays of letter-writing set out by Johnson for Boswell: 'scenes of imagery, points of conceit, unexpected sallies and artful comments' (Johnson, quoted in Boswell 1906: 166).

Chapter 3: Affect and action in CMC

1   Such environments may be game environments, such as pretend dungeons, in which people enact roles for fun. Increasingly, though, these environments are produced for other uses. Conferences or classes conducted on-line may have virtual 'discussion rooms', with virtual microphones, podia and speaker's chair; commercial web-sites may have virtual 'bars' where people may meet and chat over a virtual 'beer'.

2   The endurance characteristic of written communication has tended to disrupt the idea that communications, taken as a whole, are amenable to evaluation (ethical or otherwise) as part of comportment. A text may be (and be intended as) part of a particular exchange, but also have continued (perhaps unintended) influence outside that exchange. It is impossible to circumscribe someone's responsibility for a text, if many other people may take it up and develop it in contexts nothing like that supposed by the writer.

3   The contrast here is with non-dialogical speech, such as the advertisement or the televised political announcement.

4   The method I am describing is associated with Hans Robert Jauss.

5   This classification is repeated in *Time and Narrative* (Ricoeur 1984). The '*Verstehen*' tradition is dismissed as an unacceptable method for textual hermeneutics because it evades the problem of the temporal gap between reader and writer. '[I]ts paradox is that in abolishing the difference between other people today and other people from earlier times, it obliterates the problem of temporal distance and eludes the specific difficulty attached to the survival of the past in the present – the difficulty that brings about the difference between knowledge of others and knowledge of the past' (Ricoeur 1984: 148).

6   Unlike the addressee of a speech act, whose role involves grasping, if not accepting, the intentions of the speaker of that speech act.

7   It would be reasonable to extend this generalisation to cover media in which verbal performances are recorded, such as televised newscasts, advertisements, and political speeches. Such an extrapolation shows that technologies of communication can separate even speech from situations of dialogue.

8   With the recognition that some textual forms sustain at least temporally-extended dialogue, we can say perhaps that the second form of distanciation is something that happens to texts as their time of inscription is left behind, rather than something essential that occurs as soon as pen is set to paper. See below for further elaboration of this point.

9   This splayed referentiality is what allows Ricoeur to argue in *Time and Narrative* that fictional narrative is not falsehood but the obtaining of conditions in which truth and reference are no longer the terms in which texts are understood.

10   Equally: 'It does not suffice to say that reading is a dialogue with the author though his work, for the relation of the reader to the book [sic] is of a completely different nature' (Ricoeur 1981d: 146).

11   For example, in some areas of academic life, the reinterpretation of others' texts is as much a means of forging one's own opinions as a way of understanding others' views. The interpretive possibilities of a text, particularly the exposition of unusual or original interpretations, and the mustering of the support of canonical writers through interpretive textual exegesis, are common aspects of contemporary academic practice.

12   Most personal or informal notes and letters, and some academic writing, are written expressly to convey the views and intentions of their writers, or to sway the views or intentions of particular addressees. Most would not have been written if the writer held this goal to be unattainable.

13   An interesting distinction of this sort has been made by Deborah Tannen (Tannen 1989), and taken up by some theorists of writing. Carey McIntosh calls the sort of analysis of writing that I use, after Tannen, a 'strategies' approach, because it focuses on how texts are used; approaches such as Ricoeur's he calls a 'features' approach (McIntosh 1998: 129–30).

14   Texts of various sorts are used in conversations. People discuss texts, write notes to one another when they are expected to keep silent. Such texts tend to be interpolated, that is, not part of the wider discussion.

15   Some messages are generated automatically by robots.

16   It is not unknown in conversation, for instance in cases of mistaken identity.

17   As in other epistolary exchanges, the risk of having e-mails intercepted varies with what is being said, and its import to those who discover it. Correspondence during times of war is at risk of being intercepted, for example. If a whole correspondence is clandestine, any single interception will be significant, even if the content of the letter is not.

18   I give a more detailed discussion of temporality of CMC exchange in Chapter Four.

19   This dynamic is a little like that of an infatuated person desperately searching for significance in every *utterance* of their beloved.

20   In these cases, the relationship of the reader with the writer may be supplanted by the reader's relationship with the text, although the reader would prefer to retain the relationship with the writer.

21   This is perhaps the most important point that emerges from Derrida's *Limited Inc.* Derrida's views oscillate in the volume, in which he wishes to show how texts assert meaning independent of authorial intention, and also wishes to hold that some (mis)readings, such as John Searle's reading of him, constitute violence in text. More than an assertion of indeterminacy, this plurality of readings within the one volume supports the conclusion that our judgements of the effects of authors through texts tend to be ambivalent.

22   The third type of distanciation does not have a direct impact on understanding in on-line social relationships, since whether and how later readers interpret texts that were originally part of an exchange within a relationship doesn't affect the original relationship. The effect of this type of distanciation, when it occurs, is more subtle, in allowing participants in a discussion ongoing access to the texts of a dialogue

that has passed between them and a correspondent or correspondents. I discuss the absence of non-verbal aspects of social situations in section 3.3.3.

23   There are many discussions of this episode, which is classed by some as a 'virtual rape'. One member of LambdaMOO, calling himself Mr Bungle, used superiority in manipulating (via his computer keyboard) a dungeon environment to describe the imprisonment and sexual abuse by his 'character' of the 'character' of another person. When asked about what he considered himself to have done, Mr Bungle claimed that in a 'play' environment such as a dungeon, textual descriptions of social acts (such as rape) in no way constituted social acts, whether virtual or actual. The incident is described in Dibbell 1993.

24   An example here might be a teacher's later re-readings of her students' CMC contributions to a discussion group during a course that the teacher supervised.

25   This is a move away from treating language as ideally consisting of universal and general descriptions, but doesn't yet admit of the complex, and often ambivalent, ways in which verbal and non-verbal practices signify affectively together.

26   This latter view he criticised as a 'descriptive fallacy'.

27   See also Austin 1961.

28   He treats other aspects of social interaction, in general, as the non-linguistic conditions for successful speech acts. At various points he acknowledges their significance, but considers them too difficult to chart consistently.

29   For example, my uttering the words 'I promise to water your garden while you are away' is an illocutionary act if I say it to you as an indication of my intention to water your garden while you are away.

30   That Austin's analogue for words is non-verbal actions, and his frequent references to non-verbal expressions, should prevent us from thinking that he believes non-verbal aspects of speech situations to be irrelevant or non-affective.

31   Goffman, for example, argues that there was a tacit social convention that words signify and gestures don't (Goffman 1963). The predominance of film and television, both of which pay great, often explicit attention to gesture and facial expression, has perhaps done something to eradicate this convention.

32   From this perspective, it is quite easy to see how the emphasis on words could be modified so that other, non-verbal, and less literally uttered, aspects of a speech situation might be allowed more affective weight.

33   In Austin 1962, he reorients the contrast of truth/falsity and felicity/infelicity to make this adjustment.

34   It is important to distinguish, as Austin did not clearly do, between the pragmatic act of claiming truth, and the proposition which we take to be true or false. So long as we keep in mind that speech *acts* are pragmatic (or dramatistic, as per Altieri 1981: 78), and so concerned with people's truth claims and assumptions of truth in practical circumstances (rather than with the absolute truth of certain propositions), felicity/infelicity remains the dominant pair. The question of absolute or unconditional truth remains a peripheral one, that *might* be taken up within particular speech situations, but is not taken up in many. For further discussion of this issue see Altieri 1981: 70–81.

35   Non-ritual non-verbal actions do not represent anything, though they may sometimes be understood as representing. And non-verbal rituals, although Austin does not mention it, presumably may symbolise without representing the action performed, as the action of handing a clod of earth from one person to another can signify the transfer of land ownership.

36   This argument is made by Margaret Walker (Walker 1998: 180–6), and Cheshire Calhoun (Calhoun 1988).

37   I ask my companion for more wine only if she doesn't notice that I have finished what I had, or that I have been expectantly playing with my empty glass.

38   Weak conventionality is a property of all well-formed sentences of any natural language; strong conventionality describes formal conventions which employ rules or rule-like regularities (as do marriages or legal judgements).

39   Interestingly, although most people consider the burden of proof that spamming (bulk junk-mailing) be accepted lie with the sender, rather than the recipient, the sender goes to inordinate lengths to avoid any personal engagement with his or her addressee. Temporary e-mail addresses, to which no answers can be sent, may be used for spamming, so that no discussion can be enjoined by an addressee of junk e-mail.

40   See the further discussion in Chapter Four.

41   He suggests that some actions may give the lie to the sincerity of some speech acts (Austin 1962: 24).

42   Austin also discusses the importance of vocal cadence and inflection (Austin 1962: 74) and the significance of volume of speech (Austin 1962: 105).

43   As Stanley Cavell suggests, Austin emphasised the role of certain utterances precisely because he was intent on showing that performative utterances may be as clear and precise as statements of fact (Cavell 1995: 51). The move circumvents rather than discounts the addressees' attention and their social context, which can be expanded from Austin's own account.

44   In some wedding ceremonies, the celebrant requests anyone who believes that the marriage should not go ahead to speak up; silence is taken as tacit consent to the marriage.

45   Annette Baier makes the case for Hume in Baier 1987.

46   The specialised languages (argots, jargons) of subcultures often leak into common speech.

47   Again, the purpose to which I am putting it here is somewhat different from its most usual one.

48   It might be objected that Grice's theory is culturally specific and, as Mary Pratt has put it, makes ideological suppositions (Pratt 1986: 59–71). Arguments such as Pratt's are valid if used to claim the Gricean norms of conversation are culturally specific, since there are cultures with markedly different conversational emphases from those of English-speaking cultures. They do not show that there are any cultures that have no norms of conversation at all.

49   Grice distinguishes conversational maxims from other maxims that may apply in conversation, such as moral maxims.

50   Use of physical or verbal force usually destroys the possibility of cooperation, although it may achieve the aim of its user.

51   Grice remarks that a shared sense of what is going on may consist in as little as being together to discuss some subject or other, regardless of whether participants agree on it (Grice 1975: 46).

52   There are, of course, cases in which people make radical moves: to disrupt, to change the direction, to end, or to precipitate the end of conversation. Grice's principles cover only those communicative situations in which the efficient transmission of a message is the paramount purpose.

53   Maxims of conversation are, as Mary Pratt argues, variable across cultures. They also vary in different social situations, and across social groupings in a single society (Pratt 1986).

54   I discuss the use of representations of emotions in CMC in Chapter Four.

55   See the essays in Matsuda, Lawrence, Delgado and Crenchaw 1993, for instance that by Lawrence; Dibbell 1993; MacKinnon 1993, quoted in Butler 1997: 17–18.

56   By this argument, CMC would permit many forms of abusive action, as well as many text acts that are innocuous or positive.

57   Presumably, then, she would be happy to treat promises as undertakings to perform (or refrain from) described acts some time in the future.

58   Resistance to abuse is one form of non-cooperation that Austin does not cover, because of his use of examples in which the intentions of a speaker are presumed to be honourable. It is consistent with everything else Austin has to say about ritual actions.

59   For this reason, claims for the 'far-reaching ... consequences' of gender play on-line, such as those made by Danet 1998, seem to me to be overstated.

Chapter 4: Technical constraints on CMC

1   'Appropriative' is used here simply to signify that people are not 'taken over' by the demands of computers, but learn to use computers in ways affected also by their prior understandings of communication, of technology, of the environments into which computers are introduced. For a similar analysis, Suchman and Jordan describe in some detail the harsh effects of a male-manager-led introduction of personal computers into female-staffed secretarial offices, in which the women were prevented from adapting the technology to their prior needs and practices (in other words from appropriating the technology) (Suchman and Jordan 1997).

2   I note at this point that these structural features are to be distinguished from social features that could be treated as 'controlling factors', such as the goals of groups, and the social expectations of group members, neither of which counts as a technical constraint for my purposes.

3   Nancy Baym is one theorist who is very optimistic about 'common purpose' determining a great deal about the qualities of on-line groups (Baym 1993). Her studies of a group whose members discuss current soap operas, indeed show that this group does have a fairly clear set of purposes which structure the sorts of interactions that go on. However, it is by no means clear that all on-line groups have common purposes, just as not all other social groups have any common purpose beyond passing the time together agreeably. Nor does the eventual establishment of common purposes in some groups require the absence of confusion or conflict either before or after establishing such purposes.

4   Notably, few on-line classrooms and few workplaces allow anonymous mail or postings (although many workplaces do provide function-based e-mail accounts (such as accounts@ or info@) which may work more or less anonymously. Fora that allow multiple personae, and especially those that allow anonymous posting allow other participants less chance to grasp the characters of such people in their entirety, and so may produce relationships in which people are comparatively uncertain about people with whom they are interacting. The extent to which such uncertainty becomes problematic depends further on individual and social expectations about the acceptable uses of anonymity.

5   Most negative accounts of the advent of new media strongly resist the accusations of technological determinism, but struggle to avoid it. For an admirable non-deterministic account of a medium, see Poster 1990, in which Poster discusses through theoretical analysis and case studies the impact of television on subcultures in the USA. Joshua Meyrovitz notes that his analysis of the impact of television on print culture must be taken to be partial, because focused only on a few salient factors; yet the formalism of his analysis encourages a hasty reader to take it as comprehensive (Meyrovitz 1985).

6   See for example Suchman and Jordan 1997, Kiesler and Sproull 1987.

7   The impact of CMC on global business and finance is explored in detail by Manual Castells (Castells 1996). The exclusionary potential of the expensive hardware, software and infrastructure that CMC requires is well recognised. Steps to overcome inequalities in developed nations include budgeting for computers in state-run schools, access terminals provided for communities by local or state governments, and free courses in using computers and CMC. Such measures can take advantage

of existing infrastructure such as cable networks. In those developing nations in which infrastructure is partial or nonexistent, many communities have no access to CMC whatsoever. Many people in developing nations are simply too busy with the business of living to learn to use a public computer. Yoon's analysis of computerisation in South Korea describes a highly bureaucratised central body for computerisation, itself dominated by the interest of big business (*chaebols*), and the implementation of a computer network that did not allow CMC at all (Yoon 1996).

8 Refusal to use CMC when it is available is visible as a deprivation only if the computer becomes a dominant means for social interaction and commercial advantage.

9 Technological innovation may yet have a role to play in making CMC possible during mobility and some social activity.

10 Many network users are monitored and assessed for efficiency; privacy of conversation is limited and uncertain in the workplace.

11 Peter Danielson raises some concerns in Danielson 1996. Woodbury 1996, Ward and Stephenson 1996 and Raab 1996 all express concerns about the privacy of e-mails sent via work computers, whether these e-mails be concerned with work or not.

12 There are many accounts of monitoring of e-mail, but these tend not to concern the particular or personal content of personal communications. They are of two other classes. Some monitoring is designed to assess and to police the 'productivity' of employees and to check that they are not using work equipment for any non-work purpose. This sort of monitoring is intrusive but not illegal in most countries unless it is unannounced. The other sort of monitoring is of communications that are *de facto* in the public realm, such as those of discussion groups. They might be monitored for offensive or illegal content (such as child pornography or information on bomb-making), or for content relevant for marketing purposes (such as personal interests).

13 Many theorists of CMC have noted the comparative ease of surveillance on-line, as also the ease with which encryption can evade surveillance of the content of messages (though not of their being sent). The ways in which surveillance contributes to wariness about speech on-line have yet to be examined in detail.

14 An early commentary on computer-mediated interaction, Brook and Boal 1995, contains two articles on this limitation of human movement in the use of computers. It is usually described as a dystopian condition, analogous to being chained to a loom or other industrial tool for long hours (Lakoff 1996). Even by comparison with reading, computer-use fixes the body and range of possible movements.

15 This theme looms large in critiques of CMC and cyberspace in general. Michael Heim provided a broadly Heideggerian analysis of the orientation of word-processing packages towards efficiency, instrumentality and the treatment of all texts as bearers of information (Heim 1987, particularly 80–2, 85–91). Phil Mullins gives an illuminating discussion of personal responses to a proliferation of social possibilities in CMC (analogous to the proliferation of publicly available writing known as information overload) (Mullins 1996).

16 Anonymity is taken to be the dissociation of a message from any identifiable speaker.

17 For example, anonymous political pamphlets published in the eighteenth century were notorious for their frank, scurrilous and sometimes libellous contents.

18 The term 'deonymity' has recently been employed by Michael Bacharach and Oliver Board to describe on-line fora in which people are tied to a single user-name once and for all. That we need a special name in CMC for what is a condition of ordinary conversational discourse is perhaps indicative of its differences from such discourse (Bacharach and Board 1999).

19 See also the discussion in section 2.5.

20 There are many cases in which CMCs have enabled people to form relationships that might otherwise have been very difficult for them.

21   Indeed, sociologists focusing on varieties of discrimination tend to ask whether networks of people using CMC together sustain or limit already-existing forms of discrimination. For example, Kiesler and Sproull take up the question whether the hierarchical structures of organisations using CMC become 'flattened' by using CMC (Kiesler and Sproull 1986). Their general finding was, that 'peripheral employees' have more of a say in CMC than they had previously. Susan Herring, a linguist, found, by contrast, that women and men on four different academic discussion lists had noticeably different on-line norms of politeness, and that those norms did not do anything to allow women to make themselves heard. See, for instance, Herring 1992, 1996b; We 1994; Hall 1996; Parry and Wharton 1994. However, there is still significant debate about the findings of empirical research into sexual and other forms of discrimination in CMC.

22   A common form of discrimination is on the basis of someone's internet service provider, or ISP. Use of some ISPs, for instance those that practised mass-marketing and charged by the minute on-line, was taken as indicative of stupidity, gullibility or ignorance of existing on-line social conventions. Since a person's ISP is visible in their e-mail address, it is an easy target for discrimination, warranted or not. See for instance Grossman 1997: 31–41. Grossman discusses anonymity informally, with particular attention to the functioning of proprietary internet interfaces such as that introduced by America On-line (AOL) in 1995.

23   On a related note, feminist research into face-to-face communication, for example in participatory democracy, indicates a similar ambivalence to the summons of the physically present other. Not only may physical presence be used to intimidate or persuade, the great demand of its call places limits on the possibilities of face-to-face democratic communication for resolving differences and deciding paths of action. (See for instance Phillips 1995; Young 1990b, 1997b.)

24   My position, developed in Chapter Five, is that CMC alone does not foster intimate relationships, though it may sustain and form part of them.

25   In terms of the qualities of various sorts of message-sending, CMC is as close to simultaneous as makes no difference; it is for example at least as rapid as shouting from one mountain top to another, and rather easier on the constitution. Chat lines can enable a simultaneous exchange, and MOOs and MUDs can allow something very like a group conversation to be struck up. The speed of message transaction is high enough that conversation is possible. In MUDs and chat lines the contributions constitute series of question and answer, assertion and contradiction, joke and repartee.

26   See, for instance, Baym 1993, or Katz and Aspden 1997.

27   These styles appear frequently in informal e-mails, as detailed in Kiesler and Sproull 1986; my discussion of emoticons could also include transcriptions of non-verbal sounds, as I shall make clear presently.

28   I consider the relationship between bodily signs and linguistic signs in the section on textuality below, and show that differences between them allow for the non-representational quality of bodily signs.

29   As I note in Chapter Five, the reproach for not writing was a very common trope in letters based on classical models; more recently, too, discussions of absent letters and of the 'uninspiring letter' have figured largely in correspondences.

30   I have argued for this view elsewhere (Goulding and Rooksby 1999).

31   As to the significance of the correlation between silence and absence, it often plays an important role in the relationship between correspondents, as remarked by Janet Gurkin Altman, in generating suspense (Altman 1982: 187).

32   An important discussion of performance is that of Judith Butler. The emphasis on practice or performance is characteristic of a range of practice-theoretical approaches to self, elaborated by for example Butler 1997, 1990; Schatzki 1996; or

MacIntyre 1984. Many other writers have recently taken up the subject of social practices.

33 See, for instance, Shapiro and Schulman 1996.

34 It is not surprising that this issue has not been taken up in most professional writing on the subject of CMC, since much of that writing focuses on the workplace. Emotional breakdown, if it is considered at all in such contexts, is seen to be a failure in a person's professional responsibility, rather than a condition worthy of sympathetic treatment.

35 See section 3.2.2.

36 See, for example, Yates 1996.

37 One example is Hansard, the parliamentary debating rules, in which speakers must ensure that a reader could reliably identify the things to which they refer.

38 See section 3.3.3.

39 These three aspects of conversation situations were formalised by M.K. Halliday in his linguistic researches as field, tenor, and mode (Halliday 1979).

40 Muriel Saville-Troike, who makes this observation in a paper about silence as part of non-verbal communication, specifies that '[non-verbal communication] is more dependent [than speech] on context for its interpretation' (Saville-Troike 1985: 11).

41 I discussed context in section 3.3.

42 See section 4.5 for a more detailed discussion of place in CMC.

43 I have already addressed this subject in some detail in Chapter One, looking at the import of textual communication, treating a person's styled textual performances as but a small proportion of their total styled performances. I argued that even text that is expressive of the character of its writer incurs referential and modal opacity. In Chapter Three I deepened this account in a discussion of distanciation in text, arguing that distanciation, while not inevitable, to a large extent structures CMC relations.

44 See, for comparison, any of John Keats' travel letters. For instance: 'I'll not run over the ground we have passed that would be merely as bad as telling a dream – unless perhaps I do it in the manner of the Laputan printing press – that is I put down Mountains, Rivers, Lakes, dells, Glens, Rocks, and Clouds, with beautiful, enchanting, Gothic picturesque fine, delightful, enchanting, Grand, sublime – a few Blisters, &c. – and now you have our journey thus far' (Forman 1935: 175).

45 See sections 1.3 and 1.6.

46 The equation of capitalisation with shouting is by no means universal in CMC, but is a particular convention of Usenet.

47 The letters of Jane Welsh Carlyle, wife of Thomas Carlyle, show her different moods, most clearly if the reader is aware of the difficulties she was undergoing when many of them were written. Terseness is a particular weapon of hers against the absent-minded neglect showered on her by her husband. In her sociological research into CMC in workplaces, M. Lynne Markus encountered managers who said that they could '"read" evidence of negative emotions in the messages from their subordinates' and who made phone contact in these circumstances (Culnan and Markus 1987: 512).

48 See, for example, on the subject of rates of posting, Baym 1993: 159–60.

49 I discuss friendships of letters in detail in section 5.4.

50 Baym, for instance, accepts this position when she writes, 'Rather than accepting the filtering out of social cues, CMC users invented, and continue to invent, new ones' (Baym 1993: 152).

51 As people will, through practice, grow more familiar with the conventions of textual conversation and interaction, if emotional disconnection does indeed result partially from unfamiliarity, that disconnection will be somewhat mitigated.

52 'Secondary orality' is Walter Ong's term for oral communication that is made available by modern recording and broadcasting media. Oral presentations for

television and radio are distinguished from 'primary orality' (that existing prior to the development of such media) principally by being broadcast, and so by disabling the capacity of all to participate (Ong 1982: 37).

53 Nancy Baym describes such frustration, and common methods to limit it (Baym 1993: 145, 153).

54 This approach can broadly be deemed 'appropriative' as it treats human responses to CMC possibilities, rather than the technical possibilities alone, as determinative of the effects of CMC as part of social interaction.

55 The pattern of innovation by one group and resistance by another has been charted in Morris, Peter Collett, Marsh and O'Shaughnessy 1980, where it is described as 'gesture-resistance' (Morris, Peter Collett, Marsh and O'Shaughnessy 1980: 10).

56 That is, if our main aim in interacting with other people is the social interaction, knowing and sharing time with other people whose views match or challenge our own, and whose temperaments delight or inspire us, then we will be interested in non-verbal cues only insofar as they allow knowing and sharing. If we, like Baym, see emoticons supporting a sense of community among CMC users, then there is to all intents and purposes no difference between emoticons and facial expressions as facilitators of social interaction.

57 Such analysis points to a fundamental difficulty in classifying facial expressions and gestures as information, since 'information' is a term used to describe signs whose interpretation is fixed and unequivocal (as the zeroes and ones of binary signalling are unequivocal for the computers that exchange them). The limitations of information-theory models of human communication are well explored in, for example, Lakoff 1996 and Reddy 1993.

58 I have discussed the issue of artifice and intentionality in consideration of Edith Stein's claim that facial expressions are natural, while gesture is less so, and language hardly so at all. Stein's position was ontologically fixed, whereas I presented an alternative in which the relative degree of intentionality of facial expression, gesture and language, are not always or essentially hierarchical. See section 2.5.

59 This position corresponds roughly to the development of 'seeing aspects' that Wittgenstein described, and which has been perceptively developed by Cora Diamond (Diamond 1991).

60 Hence, what counts as a sign, as a significant aspect of a situation, may not be immediately apparent to me as I live through that situation. I may, for example, take in what is happening around me without attending to it significantly, but later draw on, and act on, certain significant aspects of a scene. More or less having the position of the sun in the sky in mind may cause me to hasten my pace as I walk towards an assignation.

61 This position is known as 'textual realism' (Ruthrof 1992: 11–12).

62 There are many other examples of the significance of non-verbal signs in inter-personal communication, too many to detail them here. The salience of any one of them, further, depends on the particular circumstances.

63 Office communications, such as reprimands, demotions and some requests, are sometimes described as peculiarly painful to the recipient when conducted via e-mail. This painfulness could be attributed to the choice of medium as much as to the choice of words, since it conflicts with the normative judgement that difficult requests and demotions should ideally be done in person.

64 I include under generic style considerations such as pace, choice of subject, and amount of detail.

65 Although, as I will explain, this is not strictly true, since the trope of togetherness in absence is an old one.

66 But social institutions, such as the court, can in some measure be separated from the place or places officially set out for them.

67 Malpas' discussion of place raises the issue of how continued inhabitation of a place produces for the individual inhabitant a *sense of place*, temporally constituted, multiplicitous yet unitary, ever-changing and yet stable. The notion of 'sense of place' stresses the affective qualities of a place for a particular person.

68 My recalling a place may happen when I am somewhere else; my imagining a place that does not exist happens from the vantage point of an existing place.

69 If the concept of place is to encompass social practices, then it also allows for the multiplicity of places in relation to a single space. Insofar as it is inhabited by people engaged in various (more or less regular) social practices, a single spatial location, the bounds of 'the Brussels town square', can incorporate many places. These may be as various as a meeting-place, a market, a theatre (achieved by setting up a soapbox or a stage) and a playground (maybe even a law court on certain days of the year), each constituted by separate, if interrelated, social practices. Each of these may constitute its own 'social space' within the town square, and although all share the same 'place' it may be remarkably difficult for individuals to move from one social space to another, since such movement involves not only spatial relocation, but social transformation.

70 Prison inhabitants often try to make a home out of a cell that they cannot leave, often with practices as simple as assigning separate places or bodily positions for each different sort of thought or activity.

71 Generations of children have made up their own imaginary worlds; they become familiar with the landscapes of Narnia, of the Magic Roundabout, or of Gotham City.

72 Other institutions such as the Church, or the Royal Society have, at various times, involved social practices knitted together to give them a place-like integrity, even though their activities have been conducted regardless of physical location.

73 Geographically dispersed institutions, such as some universities, constitute what might be called communities of discussion rather than of inhabitants.

74 There may be, at least for the travellers, no temporally splayed stock of memories, lived experiences and associations connected, for members of an institution, with any particular place.

75 For example, that I often took coffee in my local café in my home town does not mean that, if I move away and continue the institution of going to the local café for a coffee, the inhabitation continues. The places are distinct, with distinct qualities and, insofar as I think of each as a place, I will not think of them as interchangeable.

76 Bruckman's article on her MediaMOO project, written with Mitchell Resnick, describes in some details the textual 'worlds' of MOOs. One example given is of an Apple employee, Daniel Rose, entering MediaMOO for the first time. His shock at entering this strange world is, by his word, lessened when he is told that someone has described the New York Apple building in the MOO (Bruckman and Resnick 1995).

77 We would be hard pressed to agree that someone accidentally phoning up a party line, only to be abused by other people using the line, has entered the wrong place, though we might agree that they have entered the wrong conversation or the wrong group of people.

78 I discuss communities of letters in more detail in Chapter Five.

79 While tropes of mutual presence often appear, especially in their early writings, this was most often meant as a compliment on the vividness of a correspondent's letter, or as an attempt to bridge the gap between the two writers.

80 Similarly, use of the telephone, even among groups of people, does not inspire thoughts of mutual inhabitation of a shared virtual space.

81 Bruckman also invokes a parallel with Vitruvius's canons for architecture as a guide to 'designing' CMC fora (Bruckman 1995: 52).

82   Erving Goffman gives a poignant account, in *Behaviour in Public Places*, of mental patients who increasingly absent themselves from social situations, by concentrating very hard on some small object, by curling in on themselves, by refusing to meet others' eyes (Goffman 1963: 69–75).

83   Similarly, during reflection, may be described as being 'off in a world of her own' or 'off with the fairies'. The social absences of reading or other sorts of concentration are indeed unremarked in some settings; it is perhaps for the sort of harmonious absence associated with reading that users of CMC might aim.

84   Likewise, Proust's memories never brought back the places he recalled, and their poignancy exists precisely in this fact, that the sense of a place may remain strong long after one has ceased to inhabit the place, after the place, as complex of physical environment and social inhabitation, has ceased to exist.

85   This point is most powerfully put by Manuel Castells, whose work indicates clearly that the acceleration of data flows has tended to consolidate financial power in *particular physical places*, cities such as New York, Boston and London, rather than making physical places (Castells 1996). D.J. Walmsley argues that on-line communities without propinquity are ephemeral, that their members often discuss issues at a superficial level (Walmsley 2000: 10–11). Like Castells, Walmsley argues that 'IT does not annihilate markets and many location-fixed phenomena' (Walmsley 2000: 9).

86   Such dissociation is not, as Joshua Meyrovitz's arguments make clear, caused only by the use of computer-mediated communication. The mediated technologies of television and telephone, and telegraph before them, have wrought immense changes in the ways that humans relate to and are constituted by the places around them. Physical places have become less determinative of social place. People's affective relationships with commodified place are profoundly changed; people do not belong to a commodified place: it belongs to them. Commodified place is not inhabited, but rather possessed, its attributes selected and pruned for the most socially advantageous self-presentation (Meyrovitz 1995, particularly Part Two 'From print situations to electronic situations', which includes a chapter on 'Media "friends"').

87   An individual's social absence from his or her surroundings while using CMC would also be a contributor to perceiving CMC as containing places. When I join a CMC group, I disengage from the social surroundings in which my computer is set, and from (most of) the social practices of other people with whom I share those surroundings. I am, then, socially 'not there' in the same way as if I were asleep, or reading, or deliberately avoiding social contact. Increased use of CMC may in turn limit the social importance of physical presence by rendering socially acceptable a new form of social absence.

88   Each is also screened by technical means from all but a small proportion of people using computer-mediated technology at the time.

89   In MOOs, there may be other more recognisably place-like conditions determined by analogy with actual places: at a virtual conference, different discussion groups may be designated for panels, for individual sessions, for general discussion, and so on; in virtual bars designed to facilitate social interaction among business-people, detailed virtual-reality programming allows participants to order and consume food, in a complicated simulation of social milieux.

90   Of course these last are all constrained by technical parameters of the medium, as letter-writing is constrained by the technologies that are used by correspondents; but there is not, I think, a very convincing case for describing these, as Bruckman does, as 'architecture' in more than a metaphorical sense.

91   Humanist epistolary style, discussed later in this book, is famously verbose; precocity was the ideal for letter-writing in Western Europe in the late seventeenth and early eighteenth centuries (Constable 1976).

92 Somewhere between e-mail and chat, people may contribute to a discussion group at any time they choose, and do not need to send messages immediately they are written. It often does not matter who else is engaging with the discussion group at the time, and the presence of another in a discussion group, signalled by their having sent a message, is no cue to address them directly. Yet it is discussion groups that are most often considered as places.

93 Which, as I argued in the section on temporality, bear the dominant significance of 'presence' in CMC.

94 It is, for example, disrupted by the ease of entry of new members into a group, particularly if, as sometimes happens, the new members are intent on discomfiting the regulars and careless of the institutions that constitute the discussion group as a community of contributors. Many groups, as well as MUDs, vet membership applications to avoid both inappropriate contributions and to encourage a sense of the 'closed-circuit' of community.

95 See section 3.2.1.

Chapter 5: Computer-mediated friendship

1 Information transmission by computer was developed primarily for military purposes, and its ubiquity is presently sustained in large part by commercial enterprises, for whom the Internet's scope for large-scale and far-flung advertising and selling is very appealing. In and around the technical and financial aspects of CMC, however, is a wide field of primarily social relations, which are either continuations of everyday friendships or friendships made via CMC.

2 As Sherry Turkle argues, the potential of the home computer as a tool for social solidarity and political resistance to large-scale industrial organisation was recognised in the early 1970s by a sizeable number of Americans (though the original high cost of the machines excluded many from owning one, then as now) (Turkle 1995: 90–4).

3 Some writers, such as Nancy R. Duell, argue, for example, that there is very little difference between sexual intercourse and the sorts of textual-sexual experiences available via CMC (Duell 1996).

4 Of course, not all friendships are intimate. And not all are ethically sound (since friends may encourage each other in a common vice, or avoid involving themselves in each other's failings). I assume throughout this section, following Aristotle, that most people are capable of intimate friendship, and that it is better to have friends (with all attendant risks) than to live without them.

5 See also Aristotle *Magna Moralia* 1208b5: 'We see that friendship stretches through the entirety of life and is present on every occasion, and that it is a good thing'. And Aristotle *Eudemian Ethics*: 'Our entire life and voluntary association is with [people with whom we have a relation of *philia*]: for we lead our day-to-day lives with our family or relatives or friends or children or parents or wife'. These quotations also emphasise the extrinsic good of *friendship*, rather than merely the goodness of the friend.

6 Aristotle values those styles of comportment and activity that, for his account, encourage moral virtue and social harmony. His discussion of similarity, which I consider below, suggests how deeply essential stylistic conformity is for the Aristotelian picture.

7 However, even for these two sorts of *philia*, Aristotle is not talking about people befriending each other solely out of self-interest, for, as types of *philia*, these friendships include in some degree mutual regard for the other. The variety of friendships he discusses illustrates the diversity of friendships in which we may engage. His analysis of the complexity of these types of *philia*, which may occur together, suggests

that self-interests and other-interests may be entwined in our friendships in ways that are impossible to disentangle conceptually.

8   The position has been argued for by Martha Nussbaum (Nussbaum 1995).

9   Prior virtue is, however, an important part of friendship for Aristotle.

10 See section 5.3.4.

11 Today, many friends live together, in shared households, or university accommodation; such cohabitation, while not uncommon, is generally considered as a temporary stage on the way to married family life, perhaps necessitated by limited means, but not as a chosen way of life.

12 A companion of this sort may be felt as a constant presence, of which one is mindful even in absence.

13 This choice is similar in style to Aristotle's remark, at the beginning of *Nicomachean Ethics*, that ethics is only for those who already have a grounding in and practical conformity to good behaviour and activity.

14 This connection is established in Arendt 1958, particularly Chapter Two.

15 This is recommended at Aristotle 1966c: 1158b24–6.

16 Margaret Walker gives an account of moral friendships and personal integrity in black communities more often cited for their high crime rates and antisociality (Walker 1998: 123–8).

17 See for an argument to this effect Nussbaum 1995.

18 Although the rise of the vernacular as a courtly language in the countries of Western Europe transformed the face of letter writing within fifty years of his death, the humanist tradition was dominant at the time (Chartier, Boureau and Dauphin 1997, particularly Chapter Two, 'Secretaires for the people?').

19 In many cases, letter writing forged a link between people who otherwise would not have been able to share or communicate. Unlike modern electronic communication, however, the tradition of letters in Europe was not seen as a 'message' in a 'medium' but as an art, at which one might practise and excel, and through mastery of its conventions come to greater clarity, depth and spontaneity of expression (Constable 1976).

20 Of course, as the survival of many letters attests, there were also many epistolary exchanges outside of the learned tradition. As access to reading and writing became more common, more people began to exchange letters. Decreases in the cost of delivery also saw the use of letters proliferate. But for the most part, exchanging letters was not a common part of most people's lives in the West until the nineteenth century, with the increase in bourgeois travel, and eventually with cheap postal systems.

21 Some of these letters are very long. Perhaps this is partly because the still-popular mediaeval debating form, disquisition, allowed very long turns to the participants, and was in this similar to the art of written composition. Students developed facility in both disquisition and written composition through their long and arduous academic training.

22 There are among Erasmus's letters, for example, only a few to laymen and to people not in receipt of a higher education. These letters do not touch on shared intellectual interests but on the achievement of practical tasks.

23 As is evident in Erasmus's eloquent commentaries on Aristotelian adages such as 'friendship is equality', 'between friends everything is common' and 'a friend is another self' (Erasmus 1982: 29–33).

24 Erasmus's discussions of friendship are dispersed, running through works from *Enchiridion Militatis Christiani, De Contemptu Mundi, De Vidua Christiani*, his volumes of adages, and his letters. Other important sources include St Augustine 1957 and Aelred of Rievaulx 1993.

25 Yvonne Charlier's thorough study identifies the five key aspects of friendship in his correspondence as *aequalitas* (equality), *similtudo* (similarity in virtue), *benevolentia*

(generous good-will), *officia* (being useful), and *admonitio* (helping a friend to improve through criticism) (Charlier 1977: 44–7).

26 This view is very powerful in the Christian tradition, and was held notably by St Augustine, by the Cistercians (such as St Bernard of Clairvaux, and Aelred of Rievaulx), and by the movement of Devotio Moderna, with which Erasmus was associated.

27 McConica remarks that Erasmus is inconsistent in his appropriation of the Platonic picture of the relation of body and soul, since he attributes no virtue whatsoever to the body.

28 Christian attitudes towards community, for example, while valuing friendship, tended to treat it as something to be extended to all people, or at least as many as possible.

29 This is a resolution of the conundrum in Aristotle's idea of loving the virtuous man: do friends love each other for their own sakes, or because of their possession of objective virtues? And it is a resolution in favour of the latter. The example considers marriage, which Erasmus treats as a form of friendship.

30 On the subject of friendships for philosophers Erasmus comments in *On the Abundant Style* (*De Copia*) that 'the philosopher should not be deeply involved in human relationships. (This tallies splendidly with the teachings of Christ.)' (Erasmus 1978: 640).

31 This is not to say that Erasmus ignores the differences among people's dispositions and social activities. Rather, different activities of one sort or another are not goods in themselves, but the different paths along which people obtain salvation and eternal life with Christ. Prior to and more important than all kinds of social relationship is the compact of each individual with the Christian God.

32 Erasmus's position on impartiality is not a defence of epistolarity; indeed the ideas are not closely related in his thought.

33 There is, however, as I shall show, some evidence that some of his fastest friendships were with people whom he met regularly.

34 This saying he gave pride of place as the first proverb in his *Adages* (Erasmus 1982: 29–30).

35 See, for example, Erasmus 1974: 29. Poems were also used to win favour.

36 Dedication of books was often strategic, used either to advance the fortunes of a friend or of oneself, or to establish a friendship with the dedicatee.

37 I have not found any explicit justification within Erasmus's work for the friendship that does not involve shared *activities*.

38 For example, Erasmus 1988: 52–4, on the priority of love for God over love for any particular person, including a friend or a wife.

39 At the same time, shared everyday life was, for the wealthy and aristocratic at least, something to be enjoyed in itself.

40 Erasmus travelled almost constantly throughout his life, and spent up to half his days in later years reading and writing letters, habits not conducive to companionable friendship.

41 One of Erasmus's later letters contains his pen-portrait of More, showing an intimate acquaintance with his character and habits. Portraits and anecdotes are important epistolary tools for creating fictive presence (see for instance Erasmus 1975: 15–25).

42 Records show that Erasmus was frequently angry with Hermans for not replying volubly or frequently enough to his letters, and that this reluctance on his part severely damaged the friendship between them. Although this interpretation is by no means the only possible one, the collapse of Erasmus's friendship in letters with Hermans would seem to be a case in which the ties of literary connection, of fictive rather than real presence, were not able to maintain a friendship that had previously flourished.

43 See for other examples of this sort of complaint, Epistles 20, 23, 33, 34, 38, 39, 58, 81, and 83 in the same volume.

44   Later in life, Erasmus granted the letter originality as a purely literary form of self-expression, arguing that it was unlike the transcriptions of speeches. A letter from Erasmus was famously as important as an audience with him.

45   Similarly, in 1501 he wrote to a former student about the possibility of establishing friendship between them, treating as immaterial their physical separation (Erasmus 1975: 42).

46   Erasmus drew this argument from St Jerome (letter from Jerome to Nitias, quoted at Jardine 1993: 150). Jerome wrote: 'In his treatment of the exchange of letters, Turpilius the comedian said: "It is the unique way of making absent persons present." Nor did he give a false opinion, although it achieves its purpose by means of what is not true. For what, if I may speak truly, is more present between those absent from one another, than to address and hear what you value by means of letters?'.

47   See section 2.6.2.

48   I discussed the role of language as a key aspect of interpersonal understanding in relation to empathy in section 2.5.

49   Here a comparison is invited with Stein's discussion of the possibility of empathy (Stein 1989).

50   We may also, for whatever reason, *employ* our absence from correspondents to create literary or fictional selves that can exist only in the absence of a context that would dissolve them. I discuss this further in the sections on CMC friendship.

51   Though, as I have argued, intimacy and informality do not preclude careful technique in letter writing (see section 2.6.1). See, for further discussion, Chartier, Boureau, and Dauphin 1997.

52   Reading and writing abilities are learned over an extended period of time, often far longer than the period of formal schooling. See, for instance, Meyrovitz 1985: 99.

53   This is a double reading, involving on one level recognition of styles borrowed or copied from earlier archetypes, and of the meta-style of their employment, and on the other hand seeing through these the character, the particularity of the other whose writing it is.

54   Among those who write for a living, this view has always had its supporters, although it has not yet made itself felt in CMC. There has, to my knowledge, been no self-conscious attempt to forge an appropriate literary style for CMC, either within academic groups or outside them. Modulations of conversational and of literary styles both appear, and one or the other will predominate depending on the group concerned.

55   Such techniques militate against the honest expression of defects. Significantly, Erasmus does not compare faults so generously.

56   *Consilium approbat* (approving counsel), *excusatoria epistola* (apology for not writing), *hortator amicam* (encouragement of a friend), *accusat silentiam* (upbraiding a correspondent for not writing) are cited by Richard Schoeck as established tropes in letter-writing in Erasmus's time (Schoeck 1990: 69).

57   Rhetorical tropes, such as spurring activity or upbraiding uncommunicative friends, were recommended to students for overcoming such difficulties, and were common in Erasmus's letters (Erasmus 1974: 65).

58   There were numerous lengthy debates between Erasmus and his colleagues when friendships soured, often over religious issues, the most famous perhaps being his split with Martin Luther.

59   Of the four deep and passionate friendships listed by Charlier (with Thomas More, John Colet, John Fisher and Jean Vitrier), all involved some periods in which the friends shared one another's company.

60   Many of these men were not aristocrats but, like Erasmus, orphans educated by the Church.

61   The works of Julia Annas and Martha Nussbaum are some of the most notable in this area. See Nussbaum 1986; Annas 1993.

62 There are many examples of works in this recently revitalised field. Some draw inspiration from psychology (for example Dowrick 1997), others from literary and filmic sources. Some again draw from the mediaeval Christian tradition of Christian and cardinal virtues.

63 Some, usually historical rather than philosophical analyses, also mark the particular role of friendships of letters (for instance Gelles 1992, or Smith-Rosenberg 1975).

64 Feminist accounts of friendship have also paid attention to archives of letters that give quite different pictures of epistolary friendships than those of educated men in Renaissance Europe (for instance Perry 1980).

65 Taking a similar position, Marilyn Friedman gives a defence of friendship among women as having particular valuable qualities not found in other sorts of friendship.

66 This point was touched on by Carol Gilligan, whose exploration of the moral development of young boys and girls suggested that faith in systematic moral principles crumbled as children faced trying to use them to deal with the moral complexities of adult life (Gilligan 1982). The finding is also discussed in the philosophical and psychological writing inspired by Gilligan's work. It echoes Aristotle's emphasis on the virtue of friendship being an intrinsically active virtue.

67 A theory of friendship, like a theory of caring, may be a valuable thing for guiding and improving our behaviour. But our practical deliberation and comportment in relation to one another is what constitutes us as ethical subjects. So a propensity to produce good ethical theory can be undermined by a propensity to act contrary to that theory's guidance.

68 The unconditionality of friendship may pose particular risks for exploitation within friendships, when they arise in situations of structural inequality, such as in societies where women are physically and financially dependent on men. Citing the work of Claudia Card and Sandra Bartky, Bowden refers to an 'ethical lean' induced in non-reciprocal friendly relations, in which one person, typically a woman, performs 'emotional maintenance' on another who does not reciprocate. Such relationships lack the mutuality either of Aristotelian friendships, in which friends are emotionally and financially independent, or of friendships revolving around reciprocal emotional support (Bowden 1997: 92).

69 I am particularly indebted to Peta Bowden for this account of reciprocal self-disclosure.

70 This approach then could be called broadly intersubjective in the sense I used the term in Chapter Two; individuals come to understand themselves as particular selves through understanding others as selves too. See section 2.3.4.

71 The ethical possibilities of attention figure large in Murdoch 1970. See particularly 16–24.

72 Notably, Cicero seems to have some understanding of the less-than-perfect friendship (Cicero 1938). He limits the favours we may be expected to do for a friend in accordance with what we consider the friend to be able to bear (Cicero 1938: 181–3); and allows that we may have to rebuke or forgive if friends behave less than perfectly (Cicero 1938: 171, 197).

73 Of course, there are circumstances in which we feel that honesty may be damagingly painful to a friend; and circumstances in which attentive care cannot be maintained, for one reason or another. To insist on absolute honesty between friends would be to forsake discretion (Baier 1986).

74 So, for example, an incident of dishonesty, or betrayal of trust between friends, can destroy the non-conditionality of the relationship, and make trusting even in minor matters difficult to take up again.

75 The break in friendship occasioned by hypocrisy, described by Margaret Walker as misleading us 'into reasonable expectations of performance on which we might, to our grief, rely' (Walker 1998: 72), illustrates the practical dangers of deception, such as being let down.

76 For instance, Kathryn Pyne Addelson and Peta Bowden argue that most people involved in political activity are also involved in relations of care, even if only as beneficiaries (Addelson 1991: 204–5; Bowden 1997: 150–1).

77 Many discussion groups and mailing lists discuss the rules and conventions of their own discourse, and in some cases try to change or develop them. Susan Herring has remarked on the prevalence of 'meta-discussion' in discussion groups and mailing lists (Herring 1993a).

78 A smiling emoticon :) is common, as is a wink of complicity ;) . Notably, few emoticons are used to signal unhappiness, displeasure or disapproval. :(is sometimes used for unhappiness, and >:-(for crossness, but neither is common.

79 I have had several verbal reports that a smiling emoticon is, in some contexts, interpretable as a threat rather than as a show of good-will.

80 See section 2.3.

81 Husserl described the hermeneutic perfection of reliving in the smallest detail the experience of another as the precondition for fully knowing what it is that they are textually describing (Husserl 1989). Edith Stein's account of empathy showed the impossibility of such total reliving, particularly for those experiences which gain their very meaning from being the experiences of a particular person or group of people (such as being happy, or being in love, or being patriotic) (Stein 1989).

82 There may, for instance, be difficulty in feeling the quality of the addressee's silence, as opposed to reading their writings. CMC is characterised by the absence of the mute appeal, of dumb misery, and other non-verbal aspects of styled comportment apprehended by empathy.

83 Perhaps the medium itself presents a subject for shared experience for friends. The Internet may bring people together simply because they have to struggle together to use it.

Chapter 6: Politics and CMC

1 The web-sites for these CSOs are, respectively, <http://www.oxfam.org>, <http://www.amnesty.org.uk>, <http://www.greenpeace.org>, <http://www.transparencyinternational.org>. There are many thousands of such web-sites; I have given only a few for some larger Western CSOs.

2 The introduction of CMC to political activity tends to increase the extent to which overlapping or competing interests, particularly those that are globally dispersed, may act in relation to one another, either together or in opposition. CMC, part of what is usually called globalisation, furthers the deepening and thickening of transnational links of communication. The long-accepted national basis for political activity is of diminished centrality and importance for politics that encompass CMC.

3 There are innumerable discussion groups devoted to political discussion. Many CSOs have web-sites, as I have noted above. Some web-sites even specialise in providing advice to on-line political activists (Mansfield 2001).

4 The term was given its most comprehensive definition by Habermas (Habermas 1989).

5 This is a particularly important point to stress, given the common perception that national-level politics is decreasingly the level at which those political decisions affecting all are made. This, I think, justifies my claim that local discussions and cooperation on the basis of political decisions also contribute to and are part of political activity most broadly considered.

6 Recent books on the subject of political CMC often implicitly take the instrumental use of CMC as a norm. For example, Rash 1997 discusses the advantages of CMC for the two major political parties in the United States almost entirely in terms of the communicative efficiency they allow *for* these parties. Efficiency is noted in

coordinating supporters of each party, in canvassing new supporters, and in controlling the 'message' that parties give out. Rash is suspicious of participatory democracy, and devotes only 3 of 193 pages to discussion of citizen political action (Rash 1997: 179–81).

7 Indeed, use of non-empathic, although not impersonal, tactics such as coercion or threat may, at least in some circumstances, play important roles in political activity and organisation.

8 Rash claims that many commentators fear direct democracy in the US (Rash 1997: 170–1). 'The problem with rapid, ill-considered, political action, [political decision-makers] feel, is that it can lead to government by whim. A single rumor on the Web, a sensational news story, or a well-organised campaign of misinformation might create a sweeping demand to do something that could to turn out to be wrong but be difficult or impossible to change' (Rash 1997: 210–11).

9 Furthermore, it will be articulated, in debate, in the representative's own performative style, drawing on their own ways of making arguments, putting questions, and on their own knowledge of the circumstances in which their desires and needs arise.

10 Individual attention to persons' particular needs, or interests may be deemed partial; and at the higher levels of political decision-making it will almost certainly slow political processes to unworkable speeds.

11 The extremely demanding duties of contemporary politicians often make participation in both politics and a fulfilling personal life, such as raising children or caring for people who are infirm, both difficult and stressful.

12 Without structured deliberation there is no way of checking whether the persons who participate in a debate produce an outcome considered equitable to all or most. Current arrangements of limited national government *may* produce fair results, but do not always do so in democratic ways.

13 For example, the private realm is associated, in contemporary Australian politics, with personal preference and choice rather than duty or responsibility. But at the same time the private realm is often identified (by government departments, for instance) as the locus for onerous caring activities. People, typically but by no means always women, are encouraged by lack of acceptable state-funded alternatives to spend their days caring for and nursing not only children and spouse but also parents and other aged or infirm relatives.

14 Rash (1997) provides, *de facto*, a model of political activity in CMC in which personal communication has a larger role. However, the force of his analysis is to explore how large political parties use CMC. Following the attitudes of members of major political parties whom he interviewed during his research, he concludes that on-line political activity is primarily a way for large political parties to gather votes. Political activity on-line is the activity of large political parties and their supporters, a matter of information dissemination and gathering, of political campaigning, presence and ultimately of winning elections. The role of personal interaction in political CMC is treated, within this context, as a useful tool by which political party members can garner support. There is no intrinsic value in these personal relations, in either personal or political terms; rather they are instrumental for the aims of particular parties.

15 These types of political activity include volunteer work, including organisation of volunteers; participation in fund-raising, such as organising, or contributing to fêtes; belonging to and being active in political organisations; debating political issues with other citizens in the public sphere (such as through writing letters to politicians or the media, contributing to on-line political discussion, attending marches, and so on); informal support for those directly involved in politics. Kathryn Pyne Addelson's 'What do women do?' gives an account of the often underrated roles women play in politics.

16   Lister argues, in Chapter Six, that time poverty is a 'critical resource for both formal and informal forms of politics', and that women's characteristic lack of control over their own time is a primary reason for their participation in informal rather than formal politics (Lister 1997: 135–8).

17   For instance, the informal political networks of African-American women in the US are often coextensive with extended family networks, in which relations provide mutual support that straddles the personal and political realms (Lister 1997: 124). Lister in turn refers to Particia Hill Collins' analysis of working class African-American networks (Collins 1990).

18   Contracts, like other formal requirements of political activity, are also formed and maintained within particular cultural milieux. Consequently, a person's capacity to participate in political activity will depend on their sharing the understandings and values of the political community to which they belong. These may be substantive values, such as respect for persons or for the natural environment, or they may be procedural values, such as those of efficiency, and cooperation I have already mentioned. Ideals, such as impartiality, justice and fulfilment of duties are themselves values that emerge within particular social milieux, and are imparted to children by parents who take the care to educate them one way or another. In other words, political traditions are embedded within and dependent upon cultural conditions that are fostered and maintained, not within politics itself, but in homes, playgrounds, and schools.

19   Ruth Lister notes that a general recognition of difference-sensitive privacy is important in (a) resisting intrusions of the state and (b) symbolically recognising individuals' capacity for a degree of self-determination (Lister 1997: 220).

20   Opacity of the mood or intentional stance of a writer of CMCs, is of particular concern in political CMC exchanges. I discussed modal opacity in Chapter One.

21   See sections 4.3 and 4.4.

22   It can be illustrated by reference to the patterns of empathetic engagement I discussed in the second chapter of this book. Empathy with another person was shown to be possible even towards those with whom we are not intimate, although our understanding of their circumstances (their character, and the conditions under which they acted) is then limited.

23   See the discussion of artistic style, section 1.4.4.

24   It might be remarked that people acting following these norms may seem impersonal. However, in view of the prevalence of stylistic misunderstandings, it is clear that people may adopt norms of communication that seem impersonal simply to avoid misunderstandings. The style of political discussion is partially codified, as in parliamentary style manuals such as Hansard.

25   Indeed, CMC is often viewed as a communicative medium whose primary advantages are to extend already impersonal political networks, in order to gain the ear and sway the heart of a larger audience. Awareness of these possibilities must, however, be tempered by awareness of the diminution of returns as increasing numbers of individuals and groups bombard one another with e-mails.

26   Certainly few people hold that global participatory democracy is a real possibility.

27   The textuality of political CMC is likely to endure. Teleconferencing simply doesn't allow large numbers of people to debate together, and so doesn't offer the partici-patory possibilities that textual engagement can.

28   This idea is expressed succinctly, for instance, in Habermas 1990b: 199.

29   He uses this notion in several of his works, particularly in Habermas 1984, 1987, 1990. It is also present in a less developed form in Habermas 1971.

30   For instance, Habermas's key concepts include communicative action, universal pragmatics, and communicative competence.

31   It is more interesting as a possible model for CMC than other philosophical discourse models (such as the reflective equilibrium model of John Rawls, first set out in

Rawls 1971) because it specifies that discourse is incumbent upon all members of a group, and can not merely be run hypothetically in the mind of an individual member. The implication of the ISS is that moral questions can only be decided with finality if they consider the views and interests of every single affected person. In this the ISS comes closer to the ideal of participatory democracy than accounts such as Rawls's.

32 One obvious class of persons left out of discussion by the ISS is the class of those not yet born. Although this oversight raises significant questions, for reasons of space I have not discussed it.

33 Coercion is defined by Habermas as any sort of persuasion which is not 'the force of the better argument' (Habermas 1990b: 89).

34 The clarity of Habermas's conditions is designed to go some way towards explaining what may have gone wrong in particular less-than-ideal speech situations.

35 The more we consider the interrelations among members of a community, the more we might be tempted to argue that even this situation may not include all those affected by decisions deliberately made. This line of reasoning tends toward a utopian call for 'dialogue of all with all' which occurs both in Habermas's own work and in that of some of his critics. I shall not address this problem here but will do so in section 6.3.5.

36 Even very early works by Habermas stress the connection between speech and the possibility of consensus: 'What raises us out of nature is the only thing whose nature we can know: language. Through its structure, autonomy and responsibility are posited for us. Our first sentence expresses unequivocally the intention of a universal and unconstrained consensus' (Habermas 1971: 314). Later versions of the ISS still stress its function as a transcendental condition of communication. In Habermas 1984 he states that 'the medium of language and the *telos* of reaching understanding intrinsic to it reciprocally constitute one another' (Habermas 1984: 241). In Habermass 1990b he describes the ISS as being in part a set of counterfactual conditions presumed in the act of engaging in moral debate (Habermas 1990b: 68).

37 More recently, Habermas and Habermasian theorists have moved to treating the ISS as a model for *actual* debate in a range of contexts.

38 Habermas observes that 'modern societies are also characterised by the need for regulations that impinge *only* on particular interest. While these matters do require regulation, a discursive consensus is not needed; compromise is quite sufficient in this area' (Habermas 1990b: 205).

39 We can, of course, hope that the very sharing of conceptions of the good life among persons who hold different conceptions of the good life will lead, at the least, to toleration of different conceptions where those are compatible, and to the modification of conceptions of the good life to allow for toleration where they are not initially compatible. As Benhabib points out, a certain degree of variety in conceptions of the good life is accepted even by neo-Aristotelians such as Alasdair MacIntyre (Benhabib 1990b: 16).

40 Habermas's ethics follows Kant's in being deontological, formal, abstract and procedural (Habermas 1990b: 130). The difference from Kant is largely in the fact that the reasons are meant to satisfy, not oneself but all the other participants in the discussion. The sharp distinction between subject and object is preserved, but individual accountability is broadened to include the judgements of others as well as the self.

41 Communication among subjects, which Habermas contrasts with the relation between subject and object, is for him the basis of rationality. He describes communicative relations in this way: 'The focus of investigation thereby shifts from cognitive-instrumental rationality to communicative rationality. And what is paradigmatic for the latter is not the relation of a solitary subject to something in the objective world that can be represented and manipulated, but the intersubjective relation that

speaking and acting subjects take up when they come to an understanding with one another about something' (Habermas 1984: 392).

42   A clear statement of this broadened Kantian rationality is in 'Discourse ethics', in which Habermas argues that we can debate about moral rightness just as we can debate about truth. His assimilation of normative rightness and subjective authenticity to a consensual validatory model allows him to argue that the authenticity of emotions and the normative rectitude of value judgements are, just like truth, decided in intersubjective debate (Habermas 1990b).

43   Note that such participation would, according to discourse ethics, only be valuable if it were used to debate and justify moral norms. It would not be used, for instance, to debate and justify fiscal policy or administrative organisation.

44   I will take up Ess's position presently, but would like to note at this point that the definition of the scope of those participating in an ISS as 'all affected by a decision', means that a pluralist democracy such as Ess describes cannot instantiate true ISSs, but only on-going communicative action and ISSs limited to the membership of smaller groups. The problems that Ess associates with a plebiscite re-emerge as soon as debate *among* discussion groups occurs.

45   Habermas starts out from the speech act theories of John Austin and John Searle and, later, uses Noam Chomsky's notion of linguistic competence. See Chapter Three for a discussion of Austin's speech act theory.

46   Habermas allows for the possibility of a truth-like consensus, not just on matters of what is the case, but also on matters of what is right and what is sincere. In *The Theory of Communicative Action*, Habermas argues that validity pertains to the different areas of veridical truth, normative rightness and expressive authenticity (or sincerity), as well as the grounding criterion of intelligibility. In conversation, claims can be assessed in terms of each of the four, and may be questioned in any of them. Thereupon, the claim's validity in that area may be discussed.

47   True to his Kantian heritage, Habermas is more interested in defining the conditions under which ethical discourse can be said to be occurring, than he is in making substantive moral claims. He criticises Rawls, another proceduralist, for making two substantive moral pronouncements rather than remaining entirely in the procedural realm.

48   Hence, rather than trying to account for the motivational difficulty of the connection between speech and action or examining the way misunderstanding or power differences may affect political debate, Habermas is more concerned to show that consensus can be reached. Such matters are questions of rational duty, rather than of non-rational motivation.

49   Habermas's view on the transformative power of discourse is discussed in section 6.3.2.

50   Habermas's stipulation that in discourse ethics all participants must take up the position of all other participants goes some way towards mitigating the effects of a variety of styles of reasoning (see particularly Habermas 1990a). However, as I understand it, Habermas's position (in Habermas 1990a at least) is that solidarity in a universalistic morality is not a concrete practice of empathy directed towards the particular experiences of particular other people, but a more abstract sense of being bound to all other persons by an 'objectively universal' association (Habermas 1990a: 48). Still tied to discourse ethics as competitive reason-giving, this account of solidarity still fails to make room for other forms of communication that might contribute to the transformation of understanding.

51   One of the presuppositions of informal argumentation is that all participants use words in the same sense, with the same unequivocal meaning.

52   James Tully takes a similar position to mine when he argues that, in order for people to discuss any topic, they must already make assumptions, for instance about the

possibility of understanding, or the comparative consistency of uses of words in the discussion (Tully 1989: 201).

53 The criticisms raised here are aimed principally at the work contained in Habermas 1984 and 1987 as these volumes contain the fullest account of discourse ethics and the ISS.

54 Docter and Dutton found that at least some of these projects did listen to the voices of minorities. In Santa Monica, the PEN project led to the establishment of citizen discussion groups to provide better public services for homeless people. Homeless people participated in the discussion groups and contributed to the decisions made (Docter and Dutton 1998: 133–4).

55 This still leaves open the question of whether such minority groups do not have a say because they are not participating in the proper manner (i.e. following the 'specific historical values of European modernity' (Outhwaite 1994: 31)), or because their values are not taken seriously by a Habermasian procedural ethics.

56 An argument for treating electronic networks as partial public spheres is made by Becker and Wehner 2001.

57 Wayne Rash gives a comparable list (Rash 1997: 84–8), with eight categories: tactical communication, organisation, recruitment, fund-raising, strategic positioning, media relations, affinity connections (cooperation with other political organisations at a national level), and international connections. Rash focuses on CMC solely as a means of self-furtherance for major US political parties. His list gives a good sense of how the possibilities of various types of CMC are generally conceived of by political organisations in the United States. It gives less sense of how they *might* be used, either as part of cosmopolitan campaigning, within a cosmopolitan democracy, or as part of the public sphere or local government autonomy movements. And it gives no sense of the ethical issues that may arise with the increasing use of CMC as part of politics.

58 In the US, major parties have been using web-sites, e-mailouts and discussion groups since 1993, and consider these to be a major part of their election campaigns; the Republican Party also focuses its web-site on recruiting members. In Australia, also a highly technologised society, major parties have not been so rapid to take up CMC as part of promotion for their election campaigns, but do use it for coordinating campaigns and other activities. Their web-sites are less bent than the US sites on providing entertaining content or using specialised programming, and more on giving details of press releases and policies.

59 See Berg 1994 for a more detailed discussion of the distinction between technological innovation and technological assimilation.

60 This position is also argued for, in a more specifically Habermasian vein, in Becker and Wehner 2001.

61 See for example the 'Young Republicans Online Community Network' available online at <http://www.yrock.com/home/>.

62 While the efficacy of such petitions in influencing government action is difficult to estimate, their circulation does expose many computer-users to political activity.

63 Perhaps the most famous example is the Hungersite (<http://www.thehungersite.com>). Participating organisations have agreed to donate the cost of a cupful of rice every time a visitor to the site clicks on a 'hunger button'. Such web-sites are enormously popular and fairly successful in raising funds.

64 One recent example was the 2001 Christmas donation by the World Wide Web search-engine Dogpile. For each search query entered by a user of Dogpile, the company made a small contribution (below US1cent) towards provision of rice to people in famine-struck countries.

65 It is not my intention here to argue that CMC is a wholly new type of political communication, or that it enables wholly new types of political organisation. Rather my point is that CMC in some senses 'levels the playing field' in that it allows rapid

trans-global political communication not only to wealthy organisations but also to many smaller organisations. Small groups of citizens who might otherwise have remained comparatively inactive politically may join global CSOs. Small CSOs who might otherwise have had only a local field of action make use of CMC as a way to cooperate with other CSOs for common goals. Such cooperation, while already existing in many cases, is facilitated by the speed and reach of CMC.

66   I do not develop a particular account of democracy here. I accept something like the view, voiced by Thomas Pogge, that democracy requires not only universal voting, but also a range of other features such as the existence of a vote under fair conditions for all adults, a choice of candidates, and of influencing the choice of candidates, freedom of the media, freedom from extreme poverty for all voters, mutual respect among the citizenry, and an informed citizenry (Pogge 2001). For a review of the research on information technology and democracy, see Harrison and Falvey 2001.

Bibliography

Addelson, K.P. (1991) 'What do women do?', in *Impure Thoughts: Essays on Philosophy, Feminism and Ethics*, Philadelphia: Temple University Press, 188–211.

Aelred of Rievaulx (1993) *On Friendship*, trans. P. Matarasso, London, New York, Melbourne, Ontario and Auckland: Penguin.

Agre, P. (1995) 'Building community networks', in P.E. Agre and D. Schuler (eds) *Reinventing Technology, Rediscovering Community: Critical Explorations of Computing as a Social Practice*, Greenwich, CT and London: Ablex Publishing Corporation 241–8.

—— (1998) 'Designing genres for new media: social, economic and political contexts', in S.G. Jones (ed.) *Cybersociety 2.0: Revisiting Computer-mediated Communication and Community*, Thousand Oaks, London and New Delhi: Sage, 69–99.

Alexy, R. (1990) 'A theory of practical discourse', in S. Benhabib and F. Dallymayr (eds) *The Communicative Ethics Controversy*, Cambridge, MA: MIT Press, 151–92.

Altieri, C. (1981) *Act and Quality: A Theory of Literary Meaning and Humanistic Understanding*, Amherst: University of Massachusetts Press.

—— (1987) 'Style as the man: what Wittgenstein offers for speculating on expressive activity', *The Journal of Aesthetics and Art Criticism* 46: 177–92.

—— (1994) *Subjective Agency: A Theory of First-person Expressivity and its Social Implications*, Oxford and Cambridge, MA: Blackwell.

Altman, J.G. (1982) *Epistolarity: Approaches to a Form*, Columbus: Ohio State University Press.

Annas, J. (1993) *The Morality of Happiness*, New York: Oxford University Press.

Arendt, H. (1958) *The Human Condition*, Chicago: Chicago University Press.

Aretino, P. (1967) *The Letters of Pietro Aretino*, trans. T. Caldecot Chubb, Hamden, CT: Archon Books.

Aristotle (1966a) *Eudemian Ethics*, trans. J. Solomon, Oxford: Clarendon Press.

—— (1966b) *Magna Moralia*, trans. G. Stock, Oxford: Clarendon Press.

—— (1966c) *Nicomachean Ethics*, trans. D. Ross, Oxford: Clarendon Press.

Augustine (1957) *The City of God*, trans. G.G. Walsh, D. Zema, G. Morahan, D. Honan, Garden City, NY: Doubleday.

Austerlic, S. (1999) 'Internet, Emergent Culture and Design', in W. Harcourt (ed.) *Women@ internet: Creating New Cultures in Cyberspace*, London: Zed Books, 69–75.

Austin, J. (1961) 'Performative utterances', in J.O. Urmson and G.J. Warnock (eds) *Philosophical Papers*, Oxford: Clarendon Press, 233–50.

—— (1962) *How to Do Things with Words*, Oxford: Clarendon Press.

Axelrod, R.M. (1997) *The Complexity of Cooperation: Agent-based Models of Competition and Collaboration*, Princeton, NJ: Princeton University Press.

Aycock, A. and Buchignani, N. (1995) 'The E-Mail Murders: reflections on "dead" letters', in S.G. Jones (ed.) *CyberSociety: Computer-mediated Communication and Community*, Thousand Oaks, CA: Sage Publications, 10–35.

Baase, S. (1997) *A Gift of Fire: Social, Legal, and Ethical Issues in Computing*, Englewood Cliffs: Prentice Hall.

Bacharach, M. and Board, O. (1999) 'The Quality of Information in Electronic Groups'. Online. Available HTTP: <http://www.berlecon.de/iew2/papers/board.pdf> (accessed 15 June 1999).

Bachelard, G. (1994) *The Poetics of Space*, trans. Maria Jolas, Boston: Beacon Press.

Baier, A. (1985a) 'Poisoning the wells', in A. Baier, *Postures of the Mind: Essays on Mind and Morals*, Minneapolis: University of Minnesota Press, 263–91.

—— (1985b) 'What do women want in a moral theory?', *Nous* 19, 53–64.

—— (1986) 'Trust and anti-trust', *Ethics* 96(2): 231–60.

—— (1987) 'Hume, the women's moral theorist?', in E.F. Kittay and D.T. Meyers (eds) *Women and Moral Theory*, Totowa, NJ: Rowman and Littlefield, 37–55.

—— (1994) *Moral Prejudices: Essays on Ethics*, Cambridge, MA: Harvard University Press.

Baron, N.S. (1984) 'Computer-mediated communication as a force in language change', *Visible Language* XVIII(2): 118–41.

Bartky, S.L. (1997) 'Sympathy and solidarity: on a tightrope with Scheler', in D.T. Meyers (ed.) *Feminists Rethink the Self*, Boulder, CO: Westview Press, 177–96.

Bassett, C. (1997) 'Virtually gendered: life in an on-line world', in K. Gleder and S. Thornton (eds) *The Subcultures Reader*, London: Routledge, 537–50.

Baym, N.K. (1993) 'Interpreting soap operas and creating community: inside a computer-mediated fan club', *Journal of Folklore Research* 30(2/3): 143–76.

—— (1995a) 'The emergence of community in computer-mediated communication', in S.G. Jones (ed.) *CyberSociety: Computer-mediated Community and Communication*, Thousand Oaks, CA: Sage, 138–63.

—— (1995b) 'The performance of humor in computer-mediated communication', *Journal of Computer-Mediated Communication* 1(2). Online. Available HTTP <http://207.201. 161.120/jcmc/vol1/issue2/baym.html> (accessed 2 June 2000).

—— (1995c) 'From practice to culture on Usenet', in S.L. Star (ed.) *The Cultures of Computing*, Oxford: Basil Blackwell, 29–52.

—— (1998) 'The emergence of online community', in S.G. Jones (ed.) *CyberSociety: Revisiting Computer-mediated Communication and Community*, Thousand Oaks, London and New Delhi: Sage, 35–68.

Becker, B. and Wehner, J. (2001) 'Electronic networks and civil society: reflections on structural changes in the public sphere', in C. Ess (ed.) *Culture, Technology, Communication: Towards an Intercultural Global Village*, Albany, NY: State University of New York Press, 67–85.

Beebee, T.O. (1999) *Epistolary Fiction in Europe, 1500–1850*, Cambridge and New York: Cambridge University Press.

Bell, P. and Bell, R. (1993) *Implicated: the United States in Australia*, Melbourne: Oxford University Press.

Benhabib, S. (1986) *Critique, Norm and Utopia: A Study of the Foundations of Critical Theory*, New York: Columbia Press.

—— (1987) 'The "concrete" and "generalized" other', in S. Benhabib and D. Cornell (eds) *Feminism as Critique*, Minneapolis: University of Minnesota Press, 77–95.

—— (1990a) 'Afterword: communicative ethics and contemporary controversies in practical philosophy', in S. Benhabib and F. Dallmayr (eds) *The Communicative Ethics Controversy*, Cambridge, MA and London: MIT Press, 330–70.

—— (1990b) 'In the shadow of Aristotle and Hegel: communicative ethics and current controversies in practical philosophy', *The Philosophical Forum* 21(2): 1–31.

—— (1995) 'Cultural complexity, moral interdependence and the global dialogic community', in M. Nussbaum and J. Glover (eds) *Women, Culture and Development*, New York: Oxford University Press.

—— (1996) 'Toward a deliberative model of democratic legitimacy', in S. Benhabib (ed.) *Democracy and Difference*, Princeton: Princeton University Press.

Berg, A.J. (1994) 'Technological flexibility: bringing gender into technology (or was it the other way round?)', in C. Cockburn and R.F. Dilic (eds) *Bringing Technology Home: Gender and Technology in a Changing Europe*, Buckingham and Philadelphia: Open University Press, 95–110.

Berlin, I. (1976), *Vico and Herder: Two Studies in the History of Ideas*, London: Hogarth Press.

Besnier, N. (1995) 'Language and affect', *Annual Review of Anthropology* 19: 419–51.

Bjerknes, G., Ehn P. and Kyng M. (1987) *Computers and Democracy: A Scandinavian Challenge*, Aldershot: Avebury.

Blaug, R. (1996) 'New theories of discursive democracy: a user's guide', *Philosophy and Social Criticism* 22(1): 49–80.

Blum, L. (1980) *Friendship, Altruism and Morality*, Northway and Andover: Routledge.

Boal, I.A. (1995) 'A flow of monsters: Luddism and virtual technologies', in J. Brook and I.A. Boal (eds) *Resisting the Virtual Life: The Culture and Politics of Information*, San Francisco: City Lights, 3–15.

Bolter, J. (1991) *Writing Space: The Computer, Hypertext and the History of Writing*, Hillsdale, NJ: Erlbaum Associates.

Boswell, J. (1906) *The Life of Samuel Johnson*, London: J.M. Dent.

Bowden, P. (1993) 'Theoretical care: feminism, theory and ethics', *Critical Review* 33: 129–47.

—— (1997) *Caring: Gender-sensitive Ethics*, New York and London: Routledge.

Braidotti, R. (1994) 'Seduced and abandoned: the body in the virtual world', paper presented at the Institute of Contemporary Arts/Arts Councils of England conference, London.

Brand, A. (1990) *The Force of Reason: An Introduction to Habermas' Theory of Communicative Action*, Sydney: Allen and Unwin.

Brandom, R. (1984) 'Freedom and constraint by norms', in R. Hollinger (ed.) *Hermeneutics and Praxis*, Notre Dame: University of Notre Dame Press

Brenner, R.F. (1997) *Writing as Resistance: Four Women Confronting the Holocaust: Edith Stein, Simone Weil, Anne Frank, Etty Hillesum*, University Park, PA: Pennsylvania State University Press.

Bromberg, H. (1996) 'Are MUDs communities? Identity, belonging and consciousness in virtual worlds', in R. Shields (ed.) *Cultures of Internet: Virtual Spaces, Real Histories, Living Bodies*, London: Sage Publications, 143–52.

Bruckman, A. (1996) 'Finding one's own space in cyberspace', *Technology Review* 99(1): 48–54.

Bruckman, A. and Resnick, M. (1995) 'The MediaMOO project: constructionism and professional community', *Convergence* 1(1): 1–29.

Bryan, C., Tsagarousianou, R. and Tambini, D. (1998) 'Electronic democracy and the civic networking movement in context', in R. Tsagarousianou, D. Tambini, C. Bryan (eds) *Cyberdemocracy: Technology, Cities, and Civic Networks*, London and New York: Routledge, 1–17.

Butler, J. (1990) *Gender Trouble*, London: Routledge.

—— (1997) *Excitable Speech: A Politics of the Performative*, New York: Routledge.

Calhoun, C. (1988) 'Justice, care, gender bias', *Journal of Philosophy* 85: 451–63.

Campbell, J. (1989) *The Improbable Machine: What the New Upheaval in Artificial Intelligence Reveals About How the Mind Really Works*, New York: Simon and Schuster.

Card, C. (1990) 'Gender and moral luck', in O. Flanagan and A.O. Rorty (eds) *Identity, Character and Morality*, Harvard: MIT Press, 199–218.

—— (1995) *Lesbian Choices*, New York: Columbia University Press.

—— (1998) 'Women's voices and ethical ideals: must we mean what we say?', *Ethics* 99(1): 125–35.

Castells, M. (1996) *The Rise of the Network Society*, London and Malden, MA: Blackwell.

Cavell, S. (1979) *The Claim of Reason: Wittgenstein, Skepticism, Morality and Tragedy*, Oxford, Toronto, New York and Melbourne: Oxford University Press.

—— (1995) *Philosophical Passages: Wittgenstein, Austin, Emerson, Derrida*, Cambridge, MA: Blackwell.

Chafe, W. and Danielewicz, J. (1987) 'Properties of spoken and written language', in R. Horowitz and S.J. Samuels (eds) *Comprehending Oral and Written Language*, San Diego: Academic Press, 83–116.

Champagne, R. (1995) *Jacques Derrida*, New York: Twayne.

Charlier, Y. (1977) *Erasme et l'Amitie, d'apres son Correspondence*, Paris: Les Belles Lettres.

Chartier, R., Boureau, A. and Dauphin, C. (1997) *Correspondence: Models of Letter-writing from the Middle Ages to Nineteenth Century*, trans. Christopher Woodall, Cambridge: Polity Press.

Cherniak, W., Davis, C. and Deegan, M. (eds) (1996) *The Politics of the Electronic Text*, Oxford: Office for Humanities Communication, with the Centre for English Studies, University of London.

Cherny, L. and Weise, E.R. *Wired Women: Gender and New Realities in Cyberspace*, Seattle, WA: Seal Press.

Cicero, M.T. (1938) *De Senectute, De Amicitia, De Divinatione*, trans. W.A. Falconer, London: Heinemann.

—— (1948) *De Oratore, Together with De Fato, Paradoxica Stoicorum, De Partitione Oratoria*, trans. H. Rackham, London: Heinemann.

Civille, R. (1994) 'The public interest summit is today', Internet message, 29 March 1994, calling for participation.

Cocking, D. and Matthews, S. (1999) 'Friendship and the Internet', paper presented at Australian Institute of Computer Ethics Conference.

Code, L. (1996) *Rhetorical Spaces: Essays on Gendered Locations*, New York: Routledge.

Cohen, L.J. (1975) 'Spoken and unspoken meanings', in T. Sebeok (ed.) *The Tell-Tale Sign: A Survey of Semiotics*, Lisse: The Peter de Ridder Press, 19–26.

Cohen, N. (2001) 'The political potential of the Web', *Dissent* Summer: 81–3.

Cole, G.D.H. (1951) The British Labour Movement: Retrospect and Prospect. Ralph Fox Memorial Lecture, April 1951. Fabian Society, London.

Collins, P.H (1990). *Black Feminist Thought: Knowledge, Consciousness and the Politics of Empowerment*, Boston: Unwin Hyman.

Colomb, G.G and Simutis, J.A. (1996) 'Visible conversation and academic inquiry: CMC in culturally diverse classrooms', in S. Herring (ed.) *Computer-Mediated Communication: Linguistic, Social and Cross-cultural Perspectives*, Amsterdam and Philadelphia: John Benjamins Publishing Company, 146–71.

Conley, T. (1982) 'A trace of style', in M. Krupnick (ed.) *Displacement: Derrida and After*, Bloomington: Indiana University Press, 74–92.

Constable, G. (1976) 'Letters and letter-collections', in *Typologie des Sources du Moyen Âge Occidental*, vol. 17, Turnhout: Brepols.

Conway, G. (1989) *Wittgenstein on Foundations*, Atlantic Highlands: Humanities Press Inc.

Copleston, F.C. (1955) *Aquinas*, Harmondsworth, Middlesex: Pelican.

Cornell, D. (1989) *The Philosophy of the Limit*, New York: Routledge.

Crisp, Q. (1979) *How to Have a Life-Style*, New York: Methuen.

Culnan, M.J. and Markus, M.L. (1987) 'Information technologies', in F.M. Jablin, L.L. Putnam, K.H. Roberts and L.W. Porter (eds) *Handbook of Organizational Communication: an Interdisciplinary Perspective*, Newbury Park, CA: Sage, 420–43.

Curtis, P. (1997) 'Mudding: social phenomena in text-based virtual realities', in P.E. Agre and D. Schuler (eds) *Reinventing Technology, Rediscovering Community: Critical Explorations of Computing as a Social Practice*, Greenwich, CT and London: Ablex Publishing Corporation.

Danet, B. (1998) 'Text as mask: gender, play and performance on the Internet', in S.G. Jones (ed.) *CyberSociety 2.0: Revisiting Computer-mediated Communication and Community*, Thousand Oaks, London and New Delhi: Sage, 129–58.

—— (2000) 'Ethnographic studies of communication and culture on the Internet'. Online. Available HTTP <http://atar.mscc.huji.ac.il/~msdanet/overview.htm> (accessed 2 June 2000).

Danielson, P. (1996) 'Pseudonyms, mailbots and anonymous letterheads: the evolution of computer-mediated ethics', in C. Ess (ed.) *Philosophical Perspectives on Computer-Mediated Communication*, Albany: State University of New York Press, 67–94.

Davidson, D. (1986) 'Radical interpretation', in *Inquiries into Truth and Interpretation*, Oxford: Oxford University Press, 125–39.

Derrida, J. (1979) *Spurs: Nietzsche's Styles/Éperons: les styles de Nietzsche*, trans. B. Harlow, Chicago: University of Chicago Press.

—— (1988) *Limited Inc*, Evanston, IL: Northwestern University Press.

Dery, M. (1994) *Flame Wars: The Discourse of Cyberculture*, Durham, NC: Duke University Press.

Detweiler, L. (1999) 'The anonymity FAQ', Online. Available FTP <ftp://rtfm.mit.edu> as </pub/usenet/news.answers/netanonymity> (accessed 15 June 2000).

Diamond C. (1991) *The Realistic Spirit: Essays on Ludwig Wittgenstein*, Cambridge, MA: MIT Press.

Dibbell, J. (1993) 'A rape in Cyberspace (or TINYSOCIETY and how to make one)', *The Village Voice*. Online. Available FTP <ftp://ftp.lambda.moo.mud.org/pub/MOO/papers/VillageVoice.txt> (accessed 15 November 2001).

Docter, S. and Dutton, W. (1998) 'The First Amendment online: Santa Monica's Public Electronic Network', in R. Tsagarousianou, D. Tambini, C. Bryan (eds) *Cyberdemocracy: Technology, Cities, and Civic Networks*, London and New York: Routledge, 125–47.

Dowrick, S. (1997) *Forgiveness and Other Acts of Love*, Victoria: Ringwood.

Dreyfus, H. (1995) 'From Socrates to expert systems: the limits and dangers of calculative rationality', paper presented at the University of Western Australia.

Duchêne, R. (1970) *Madame de Sévigné et la Lettre d'Amour*, Paris: Bordas.

Duell, N.R. (1996) 'Our passionate response to virtual reality', in S. Herring (ed.) *Computer-mediated Communication: Linguistic, Social and Cultural Perspectives*, Amsterdam and New Philadelphia: J. Benjamin, 129–46.

Dunlop, C. and Kling, R. (1996) (eds), *Computerisation and Controversy: Value Conflicts and Social Choices*, second edition, Boston: Academic Press.

Emmet, D. (1966) *Rules, Roles and Relations*, London and New York: Macmillan; St Martin's Press.

Erasmus, D. (1974) *Letters 1–141*, trans. R.A.B. Mynors and D.F.S. Thomson, Toronto, Buffalo and London: University of Toronto Press.

—— (1975) *Letters 142–297*, trans. R.A.B. Mynors and D.F.S. Thomson, Toronto, Buffalo and London: University of Toronto Press.

—— (1978) *De Copia, De Ratio Studii*, trans. B.I. Knott, Toronto, Buffalo and London: University of Toronto Press.

—— (1982) *Adages Ii1–Iv100*, trans. M.M. Phillips, Toronto, Buffalo and London: University of Toronto Press.

—— (1985) *De Conscribendis Epistolis, Formula, De Civilitate*, trans. C. Fantazzi, Toronto, Buffalo and London: University of Toronto Press.

—— (1988) *Enchiridion Militatis Christiani, De Contemptu Mundi, De Vidua Christiani*, trans. C. Fantazzi, Toronto, Buffalo and London: University of Toronto Press.

—— (1989) *Letters 1015–1055*, trans. R.A.B. Mynors, Toronto, Buffalo and London: University of Toronto Press.

Ess, C. (1996) 'The political computer: democracy, CMC and Habermas', in C. Ess (ed.) *Philosophical Perspectives on Computer-Mediated Communication*, New York: State University of New York Press, 197–222.

Faderman, L. (1981) *Surpassing the Love of Men: Romantic Friendship and Love Between Women from the Renaissance to the Present*, New York: William Morrow.

Felman, S. (1980) *La Scandale du Corps Parlant: Don Juan avec Austin, ou Seduction en Deux Langues*, Paris: Seuil.

Ferguson, O.W. (1966) 'Nature and friendship: the personal letters of Jonathon Swift', in H. Anderson, P.B. Daghlian and I. Ehrenpreis (eds) *The Familiar Letter in the Eighteenth Century*, Lawrence: Kansas University Press.

Fitzgerald, P. (1985) *Charlotte Mew and her Friends*, London: Harvill.

Fitzgerald, J.T. (ed.) (1997) *Greco-Roman Perspectives on Friendship*, Atlanta, GA: Scholar's Press.

Forman, M.B. (ed.) (1935) *Collected Letters of John Keats*, second edition, Oxford: Oxford University Press.

Foucault, M. (1986) *The Care of the Self*, trans. R. Hurley, New York: Vintage Books.

Fraser, N. (1989) *Unruly Practices: Power, Discourse and Gender in Contemporary Social Theory*, Cambridge: Polity Press.

—— (1997) 'Rethinking the public sphere', in *Justice Interruptus: Critical Reflections on the 'Postsocialist' Condition*, New York and London: Routledge, 69–98.

Frederick, H. (1993) 'Computer networks and the emergence of global civil society', in L. Harasim (ed.) *Global Networks: Computers and International Communication*, Cambridge, MA and London: MIT Press, 283–96.

Friedman, M. (1989a) 'Feminism and modern friendship: dislocating the community', *Ethics* 99, 60–79.

—— (1989b) 'Friendship and moral growth', *Journal of Value Inquiry* 23.

—— (1993) *What are Friends For? Feminist Perspectives on Relationships and Moral Theory*, Ithaca, NY: Cornell University Press.

Frings, M. (1996) *Max Scheler: A Concise Introduction into the World of a Great Thinker*, second edition, Milwaukee: Marquette University Press.

Gadamer, H.G. (1998) *Truth and Method*, trans. J. Weinsheimer and D.G. Marshall, second edition, New York: Continuum.

Gandy, O. (1993) *The Panoptic Sort: A Political Economy of Personal Information*, Boulder, CO: Westview Press.

Gaskin, J.E. (1997) *Corporate Politics and the Internet*, Upper Saddle River, NJ: Prentice Hall.

Geertz, C. (1975) *The Interpretation of Cultures: Selected Essays*, London: Hutchison.

Gelles, E.B. (1992) *Portia: The World of Abigail Adams*, Bloomington and Indianap olis: Indiana University Press.

Genova, J. (1995) *Wittgenstein: A Way of Seeing*, New York: Routledge.

Gilligan, C. (1982) *In a Different Voice: Psychological Theory and Women's Development*, Cambridge, MA: Harvard University Press.

Gleason, M. (1995) *Making Men: Sophists and Self-presentation in Ancient Rome*, Princeton, NJ: Princeton University Press.

Goffman, E. (1963) *Behavior in Public Places: Notes on the Social Organization of Gatherings*, New York and London: Free Press and Collier Macmillan Publishers.

Goodman, N. (1975) 'The status of style', *Critical Inquiry* 1: 799–811.

Goulding, P. and Rooksby, E. (1999) 'Trust and on-line teaching: some reflections', *Proceedings of AICEC99*, 169–79.

Gramm-Hanssen, K. (1996) 'Objectivity in the description of nature: between social construction and feminism', in N. Lykke and R. Braidotti (eds) *Monsters, Goddesses and Cyborgs: Feminist Confrontations with Science, Medicine and Cyberspace*, London and New Jersey: Zed Books, 88–102.

Grice, H.P. (1975) 'Logic and conversation', in P. Cole and J.L. Morgan (eds) *Syntax and Semantics*, New York: Academic Press, 41–58.

Grossman, W. (1997) *net.wars*, New York: New York University Press.

Grundy, I. (1986) 'The techniques of spontaneity: Johnson's developing epistolary style', in P.J. Korshin (ed.) *Johnson after Two Hundred Years*, Philadelphia: University of Pennsylvania Press, 211–24.

Habermas, J. (1971) *Knowledge and Human Interests*, trans. J.J. Shapiro, second edition, Boston: Beacon Press.

—— (1984) *The Theory of Communicative Action*, vol. 1, *Reason and the Rationalization of Society*, trans. T. McCarthy, Boston: Beacon Press.

—— (1985) 'Question and counterquestion', trans. J. Bohman, in R. Bernstein (ed.) *Habermas and Modernity*, Cambridge MA: MIT Press.

—— (1987) *The Theory of Communicative Action*, vol. 2, *Lifeworld and System: A Critique of Functionalist Reason*, trans. T. McCarthy, Boston: Beacon Press.

—— (1989) *Structural Transformation of the Public Sphere: An Inquiry into a Category of Bourgeois Society*, trans. T. Burger with F. Lawrence, Cambridge, MA: MIT Press.

—— (1990a) 'Justice and solidarity: on the discussion concerning "Stage 6"', *Philosophical Forum* 21(2): 32–52.

—— (1990b) *Moral Consciousness and Communicative Action*, trans. C. Lenhardt and S.W. Nicholsen, Cambridge, MA: MIT Press.

—— (1993) *Justification and Application: Remarks on Discourse Ethics*, trans. C. Cronin, Cambridge: Polity Press.

—— (1998) *The Inclusion of the Other: Studies in Political Theory*, trans. C. Cronin, P. de Grieff (eds), Cambridge, MA: MIT Press.

Hall, K. (1996) 'Cyberfeminism', in S. Herring (ed.) *Computer-Mediated Communication: Linguistic, Social and Cultural Perspectives*, Amsterdam and New Philadelphia: J. Benjamin, 147–72.

Hall, S. (1991) 'The local and the global: globalization and ethnicity', in A. King (ed.) *Culture, Globalization and the World-System*, Houndsmill and London: Macmillan, 19–41.

Halliday, M.K. (1979) *Language as Social Semiotic: The Social Interpretation of Language and Meaning*, London: Arnold.

Hamelink, C.J. (1991a) *Communication: The Most Violated Human Right*, Stockholm: Inter Press Service dispatch.

—— (1991b) 'Global communication: plea for civil action', in B.V. Hofsten (ed.) *Informatics in Food and Nutrition*, Stockholm: Royal Academy of Sciences.

Harries, K. (1968) 'Wittgenstein and Heidegger: the relationship of the philosopher to language' *Journal of Value Inquiry* 2: 281–91.

Harrison, T. and Falvey L. (2001) 'Democracy and new communication technologies', in W.B. Gudykunst (ed.) *Communication Yearbook 25*, Mahwah, NJ: Lawrence Erlbaum.

Hasan, R. (1971) 'Rime and reason in literature', in S. Chatman (ed.) *Literary Style: A Symposium*, London and New York: Oxford University Press, 299–329.

Hausheer, R. (1996) 'Three major originators of the concept of *Verstehen*: Vico, Herder, Schleiermacher', in A. O'Hear (ed.) *Verstehen and Humane Understanding*, Cambridge and New York: Cambridge University Press.

Hawthorne, S. and Klein, R. (eds) (1999) *Cyberfeminism: Connectivity, Critique and Creativity*, North Melbourne: Spinifex Press.

Hayakawa, S. (1939) *Language in Action*, New York: Harcourt, Brace and Company.

Hayles, K.N. (1993) 'Virtual bodies and flickering signifiers', *October 66*: 69–91.

Heaton, L. (2001) 'Preserving communication context: virtual workspace and interpersonal space in Japanese CSCW', in C. Ess (ed.) *Culture, Technology, Communication: Towards an Intercultural Global Village*, Albany, NY: State University of New York Press, 213–40.

Heim, M. (1986) 'Humanistic discussion and the on-line conference', *Philosophy Today* 30: 278–88.

—— (1987) *Electric Language*, New Haven: Yale University Press.

Held, D. (1995) *Democracy and the Global Order: From the Modern State to Cosmopolitan Governance*, Stanford, CA: Stanford University Press.

—— (1998) 'Democracy and globalization', in D. Archibugi, D. Held and M. Köhler (eds) *Re-Imagining Global Community: Studies in Cosmopolitan Democracy*, Cambridge: Polity Press, 11–27.

Herder, J.G. (1967) *Sämtliche Werke*, vol. 5, Hildesheim and New York: Georg Olms Verlag.

Herring, S. (1992) 'Gender and participation in computer-mediated linguistic discourse', paper presented at the Annual Meeting of the Linguistic Society of America (Philadelphia, PA, 9–12 January), Document ED345552, Washington, DC: ERIC Clearinghouse on Languages and Linguistics.

—— (1993a) 'Macrosegmentation in postings to two electronic "lists"', paper presented at the Georgetown University Round Table on Languages and Linguistics, Pre-session on Discourse Analysis: Written Texts.

—— (1993b) 'Men's language: a study of the discourse of the LINGUIST list', in A. Crochétiere, J.C. Boulanger and C. Ouellen (eds) *Les Langues Menacées: Actes du XVe Congres International des Linguistes*, vol. 3, Québec: Les Presses de l'Université Laval, 347–50.

—— (1994) 'Politeness in computer culture: why women think and men flame', in M. Bucholtz, A.C. Liang, L. Sutton and C. Hines (eds) *Cultural Performance: Proceedings of the Third Berkeley Women and Language Conference*, Berkeley: Berkeley Women and Language Group, 278–94.

—— (1996a) 'Gender and democracy in computer-mediated communication', in R. Kling (ed.) *Computerization and Controversy: Value Conflicts and Social Choices*, second edition, New York: Academic.

—— (1996b) 'Posting in a different voice: gender and ethics in computer-mediated communication', in C. Ess (ed.) *Philosophical Perspectives on Computer-Mediated Communication*, Albany NY: State University of New York Press, 115–45.

Hiltz, S.R. (1984) *Online Communities: A Case Study of the Office of the Future*, Norwood, NJ: Ablex.

Hollis, M. (1987) *The Cunning of Reason*, Cambridge and New York: Cambridge University Press.

Hudson, N. (1994) *Writing and European Thought 1600–1850*, Cambridge, New York and Melbourne: Cambridge University Press.

Hunter, L. (1999) *Critiques of Knowing: Situated Textualities in Science, Computing and the Arts*, London and New York: Routledge.

Husserl, E. (1931) *Ideas: General Introduction to Pure Phenomenology*, trans. W.R.B. Gibson, London: Allen and Unwin; New York: Humanities Press.

—— (1973) *Cartesian Meditations: An Introduction to Phenomenology*, trans. D. Cairns, The Hague: Martinus Nijhof.

—— (1989) *Ideas Pertaining to a Pure Phenomenology and to a Phenomenological Philosophy*, trans. R. Rojcewisy and A. Schuwer, Dordrecht and London: Kluwer.

Introna, L. (1999) 'Virtuality and morality: on (not) being disturbed by the other', unpublished manuscript.

Jardine, L. (1993) *Erasmus, Man of Letters: The Construction of Charisma in Print*, Princeton, NJ: Princeton University Press.

Jauss, H.R. (1982) *Aesthetic Experience and Literary Hermeneutics*, trans. M. Shaw, Minneapolis: University of Minnesota Press.

Johnson, M. (1974) *The Body in the Mind: The Bodily Basis of Meaning, Imagination and Reasoning*, Chicago and London: University of Chicago Press.

Jones, S.G. (1995) 'Understanding community in the information age', in S.G. Jones (ed.) *CyberSociety: Computer-mediated Communication and Community*, Thousand Oaks, CA: Sage Publications, 10–35.

—— (1998) 'Information, Internet and community: Some notes towards an understanding of community in the information age', in S.G. Jones (ed.) *CyberSociety 2.0: Revisiting Computer-mediated Communication and Community*, Thousand Oaks, London and New Delhi: Sage, 1–34.

Jordan, T. (1999) *Cyberpower: The Culture and Politics of Cyberspace and the Internet*, London and New York: Routledge.

Karg-Elert, S. (1931) *Polaritätslehre*, Berlin: Simon.

Katz, J.E. and Aspden, P. (1997) 'A nation of strangers?', *Communications of the ACM* 40(12): 81–6.

Kerr, E.B. and Hiltz, S.R. (1982) *Computer-Mediated Communication Systems*, New York: Academic Press.

Kersenboom, S. (1996) *Word, Sound, Image: The Contemporary Tamil Text*, Providence, RI: Berg Publishers.

Kiesler, S. and Sproull, L. (1986) 'Reducing social context cues: electronic mail in organizational communication', *Management Science* 32(11): 1492–512.

—— (eds) (1987) *Computing and Change on Campus*, Cambridge, New York, New Rochelle, Melbourne and Sydney: Cambridge University Press.

Kiesler, S., Siegel, S. and McGuire, T.W. (1984) 'Social psychological aspects of computer mediated communication', *American Psychologist* 39(10): 1123–34.

Koehler, J.W., Dupper, T., Scaff, M.D., Reitberger, F. and Paxon, P. (1998) *The Human Side of Intranets: Content, Style and Politics*, Boca Raton, FL: St Lucie Press.

Koehn, D. (1998) *Rethinking Feminist Ethics: Care, Trust, Empathy*, London and New York: Routledge.

Korenman, J. and Wyatt, N. (1996) 'Group dynamics in an e-mail forum', in S. Herring (ed.) *Computer-Mediated Communication: Linguistic, Social and Cross-cultural Perspectives*, Amsterdam and Philadelphia: John Benjamins Publishing Company, 212–35.

Kramerae, C. (1998) 'Feminist fictions of future technology', in S. G. Jones (ed.) *CyberSociety 2.0: Revisiting Computer-mediated Communication and Community*, Thousand Oaks, London and New Delhi: Sage Publications, 100–28.

Kymlicka, W. and Nelson, W. (1996) 'Return of the citizen: a survey of recent work on citizenship theory', *Ethics* 104: 352–81.

Laclau, E. and Mouffe, C. (1995) *Hegemony and Socialist Strategy*, trans. W. Moore and P. Cammack, London: Verso.

Lakoff, G. (1996) 'Body, brain and communication', interview with I.A. Boal. In J. Brook and I.A. Boal (eds) *Resisting the Virtual Life: The Culture and Politics of Information*, San Francisco: City Lights.

Lang, B. (1978) 'Style as instrument: style as person', *Critical Inquiry* 4: 715–39.

—— (1990) *The Anatomy of Philosophical Style*, Oxford and Cambridge, MA: Basil Blackwell.

Langford, D. (1996) 'Ethics and the Internet: appropriate behavior in electronic communication', *Ethics and Behavior* 6(2): 91–106.

Langham, D. (1994) 'Preserving democracy in cyberspace: the need for a new literacy', *Computer-Mediated Communication Magazine* 1(4): 7. Online. Available HTTP <http://www.december.com/cmc/mag/2994/aug/literacy.html> (accessed 26 December 2001).

Lanham, R. (1974) *Style: An Anti-textbook*, New Haven: Yale University Press.

—— (1993) *The Electronic Word: Democracy, Technology and the Arts*, Chicago: University of Chicago Press.

Lawley, E.L. (1992) 'Discourse and distortion in computer-mediated communication'. Online. Available HTTP <http://www.itcs.com/elawley/discourse.html> (accessed 9 November 2001).

Lawrence, C.R. III (1993) 'If he hollers, let him go: regulating racist speech on campus', in M.J. Matsuda, C.R. Lawrence III, R. Delgado and K.W. Crenchaw (eds) *Words that Wound: Critical Race Theory, Assaultive Speech and the First Amendment*, Boulder, CO: Westview Press, 168–89.

Lee, E. (1997) *The Labor Movement and the Internet: The New Internationalism*, London and Chicago: Pluto Press.

Lipps, T. (1903–6) *Aesthetik*, Berlin: B.G. Teubner.

Lister, R. (1997) *Citizenship: Feminist Perspectives*, Houndsmill: Macmillan.

Loader, B. (ed.) *The Governance of Cyberspace: Politics, Textuality and Global Restructuring*, London: Routledge.

Lugonès, M. (1987) 'Playfulness, "world-travelling" and loving perception', *Hypatia* 2(2): 3–19.

MacIntyre, A. (1984) *After Virtue*, second edition, Notre Dame, IN: Notre Dame Press.

MacKinnon, C. (1993) *Only Words*, Cambridge, MA: Harvard University Press.

Malandro, L.A. and Barker, L. (1985) *Non-Verbal Communication*, Reading, MA, Menlo Park, CA, London, Amsterdam, Don Mills, Ontario and Sydney: Addison-Wesley Publishing Company.

Malpas, J.E. (1994) 'A taste of madeleine: notes towards a philosophy of place', *International Philosophical Quarterly* 34: 433–51.

Manley, L. (1980) *Convention 1500–1750*, Cambridge, MA: Harvard University Press.

Mansbridge, J. (1980) *Beyond Adversary Democracy*, New York: Basic Books.

Mansfield, H. (2001) 'Tips for e-activists'. Online. Available HTTP <http://www.eactivist.org/tips_for_eactivists.html> (accessed 12 November 2001).

Marsden, J. (1996) 'Virtual sexes and feminist futures: the philosophy of cyberfeminism', *Radical Philosophy*, 78: 6–16.

Marvin, L.-E. (1995) 'Spoof, spam, lurk and lag: the aesthetics of text-based virtual realities', *Journal of Computer-Mediated Communication* 1(2). Online. Available HTTP <http://shim.huji.ac.il/jcmc/vol1/issue2/vol1no2.html> (accessed 3 June 2001).

Matheson, K. (1992) 'Women and computer technology: communicating for herself', in M. Lea (ed.) *Contexts of Computer-Mediated Communication*, New York: Harvester Wheatsheaf, 66–88.

Matsuda, M. (1993) *Words that Wound: Critical Race Theory, Assaultive Speech and the First Amendment*, Boulder, CO: Westview Press.

McConica, J. (1991) *Erasmus*, New York: Oxford.

McIntosh, C. (1998) *The Evolution of English Prose 1700–1800: Style, Politeness and Print Culture*, Cambridge, New York and Melbourne: Cambridge University Press.

McLuhan, M. (1962) *The Gutenberg Galaxy: The Making of Typographic Man*, London: Routledge and Kegan Paul.

Merleau-Ponty, M. (1962) *The Phenomenology of Perception*, London: Routledge and Kegan Paul.

——(1964) *The Primacy of Perception: And Other Essays on Phenomenological Psychology, the Philosophy of Art, History and Politics*, Evanston, IL: Northwest University Press.

Meyers, D.T. (1993) 'Moral reflection: beyond impartial reason', *Hypatia* 8(3): 21–47.

Meyrovitz, J. (1985) *No Sense of Place: The Impact of Electronic Media on Social Behaviour*, New York: Oxford University Press.

Mill, J.S. (1963) *Essays on Politics and Culture* (ed.) G. Himmelfarb, Garden City, NY: Anchor Books.

Mitchell, W. (1995) *City of Bits: Space, Place and the Infobahn*, Cambridge, MA: Harvard University Press.

Moles, A. (1966) *Information Theory and Aesthetic Perception*, trans. J.F. Cohen, Urbana: University of Illinois Press.

Moon, D. (1995) 'Practical discourse and communicative ethics', in S.K. White (ed.) *The Cambridge Companion to Habermas*, Cambridge: Cambridge University Press, 143–64.

Morley, D. and Robins, K. (1995) *Spaces of Identity: Global Media, Electronic Landscapes and Cultural Boundaries*, New York and London: Routledge.

Morris, D., Collett, P., Marsh, P. and O'Shaughnessy, M. (1980) *Gestures: Their Origins and Distribution*, New York: Stein and Day.

Mulligan, K. (1987) 'Promising and other social acts: their constitution and structure', in K. Mulligan (ed.) *Speech Act and Sachverhalt: Reinach and the Foundations of Realist Phenomenology*, Dordrecht: Martinus Nijhof, 29–90.

Mullins, P. (1996) 'Sacred text in the sea of texts: the Bible in North American electronic culture', in C. Ess (ed.) *Philosophical Perspectives on Computer-Mediated Communication*, Albany: State University of New York Press, 271–302.

Murdoch, I. (1962) 'Metaphysics and ethics', in D.F. Pears (ed.) *The Nature of Metaphysics*, London: Macmillan and Co.; New York: St Martin's Press, 99–123.

—— (1970) 'The idea of perfection', in *The Sovereignty of Good*, London: Routledge and Kegan Paul, 1–45.

Myers, S.H. (1990) *The Bluestocking Circle: Women, Friendship and the Life of the Mind*, New York: Oxford University Press.

Negroponte, N. (1995) *Being Digital*, Rydalmere, NSW: Hodder and Stoughton.

Nestor, P. (1985) *Female Friendships and Communities: Charlotte Bronte, George Eliot, Elizabeth Gaskell*, Oxford: Clarendon Press; New York: Oxford University Press.

Noddings, N. (1984) *Caring: A Feminist Approach to Ethics and Moral Education*, Berkeley, CA: University of California Press.

Nussbaum, M. (1986) *The Fragility of Goodness: Luck and Ethics in Classical Tragedy and Philosophy*, Cambridge and New York: Cambridge University Press.

—— (1995) 'Aristotle on human nature and the foundation of ethics', in R. Harrison and J. Altham (eds) *World, Mind and Ethics: Essays on the Philosophy of Bernard Williams*, Cambridge: Cambridge University Press.

Ohmann, R. (1971) 'Speech, action and style', in S. Chatman (ed.) *Literary Style: A Symposium*, London and New York: Oxford University Press, 241–59.

Okin, S.M. (1989) *Justice, Gender and the Family*, New York: Basic Books.

Ong, W. (1982) *Orality and Literacy: The Technologizing of the Word*, London: Methuen.

Outhwaite, W. (1994) *Habermas: A Critical Introduction*, Cambridge: Polity Press.

Parkes, M. (1996) 'Making friends in cyberspace', in *Journal of Communication* 46(1): 82.

Parry, L. and Wharton, R. (1994) 'Networking in the workplace: the role of gender in electronic communications', in U. Gattiker (ed.) *Women and Technology*, Berlin and New York: De Gruyter, 65–92.

Pateman, C. (1970) *Participation and Democracy*, Cambridge: Cambridge University Press.

Patience, A. (2000) 'Beyond the silencing academy', in P. James (ed.) *Burning Down the House: The Bonfire of the Universities*, Carlton, Australia: Association for the Public University, with Arena Publications, 32–45.

Paulson, W.R. (1988) *The Noise of Culture: Literary Texts in a World of Information*, Ithaca and London: Cornell University Press.

Peirce, C.S. (1917) *Collected Papers*, vols. 1–6, Cambridge, MA: Harvard University Press.

—— (1974) *Collected Papers*, vols. 1–6, (eds) C. Hartshorne and P. Weiss, Cambridge, MA: Harvard University Press.

Perry, R. (1980) *Women, Letters and the Novel*, New York: AMS Press.

Petrarch, F. (1975–85) *Letters on Familiar Matters*, trans. A. Bernado, Albany: State University of New York Press, 3 volumes.

Phillips, A. (1991) *Engendering Democracy*, Cambridge: Polity Press.

—— (1995) *The Politics of Presence*, Oxford: Clarendon Press; New York: Oxford University Press.

Phillips, S.V. (1985) 'Interaction structured through talk and interaction structured through "silence"', in D. Tannen and M. Saville-Troike (eds) *Perspectives on Silence*, Norwood, NJ: Ablex Publishing Corporation, 165–84.

Plant, S. (1993) 'Beyond the screens: film, cyberpunk and cyberfeminism', *Variant* 14: 12–17.

Pogge, T. (2001) 'Achieving democracy', *Ethics and International Affairs* 15(1): 3–23.

Poster, M. (1990) *The Mode of Information: Poststructuralism and Social Context*, Cambridge: Polity Press in association with Basil Blackwell.

Pratt, M.L. (1977) *Toward a Speech Act Theory of Literary Discourse*, Bloomington and London: Indiana University Press.

—— (1986) 'Ideology and speech act theory', *Poetics Today* 7(1): 59–71.

Prins, G. and Sellwood, E. (1998) 'Global security problems and democratic process', in D. Archibugi, D. Held and M. Köhler (eds) *Re-Imagining Global Community: Studies in Cosmopolitan Democracy*, Cambridge: Polity Press, 252–72.

Raab, C. (1996) 'Privacy and trust: information, government and ITC', *Proceedings of ETHICOMP96*, 200–17.

Rash, W. (1997) *Politics on the Nets: Wiring the Political Process*, New York: W.H. Freeman.

Rawls, J. (1971) *A Theory of Justice*, Cambridge, MA: Belknap Press.

Raymond, J. (1986) *A Passion for Friends: Towards a Philosophy of Female Affection*, Boston: Beacon Press.

Reddy, M. (1993) 'The conduit metaphor', in D. Ortony (ed.) *Metaphor and Thought*, second edition, Cambridge: Cambridge University Press.

Reid, E. (1992) 'Electropolis: communication and community on Internet Relay Chat', *Intertrek* 3(3): 7–15.

—— (1995) 'Virtual worlds: culture and imagination', in S.G. Jones (ed.) *CyberSociety: computer-mediated Communication and Community*, Thousand Oaks, CA: Sage Publications, 164–83.

Resnick, M., Bruckman, A. and Martin, F. (1996) 'Pianos not stereos: creating computational toolkits', *Interactions* 3(6).

Richetti, J. (1983) *Philosophical Writing: Locke, Berkeley, Hume*, Cambridge, MA: Harvard University Press.

Ricoeur, P. (1976) *Interpretation Theory: Discourse and the Surplus of Meaning*, Fort Worth, TX: Texas Christian University Press.

—— (1977) 'Writing as a problem for literary criticism and philosophical hermeneutics' *Philosophical Exchange* 2(3): 3–15.

—— (1978) *The Rule of Metaphor: Multi-disciplinary Studies of the Creation of Meaning in Language*, trans. R. Czerny, K. McLaughlin and J. Costello SJ, London and Henley: Routledge and Kegan Paul.

—— (1981a) 'Appropriation', in P. Ricoeur, *Hermeneutics and the Human Sciences: Essays on Language, Action and Interpretation*, trans. J.B. Thompson, Cambridge and New York: Cambridge University Press; Paris: Édition de la Maison des Sciences de l'Homme, 182–96.

—— (1981b) 'The model of the text', in P. Ricoeur, *Hermeneutics and the Human Sciences: Essays on Language, Action and Interpretation*, trans. J.B.Thompson, Cambridge and New York: Cambridge University Press; Paris: Édition de la Maison des Sciences de l'Homme, 197–221.

—— (1981c) 'The task of hermeneutics', in P. Ricoeur, *Hermeneutics and the Human Sciences: Essays on Language, Action and Interpretation*, trans. J.B.Thompson, Cambridge and New York: Cambridge University Press; Paris: Édition de la Maison des Sciences de l'Homme, 43–62.

—— (1981d) 'What is a text? Explanation and understanding', in P. Ricoeur, *Hermeneutics and the Human Sciences: Essays on Language, Action and Interpretation*, trans. J.B.Thompson, Cambridge and New York: Cambridge University Press; Paris: Édition de la Maison des Sciences de l'Homme, 145–64.

—— (1984) *Time and Narrative*, trans. K. McLoughlin and D. Pellauer, Chicago: University of Chicago Press.

Robinson, J. (1984a) 'General and individual style in literature', *The Journal of Aesthetics and Art Criticism* (4): 147–58.

—— (1984b) 'Style and personality in the literary work', *Philosophical Review* 94: 227–47.

Ronell, A. (1989) *The Telephone Book: Technology, Schizophrenia and Electronic Speech*, Lincoln: University of Nebraska Press.

Rorty, A.O. and Wong, D. (1990) 'Aspects of identity and agency', in O. Flanagan and A.O. Rorty (eds) *Identity, Character and Morality*, Cambridge, MA: MIT Press, 19–36.

Rose, M. (1993) *The Internet Message: closing the book with electronic mail*, Englewood Cliffs, NJ: PTR Prentice Hall.

Rosenau, J. (1998) 'Governance and democracy in a globalizing world', in D. Archibugi, D. Held and M. Köhler (eds) *Re-Imagining Global Community: Studies in Cosmopolitan Democracy*, Cambridge: Polity Press, 28–57.

Rouse, J. (1987) *Knowledge and Power: The Construction of Knowledge in the Sciences*, Ithaca: Cornell University Press.

Rousseau, J.J. (1978) *The Social Contract, with Geneva Manuscript and Political Economy*, ed. R.D. Masters, trans. J.R. Masters, New York: St Martin's Press.

Rubin, L. (1985) *Just Friends: The Role of Friendship in our Lives*, New York: Harper and Row.

Ruesch, J. and Kees, W. (1972) *Nonverbal Communication: Notes on the Visual Perception of Human Relations*, Berkeley and London: University of California Press.

Ruthrof, H. (1992) *Pandora and Occam: The Limits of Language and Literature*, Bloomington and Indianapolis: Indiana University Press.

—— (2000) *The Body in Language*, London: Cassell.

Saunders, G.R. (1985) 'Silence and noise as emotional management styles: an Italian case', in D. Tannen and M. Saville-Troike (eds) *Perspectives on Silence*, Norwood, NJ: Ablex Publishing Corporation, 35–68.

Saville-Troike, M. (1985) 'The place of silence in an integrated theory of communication' in D. Tannen and M. Saville-Troike (eds) *Perspectives on Silence*, Norwood, NJ: Ablex Publishing Corporation, 3–20.

Schatzki, T. (1996) *Social Practices: A Wittgensteinian Approach to Practices and the Social*, Cambridge: Cambridge University Press.

Scheler, M. (1971) *Wesen und Formen der Sympathie*, Bern and Munich: Francke.

Schoeck, R. (1990) *Erasmus of Europe: The Making of a Humanist*, Savage, ND: Barnes and Noble Books.

Schuler, D. (1994) 'Community networks: building a new participatory medium', *Communication of the ACM* 37(1): 39–51.

—— (1996) *New Community Networks: Wired for Change*, New York: ACM Press.

Selfe, C. (1988) 'The humanisation of computers: forget technology, remember literacy', *English Journal* 69–71.

Shapiro, D.E. and Schulman, C.E. (1996) 'Ethical and legal issues in e-mail therapy', *Ethics and Behavior* 6(2): 107–24.

Smith-Rosenberg, C. (1975) 'The female world of love and ritual: relations between women in nineteenth-century America', *Signs: Journal of Women in Culture and Society* 1(1): 38–54.

Spencer, V. (1996) 'Towards an ontology of holistic individualism: Herder's theory of identity, culture and community', *History of European Ideas* 23(3): 245–60.

Spender, D. (1993) *Nattering on the Net: Women, Power and Cyberspace*, Sydney: Spinifex Press.

Standage, T. (1998) *The Victorian Internet: The Remarkable Story of the Telegraph and the Nineteenth Century's Online Pioneers*, London: Weidenfeld and Nicholson.

Star, S.L. (1991) 'Power, technology and the phenomenology of conventions: on being allergic to onions', in J. Law (ed.) *A Sociology of Monsters: Essays on Power, Technology and Domination*, Albany, NY: SUNY Press.

—— (1995) *The Cultures of Computing*, Oxford and Cambridge, MA: Blackwell.

—— (1996) 'From Hestia to homepage: feminism and the concept of home in cyberspace', in N. Lykke and R. Braidotti (eds) *Monsters, Goddesses and Cyborgs: Feminist Confrontations with Science, Medicine and Cyberspace*, London and New Jersey: Zed Books, 30–46.

Stein, E. (1986) *Life in a Jewish Family: Her Unfinished Autobiographical Account*, Washington, DC: ICS Publications.

—— (1989) *On the Problem of Empathy*, trans. W. Stein, Washington DC: ICS Publications.

Stivale, C.J. (1996) 'Spam: heteroglossia and harassment in cyberspace', in D. Porter (ed.) *Internet Culture*, New York, London: Routledge, 133–44.

Stone, R.A. (1991) 'Will the real body please stand up? boundary stories about virtual cultures', in M. Benedikt (ed.) *Cyberspace: First Steps*, Cambridge, MA: MIT Press, 81–118.

—— (1995) *The War of Desire and Technology at the Close of the Mechanical Age*, Cambridge, MA: MIT Press.

Strawson, P.F. (1959) *Individuals: An Essay in Descriptive Metaphysics*, London: Methuen.

Suchman, L. and Jordan, B. (1997) 'Computerization and women's knowledge', in P.E. Agre and D. Schuler (eds) *Reinventing Technology, Rediscovering Community: Critical Explorations of Computing as a Social Practice*, Greenwich, CT and London: Ablex Publishing Corporation.

Swift, J. (1948) *Journal to Stella*, ed. H. Williams, Oxford: Clarendon Press.

Tambini, D. (1998) 'Civic networking and universal rights to connectivity: Bologna', in R. Tsagarousianou, D. Tambini, and C. Bryan (eds) *Cyberdemocracy: Technology, Cities, and Civic Networks*, London and New York: Routledge, 84–109.

Tannen, D. (1984a) *Coherence in Spoken and Written Discourse*, Norwood, NJ: Ablex Publishing Corporation.

—— (1984b) *Conversational Style: Analyzing Talk Among Friends*, Norwood, NJ: Ablex Publishing Corporation.

—— (1989) *Talking Voices: Repetition, Dialogue, and Imagery in Conversational Discourse*, Cambridge and New York: Cambridge University Press.

—— (1990) *You Just Don't Understand: Men and Women in Conversation*, New York: Morrow.

Tannen, D. and Lakoff, R. (1994) 'Conversational strategy and meta-strategy in a pragmatic theory', in D. Tannen *Gender and Discourse*, New York: Oxford University Press, 137–74.

Tasker, Y. (1998) *Working Girls: Gender and Sexuality in Popular Cinema*, London and New York: Routledge.

Tsagarousianou, R. (1998a) 'Back to the future of democracy? New technologies, civic networks and direct democracy in Greece', in R. Tsagarousianou, D. Tambini, C. Bryan (eds) *Cyberdemocracy: Technology, Cities, and Civic Networks*, London and New York: Routledge, 41–59.

—— (1998b) 'Electronic democracy and the public sphere', in R. Tsagarousianou, D. Tambini, C. Bryan (eds) *Cyberdemocracy: Technology, Cities, and Civic Networks*, London and New York: Routledge, 167–78.

Tracey, J. (1996) *Erasmus of the Low Countries*, Berkeley and Los Angeles, CA: University of California Press.

Tully, J. (1989) 'Wittgenstein and critical interpretation', *Political Theory* 17(2): 172–204.

Turkle, S. (1994) 'Constructions and reconstructions of self in virtual reality: playing in the MUDs', *Mind, Culture and Activity* 1: 158–67.

—— (1995) *Life on the Screen: Identity in the Age of the Internet*, New York: Simon and Schuster.

Turkle, S. and Papert, S. (1990) 'Epistemological pluralism: styles and voices within the computer culture', *Signs: Journal of Women in Culture and Society* 16(1): 128–57.

—— (1984) *The Second Self: Computers and the Human Spirit*, New York: Simon and Shuster.

Ullman, E. (1995) 'Out of time: reflections on the programming life', in J. Brook and I.A. Boal (eds) *Resisting the Virtual Life: The Culture and Politics of Information*, San Francisco: City Lights, 131–44.

Ullmann, S. (1971) 'Stylistics and semantics', in S. Chatman (ed.) *Literary Style: A Symposium*, London and New York: Oxford University Press, 133–55.

Ulmer, G. (1985) *Applied Grammatology: Post(e)-pedagogy From Jacques Derrida to Joseph Beuys*, Baltimore: Johns Hopkins University Press.

Valdès, M. (ed.) (1991) *A Ricoeur Reader: Reflection and Imagination*, Toronto and Buffalo: University of Toronto Press.

Walmsley, D.J. (2000) 'Community, place and cyberspace', *Australian Geographer* 31(1): 5–19.

Walker, M. (1998) *Moral Understandings: A Feminist Study in Ethics*, London: Routledge.

Walther, J. (1996) 'Computer-mediated communication: impersonal, interpersonal and hyperpersonal interaction', *Communication Research* 23(1): 3–43.

Walther, J. and Burgoon, J.K. (1992) 'Relational communication in computer-mediated interaction', *Communication Research* 19(1): 50–88.

Ward, J. and Stephenson, C. (1996) 'People-centred information systems development', *Proceedings of ETHICOMP96*, 275–92.

Ward, M. (2000) 'Internet "divides society"', BBC News report, Tuesday 23 May 2000. Online. Available HTTP <http://news.bbc.co.uk/hi/english/sci/tech/newsid_760000/760867.stm> (accessed 25 May 2000).

Wardhaugh, R. (1996) *An Introduction to Sociolinguistics*, second edition, Oxford and Cambridge, MA: Blackwell.

Warnke, G. (1995) 'Discourse ethics and feminist dilemmas of difference', in J. Meehan (ed.) *Feminists Read Habermas: Gendering the Subject of Discourse*, New York: Routledge, 247–62.

We, G. (1994) 'Cross-gender communication in cyberspace', *Electronic Journal of Virtual Culture* 2(3). Online. Available FTP <ftp://byrd.mu.wvnet.edu/pub/ejvc/WEV2N3> (accessed 3 June 2000)

Weisband, S.P. (1987) 'Instrumental and symbolic aspects of an executive information system', in S. Kiesler and L. Sproull (eds) *Computing and Change on Campus*, Cambridge, New York, New Rochelle, Melbourne and Sydney: Cambridge University Press, 150–70.

Werry, C. (1996) 'Linguistic and Interactional features of Internet Relay Chat', in Susan Herring (ed.) *Computer-Mediated Communications, Linguistic Social and Cross-cultural Perspectives*, Amsterdam and Philadelphia: John Benjamins Publishing Company, 47–64.

Wexelblat, A. (1991) 'Giving meaning to place: semantic spaces', in M. Benedikt (ed.) *Cyberspace: First Steps*, Cambridge and London: MIT Press, 255–72.

Wittgenstein, L. (1958) *Philosophical Investigations*, trans. G.E.M. Anscombe, New York: Macmillan.

Wojtyla, K. (1979) *The Acting Person*, Dordrecht, Boston and London: Reidel.

Wolfflin, H. (1953) *Classic Art: An Introduction to the Renaissance*, trans. P. and L. Murray, London: Phaidon.

Wollheim, R. (1987) 'Pictorial style: two views', in B. Lang (ed.) *The Concept of Style*, Pennsylvania: University of Pennsylvania Press, 129–45.

Woodbury, M. (1996) 'E-mail, voice-mail and privacy: what policy is ethical?', *Proceedings of ETHICOMP96*, 44–68.

Woolgar, S. and Grint, K. (1996) *The Machine at Work: Technology, Organisation and Work*, Cambridge: Polity Press, in association with Blackwell.

Yates, S. (1996) 'Oral and written aspects of computer conferencing: a corpus-based study', in S. Herring (ed.) *Computer-Mediated Communication: Linguistic, Social and Cross-cultural Perspectives*, Amsterdam and Philadelphia: John Benjamins Publishing Company, 29–46.

Yoon, S.H. (1996) 'Power online: a poststructuralist perspective on computer-mediated communication', in C. Ess (ed.) *Philosophical Perspectives on Computer-mediated Communication*, Albany: State University of New York Press, 171–96.

Young, I.M. (1990a) 'Impartiality and the civic public: some implications of feminist critiques of moral and political theory', in *Throwing Like a Girl, and Other Essays in Feminist Philosophy and Social Theory*, Bloomington and Indianapolis: Indiana University Press, 93–113.

—— (1990b) 'Polity and group difference: a critique of the ideal of universal citizenship', in *Throwing Like a Girl, and Other Essays in Feminist Philosophy and Social Theory*, Bloomington and Indianapolis: Indiana University Press, 114–40.

—— (1997a) 'Asymmetrical reciprocity: on moral respect, wonder, and enlarged thought', *Constellations: An International Journal of Critical and Democratic Theory* 3(3): 48–69.

—— (1997b) 'Communication and other: beyond deliberative democracy' in *Intersecting Voices: Dilemmas of Gender, Political Philosophy, and Policy*, Princeton, NJ: Princeton University Press, 60–74.

Index